Quality Control and Waste Utilization of Agriculture and Dairy Products

About the Editors

Dr. Naveen Kumar is presently working as faculty of Food Technology at Amity Institute of Biotechnology, Amity University Rajasthan, Jaipur. He has done his M.Sc. (Food Technology) from Guru Jambheshwar University of Science and Technology, Hisar (HR) and PhD (Dairy Chemistry) from National Dairy Research Institute, Karnal (HR). He is actively engaged in creative teaching, innovative research and high impact societal service programs that have improved Food processing, safety, and quality. His area of interest for research includes detection of adulterants and contaminantsin various agricultural and food samples, food fortification and enrichment, waste utilization, design and fabrication of various analytical methods as evident from his technical publications (over 30) in reputed journals and symposia besides reviewing several research articles for national and international journals. He has published many book chapters and edited 3 books. He has developed well equipped laboratory (Food Safety and Nanotechnology) for basic and applied scientific research. He has guided several B. Tech., M.Sc. and M. Tech. students for their minor and major research projects. PhD scholars under his guidanceare presently working on developing colorimetric methods for the rapid detection of various contaminants in food products. He is a life time member of Dairy Technology Society of India (DTSI). He has been awarded with Young Scientist award for his excellent research contribution in the field of food safety and nanotechnology.

Dr. Ravinder Kaushik is working as Assistant Professor in the School of Bioengineering and Food Technology, Shoolini University, Solan (Himachal Pradesh), India. He has done M.Sc. and M.Tech (with distinction) in Food Technology and PhD in Dairy Chemistry with specialization in Micronutrient Fortification and Functional Foods. He has published more than 30 International and National research articles, 12 book chapters. He has also attended more than 10 International and national conferences. He is Editor of International Journal of Food and Fermentation and International Journal of Food and Nutrition and referee of more than 15 International and National Journals. He has applied 3 national patents. He has guided 18 M.Sc., 2 M.Phill and 3 PhD students and at present guiding 3 M.Sc. and 3 PhD students. His area of interest for research includes micronutrient fortification, bakery and application of herbs in Food Industry. He was recipient of ICAR Scholarship and Certificate of appreciation for outstanding research during PhD by NDRI, Karnal. He is an external examiner for CSK Palampur, ITM University, Gwalior and MM University, Ambala.

Dr. Prince Chawla is working as Assistant Professor in the School of Bioengineering and Food Technology, Shoolini University, Solan, Himachal Pradesh. He is M.Sc. (Food Science and Technology) from CDLU, Sirsa and currently pursuing PhD (Food Technology) from Shoolini University, Solan. He has over 4 years of Research and Teaching experience from ICAR-NDRI and Shoolini University. He has published 10 international publications and 4 book chapters in various reputed journals and books. He has edited one book on Human Health and Nutrition. He has applied 1 national patent. He has presented more than 30 papers in international and national conferences. He is a recognized reviewer of Elsevier. Also, he has reviewed several international research articles.

Quality Control and Waste Utilization of Agriculture and Dairy Products

Naveen Kumar
Amity Institute of Biotechnology
Amity University Rajasthan
Jaipur, Rajasthan, India

Ravinder Kaushik

Prince Chawla

School of Bioengineering and Food Technology
Shoolini University, Solan
Himachal Pradesh

NEW INDIA PUBLISHING AGENCY
New Delhi – 110 034

NEW INDIA PUBLISHING AGENCY
101, Vikas Surya Plaza, CU Block, LSC Market
Pitam Pura, New Delhi 110 034, India
Phone: + 91 (11) 27 34 17 17 Fax: + 91 (11) 27 34 16 16
Email: info@nipabooks.com
Web: www.nipabooks.com

Feedback at feedbacks@nipabooks.com

ISBN: 978-93-87973-20-6

Composed and Designed by NIPA

Preface

Agriculture and Food Technology are directly associated with each other. Agriculture produces raw food commodities and other valuable products which are harvested and processed to food products. The agricultural practices could affects the quality of raw as well as processed food products, hence good agriculture practices produce high quality food products with enhanced shelf-life with admirable sensory properties. The present book consists of inter-relationship between agriculture and food. The hot topics of present and future are compiled in form of different chapters. Agriculture waste is mainly burned which creates smog, therefore its transformation into biochar or fodder is a new eco-friendly and economical method. India is suffering from hunger and hidden hunger and at the same time lots of agriculture produce are waste due to postharvest losses. How post-harvest losses can be minimized is also described. The key weapon/deterrent to overcome hidden hunger is micronutrient fortification. The important micronutrients are iron, calcium, zinc, vitamin D and vitamin A, respectively. Adulteration of ghee is a common practice in India, therefore different analytical methods to asses' purity are discussed. Essential oil gives flavor, nutrients and protection against microorganisms and enhance shelf-life and sensory attributes. Meat processing industries produces hides, skin, organs, and bones as waste product, how they utilized as value added products is also discussed. The processing equipment's are source of contamination. It can be minimized by exact design of food processing equipment. Novel processing techniques such as gamma irradiation are highly useful and it is used for modification of starch, whereas, pulse electric field is used to inactivate microorganism and food processing. Probiotics are heath beneficial microorganisms. New probiotic microorganism are invented and there use for human health is also documented. Nutrigenomics is emerging field which is highly useful in food industry. Chitosan is used in food industry for long time, however its use in dairy sector is limited. Its application in dairy industry is also important for improving dairy products. Adulteration is wound to food industry. Different types of adulterants and their control is discussed. Agriculture crops are infested by pests and for pest management organophosphorus pesticides are used. They are highly toxic to humans. There detection in food samples are discussed in last. The whole book discussed about new approaches in agriculture and food sector. This book could be a new dimensions to agriculture and food sector.

Editors

Contents

List of Contributors

Ami Patel, Assistant Professor, Department of Dairy Microbiology, Mansinhbhai Institute of Dairy and Food Technology, Mehsana, Gujarat

Anil Panghal, Lovely Professional University, Phagwara, Punjab

Ankit Goyal, Assistant Professor, Department of Dairy Chemistry, Mansinhbhai Institute of Dairy and Food Technology, Mehsana-384002, Gujarat

Ankit Singla, Regional Centre of Organic Farming, Department of Agriculture, Cooperation and Farmers Welfare, Ministry of Agriculture and Farmers Welfare, Bhubaneswar, Odisha

Anupama Sharma, Project Coordinator, Veterinary Parasitology, SKUAST-J, Jammu, J&K

Apurva Sharma, Dairy Chemistry Division, ICAR-National Dairy Research Institute Karnal-132 001, Harayana

Arvind, Division of Livestock Products Technology, ICAR-IVRI, Bareilly, Uttar Pradesh

Beenu Tanwar, Assistant Professor, Department of Dairy Technology, Mansinhbhai Institute of Dairy and Food Technology, Mehsana,Gujarat

Chitra Gupta, Dairy Chemistry Division, ICAR-National Dairy Research Institute Karnal-132 001, Harayana

D.C. Saxena, Department of Food Engineering and Technology, Sant Longowal Institute of Engineering & Technology, Longowal – 148106, Punjab

Diwas Pradhan, Dairy Microbiology Division, ICAR-National Dairy Research Institute Karnal-132001, Haryana, India

Gagnesh Sharma, Regional Centre of Organic Farming, Department of Agriculture, Cooperation and Farmers Welfare, Ministry of Agriculture and Farmers Welfare, Bhubaneswar, Odisha

Gopikrishna G., Assistant Professor, Department of Dairy & Food Technology, Shri G.N. Patel Dairy Science & Food Technology College, SDAU, Gujarat

Harish Kumar, Department of Food Technology, Akal College of Agriculture, Eternal University Baru Sahib-173-101, Himachal Pradesh

Heena Sharma, Dairy Technology Division, ICAR-National Dairy Research Institute, Karnal-132 001, Harayan

Joginder Singh Duhan, Department of Biotechnology, Chaudhary Devi Lal University Sirsa-125 055 (India)

Kamal Gandhi, Scientist, Dairy Chemistry Division NDRI, Karnal 132 001, Harayana

Karuna Meghawal, Dairy Chemistry Division, Mansinhbhai Institute of Dairy and Food Technology (MIDFT), Mehsana-384002, Gujarat

Kazuyuki Inubushi, Bioresource Science, Graduate School of Horticulture, Chiba University Matsudo-271-8510, Chiba, Japan

Khalid Bashir, National Institute of Food Technology Entrepreneurship and Management (NIFTEM), Kundli-131028, Haryana

Kulsum Jan, School of Bioengineering and Food Technology, Shoolini University, Solan Himachal Pradesh

Lovepreet Gill, Chaudhary Devi Lal University, Sirsa, Haryana

Madhavi T.V., Assistant professor, Department of Dairy Microbiology, College of Dairy Technology PV Narasimha Rao Telangana State University, Telangana

Manvesh Kumar Sihag, Assistant Professor, Dept. of Dairy Chemistry, Mansinhbhai Institute of Dairy and Food Technology, Mehsana-384002, Gujarat

Naveen Kumar, Amity Institute of Biotechnology, Amity University, Jaipur, Rajasthan

Navnidhi Chhikara, Lovely Professional University, Phagwara, Punjab

Nihir Shah, Assistant Professor, Department of Dairy Microbiology, Mansinhbhai Institute of Dairy and Food Technology, Mehsana-384002, Gujarat

Nitika Sandhu, Post doctorate Fellow, Division Plant Breeding, Genetics and Biotechnology International Rice Research Institute, Manila, Philippines

Pardeep Kumar Sadh, Department of Biotechnology, Chaudhary Devi Lal University, Sirsa, Haryana

Parmar Manish Kumar, College of Dairy Science, Kamdhenu University, Gujarat

Pratap Singh, College of Dairy Science, Kamdhenu University, Gujarat

Prince Chawla, Shoolini University, Solan, Himachal Pradesh, India

Priti Saha, National Dairy Research Institute, Karnal, Haryana

Priyanka Singh Rao, Dairy Chemistry Division, ICAR-National Dairy Research Institute Karnal, Haryana

Ravinder Kaushik, Assistant Professor, School of Bioengineering and Food Technology, Shoolini University, Himachal Pradesh

Richa Singh, Dairy Chemistry Division, ICAR-National Dairy Research Institute, Karnal-132 001, Harayan

Sandeep Kumar, Department of Biotechnology, Chaudhary Devi Lal University Sirsa, Haryana

Sanju B. Dhull, Chaudhary Devi Lal University, Sirsa, Haryana

Seema Rana, Senior Research Fellow, Dairy Chemistry Division NDRI, Karnal, Haryana

Shilpa Shree, Dairy Chemistry Division, ICAR-National Dairy Research Institute, Karnal-132 001, Harayan

Shumaila Jan, Department of Food Engineering and Technology, Sant Longowal Institute of Engineering and Technology, Longowal – 148106, Punjab

Subhash Prasad, Assistant Professor, Dairy Engineering Department, College of Dairy Science Amreli, Kamdhenu University, Gandhinagar, Gujarat

Sudheendra CH. V. K., Assistant professor, Department of Dairy Microbiology, Dairy Science College, Kamdhenu University, Gujarat

Sudheer Kumar, Division of Livestock Products Technology, ICAR-IVRI, Bareilly, Uttar Pradesh, India

Sumit Arora, Dairy Chemistry Division, ICAR-National Dairy Research Institute, Karnal-132 001, Harayan

Surbhi Sharma, Chaudhary Devi Lal University, Sirsa, Haryana

Suresh Kumar Rohilla, Department of Biotechnology, Chaudhary Devi Lal University Sirsa Haryana

Tanmay Hazra, Assistant Professor, Dairy chemistry Department, College of Dairy Science Amreli, Kamdhenu University, Gandhinagar, Gujrat

Tarun Pal Singh, Division of Livestock Products Technology, ICAR-IVRI, Bareilly, Uttar Pradesh, India

Varsha Singla· TFS Lab., Dairy Microbiology Division, National Dairy Research Institute Karnal, Haryana, India

Vivek Sharma, National Dairy Research Institute, Karnal, Haryana

1

Recent Developments in Reducing Postharvest Losses of Food in India

Subhash Prasad and Tanmay Hazra

Abstract

Food lost during the production chain is referred to as postharvest loss. Reducing postharvest loss can effectively feed starving mouths while conserving resources and decreasing the pressure to produce more. There are five main areas where postharvest loss can be reduced – harvest, storage, transportation, processing, and retail. New approaches and technologies in each of these areas will increase the amount of food available for human consumption. The total loss due to poor post-harvest processing of agricultural products in India when valued in terms of monetary reflects a tremendous loss in the economy. Annual value of harvest and post-harvest losses of major agricultural produces at national level to be of the order of Rs. 92,651 Crore calculated using production data of 2012-13 at 2014 wholesale prices. Deficits in food items or financial loss should not have occurred if postharvest losses were reduced through proper processing and preservation from harvest to consumption. Both the government and private sector need to invest in research so as to improve and modernize post-harvest facilities for attaining more efficient market infrastructure and distribution channels. Research and extension activities have to be closely coordinated particularly in the public sector for the benefit of farmers, traders and consumers.

Keywords: Post-harvest losses, Damage, Packaging, Value Addition and Preservation, Consumer preferences

1. Introduction

Post-harvest food loss is defined as measurable qualitative and quantitative food loss along the supply chain, starting at the time of harvest till its consumption or other end uses (Hodges *et al.*, 2011). Every year, an estimated 1.3 billion ton - roughly one-third - of the food produced for human consumption worldwide is lost or wasted. In industrialized countries, significant waste occurs at the consumption stage, while in low income countries, food losses take place primarily during the early and middle stages of the supply chain. Empirical evidence on the extent of post-harvest food losses is scarce and estimates vary substantially, between countries and regions as well 2 as between different types of products. Some estimates for average losses in East and Southern Africa, for instance, put Post-harvest losses for grains at 10-20% (in term of weight loss), with some regions reaching as high as 25-35%. In South and Southeast Asia, rice physical losses are 10–25% and quality losses can discount prices by up to 30% (Gummert, 2013 ; Manners-Bell and Miroux, 2013; FAO, 2011). Peculiarly, current values related to post-harvest losses have no much difference about the early cited values, the first world food conference in 1974 identified reduction of post-harvest losses as part of the solution in addressing world hunger. At this time, an overall estimate for post-harvest losses of 15%, more previous extensive studies suggested that about 15% of grain may be lost in the post-harvest system (Liang *et al.*, 1993; Parfitt *et al.*, 2010). As for individual case, rice in Asia, the estimated quantitative losses ranged from 10 to 37% in 1994 and was from 13-15% by 2004 (FAO, 1994; Smil, 2004; Grolleaud, 2002). That does not mean there was no progress or reduction in post-harvest, but it is shows that current global losses cannot be quantified whoever post-harvest loss data for developing countries was collected over many years ago, (Parfitt *et al.*, 2010).

In India, the production is about 450 million tons of raw food materials of plant and animal origin which are refined, stored and transformed into various usable products using conventional and modern post-harvest and food processing technology, out of this amount there is 10% post-harvest losses in durables (Cereals, pulses and oilseeds), 20% losses in semi-perishables (Potato, onion, sweet potato, tapioca) and around 25% in products like milk, meat, fish and eggs. Furthermore, In India, annual storage losses estimated to be 14 million ton of food grains worth $ 16,000 million every year. About from 30% to 40% of the fruits and vegetables grown in India (40 million tons amounting to US$ 13 billion) get wasted annually due to gaps in the cold chain such as poor infrastructure, insufficient cold storage capacity, unavailability of cold storages in close proximity to farms, poor transportation infrastructure, etc. This results in instability in prices and farmers cannot get remunerative prices beside rural impoverishment and farmers' frustrations (Rajasri *et al.*, 2010; Maheshwar and Chanakwa, 2006; Rolle, 2006; Ali, 2004).

On the basis of production and wholesale market price in India, The Associated Chambers of Commerce and Industry of India (ASSOCHAM) found that fruits and vegetables post-harvest losses reached amount of $33,745 million in 2011-12 and may cross $33,745 million in 2013-14. Unavailability of cold storages in India is just one of major reasons for these losses, since operating costs for

Indian cold storage units are a whopping over $60 per cubic metre per year compared to less than $30 in the west. Energy expenses make up about 28% of the total expenses for Indian cold storages compared to 10% in the West. These factors make setting up of cold storages difficult, unviable and uneconomical (Maheshwar and Chanakwa, 2006).

In last decades different organizations and institutions in India, including; governmental organization; National/international research institutes and universities; private sector; Non-governmental organizations (NGOs) etc. have been involved and played different rules in post-harvest losses and their effect. Compared to other Developing Countries, Indian Government has different organizations and departments involved in postharvest losses issues, i.e. Department of Agriculture and Cooperation (DAC) which follows Ministry of Agriculture and has the Agricultural Marketing Advisor, DAC active in cooperative education & training, information technology and agricultural marketing with providing different post-harvest commodity profiles, DAC supervise the Directorate of Marketing & Inspection (DMI) which is running national level surveys and statistics within the country. Also; Department of Agricultural Research and Education (DARE), which leads Indian Council of Agricultural Research (ICAR) the autonomous organisation with separate thrust area in reduction of post-harvest losses, value addition to agricultural produce, processing and utilization of by-products. ICAR also has established the Central Institute of Post-Harvest Engineering and Technology (CIPHET) in 1989 and now CIPHET is running different projects including assessment of post-harvest losses, application of modern technologies, low cost cold chain transport and storage and many other post-harvest related works. In addition, The Department of Food and Public Distribution in Ministry of Consumer Affairs, Food and Public Distribution (MCAFPD) has a primary Policy objective to ensure food security for the country through timely and efficient procurement and distribution of foodgrains, this involves procurement of various foodgrains, building up and maintenance of food stocks, their storage, movement and delivery to the distributing agencies and monitoring of production, stock and price levels of foodgrains.

2. Objectives of Applying Post Harvest Technology

a) To maintain quality (appearance, texture, flavor and nutritive value)

b) To protect food safety

c) To reduce losses (both physical and in market value) between harvest and consumption.

3. Post-Harvest System Activities and Operations

The post-harvest system encompasses a sequence of activities and operations that can be divided into two groups:

3.1 Technical Activities

(a) Harvesting

The time of harvesting is determined by degree of maturity. A distinction should be made between maturity of stalks (straw), seedpods and seeds for cereals and pulses that affects successive operations, particularly storage and preservation.

(b) Field Drying

(i) **Pre-harvest drying:** It is done mainly for cereals and pulses. Extended pre-harvest field drying ensures good preservation but also heightens the risk of loss due to biological attack (birds, rodents, insects etc.) and moulds which is encouraged by weather conditions. On the other hand, harvesting before maturity entails the risk of loss through moulds and decay of seeds.

(ii) **Post-harvest drying**: The length of time needed for full drying of seedpods and grains depends considerably on weather and atmospheric conditions. The harvest is exposed of wandering livestock and the depredations of birds, rodents or small ruminants for lengthy drying such as cribs or even unroofed threshing floors or terraces. Apart from the actual wastage, the droppings left by these marauders often result in higher losses than what they actually eat. On the other hand, if grain is not dry enough, it is vulnerable to mould and can rot during storage. Moreover, if grain is too dry it becomes brittle and can crack after threshing, during hulling or milling. This applies especially to rice if milling takes place for a long time (two to three months) after the grain has matured. It can cause heavy losses. During winnowing, broken grain can be removed with the husks and is also more susceptible to certain insects (e.g. flour beetles and weevils). Lastly, if grain is too dry, corresponds to loss of weight and hence loss of money at the time of sale.

(c) Threshing and cleaning

If a harvest is threshed before it is dried enough, this operation will most probably be incomplete. Furthermore, if grain is threshed when it is too damp and then immediately heaped up or stored (in a granary or bags), it will be much more susceptible to attack from micro-organisms, thus limiting its preservation.

(d) Storage

Facilities, hygiene and monitoring must all be adequate for effective, long-term storage. In closed structures (granaries, warehouses, hermetic bins), control of cleanliness, temperature and humidity is particularly important. Damage caused by pests (insects, rodents) and moulds can lead to deterioration of facilities and result in losses in quality and food value as well as quantity.

(e) Processing

Excessive hulling or threshing can also result in grain losses, particularly in the case of rice (hulling) which can suffer cracks and lesions. The grain is then not only worth less but also becomes vulnerable to insects such as the rice moth (*Corcyra cephalonica*).

(i) **Primary processing**: It includes cleaning, classification, dehulling, pounding, grinding, packaging, soaking, winnowing, drying, sieving, whitening, milling etc.

(ii) **Secondary processing:** It comprises of mixing, cooking, frying, moulding, cutting, extrusion etc.

3.2 Economic Activities

(a) **Product evaluation**: Product evaluation is done mainly for quality control and preparation of standard recipes to increase the food value.

(b) **Packaging:** It comprises of weighing, labeling and sealing.

(c) **Transporting**: Much care is needed in transporting a mature harvest, in order to prevent detached grain from falling on the road before reaching the storage or threshing place. Collection and initial transport of the harvest thus depend on the place and conditions where it is to be stored, especially with a view to threshing.

(d) **Marketing**: Marketing is the final and decisive element in the post-harvest system. It can occur at various points in the agrofood chain, particularly at some stage in processing. Moreover, it cannot be separated from transport which is an essential link in the system viz. publicity, selling, distribution etc.

(e) **Consumer preferences:** Driven by increasing consumer demand for healthier, safer, and more environmentally friendly food products, the use of food labeling has become increasingly important in recent years. The use of credible labels allows firms to signal quality or the presence of specific desirable attributes, and in so doing to create the potential for premiums based on this signal. Caswell and Padberg (1992) discuss the possibility of food labels as the answer to the imperfect information dilemma in food safety. Also Caswell and Mojduszka (1996) argue that quality signaling through product labeling promotes market incentives with relatively limited government involvement. It includes product evaluation, consumer education.

(f) **Information and communication**: It is worth noting that this intervention differs from the previous studies in that it involves public (satellite) payphones rather than cell phones or internet kiosks.This intervention occurred in places where neither cell phones nor fixed linephones were available. The treated villages were located in zones where cell phone coverage was technically and economically unfeasible. The satellite technology implemented did not require villages to posses fixed lines or electrical supply in order to enjoy the service. Therefore, phone placement only followed the criteria of being provided to villages without prior access to ICT. This coupled with differences in timing for phone placement that were uncorrelated with base line previous studies regarding endogenous placement of ICT with respect to the outcomes of interest.

(g) **Administration and management**: It is one of the important activities. Proper administration will lead to the proper management of agricultural products. Thus reduces the loss of agricultural products and increases the efficiency of attached member as well as in terms of monetary

4. Post-Harvest Losses

"Losses are a measurable reduction in foodstuffs and may affect either quantity or quality" (Tyler and Gilman, 1979). They arise from the fact that freshly harvested agricultural produce is a living thing that breathes and undergoes changes during post-harvest handling. Loss should not be confused with damage, which is the visible sign of deterioration, for example, chewed grain and can only be partial. Damage restricts the use of a product, whereas loss makes its use impossible.

4.1 Types of Losses

The first distinction in agro-food losses is that between quantity and quality.

(a) Quantitative loss is a loss in terms of physical substance, meaning a reduction in weight and volume and can be assessed and measured.

(b) Qualitative loss, however, is concerned particularly with the food and reproductive value of products and requires a different kind of evaluation.

It should be noted that we shall not consider losses occurring during the production period and caused by various crop pests (insects, weeds, disease), even though they have a major influence on food preservation conditions and account in part for the nature and size of post-harvest losses.

After describing direct and indirect losses, we shall thus look at weight loss, then quality loss, food loss, seed viability loss and commercial loss. We should not forget the existence of moisture content and the difference between damage and loss.

(i) **Moisture content**: In bio-chemical terms, organic products are composed of dry matter and water. The moisture content is the amount of free water within a given product and is expressed either as a decimal proportion or a percentage. For example, with cereals, a 13% moisture content is considered a guarantee of satisfactory grain preservation. In agriculture, moisture content or humidity rate is usually indicated as a proportion of the moist product; i.e. the moisture content is the proportion of the weight of moisture to the total weight of dry matter and moisture.

(ii) **Damage**: Damage is a clear deterioration in the product, e.g. broken or pitted grain, which affects more its quality than its quantity and can in the long-term result in a definite loss. Both damage and loss should be quantified in terms of weight and cost.

(iii) **Direct and indirect losses**: Direct losses occur when the disappearance of a foodstuff is caused by leakage (for example, spillage from bags) or consumption by pests (insects, rodents, birds), whereas indirect losses occur when a reduction in quality leads to the consumer's refusal to purchase.

(iv) **Weight loss:** While weight loss is easy to observe and measure, it does not necessarily mean food loss, since it can result simply from a reduction in moisture content. Moisture loss during drying is therefore not a food loss. On the other hand, an abnormal increase in weight through moisture absorption following rainfall on stocks left in the open can cause serious damage resulting in loss. Weight loss can be caused by leakage, during transport for example, if sacks have holes or are insecurely attached. It is often the result of prolonged infestation and consumption by insects, rodents and birds or poor packaging. Weight loss from pests is not immediately apparent and may deceive an inexperienced purchaser. It can be checked by taking an equivalent amount of clean, healthy cereal, milling the two samples and weighing the flour from each. The poorer sample will produce less flour. This method can also be used to check whether the weight is really correct, for it is easy to increase it by moistening the grain or adding foreign bodies such as pebbles, earth or waste material.

(v) **Quality loss**: Quality criteria cover a wide range and are concerned both with external features, shape and size and with odour and taste. The cultural factors that can influence diets and food habits must also be borne in mind.The cleanliness and healthy condition of a product are primary concerns for the market and correspond to what is referred to as a "sound, legal and merchantable" product in commercial law. For example, if a trader takes a handful of grain from a sack, he can quickly see if it releases dust and work out if this is the result of insect infestation. Similarly, a bad smell can arouse suspicions that rodents have been at the grain, verifiable by the presence of rat or mouse droppings and hair. Many other objects can be mixed in with a foodstuff and reduce its value: bad grain, scraps of straw or other plant residue, soil, pebbles, bits of glass, etc. All such objects are hard to remove but some of them represent a greater risk of contamination than others: the soluble excreta of pests, oils, pesticides, pathogenic organisms spread by rodents and toxins from fungi and moulds. It goes without saying that the presence of foreign bodies, which can distort the weight of a batch being sold, also affects the quality and thus the market value of a product.

(vi) **Food loss:** While food loss clearly results from a loss in quantity, it also results, but more insidiously, from a loss in quality and edibility, making it unfit for human consumption. Staple foods contain not only essential nutrients but also important vitamins. For instance, grain hearts are rich in protein and vitamins; however, they are also the preferred target of rodents and insects. The various nutritive parts of products are thus the prey of different families of parasites. Weevils feed especially on the endosperm, the inside of the seed, which is rich in carbohydrates, while many parasites attack the cereal cover, which is rich in vitamins. Vitamin content is also affected by humidity during storage and by mould infection.

(vii) **Seed viability loss**: Seed set aside for sowing, like any product used for reproduction, is preserved with great care in order to maintain its full germinative potential. As noted above, the protein-rich grain heart can be a favourite target of certain pests. Atmospheric conditions also play a part, as they can weaken the seed's productive potential; variations in light, temperature and humidity, leading to excessive respiration, are particularly responsible here.

(viii) **Commercial loss:** Commercial loss is the translation of the various types of loss listed above into economic and monetary terms. Although the price of a foodstuff is usually based on weight, many other factors play a part.

This applies especially to the qualitative elements emphasized above, starting with cleanliness and purity, which will be all the more sought after if supplies are abundant in the market-place. Reference to abundance brings us to the key economic factor of the supply-and-demand situation at a given moment.

A producer's ability to take advantage of a time when the scarcity of a commodity pushes up the price, is an element in good marketing management of his production, based on information and foresight. This assumes good organization, in which structural and not only market-situational factors are taken into account (for example, having enough storage facilities available and in good condition to be able to hold on to the harvest until the price rises) as well as keeping abreast of long-term developments, such as socio-cultural changes, which affect the future. Although this kind of market-oriented attitude depends on an individual's skills, it also has some collective aspects that deserve development. For the present, we would note that the ability to capitalize on a product depends on a number of technical and economic factors, in which the quality of the merchandise plays an increasingly important role but so also do the human qualities of the producer and hence, the training that readies him to take his place as an economic player in the life of his country.

(ix) **Irreducible losses and compensation**: While loss of weight during drying is normal and measurable, there are other, said "irreducible" losses, which arise basically from respiration of the product and mechanical rubbing of grain against itself, as well as the breakage inevitable with certain machines. It should therefore always be remembered that losses, whether pre-harvest or post-harvest (i.e. in production, distribution, storage or marketing) cannot be materially reduced to zero and that they have to be compensated for through extra production. The production increase rate must be progressively higher than that of losses, if such compensation is to be adequate, so that compensation for a 20 % loss will require 25 % more production, for a 40 % loss, 66 % more and for a 60 % loss, 150 % more.

5. Post-Harvest Losses in India

A comprehensive nation-wide quantitative assessment of harvest and post-harvest losses for 46 agricultural produces was carried out to estimate the extent of harvest and post-harvest losses (DARE/ICAR, 2011) (Fig.1).

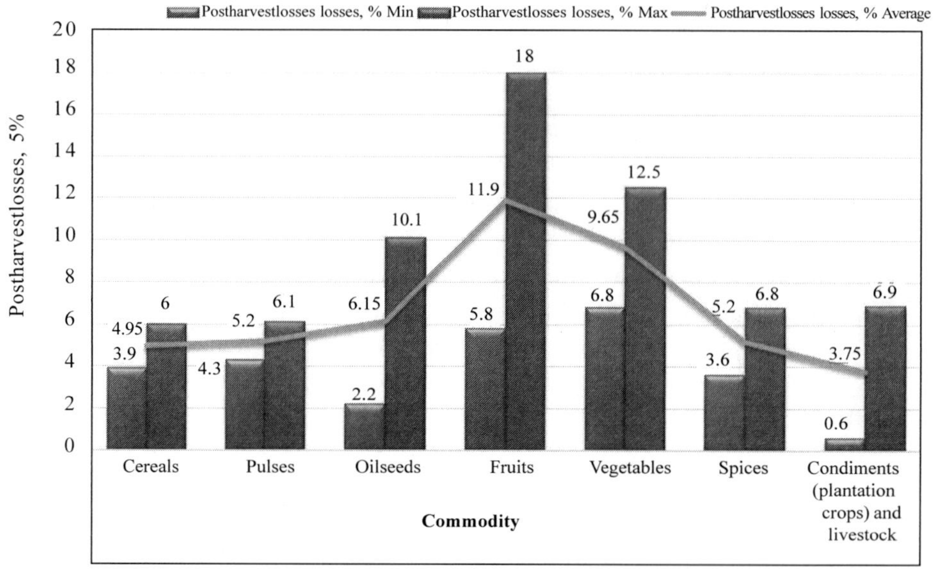

Fig. 1: Harvest and post-harvest losses in different commodities from nation scale quantitative assessment in India 2011

The Central Institute of Post-Harvest Engineering and Technology (CIPHET), Ludhiana has estimated the annual value of harvest and post-harvest losses of major agricultural produces at national level to be of the order of Rs. 92,651 crore calculated using production data of 2012-13 and 2014 wholesale prices. Annual wastage of agricultural produce, milk, meat, marine and poultry products as assessed by CIPHET, Ludhiana.

Table 1: Annual wastage of agricultural produce, milk, meat, marine and poultry products as assessed by CIPHET, Ludhiana (2012-13)

Commodity/Crop	Losses during Transportation(%)	Losses during Farm Operations (including transportation loss)(%)	Losses during Storage(%)	Overall Total Loss(%)	Monitory value of the loss (in Rs. crore)
Milk	0.02	0.71	0.21	0.92	4409
Meat	0.00	1.99	0.72	2.71	1235
Marine Fish	0.91	9.61	0.91	10.52	4315
Inland Fish	0.17	4.18	1.05	5.23	3766
Egg	0.36	4.88	2.31	7.19	1320
Poultry Meat	0.66	2.74	4.00	6.74	3942
Cereals				4.65-5.99	20698
Pulses				6.36-8.41	3877
Oilseeds				3.08-9.96	8278
Fruits & Vegetables				4.58-15.88	40811

Table 2: Post Harvest Losses in India: Summary of Results assessed by CIPHET, Ludhiana (2012-13)

Crop	% Loss (minimum)	% Loss (maximum)
Cereals	4.65 (Maize)	6.0 (Sorghum)
Pulses	6.36 (Pigeon pea)	8.41(Chick pea)
Oilseeds	3.08 (Cottonseed)	9.96 (soybean)
Fruits	6.70 (Papaya)	15.88 (Guava)
Vegetables	4.58 (Tapioca)	12.44 (Tomato)
Livestock Produce	0.92 (Milk)	10.52 (Marine Fish)

6. Causes of Postharvest Losses

Postharvest losses are caused by both external and internal factors.

(a) External Factors Which Lead to Postharvest Losses

(i) Mechanical Injury

Fresh fruits and vegetables are highly susceptible to mechanical injury owing to their tender texture and high moisture content. Poor handling, unsuitable packaging and improper packing during transportation are the cause of bruising, cutting, breaking, impact wounding, and other forms of injury in fresh fruits and vegetables.

(ii) Parasitic Diseases

The invasion of fruits and vegetables by fungi, bacteria, insects and other organisms, is a major cause of postharvest losses in fruits and vegetables. Microorganisms readily attack fresh produce and spread rapidly, owing to the lack of natural defense mechanisms in the tissues of fresh produce, and the abundance of nutrients and moisture which supports their growth. Control of postharvest decay is increasingly becoming a difficult task, since the number of pesticides available is rapidly declining as consumer concern for food safety is increasing.

(b) Internal Factors

Fruit and vegetable tissues are still alive after harvest, and continue their physiological activity. Physiological disorders occur as a result of mineral deficiency, low or high temperature injury, or undesirable environmental conditions, such as high humidity. Physiological deterioration can also occur spontaneously owing to enzymatic activity, leading to over ripeness and senescence, a simple aging phenomenon.

7. Adaptions of New Technologies for Reducing Post-Harvest Losses in India

Adaptions of new technologies for reducing post-harvest losses. For the ability of adaptions new technology which help in reducing post-harvest losses, a study based on survey conducted with small rice millers of Orissa in 1996 on modern trend of rice processing and by product as step to reduce post-harvest losses due to old traditional milling methods, 33.64% of rice miller owners were interested to modify their rice millers and 16.16 of them were satisfied with the existing systems and have no desire to shift towards new technology (Dash *et al.* 1996). And this percentage was lower than early percentage of rice huller owner, where 30% of rice huller owner were satisfied over their own practice and didn't want to shift to modern rice milling (Dash *et al.* 1993). A project implemented by International Development Enterprises (IDE) in India with funds received from the Crop Post-Harvest Programme (CPHP) of the Department for International Development (DFID), it was implemented in partnership with international non-governmental organization (IntNGO) based in the UK also with different Indian partners including different research institutes and non-governmental organization (NGO) based in the region Himachal Pradesh to develop and commercialize of suitable cardboard carton packaging for tomatoes as the main task (Phansalkar, S.J. 2003). By the end of the first phase of the project in June 2001 a prototype corrugated cardboard carton (CCC) had been developed and tested. By early 2002, the producers had an agreement with a manufacturer to produce 100,000 cartons with credit arrangements with a local bank. This case study considered new approach that combined both conventional development and aid projects, the geographic focus of the project and selection of local NGO partners built on existing activities and relationships of IDE and Helped the poor and non-poor cope with environmental policy changes (Hall *et al.*, 2003) 9 Based on the principle of direct evaporative cooling zero energy cool chambers have been developed. It does not require any electricity or power to operate, materials required like bricks, sand, bamboo etc. available easily and cheaply, Cool chambers can reduce temperature by 10°C and maintain high humidity of about 95% that can increase shelf life and retain quality of horticultural produce. National Horticulture Board is giving 100% grant in aid for the benefit of the farmer. (Kitinoja *et al.*, 2011; Roy and Pal, 1991), later Kaushalya Foundation revisited the idea and has completed the constructed 300 PZECC out of 500 for farmers in Patna, Naland and Vaishali district in Bihar. Other simple technology was a simple shade structure for field packing results in 1% weight losses for spinach as compared to 5% weight loss when packed during the same time period under sun (Kitinoja *et al.*, 2010). With near cooling concept, a cool storage shed introduced by CTI (Compatible Technology International) the international non-profit volunteer organization, CTI's cool storage shed make farmers can extend the shelf-life of their fruits and vegetables by storing their crops just 1, 2 or 3 additional months, they can sell their harvest in the off season, when market prices are much higher. Additionally, farmers using the storage shed have more time to process their crops into value-added products. The cool storage shed is currently used in India, where it's enabled farmers to triple their earnings, CTI primarily is focusing on helping small farmers address their post-harvest challenges. For technology produced and distributed by government, Ayyappan (2012) mentioned that ICAR Developed and commercialized around 60 processing machineries and technologies for post-harvest loss reduction and value addition. Along the lines of technology introduced to India for reducing post-harvest losses, IRRI showed safe storage in the smaller Super Grain bags (60 kg) as hermetic storage of rice and corn seed with good results for long storage periods of 90-280 days with germination rates at the end of the period from 95 to 98.3%. Super Grain bags are now used on a large scale by Bayer Crop Sciences for rice seed storage in India (Villers and Gummert, 2009).

8. Recent Developments in Reducing Postharvest Losses

Raw Material

No matter how perfect postharvest operations are, good returns cannot be obtained from poor quality raw materials. The selection of suitable varieties is, therefore, essential. Linking production to postharvest operations is essential to optimizing results.

Varietal differences in storability

Some varieties of the same crop store better than others. Therefore, to reduce food loss and to achieve maximum shelf-life, only varieties known to store well should be stored.

Harvesting

Harvesting should be carried out as carefully as possible to minimize mechanical injury such as scratches, punctures and bruises to the crop. This should be carried out during the cool part of the day, which is early morning and late evening harvest crop at a matured green state.

Handling

Mechanical injury provides sites for pest attack and increases physiological losses. Therefore, avoid mechanical injury to the crop while handling. Because of their soft texture, all agricultural products should be handled gently to minimize bruising and breaking of the skin. Bruising renders the product unsaleable to most people although it usually has minor effect upon the nutritional value. The skin of agricultural products is an effective barrier to most of the opportunistic bacteria and fungi that cause rotting of the tissues. Breaking of the skin also stimulates physiological deterioration and dehydration. Careful digging and movement of roots and tubers significantly reduces post-harvest losses. Reducing the numberof times the commodity is handled reduces the extent of mechanical damage. Crops should not be heaped at collection centre on the farm as this will lead to rapid spoilage particularly of fruits at centre of the heap. Fruits and vegetables should not be exposed to the sun. Crops should be transferred promptly after harvest to a clean, cool, well-ventilated shed.

Sorting and cleaning

Sort out damage crops from undamaged crops. Remove dirt from sound crop before putting into transport containers.

Packing

Increased use of corrugated cartons for local distribution of produce could be accomplished with improvement in the quality of boxes produced in India. The ventilated CFB box which contains ventilated partitions, and which was developed at the IARI was found to be ideal for the packaging and transportation of fruits, owing to the comparably minimal level of bruising observed in these boxes. Cushioning materials used in the packaging of fruits and vegetables in wooden boxes include dry grass, paddy straw, leaves, sawdust, paper shreds etc., all of which end up as garbage and add to environmental pollution in cities. Moulded trays or cardboard partitions used in CFB boxes are, however, easily recycled.

Transportation

Load and unload transport vehicles carefully. Use clean, well-ventilated vehicle covered at the top for transportation. Transport crops during the cool part of the day by driving carefully over smooth roads to minimize damage to crop. Attention must be given to commodity compatibility within a load. Ethylene-sensitive commodities such as lettuce should not be shipped with ethylene generators such as apples. A complete description of compatible and incompatible commodities is available (Ashby *et al.*, 1987). The most common cause of freight claims is load shifting and crushing, but the costliest claims are the result of inadequate temperature control (Beilock, 1988). Other transportation steps are also important in quality maintenance, for example, from field to packing facility and from wholesale distribution point to retail outlet. The same principles that apply to long distance ones, apply to short-distance shipments, but handling practices tend to receive less attention when the shipping distance is short. Fields and rural roads are usually bumpier than highways; thus, vehicles hauling the harvested crop from field to packaging house are generally not as capable of preventing shock and vibration damage as the tractor-trailer rigs will do. The delay of cooling of a crop is affected by the time required to load a vehicle in the field, the distance from field to packinghouse, the speed of the vehicle and the number of vehicles waiting to be unloaded at the packinghouse (Garner *et al.*,1987).

Railways and roads are two important transportation systems for the movement of goods in India. The use of railways for the transportation of fruits and vegetables in India could be greatly enhanced by: making provisions for cooling and ventilation, providing improved handling facilities at platforms and providing storage space to accommodate the goods upon arrival at their destinations. Similarly road services could be considerably improved by widening roads, upgrading surfaces and through the introduction of one way traffic. Long waits at level crossings should be avoided by introducing flyovers at intersections in order to increase the speed and movement of goods by road. Facilities such as sheds, for temporary cool storage should be available on highways and major roads.

Packaging and storage

On Farm Storage: On farm storage is required in remote and inaccessible areas of India, to reduce losses in highly perishable fresh agricultural produce. The high cost and high energy requirements of refrigeration, and the difficulty of installing and running refrigerated facilities in remote areas of India, precludes the use of refrigerated storage in many parts of India. Low-cost, low-energy, environmentally friendly cool chambers made from locally available materials, and which utilize the principles of evaporative cooling, were therefore developed in response to this problem. These cool chambers are able to maintain temperatures at 10–15°C below ambient, as well as at a relative humidity of 90%, depending on the season.

Perforated Films: Perforated films used for packing the fruits and vegetables and kept the product safe on the basis of the amount of escaped gasses via perforated layer as well as the gasses enters from polymeric film is balanced with the throughout gasses movement rate of perforated film (Fishman *et al.*, 1996). In the case of perforated film packaging the cool air has been supplied for providing a suitable temperature to the packed fruits and vegetables.

Control Atmosphere/Modified Atmosphere Storage: The controlled atmosphere (CA) storage in which high level of carbon dioxide (CO_2) and low level of oxygen (O_2) are maintained, is one of the most significant contribution to the storage technology. When combined with refrigeration, it markedly retards the respiratory activity and may delay softening, yellowing, quality changes, and other deteriorative processes. However, important factor in CA storage is the tolerance or susceptibility of the fruits and vegetables to the injury caused by decreased O_2 and increased CO_2 concentration. The relative tolerance of individual fruits and vegetables varies considerably and is largely dependent on temperature, age, morphology and the anatomy of the horticultural products.

In this system, the produce is held under the atmospheric conditions modified by package, over wrap, box liner or pallet cover. The first requirement of the controlled atmosphere is a gas-tight envelope around the produce and the second requirement is some means of maintaining the concentration of CO_2 and O_2 at a desired level. The fruit that has derived the most benefit from CA storage is apple. Among the tropical fruits, the best atmosphere for storage of mangoes is 5 % CO_2 and 5 % O_2 at 13°C.

The beneficial effect of CA storage are (1) prolonged storage life of perishables by arresting the respiration and senescence process, (2) reduction in sensitivity to ethylene, and (3) decrease in the incidence and severity of disease causing organisms such as fungi, bacteria, insects and pests, in selected commodities. The CA storage proves beneficial for fruits and vegetables that deteriorate rapidly or those that complete ripening after harvest.

Active packaging: Increased demand of fresh fruits and vegetables needs efficient packaging, which can restore the product quality up to long time (processing to consumption). Several intensive studies occurred for developing the advance packaging technique because controlling the fruits and vegetables deterioration with the help of traditional packaging technologies is impossible.

Active packaging is very efficient and successfully used for packing the fresh fruits and vegetables and provides better packing characteristics at marginal cost (Mehyar *et al.*, 2011) Quality of the packed product cannot be efficiently maintained with general packaging technologies due to which a suitable and advanced packaging technique has been developed for controlling the deterioration and enhance the shelf life of fruits and vegetables by adding active ingredients in the packaging materials. Active packaging is very useful for preserving the perishable fruits and vegetables because of this modern packaging technique, different types of indicators (colour indicators, oxygen indicators and CO_2 indicators etc.) also can be used for alarming the condition of packed products which facilitates the hygienic quality control. Ozdemir and Floros (2004) stated that active packaging provides efficient barrier to the moisture and gasses migration, minimize the chances of contamination from outside and facilitate the handling process throughout the storage and marketing periods.

Waxing: The outer surface of fruits and vegetables (excluding under-ground ones) have a natural waxy layer, which is partly removed during handling and washing. An extra discontinuous layer of wax applied artificially, provides the necessary protection against the entry of decay organisms. The practical benefit from wax coating is usually a reduction in evaporation and respiration. It has been reported that where refrigerated storage facilities are not available, protective skin coating with wax is one of the methods developed for increasing the storage life of fruits and vegetables.

Cold/Cool Chain

The cold chain industry is emerging as a fast-growing business sector in India, with developments in the food processing sector, organized retail and government initiatives driving growth. To develop a world-class cold chain infrastructure, government and industry bodies need to work in collaboration to encourage the adoption of better and more efficient refrigeration technologies that can prolong the shelf life of food products and bring commensurate economic returns to the farmers. The technology of construction has undergone a phenomenal change from conventional brickwall construction to sandwich insulated panel and reinforced concrete (RCC) structures to pre-engineered buildings (PEB) steel structures. Energy-efficient practices like energy recovery systems, energy-efficient designs of refrigeration equipment and automation are some of the innovative features. Efforts need to be made in order to introduce the concept of green technology, as also the use of renewable energy for the cold chain sector. Special emphasis needs to be laid on development of reefer infrastructure in view of India's exports thrust and potential. Besides, to boost the investments, financial institutions should play a major role to encourage the investment in cold chain industry in terms of term loan sanctioning, nominal interest rates and disbursement. The growth cannot happen without their support. The state government must make a step towards subsidizing the electrical tariffs, encouraging use of renewable energies, etc in order to boost the development of cold chain infrastructure in India.

Diversification and value addition

In the past, fruits and vegetables were processed primarily into jams, jellies, chutneys, etc. Canning and dehydration were considered to be the most sophisticated methods of processing, prior to the discovery of rapid freezing. In recent times, considerable emphasis has been placed on the handling of fresh fruits and vegetables. Canning has become practically obsolete and methods such as aseptic packaging, cryogenic freezing, deep freezing accelerated freeze drying, controlled and modified atmosphere storage, shrink wrapping etc. have been increasingly used in extending the shelf life of fruits and vegetables. These technologies must be adopted if India is to keep pace with the rest of the World.

Value of postharvest research and development

They identified the following five reasons to justify an increased commitment to postharvest research by the international agricultural system:

1. High internal rates of return,
2. International public good character,
3. Effect on poverty,
4. Effect on food security and health, and
5. Effect on sustainable use of resources.

Public awareness

Public awareness campaigns must be implemented in order to increase awareness of the costs and implication of losses after harvest/production. Fixed targets must also be established to curb postharvest losses, along the same lines as those used in family planning and other time bound national programs. Public awareness campaigns should involve scientists, as well as extension and social worker organizations, and should incorporate the use of audio visual aids and the mass communication systems, including both print and electronic media.

The Government of India is committed to providing a massive thrust to food processing and other agro-based industries in an endeavor to increase the income of farmers, create employment opportunities, diversify the rural economy and foster rural industrialization. This sector has a critical role in improving agricultural productivity, reducing waste in fruits, vegetables and other perishable food items, and improving food availability for the domestic market as well as for export markets. Fresh and processed fruits and vegetables offer opportunities for both the domestic market and for international trade. In today's liberalized policy environment, India is well placed for both local and foreign investment in the food processing sector.

9. Government of India Recent Implementing Schemes to Reduce to Postharvest Losses

To curb the losses in supply chain of agriculture produce and to improve the existing infrastructure for food processing, the Ministry of Food Processing Industries has been implementing the Schemes of Mega Food Parks; Integrated Cold Chain, Value Addition and Preservation Infrastructure; and Setting up/ Modernization of Abattoirs.

The scheme for **Mega Food Parks** aims to provide modern infrastructure for food processing units in the country on pre-identified cluster basis. Under the scheme, grant-in-aid is provided @ 50% of the eligible project cost in general areas and 75% thereof in difficult areas and hilly areas i.e., North East Region including Sikkim, J&K, Himachal Pradesh, Uttarakhand and ITDP notified areas of the states, subject to a maximum of Rs.50.00 crore per project. A total of 42 Mega Food Park projects have been approved by the Government to be set up in the country.

The Scheme for Setting up/ Modernization of Abattoirs aims to provide hygienic finished meat and meat products, slaughter waste management and pollution control. The Scheme envisaged grant-in-aid @ 50% of the project cost in general areas and 75% for North- Eastern region subject to a maximum of Rs.15.00 Crore per project. So far, 41 Abattoir projects have been sanctioned.

The Scheme of Cold Chain, Value Addition and Preservation Infrastructure aims at arresting post-harvest losses of horticulture & non-horticulture produce and providing remunerative price to farmers for their produce. Under the scheme, financial assistance is provided in the form of grant-in-aid of maximum Rs.10 crore per project for setting up of integrated cold chain and preservation infrastructure facilities without any break from the farm gate to the consumer.

The integrated cold chain and preservation infrastructure can be set up by individuals, groups of entrepreneurs, cooperative societies, Self Help Groups (SHGs), Farmer Producer Organizations (FPOs), NGOs, Central/State PSUs, etc. The scheme is primarily private sector driven and proposals under this scheme are invited through Expression of Interest (EOI). The scheme is available in all States/UTs and rural & urban areas. So far, 134 Integrated Cold Chain Projects have been sanctioned by the Ministry in the country to reduce the cold chain gap. Of this, 88 Integrated Cold Chain projects have achieved completion and commenced commercial operation, 46 Integrated Cold Chain projects are in various stages of implementation. The impact of these 134 integrated Cold Chain projects being assisted by Ministry in the country under the Scheme of Cold Chain,

Value Addition and Preservation Infrastructure in respect of expected capacity creation is 4.92 Lakh MT of Cold Storage/Controlled Atmosphere/Deep Freezer, 113.90 MT/Hour of Individual Quick Freezer (IQF), 54.65 Lakh Litter Per Day of Milk Storage/Processing and 761 Number of Reefer Vans. Capacity created from 88 completed cold chain projects is 3.31 Lakh MT of Cold Storage/CA/ Deep Freezer, 77.15 MT/Hr of Individual Quick Freezing, 31.80 Lakh Litre Per Day of Milk Processing/Storage and 423 Number of Reefer Vans. State wise funds are not allotted under the scheme of Cold Chain, Value Addition and Preservation Infrastructure.

10. Conclusion

India is second largest producer of food next to China with estimated food processing industry size at US$ 70 billion. In 2012, the production was 257 million tonnes of food grain (rice, wheat, coarse grains and pulses), 75 million tonnes of fruits and 149 million tonnes of vegetables. Out of these amounts, only 2.2 % of these are processed. In contrast, countries like USA (65%) and China (23%) are far ahead of India in reducing the wastage and enhancing the value addition and shelf life of the farm products. The losses in postharvest sector are estimated to be from 10 to 25% in durables, semi-perishables and products like milk, meat, fish and eggs. The estimated losses in fruits and vegetables are higher and reached from 30 to 40%. These %ages are not acceptable and adversely affect the Indian economy. To prevent such amount of losses, different organizations in India have been trying to find solution for serious issue related to post-harvest. A number of deficiencies currently exist in the postharvest management and processing of food in India. Handling of raw produce through many stages of middlemen, Processing is mostly controlled by urban rather than rural entrepreneurs which leads to losses in valuable by products, Non-availability of adequate and efficient equipment and machinery to be used in catchment areas, Low level of entrepreneurial urge in rural areas due to constraints of awareness, finance, assured market and proper training on technology and a fragmented and inefficient value chain.

Action must be taken in order to upgrade systems like modern post-harvest equipment, latest packaging and storage system, cold chain facilities, diversification and value addition, postharvest research and Public awareness in order to reduce the levels of postharvest losses in India.To curb the losses in supply chain of agriculture produce and to improve the existing infrastructure for food processing, the Ministry of Food Processing Industries has been implementing the Schemes of Mega Food Parks; Integrated Cold Chain, Value Addition and Preservation Infrastructure; and Setting up/ Modernization of Abattoirs

References

Ashby BH, Hinsch RT, Risse IA, Kindya WG, Craig WL, Turczyn MT.,1987. Protecting Perishable Foods during Transport by Motor Truck. USDA Handbook No. 669. U.S. Govt. Printing Office, Washington, D.C.

Ayyappan, S. 2012. Feeding over a billion forever: challenges and priorities for ICAR in the next decade. ACIAR Seminar Series presentation, 18 January 2012, Canberra, Australia.

Beiioclt, R.,1988. Losses in the logistical system: The case of perishables. *J. Food Dist. Res.*, ll 9(2): 20-28.

Caswell, J.A. and Mojduszka, E.M.; 1996 "Using Informational Labeling to Influence the Market for Quality in Food Products." *American Journal Agriculture Economics*, 78: 1248-1253.

Caswell, J. A. and Padberg, D. I., 1992 "Toward a more Comprehensive Theory for Food Labels." *American Journal Agriculture Economics* 74: 460- 468.

DARE/ICAR (Department of Agricultural Research and Education/ Indian Council of Agricultural Research). 2011. Post-harvest Management and Value-addition, DARE/ICARAnnual Report 2010–11, Ministry of Agriculture, India. P: 57-62.

Dash, S. K., Bakhara, C.K. and Mohanty, S.N. 1993. Status of small rice hullers of Orissaand response of the millers on modernization of hullers. *Agric. Engng. Today*. 17 (3-4): 73-78.

Dash, S. K., K Khan, M.D., Bakhara, C.K. and Mohanty, S.N. 1996. Study on the responseof small millers of Orissa to modernization. *Curr. Agric. Res.* 9(1-2): 39-41.

Fishman, S., Rodov, V. and Ben-Yehoshua, S. 1996. Mathematical model for perforation effect on oxygen and water vapour dynamics in modifiedatmosphere packages. *Journal of Food Science*, 61: 956-961

Garner, J.C., Prussia, S.E., Shewfelt, R.L., Jordan, J.L.,1987. Peach quality after delays in cooling. American Society of Agricultural Engineers Tech. Paper number B7-6501 St. Joseph, Michigan.

Grolleaud, M. 2002 Post-harvest losses: discovering the full story. Overview of the phenomenon of losses during the post-harvest system. Rome, Italy: FAO, Agro Industries and Post-Harvest Management Service.

Gummert, M. 2013. Reducing rice postharvest losses. Developed by M. Gummert with funding for IRRI's postharvest projects provided by the Asian Development Bank (ADB), the Swiss Agency for Development and Cooperation (SDC), and the Deutsche Gesellschaftfür Internationale Zusammenarbeit (GIZ).

Hall A. J., Yoganand, B., Sulaiman R. V., and Clark N. G. (Eds.). 2003. Post-harvest innovations in innovation: reflections on partnership and learning. Crop Post-Harvest Programme (CPHP), South Asia, C/o International Crops Research Institute for the Semi-Arid Tropics (ICRISAT), Patancheru 502 324, Andhra Pradesh, India: Crop Post Harvest Programme South Asia. 180 pp.

Hodges, R.J., Buzby, J.C. and Bennett, B., 2011. "Postharvest losses and waste in developed and less developed countries: opportunities to improve resource use." *Journal of Agricultural Science* 149:37-45.

Kitinoja, L., A.l. Hassan, H.A., Saran S. and Roy S.K. 2010. Identification of appropriate postharvest technologies for improving market access and incomes for small horticultural farmers in sub-Saharan Africa and South Asia. Invited paper in three parts for the IHC Postharvest Symposium Lisbon, August 23, 2010. *Acta Hortic.*

Kitinoja, L., S. Saran, S.K. Roy, and A.A. Kader. 2011. "Postharvest Technology for Developing Countries: Challenges and Opportunities in Research, Outreach and Advocacy." *J of the Science of Food and Agriculture* 9: 97–603.

Maheshwar, C. and Chanakwa, T.S. 2006. Postharvest Losses Due To Gaps in Cold Chain in India: A Solution. *Acta Hort*. (ISHS) 712:777-784.

Manners-Bell, J. and Miroux A. 2013. Logistics as Solutions and New Opportunities: The Role of Logistics in Reducing Post-Harvest Losses. Global Agenda Council on Logistics & Supply Chain Systems, 2012-2014. Published by World Economic Forum, Geneva, Switzerland, 2013

Mehyar, G.F. and Han, J.H. 2011. Active Packaging for Fresh-Cut Fruits and Vegetables, Edited by Aaron L. Brody, Hong Zhuang and Jung H. Han. Blackwell Publishing Ltd, pp. 267-284.

Ozdemir, M. and Floros, J.D. 2004. Onions: Postharvest Operation,Organisation:Massey University, Private Bag, Active food packaging technologies. *Critical Review Food Nutrition*, 44:185–193.

Parfitt, J., Barthel, M. and Macnaughton, S. 2010. Food waste within food supply chains: quantification and potential for change to 2050. *Phil. Trans. R. Soc. B* (2010) 365.

Phansalkar, S.J. 2003. Evolving technology through collaboration and partnership: the case of IDE(I)'s work with tomato packaging in Himachal Pradesh, India. Pages 32–44

Rajasri, M., Sambasiva Rao P. and MeenaKumari, K.V.S. 2010. Inert dusts better alternatives to manage Angoumois grain moth Sitotrogacerealella in stored rice 29th Congress of the International Seed Testing Association (ISTA), Cologne, Germany, 16-22 June 2010.

Rolle, R. S. (ed.) 2006. Improving postharvest management and marketing in the Asia Pacific region: issues and challenges trends in the fruit and vegetable sector. Tokyo, Japan: FAO, Asian Productivity Organisation (APO).

Roy, S.K. and Pal, R.K. 1991. A low cost zero energy cool chamber for short-term storage of mango. *Acta Hort* 291:519-524.

Smil, V. 2004. Feeding the world: how much more rice do we need? In Rice is life, scientific perspectives for the 21st century. Proc. of the World Rice Research Conf. held in Tokyo and Tsukuba, November 2004, Japan, pp. 21–23.

Tyler, P.S. and Gilman, G.A.,1979. L'évaluation des pertes post-récolte», Séminaire de Bamako, pp.137-151.

Villers, P. and Gummert, M. 2009. Seal of Approval. Rice Today, January-March 2009. pp. 36-37.

2

Agricultural Waste to Biochar A New Eco-friendly Approach in Indian Scenario

Ankit Singla, Varsha Singla, Harish Kumar, Gagnesh Sharma and Kazuyuki Inubushi

Abstract

India ranks in the world's five largest producers of over 80% of agricultural produce items. Processing of agricultural produce generates substantial amount of crop residues which can have tremendous value to farmers. However, a large portion of the residues is burned on farm primarily to clear the field from straw and stubble; which affects the environment, soil health and crop yield.The conversion of crop residues to eco-friendly and valuable product like biochar is need of the hour. Biochar is an organic amendment which slowly releases C in the soil, and is stable over the years. Various applications of biochar like reduction in greenhouse gases emission, sequestering C in the soil, increasing crop yield, used as combusting fuel and livestock feedmakes it a promising candidate for sustainable agriculture and environment.

Keywords: Agriculture, Crop Residue, Biochar, Greenhouse Gases, Soil Health

1. Introduction

Agriculture plays a vital role in India's economy. Along with fisheries and forestry, agriculture is one of the largest contributors to the gross domestic product in our country. Among the rice growing countries in the world, India has the largest cultivation area. India ranks next to the China in rice, wheat, vegetables, and fruits production, and is the largest producer of the spices. The production of crops leads to the generation of residues which needs proper utilization. In our country, these crop residues are mainly used for animal feeding, biomanure making and as the fuel for domestic and industrial use. Besides these, we are generating a large quantity of surplus residues which are often burnt on-farm.

Burning of crop residue causes environmental pollution by emission of greenhouse gases (GHG) along with loss of nutrients and microbial flora in soil environment; which leads to decrease the soil fertility and ultimately the crop yield. Moreover, India's population is increasing day by day which pressurize the agriculture to feed the more people with limited natural resources. This necessitates the use of excessive chemical fertilizers for crop production which also leads to a number of negative impacts on the environment including the emission of GHG. So, we need sustainable use of the agricultural residues. At present, biochar is one of the most preferential option for the proper utilization of agricultural waste. Biochar is a stable, recalcitrant organic C compound that is the product of thermal degradation of organic matter (including crop residues) in the absence of air (pyrolysis). Biochar has the potential to be used for a wide range of applications. Biochar input to the soil has been reported to boost soil fertility and improve soil quality resulting in increased crop yield. Soil benefits also include raising soil pH, increasing water holding capacity, improving cation exchange capacity and retaining nutrients. Biochar is a low-cost product and has been tipped as an excellent soil amendment for sequestering C, for increasing soil organic carbon, water retention and to provide a preferred habitat for soil microbes. It could be used as combusting fuel, electrode for microbial fuel cell, livestock feed, and also helps in the removal of pollutants. A developing nation like India strongly requires the production of eco-friendly biochar. However, it is true that only very limited knowledge or practical utility of biochar is in the process of Indian agricultural system which should be promoted to get the sustainable use of crop residues. Countries like USA, China, Japan, UK, Germany, Australia, South Korea etc. are gaining a lot of benefits by using the biochar. This chapter highlights the importance of biochar which can be implemented in Indian scenario too.

2. Agricultural Crop Production and Residue Generation in India

2.1 Agricultural Crop Production

It is estimated that more than 58 % of the rural households depend on the agriculture as their principal means of livelihood. As per estimates by the Central Statistics Office, the share of agriculture and allied sectors (including agriculture, livestock, forestry and fishery) was 15.35 % of the gross value added during 2015-16 at 2011-12 prices. India is the largest producer, consumer and exporter of spices and spice products. India's fruit production has grown much faster than vegetables, making it the second largest fruit producer in the world. India's horticulture output, comprising fruits, vegetables and spices, was estimated to be 283.4 MT in 2015-16. It ranks third in farm and agriculture outputs. Agricultural export constitutes 10 % of the country's exports and is the fourth-largest exported principal commodity. As per the 3rd Advance Estimates, India's foodgrain production has increased marginally to 252.23 MT in the year 2015-16. Production of pulses in India is estimated at 17.06 MT.

2.2 Crop Residue Generation

On the annual basis, 686 MT gross residue is generated in India. Out of this, 545 MT is contributed by cereals, oilseed, pulses and sugarcane crops together; 61 MT by horticultural crops (coconut, banana and areca nut) and 80 MT by others (cotton and jute) (Fig. 1). At crop group level, cereal contributes the highest amount; 368 MT (54%) followed by sugarcane 111 MT (16 %). At individual crop level, rice contributes the highest amount (154 MT) gross residue followed by wheat (131 MT) (Hiloidhari *et al.*, 2014).

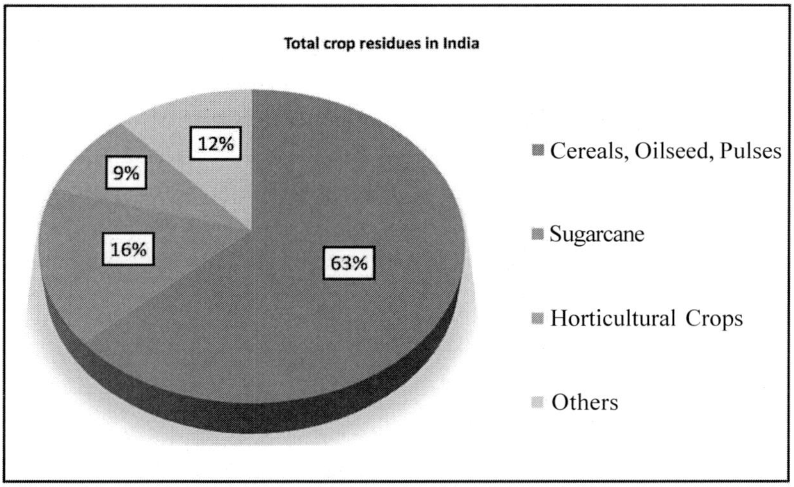

Fig. 1: Crop wise contribution of total residues generation in India

Considering the surplus portions of residues available from the selected crops, annual national potential is around 234 MT, i.e. 34% of the gross residue generated in India. The group of cereals contribute the highest amount of surplus residue (89 MT) followed by sugarcane (56 MT), others (47 MT), horticultural (23 MT), oilseeds (14 MT) and pulses (5 MT) (Fig. 2). At individual crop level, the maximum amount of surplus residue is contributed by sugarcane (56 MT), followed by cotton (47 MT) and rice (43MT).

Although, rice produces the highest amountof gross residue among all the crops, its surplus residue production is less than sugarcane. This is because rice residues (husk and straw) compared to sugarcane residues (bagasse, leaves and tops) can be used as cattle feed, animal feed, packing material, heating and cooking fuel. Surplus residue potential from banana and coconut (horticultural crops) is also significant in India and is estimated as 12 MT and 10 MT, respectively (Hiloidhari *et al.*, 2014).

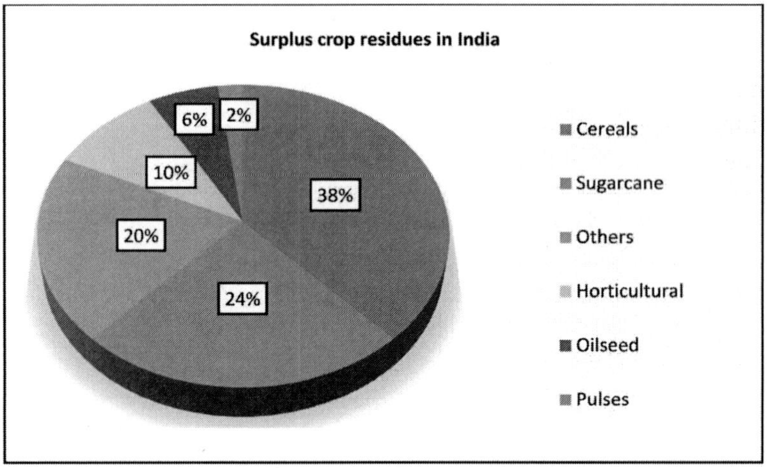

Fig. 2: Crop wise contribution of surplus residues generation in India

Residue potential varies significantly among the states of India. In terms of gross potential, it ranges from a minimum value of 0.21 MT in Mizoram to a maximum value of 121 MT in Uttar Pradesh. Sugarcane is widely cultivated in the state followed by wheat and rice. These three crops together contribute more than 90% residue generated in the state. Punjab, another agriculturally advanced state of India produces 83 MT gross residues. Concerning the surplus residue potential, Uttar Pradesh produces the highest amount (40MT) followed by Maharashtra (31MT) and Punjab (28MT) (Hiloidhari *et al.*, 2014).

2.3 Fate of Crop Residues and Negative Impacts of Residues' Burning

The crop residues are used for animal feeding, soil mulching, biomanure making, that ching for rural homes and fuel for domestic and industrial use. The utilization of crop residues varies across different states of the country. The residues of cereal crops are mainly used as cattle feed. Rice straw and husk are used as domestic fuel or in boilers for parboiling rice. Farmers use crop residues either themselves or sell it to landless households or intermediaries, who further sell them to industries. The residues of cotton, chilli, pulses and oilseed crops are mainly used as fuel for household needs. The shells of coconut, stalks of rapeseed and mustard, pigeon pea, jute, mesta, and sunflower are used as domestic fuel. Residues of groundnut are burnt as fuel in brick kilns and lime kilns. However, a large portion of the residues is burnt on-farm primarily to clear the field for sowing of the succeeding crop. The residues of rice, wheat, cotton, maize, millet, sugarcane, jute, rapeseed-mustard and groundnut are typically burnt on-farm across different states of the country. The problem is more severe in the irrigated agriculture, particularly in the mechanized rice-wheat system of the northwest India (Asadullah *et al.*, 2008). Sugarcane tops are either used for feeding of dairy animals or burnt on-farm for growing a ratoon crop in most parts of the country. In states like Punjab and Haryana, where crop residues of rice are not used as cattle feed, a large amount is burnt on-farm. According to the estimates of Sardar Patel Renewable Energy Research Institute (2004), about 72 MT crop residues are burnt on-farm; while, Pathak *et al*., (2010) have estimated it to be 93 MT. It was estimated that 22% of rice straw and 10% of wheat straw are burned *in-situ* in Uttar Pradesh (Beri *et al*., 2003). In case of fibre crops, approximately 80% of the residues are from cotton and are subjected to on-farm burning.

Burning of crop residues leads to the emission of trace gases: carbon dioxide (CO_2), methane (CH_4), carbon monoxide (CO), nitrous oxide (N_2O), oxides of nitrogen (NO_X) and sulphur (SO_X), and other hydrocarbons to the atmosphere. The increase in the atmospheric concentration of greenhouse gases (GHG) also causing the global warming. The global temperatures have increased 0.8^{o} over the past century and are predicted to increase another 1.1 to 6.4 degrees over the next century (Peters *et al*., 2013). There is a growing consensus that the warming is at least a consequence of increasing anthropogenic GHG. It is estimated that global GHG emission has increased by 70% between the years 1970 to 2004 (IPCC, 2007). The increase in the concentration of N_2O also leads to the depletion of the stratospheric ozone layer (Ravishankara *et al*., 2009).

The burning of crop residues also causes loss of plant nutrients like N, P, K and S. The burning of crop residues is the wastage of valuable resources which could be a source of C, bio-active compounds, feed and energy for rural households and small industries. Heat generated from the burning of crop residues elevates the soil temperature causing death of active beneficial microbial population, though the effect is temporary, as the microbes regenerate after a few days. Repeated burning in a field, however, permanently diminishes the microbial population. The burning of crop residues immediately increases the exchangeable ammonium-N (NH_4^+-N) and bicarbonate- extractable P content, but there is no build-up of nutrients in the soil profile. Long-term burning also reduces total N and C, and potentially mineralizable-N in the upper soil layer (Blanco-Canqui and Lal, 2009). It was reported that one ton of rice straw on burning can release about 3 kg particulate matter, 60 kg CO, 1460 kg CO_2, 199 kg ash and 2 kg SO_2 (Gadi *et al*., 2003).

3. Biochar: A Promising Solution for Conversion of Agricultural Waste

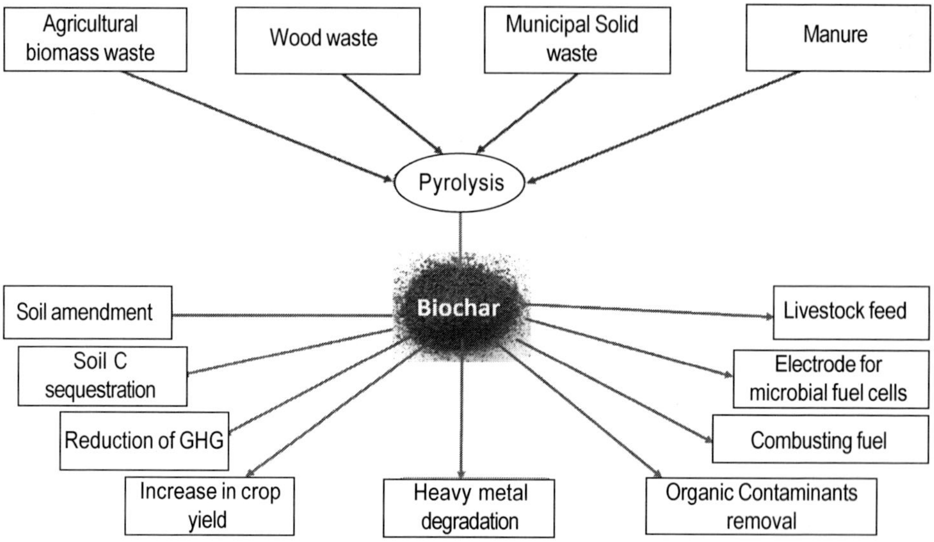

Fig. 3: Formation and applications of biochar

3.1 General Characteristics of Biochar

Biochar is a fine-grained, black, solid, C-rich (70–80%) porous substance produced from the thermal decomposition of various biological wastes (e.g. wood waste, agricultural biomass waste, municipal solid waste and manures) in the absence of oxygen (Lehmann *et al.*, 2002) (Fig. 3). Biochar has large surface area and high porosity, tending to increase with increasing pyrolysis temperature until around 850 (Brown *et al.*, 2006). Many biochar products have alkaline pH (Spokas *et al.*, 2012; Singla and Inubushi, 2014a), which can decrease soil acidity, creating a more favourable habitat for many plants and microbes. Biochar has the high capacity to adsorb cations and anions from solutions, including a variety of organic compounds.

3.2 Types of Biochar

There are two processes for biomass pyrolysis, slow pyrolysis (SP) and fast pyrolysis (FP). SP is characterized by slow heating (minutes to hours) of the organic material to ~400 in the absence of oxygen and relatively long solids and gas residence times (typically several minutes to hours) (Bruun *et al.*, 2012). The FP technology is typically more complicated. Small-grained organic material is blown into a hot reactor (~450-700) and exposed to heat transfer for just a few milliseconds to seconds (Laird *et al.*, 2009). SP and FP results in biochars with different physico-chemical properties (Table 1). Char contains varying amount of C, typically ranging from 60-90% (Gaur and Reed, 1995). Apart from SP and FP, 'intermediate pyrolysis (IP)' has also been used to describe biomass pyrolysis in a certain type of commercial screw-pyrolyser – the Haloclean reactor (Hornung *et al.*, 2006); Table 1.Very fast pyrolysis, also referred as 'flash pyrolysis' (Demirbas and Arin, 2002), is usually in the context of laboratory studies involving rapid movement of substrate through a heated tube under gravity or in a gas flow. Higher temperatures and shorter residence times than FP are used, the main product distributions are similar to FP.

Table 1: Product yield for different types of biochar

	Char (%)	Liquid (%)	Gas (%)
Slow pyrolysis (SP)	25-35	20-50	20-50
Fast pyrolysis (FP)	10-25	50-70	10-30
Intermediate pyrolysis (IP)	30-40	35-45	20-30

3.3 Uses of Biochar

3.3.1 Biochar as soil amendment

One of the most commonly studied applications of biochar is its use as an agricultural soil amendment (Fig. 3). Biochar application can improve chemical, biological, and physical properties of the soil. Because of its porous structure, biochar creates a habitat for beneficial microorganisms, increasing total stored macronutrient content, cation-exchange capacity, water absorption capacity, and organic matter content such as soil organic carbon and total N(Lehmann *et al.*, 2011; Singla *et al.*, 2014a). It offers an opportunity to save N fertilizers in the field. In most cases, it also increases soil pH, making it a great replacement for the traditional practice of using lime to raise the pH. The application of biochar in the soil results in the availability of macro and micro elements such as P, K, Mg, Ca, Mo, and B (Silber *et al.*, 2010). Ammonia exposed to biochar surfaces is known to react with surface oxygen groups, which leads to the formation of amines and amides under ambient (<100°C) conditions or ammonium salts, depending on the specific type of chemical reactions. The polar groups on biochar surfaces act as water adsorption centres and facilitate the formation of water clusters on the carbon surfaces. Additionally, the porous structure of biochar that retained water can result in better nutrient availability by decreasing the discharge of total N and P (Spokas *et al.*, 2012; Xie *et al.*, 2016).

3.3.2 Biochar in C sequestration and crop yield

The application of biochar can be helpful in sequestering C in the soil resulting in the reduction of GHG emission in the atmosphere (He *et al.*, 2016). However, the impact of biochar on different GHG including CO_2, CH_4, and N_2O can vary significantly (Spokas *et al.*, 2012; Singla and Inubushi, 2013; Singla *et al.*, 2014b). Biochar amendments generally reduces CO_2 production by improving carbon stabilization. However, no significant effect was observed on soil CO_2 respiration that was measured in the field (Castaldi *et al.*, 2011). Paddy CH_4 emissions significantly decreased under biochar amendments, which did not result from the inhibition of methanogenic growth but resulted from the significant decrease of the ratio of methanogenic to methanotrophic abundances (Feng *et al.*, 2012). The decrease in N_2O emission is hypothesized as a result from an impact on the N fixing microorganisms, and other influences on the microbial population by the biochar (Lehmann *et al.*, 2011). However, contrary to the above, some of the reports have also found the increased emission of GHG after biochar application (Saarnio *et al.*, 2013; Singla and Inubushi, 2014b, Singla *et al.*, 2014b). It appears that the amount of GHG emission will depend on the physical and chemical properties of the biochar, the type of the soil, the microbiological circumstances, and the water and fertilizer management.

The increase in soil nutrients, organic matter content and microbial activities by biochar application can lead to increased crop yield over short term as well as long term (Singla *et al.*, 2014a; Paneque *et al.*, 2016; Qin *et al.*, 2016). Asai *et al.*, (2009) reported decreased yield of rice by the application of biochar without N fertilizer. It indicates that the addition of N-source with biochar seems to be essential for the crop improvement. The maintenance of C:N ratio is also required to increase crop yield as the high rate of biochar application to the soil caused low grain yield because of limitations in N availability for plant growth resulting from biochar properties such as low mineral element and high C:N ratios (Asai *et al.*, 2009, Singla *et al.*, 2014b). In addition, Yamato *et al.*, (2006) reported that multiple applications of biochar and fertilizer resulted in more stable crop yields than a single application of fertilizer or biochar. The activities of certain enzymes e.g., alkaline phosphatase, aminopeptidase and *N*-acetylglucosaminidase have been reported to increase after the application of biochar which also helps in the improvement of soil biological performance and crop yield.

3.3.3 Biochar in pollutants degradation

Biochar offers promise as a low-cost alternative to current strategies like filtration and bio-retention for removal of the pollutants. Because of its high affinity to adsorb molecular ions, biochar has demonstrated excellent potential in a variety of toxicological mediation strategies. It has shown effectiveness in mitigating aqueous metals, suspended solids, organic compounds, and organic hydrocarbons in a variety of industrial applications including urban and residential storm water runoff, resource extraction runoff, industrial yard runoff, and industrial wastewater filtration. The large specific surface area, porous structure, surface functional groups of biochar are the important features promising their high removal efficiencies of contaminants. Column filtration tests with biochar (green waste, poultry litter, waste wood, digester waste) showed toxic metal (Cd, Cr, Cu, Pb, Ni, and Zn) reduction ranging from 17-75% depending on the metal, total suspended solid reduction of around 86%, and up to 100% efficiency at removing some polycyclic aromatic hydrocarbons (Reddy *et al.*, 2014). Apart from heavy metals and organic contaminants, other pollutants such as ammonium/ nitrate, phosphate and fluoride could also be removed by the application of biochar (Hollister *et al.*, 2013). Other uses of biochar in urban storm water filtration scenarios include incorporation into rain gardens and sensitive buffer strips to bolster bio-retention attributes.

3.3.4 Biochar as a fuel

Biochar can also be an appropriate material for direct combustion/co-combustion with low rank coals for heat production because it has considerably higher energy densities which iscomparable to lignite (Liu *et al.*, 2013). Biochar may also be used as a sustainable electrode material for the electricity production in microbial fuel cells which can reduce the energy and C footprint associated with electrode manufacturing (Huggins *et al.*, 2014). It was estimated that the use of biochar results in a reduction of 90% power output cost compared to commonly used granular activated C or graphite granule.

3.3.5 Biochar as a feed for livestock

In addition to all above properties, biochar can have various beneficial effects on livestock production when ingested as a feed supplement or used in feed processing. When added as a supplement to recommended feed @ 0.2%; biochar (corn cob, canarium seed) can increase total weight and improve total body characteristics of broiler chicken (Kana and Teguia, 2011). This has been repeated in studies with cattle showing an increase up to 25% in body weight while feeding @ 0.5% biochar (rice husk). It has also resulted in reducing methane emissions in livestocks up to 22%.

4. Conclusion

Efficient agricultural production should not deal only with the processing of raw material to product formation but also includes the utilization of left over residues. Biochar is an efficient C source which can be produced from variety of biological wastes. Many developed and developing nations have adopted the production of biochar for various purposes. India is generating a huge quantity of surplus agricultural residues which has immense potential and it should be harnessed into biochar.

References

Asadullah, M., Rahman, M.A., Ali, M.M., Motin, M.A., Sultan, M.B., Alam, M.R. and Rahman, M.S., 2008. Jute stick pyrolysis for bio-oil production in fluidized bed reactor. *Bioresource Technology*, 99:44-50.

Asai, H., Samson, K.B., Stephan, M.H., Songyikhangsuthor, K., Homma, K., Kiyono, Y., Inoue, Y., Shiraiwa, T. and Horie, T., 2009. Biochar amendment techniques for upland rice production in Northern Laos: 1. Soil physical properties, leaf SPAD and grain yield. *Field Crops Research,* 111:81-84.

Beri, V., Sidhu, B.S., Gupta, A.P., Tiwari, R.C., Pareek, R.P., Rupela, O.P., Khera, R. and Singh, J., 2003. Organic Resources of a part of Indo-Gangetic Plain and their utilization. Department of Soils, PAU, Ludhiana, India, p.93.

Blanco-Canqui, H. and Lal, R., 2009. Crop residue removal impacts on soil productivity and environmental quality. *Critical Reviews in Plant Science*, 28:139-163.

Brown, R.A., Kercher, A.K., Nguyen, T.H., Nagle, D.C. and Ball, W.P., 2006. Production and characterization of synthetic wood chars for use as surrogates for natural sorbents. *Organic Geochemistry*, 37:321-333.

Bruun, E.W., Ambus, P., Egsgaard, H. and Hauggaard-Nielsen, H., 2003. Effects of slow and fast pyrolysis biochar on soil C and N turnover dynamics. *Soil Biology and Biochemistry*, 46:73-79.

Castaldi, S., Riondino, M., Baronti, S., Esposito, F.R., Marzaioli, R., Rutigliano, F.A., Vaccari, F.P. and Miglietta, F., 2011. Impact of biochar application to a Mediterranean wheat crop on soil microbial activity and greenhouse gas fluxes. *Chemosphere*, 85:1464-1471.

Demirbas, A. and Arin, G., 2002. An Overview of Biomass Pyrolysis. *Energy Sources*, 24: 471-482.

Feng, Y., Xu, Y., Yu, Y., Xie, Z. and Lin, X., 2012. Mechanisms of biochar decreasing methane emission from Chinese paddy soils. *Soil Biology and Biochemistry*, 46:80-88.

Gadi, R., Kulshrestha, U.C., Sarkar, A.K., Garg, S.C. and Parashar, D.C., 2003. Emissions of SO_2 and NO_x from bio-fuels in India. *Tellus B*, 55:787-795.

Gaur, S. and Reed, T.B., 1995. An Atlas of Thermal Data for Biomass and Other Fuels. National Renewable Energy Laboratory, Golden, Colorado, USA.

He, Y., Zhou, X., Jiang, L., Li, M., Du, Z., Zhou, G., Shao, J., Wang, X., Xu, Z., Hosseini Bai, S. and Wallace, H., 2016. Effects of biochar application on soil greenhouse gas fluxes: a meta analysis. *Global Change Biology Bioenergy*, doi: 10.1111/gcbb.12376 (in press).

Hiloidhari, M., Das, D. and Baruah, D.C., 2014. Bioenergy potential from crop residue biomass in India. *Renewable and Sustainable Energy Reviews*, 32:504-512.

Hollister, C.C., Bisogni, J.J. and Lehmann, J., 2013. Ammonium, nitrate, and phosphate sorption to and solute leaching from biochars prepared from corn stover (L.) and oak wood (spp.). *Journal of Environmental Quality*, 42:137–144.

Hornung, A., Apfelbacher, W., Koch, W., Linek, A., Sagi, S., Schoner, J., Stohr, J., Seifert, H.,Tumiatti, V. and Lenzi, F., 2006. Thermo-chemical conversion of straw - Haloclean intermediate Pyrolysis. 17th International Symposium on Analytical and Applied Pyrolysis.

Huggins, T., Wang, H., Kearns, J., Jenkins, P. and Ren, Z.J., 2014. Biochar as a sustainable electrode material for electricity production in microbial fuel cells. *Bioresource Technology*, 157:114-119.

IPCC., 2007. Changes in atmospheric constituents and in radiative forcing, *In*: Climate change, the physical science basis, contribution of working group I to the fourth assessment report of the intergovernmental panel on climate change, Cambridge University Press, Cambridge, UK.

Kana, J.R. and Teguia, A., 2011. Growth performance and carcass characteristics of broiler chickens fed diets supplimented with graded levels of charcoal from maize cob or seed of *Canarium schweinfurthii* Engl. *Tropical Animal Health and Productivity*, 43:51-56.

Laird, D.A., Fleming, P., Wang, B., Horton, R. and Karlen, D., 2010. Biochar impact on nutrient leaching from a midwestern agricultural soil. *Geoderma*, 158:436-442.

Lehmann, J., Silva, J.P. Jr., Rondon, M., Cravo, M.S., Greenwood, J., Nehls, T., Steiner, C. and Glaser, B., 2002. Slash-and-char: a feasible alternative for soil fertility management in the central Amazon. *In*: *Proceedings of the World Congress of Soil Science*, Thailand.

Lehmann, J., Rillig, M.C., Thies, J., Masiello, C.A., Hockaday, W.C. and Crowley, D., 2011. Biochar effects on soil biota - a review. *Soil Biology and Biochemistry,*43:1812-1836.

Liu, Z., Quek, A., Kent Hoekman, S. and Balasubramanian, R., 2013. Production of solid biochar fuel from waste biomass by hydrothermal carbonization. *Fuel*, 103:943-949.

Paneque, M., José, M., Franco-Navarro, J.D., Colmenero-Flores, J.M. and Knicker, H., 2016. Effect of biochar amendment on morphology, productivity and water relations of sunflower plants under non-irrigation conditions. *Catena*, 147:280-287.

Pathak, H., Bhatia, A., Jain, N. and Aggarwal, P.K. 2010. Greenhouse gas emission and mitigation in Indian agriculture – A review, *In*: ING Bulletins on Regional Assessment of Reactive Nitrogen, Bulletin No. 19 (Ed. Bijay-Singh), SCON-ING, New Delhi, pp.1-34.

Peters, G.P., Andrew, R.A., Boden, T., Canadell, J.G., Ciais, P., Quéré, C.L., Marland, G., Raupach, M.R. and Wilson, C., 2013. The challenge to keep global warming below 2! . *Nature Climate Change,* 3:4-6.

Reddy, K.R., Xie, T. and Dastgheibi, S., 2014. Evaluation of Biochar as a Potential Filter Media for the Removal of Mixed Contaminants from Urban Strom Water Runoff. *Journal of Environmental Engineering*, 140:1-10.

Qin, X., Li, Y.E., Wang, H., Liu, C., Li, J., Wan, Y., Gao, Q., Fan, F. and Liao, Y., 2016. Long-term effect of biochar application on yield-scaled greenhouse gas emissions in a rice paddy cropping system: A four-year case study in south China. *Science of The Total Environment*, 569:1390-1401.

Saarnio, S., Heimonen, K. and Kettunen, R., 2013. Biochar addition indirectly affects N_2O emissions via soil moisture and plant N uptake. *Soil Biology and Biochemistry*, 58:99-106.

Silber, A., Levkovitch, I. and Graber, E., 2010. pH-dependent mineral release and surface properties of cornstrawbiochar: Agronomic implications. *Environmental Science and Technology*, 44:9318-9323.

Singla, A. and Inubushi, K., 2013. CO_2, CH_4 and N_2O production potential of paddy soil after biogas byproducts application under waterlogged condition. *International Journal of Agriculture, Environment and Biotechnology*, 6:233-239.

Singla, A. and Inubushi, K., 2014a. Effect of biochar on CH_4 and N_2O emission from soils vegetated with paddy. *Paddy and Water Environment*, 12:239-243.

Singla, A. and Inubushi, K., 2014b. Biogas byproducts affecting N_2O, CO_2 and CH_4 production potential of Regosol soil under aerobic incubation. *HortResearch*, 68:7-13.

Singla, A., Dubey, S.K., Singh, A. and Inubushi, K., 2014a. Effect of biogas digested slurry-based biochar on methane flux and methanogenic archaeal diversity in paddy soil. *Agriculture, Ecosystems and Environment*, 197:278-287.

Singla, A., Iwasa, H. and Inubushi, K., 2014b. Effect of biogas digested slurry based-biochar and digested liquid on N_2O, CO_2 flux and crop yield for three continuous cropping cycles of komatsuna (*Brassica rapa* var. perviridis). *Biology and Fertility of Soils*, 50:1201-1209.

Spokas, K.A., Cantrell, K.B., Novak, J.M., Archer, D.W., Ippolito, J.A., Collins, H.P., Boateng, A.A., Lima, I.M., Lamb, M.C., McAloon, A.J., Lentz, R.D. and Nichols, K.A., 2012. Biochar: a synthesis of its agronomic impact beyond carbon sequestration. *Journal of Environmental Quality*, 41:973–989.

Xie, T., Sadasivam, B.Y., Reddy, K.R., Wang, C. and Spokas, K., 2016. Review of the effects of biochar amendment on soil properties and carbon sequestration. *Journal of Hazardous, Toxic, and Radioactive Waste*, 20:1-14.

Yamato, M., Okimori, Y., Wibowo, I. F., Anshori, S. and Ogawa, M., 2006. Effects of the application of charred bark of *Acacia mangium* on the yield of maize, cowpea and peanut, and soil chemical properties on South Sumatra, Indonesia. *Soil Science and Plant Nutrition*, 52:489-495.

3

Meat, Fish and Poultry Waste A Challenge or An Opportunity

Sanju B. Dhull, Anil Panghal, Navnidhi Chhikara
Prince Chawla, Lovepreet Gill and Surbhi Sharma

Abstract

The interest in the utilization of industrial by-products is increasing day by day and is major reason for exploring different meat, poultry and fish industry waste and optimization of extracting conditions of different valuable compounds. Utilization of these by-products in effective manner can be positive for meat industry economy as well as environmental pollution of the country. Besides the potential revenue losses, non-utilized or underutilized by-products accounts for the extra cost for their disposal. Meat producers are converting these by-products into value added edible and inedible form. Among the most prominent current uses of meat, poultry and fish waste are food ingredients, water treatment, cosmetic and personal care products, biogas/biodiesel, biomedical and pharmaceutical application. Several studies have dealt with the production of several value-added products such as gelatin, collagen, enzymes, specific proteins, bioactive peptides, chitin, chitosan, and pigments from the meat industries waste. Recently, in the food and pharmaceutical industry, an increasing number of new applications have been found for products generated from meat, poultry and fish industry waste; in different products as foaming agents, emulsifiers, biodegradable film-forming materials, colloid stabilizers, and microencapsulating agents, in line with the growing trend to replace synthetic agents with more natural ones.

Keywords: Meat waste, poultry, fish, collagen, bioactive peptide, by-products

1. Introduction

"Food wastes" are usually derived during processing of raw materials to finished product and result in liquidor solid residues of high organic load. Food wastes are produced throughout all the food life cycle. According to the Food and

Agriculture Organization, globally about one-third of the edible parts of food produced gets lost or wasted, roughly accounting 1.3 billion ton/year. It reflects not only the food processing wastes, but also the "food losses" (Gustavsson *et al.*, 2011). Excluding the agricultural food losses,42% of the food waste is produced by households, 38% during food processing, and 20% is distributed along the whole chain. Generally, the food wastes are derived from the processing of raw materials where high valued nutritionally rich portion is extracted or separated and processed from the remains within edible components or little nutritional value (Oreopoulou and Russ, 2007). The slaughter houses along with the meat processing units generate a significant amount of solid and liquid by-products. In order to give an idea of the amount of the generation of the different waste streams, table 1 shows the quantity of waste produced and the percent ratio between amount of waste and amount of production of each industrial sector (Segree and Falasconi, 2011).

Table 1: Estimated waste in the food industry

Industrial Sector	Amount of waste(000t)	Waste%
Meat and meat products	150	2.5
Fish and fish products	8	3.5
Fruits and vegetables	279	4.5
Vegetable and animal oils and fats	73	1.5
Dairy and ice cream industry	404	3
Grain and starch products	245	1.5
Other food products	239	2
Drinks and beverage industry	492	2
Total	1890	2.6

Source: Baiano (2014)

With the increase in world population and the existing shortage of high quality lowcost foods, recovery of nutrients from presently waste sources and their utilization as foods or feeds will help to fill the gap between the world population and food supplies. Until a few decades ago, food industry by-products were considered either used as animal feed or brought to landfills for composting. The waste has strong economic potential in production of new products and functional ingredients. This practice has recently changed for several reasons including the growing concern for environment; more stringent regulations to minimize the impact of waste on human health; high disposal costs of wastes and the growing awareness of the potential benefits deriving from marketable components present in food industry by-products (Laufenberg *et al.*, 2003). Meat packing and citrus processing industries are good examples of substantial and successful processing of waste utilization already in effect (Burch *et al.*, 1963).

1.1 Meat, Poultry and Fish Industry Waste

India is bestowed with vast livestock wealth and it is growing at the rate of 6% per annum (Jayathilakan *et al.*, 2012). By slaughtering and processing of meat animal, only one third is recovered as meat while the rest is comprised of coproducts and waste, which need to be further processed and utilized. Traditional edible meat by-products have been gradually disappearing from market because of health and economic return concerns. Nonutilization or underutilization of these byproducts not only lead to loss of potential revenues to industries but also lead to the added and increasing cost of disposal of these by-products. Besides pollution and hazard aspects, meat, poultry and fish processing industry wastes have a potential for recycling waste material or for conversion into useful products of higher economic value. Sometimes, traditions, culture and religion are important when a meat byproduct is being utilized for food. Regulatory requirements are also important because in many countries the use of meat by-products is restricted for reasons of food safety and quality. However, by-products such as blood, liver, lung, kidney, brains, spleen and tripe have good nutritive value. Also, the growth and economy of egg production and poultry processing industries depends largely on efficient utilization of waste products. On the basis of live weight of animal the by-products account for almost 60% and out of this 40% are edible and 20% are inedible (Chatli *et al.*, 2005). FAO (2008) reported that about 107 million livestock and more than 650 million poultry birds were slaughtered in India annually, leading to the production of 6.3 million tones meat. It leaves huge loads of by-products which is further increased by dead and fallen animals. In India, the value of unprocessed by-products produced from buffalo and sheep slaughtering was reported to be quite high. Further it is reported that if these by-products are processed then the returns will be almost equal to the value of the meat derived from an animal while nonutilization of these by-products may create major aesthetic and catastrophic health problems. Value addition of animal by-products mainly has two benefits. Firstly, the meat processing industry gets additional revenue by producing industrial, household, cosmetics, pharmaceutical and medical products; livestock feed additives and pet foods *etc.* that otherwise would have been unrealized. Secondly, the costs of disposing of these environment and health threatening secondary items are avoided. Also, utilization of these by products as compost/fertilizer can contributes a lot in organic farming and will reduce the use of synthetic fertilizers. Therefore, the potential and scope of meat industry byproduct utilization is really great which will result in industrial development, environmental management, new employment generation, and better returns to the producers. Additionally, animal by-productsand wastes are a good source of renewable energy as well its production is economically feasible (Jayathilakan *et al.*, 2012).

2. Meat Industry

Meat by-products are produced by slaughter houses, meat processors, wholesalers and rendering plant, respectively. The waste of slaughter house consists of the portion of a slaughtered animal that cannot be sold as meat or used in meat-products. Meat processing waste includes bones, blood and internal organs, skin, and the contents of the gastro-intestinal tract etc. and it varies with the type of animal (Sielaff, 1996; Grosse, 1984). The specific amount of waste generated for each type of animal is given in table 2.

Table 2: The specific waste index for slaughter houses with respect to the type of animal

Animal	Specific waste index
Cow	0.56
Calf	0.87
Pig	0.2
Sheep	0.1

Source: Russ and Pittroff (2004).

By-products including organs, bone and blood, fat or lard, skin, feet, abdominal content and intestine of cattle, pigs and lambs represents 66.0, 52.0 and 68.0% respectively of the live weight (Irshad *et al.*, 2015). Historically, in Asia, by-products were a favorite food, but because of increasing health concerns focus on non-food usessuch as pet foods, animal feed, pharmaceuticals and cosmetics have increased (Rivera *et al.*, 2000). Also, more than half of the animal by-products have unusual physical and chemical characteristics, therefore, not found suitable for normal consumption. As a result, a valuable source of potential revenue is lost, and the cost of disposing of these products is increasing. In addition to economic losses, unused meat products cause serious environmental pollution. However with improved utilization, meat by-products can give a good profit to meat processors. Efficient utilization of meat by-products is important for the profitability of the meat industry. The United States Department of Agriculture Economic Research Service has found that by-products from beef had generated 11.4% of the gross income while the figure for pork was 7.5%.

2.1 Types of Meat Industry Waste

The majority of the waste, in the meat industry is produced during slaughtering (Table 3, 4). Slaughter house waste consists of the portion of a slaughtered animal that cannot be sold as meat or used in meat-products. Meat industry waste has been classified as follows:

2.1.1 On the Basis of Edibility

Edibility of a food sample is controlled by custom, religion, consumer acceptance, reputation, availability of the product, economics and hygiene conditions. Animal by-products can be classified on the basis of their utilisation as food such as:

- **Edible by-products** are those which can be consumed as a foodby human beings. These include liver, kidney, heart, brain, intestine, tongue, spleen etc. They are also called as variety meats. Slaughtered animal species, sex, live weight, fatness and methods of slaughtering affect the usability of by-products. Biologically, the most non-carcass part which is properly cleaned, handled and processed is suitable for edible purpose.
- **Inedible by-product** are those which cannot beconsumed as food source by human beings e.g. hides, skins, ear, snout, gallbladder, foetus, hoofs, horns, hair, bristles etc. All parts of dead animal or condemned meat and organs also come in this category.

2.1.2 On the Basis of Collection

Animal by-products are also divided into principal/primary and secondary by-products (Sharma and Sharma, 2011).

- **Principal by-products**- the by-products directly harvested from the animals e.g. hides and skins, bones, blood, hoofs and horns.
- **Secondary by-products**-the by-products derived from principal or primary by-productse.g. bones yields like bone meal, fat, gelatine, buttons, cutlery handles etc. Likewise intestines may yield casings, catgut, tennis strips etc. as secondary by-products.

2.1.3 On the Basis of Utilisation

The animal by-products needs to be utilized properly in order to ensure better returns, supply highly nutritive livestock feed (meat meal, carcass meal, bone meal etc.), establish secondary rural industries, generate employment, check the pollutionand bring crop improvement in the form of manure and fertilizer. Sharma and Sharma, (2011) classified waste on the basis of their utilization as following:

- **Agricultural by-products**- meat meal, bone meal, fertilizer etc.
- **Industrial by-products**- glue, gelatine, casings etc.
- **Pharmaceutical by-products**- pepsin, insulin, hormones, bio-chemicals etc.

Table 3: Approximate yield of waste from large animals

S. No.	Meat/By Products	Percent Yield
1.	Meat (boneless)	28.57
2.	Bone, head, feet	22.85
3.	Paunch content and waste	16.00
4.	Hide	7.57
5.	Blood	3.14
6.	Lungs and oesophagus	2.00
7.	Liver	1.42
8.	Stomach	0.71
9.	Heart	0.42
10.	Head meat and brain	0.28
11.	Tongue	0.28
12.	Spleen	0.28
13.	Kidneys	0.14
14.	Fat	1.71
15.	Casings	2.00
16.	Other offal (udder, tail end)	4.00
17.	Urine, body fluid, bile, dung	3.50

Source: Chatterjee *et al.*(1991)

Table 4: Approximate yield of waste from small animals

S. No.	Meat/By Products	Percent Yield
1.	Dressed weight	40.00
2.	Paunch contents	20.00
3.	Skin	9.20
4.	Gut and tripe	8.00
5.	Head	5.60
6.	Blood	3.00
7.	Fatty tissue	2.00
8.	Lungs and oesophagus	1.00
9.	Liver	1.20
10.	Hoofs	0.80
11.	Heart	0.40
12.	Kidney	0.40
13.	Spleen	0.20
14.	Pancreas	0.16

Source: (Chatterjee *et al.*, 1991)

2.2 Nutritive Value of Meat Waste

Meat by-products contain many nutrientslike essential amino acids, fatty acids, vitamins, hormones and minerals, therefore, can be used as food and medicines. Some examples are lung, kidney, brain, spleen, and tripe. Some organ meat, including liver and kidney, also contains a higher level of carbohydrate than other meat materials (Devatkal *et al.*, 2004b).

- **Fat:** Fat content of pork tail is observed to be highest while moisture content to be lowest of all meat by-products.
- **Protein:** The protein level of liver, tail, ears and feet of cattle is nearly equal to lean meat tissue (Unsal and Aktas, 2003) whereas brain, chitterlings and fatty tissue have lowest protein content comparatively. USDA reported that mechanically deboned beef and pork contain at least 14% protein. The by-products contain a larger amount of amino acids like proline, hydroxyproline and glycine, but lower level of tryptophan and tyrosine.
- **Vitamins and minerals:** Vitamin content of organ meats is usually higher than that of lean meat tissue. Organs such as kidney and liver contain very high amount of riboflavin (1.697–3.630 mg/100 g), which is 5–10 times more than that of lean meat. Liver is observed as best source of niacin, vitamin B_6, folacin, vitamin B_{12}, ascorbic acid and vitamin A, whereas, kidney as a good source of vitamin B_6, B_{12}, and folacin. Lamb kidneys, pork, liver, lungs, and spleen portions are rich in iron, as well as vitamins. The livers of beef, lamb and veal contains highest copper content contributing 90–350% of the RDA (2 mg/day). Highest amount of manganese (0.128–0.344 mg/100 g) is found in liver while thymus and sweet breads contains highest level of phosphorus (393–558 mg/100 g) and potassium (360–433 mg/100 g) (Devatkal *et al.*, 2004). Sodium content of most of the by-products is at or below the levels found in lean tissue, with the exception of brain, kidney, lungs, spleen and ears. Highest calcium content (315–485 mg/100 g) is observed in mechanically deboned meat.
- **Fatty acids:** Many organ meats contain more polyunsaturated fatty acids than lean muscle. Different organs such as heart, liver, brain, chitterlings, kidney and lungs contains lowest level of monounsaturated fatty acids while highest level of polyunsaturated fatty acids (Liu, 2002). High level of cholesterol (3-5times, 260–410 mg/100 g) and phospholipids is found in organ meats than in lean meat. Brains contain highest level of cholesterol (1,352–2,195 mg/100 g) and phospholipids compared to other meat by-products and organs. For this reason, the United States Department of Health recommends that these by-products should be eaten in limited amounts, because of health concerns. In addition, some other reasons for limited consumption are high cholesterol content of organ meats, and the possible accumulation of pesticides, drug residues and toxic heavy metals in different organs respectively.

2.3 Utilisation of Meat Industry Waste

Meat industry waste can be converted into valuable processed food, pharmaceutical and microbiological products (Fig. 1).

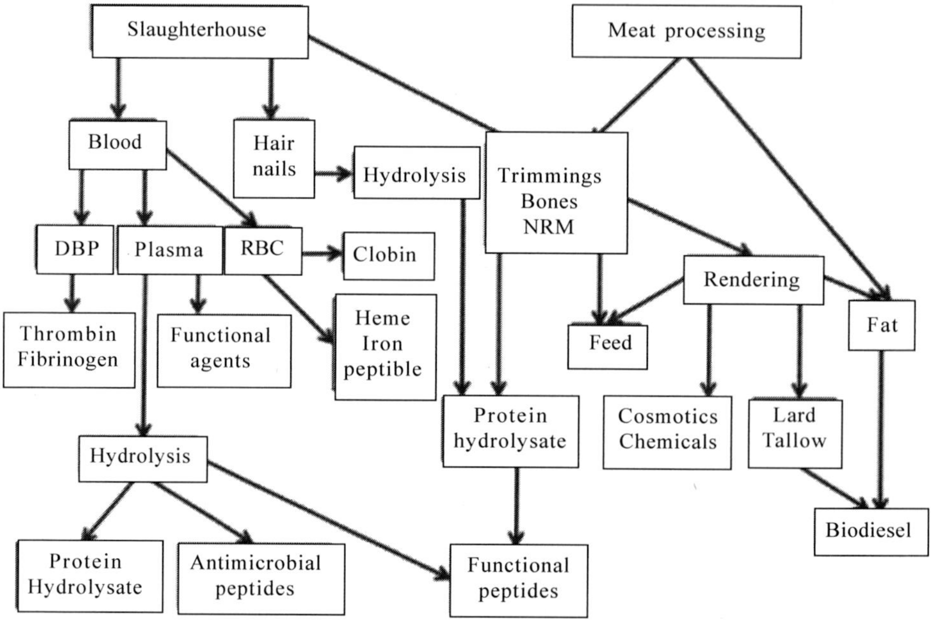

Fig. 1: Flow diagram of main routes for value-addition to meat by-products (Toldrá *et al.*, 2012)

2.3.1 Blood Utilisation

Blood generally obtained from bovine and porcine sources is made up of red blood, white blood cells and platelets and the plasma fraction. Animal blood is one of main edible by-product of meat industry and is a rich source of protein and iron (Wan *et al.*, 2002). Blood constitute about 2.4 to 8% of the total body weight. Blood of a healthy animal is nutritionally rich and free from living microorganisms, especially pathogens. Typical composition of bovine blood consists of 80.9% water, 17.3% protein, 0.23% lipid, 0.07% carbohydrate, and 0.62% minerals (Duarte *et al.,* 1999). Blood can be used in food industry as a color additive, emulsifier, stabilizer, clarifierand as a nutritionaml component (Silva and Silvestre, 2003: Jyantilakan *et al.*, 2012; Rahman *et al.*, 2014). After removal ofhemoglobin, cellular fractions of blood may be used as color enhancer and fat replacerin meat products. Blood is used to prepare blood cake, blood sausages, bread, biscuits, blood puddings and blood curd in many European and Asian countries (Ghost, 2001; Jack and Yun-Hwa, 2011). Some other food applications of blood are as a milk substitute, protein supplement, a lysine supplement or a vitamin stabilizer, and an excellent source of most of the trace minerals. Non-food applications of blood are as a binder, fertilizer and blood meal in animal feed stuff (Jyantilakan *et al.*, 2012).

The utility of Blood factor XIII which is a transglutaminase (TGase) isolated from animal blood and organs is of great importance in food research. It is an enzymogen present in plasma, placenta and platelets and was first extracted from bovine blood in 1983.TGase improved the binding ability of fresh meat products and also enhanced the cross-linking between myosin and proteins of other food source (soy, casein and gluten). Moreover,the restructured meat products can be processed without heating, and their salt and phosphate content can be reducedby TGase addition (Jyantilakan *et al.*, 2012).

2.3.2 Blood Plasma Utilization in Food

Blood proteins present in plasmahave good functional properties such as foaming (Del *et al.*, 2008), gelation and emulsification (Silva and Silvestre, 2003) that accounts for its use in food industry. Blood plasma forms a gel at a protein concentration of 4.0–5.0% which appears very similar to cooked egg whites and gel strength increases with increasing the concentration. This gelling property can be used to replace egg whites in the baking industry (Ghost, 2001).The binding strength depends on moisture, temperature, pH and size of meat cuts. Plasma addition also improved the color characteristics of cooked ham and hot dogs. Cooked ham with 1.5- 3.0% frozen blood plasma, and hot dogs with 2.7% added plasma, were found more appealing in color in comparision to samples without plasma (Autio *et al.*, 1985).

2.3.3 Medicinal and Pharmaceutical Uses

Several fractions of blood have many therapeutic and microbiological applications e.g. as a necessary ingredient in blood agar, as a nutrient for tissue culture media and as peptones for microbial growth (Kurbanoglu and Kurbanoglu, 2004). Liquid plasma is its largest fraction (63.0%), consisting of 3.5% albumin and 4.0% globulin and fibrinogen. Some components of blood such as albumins, globulins, glycerophosphates, sphingomyelins, and catalase are used for biological assay while many other such as fibrinogen, immunoglobulins, fibrinolysin, serotonin, kalikreninsa and plasminogen are isolated for chemical or medical uses(Young and Lawrie, 2007). Purified bovine albumin is used in testing for the Rh factor in human beings,as a stabilizer in different vaccines for antibiotic sensitivity tests and in replenishing blood or fluid loss in animals (Jyantilakan *et al.*, 2012).

2.4 Hides and Skins

In world's leather market,10-12% share comes from India. India is the world's largest producer as well as exporter of hides/skins and their products. Hides are significant portion of animal body weight ranging from 4.0 to 11 % varying with animals, for e.g. 5.1–8.0% of cattle body weight, 3–8% in swine and 11.0–11.7% in sheep (Benjakul *et al.*, 2009). India produces 23.2 million cattle hides, 20.3 million buffalo hides, 90.6 million goat skins and 37.3 million sheep skins as primary/principal by-product (FAO, 2014). These raw hides and skin provides 10-15% of the total value from slaughtered animals. This value can be enhanced by processing hides into leather bags and shoes, glue and edible gelatin, cosmetics, rawhide, athletic equipment, reformed sausage casings and sausage skins (Benjakul *et al.*, 2009).

After the skin is removed from animal body, curing is done to reduce microbial and enzymatic decomposition. Four different methods are used for curing of animal hides; salt curing, air drying, mixer curing and raceway curing (Jyantilakan *et al.*, 2012). In U.K. and some European and Asian countries, pork skin is used as snack food (pork rind) and prepared by immersing, boiling, drying and then frying, also called as "pork scratching". Pork skin is similar to human skin, and can be used for dressing of burns or skin-ulcers. For dressing purposes, pork skin is cut into strips or a patch, shaved of hair, split to a thickness of 0.2–0.5 mm, cleansed, sanitized and packaged. This skin can be used for skin grafting but care should be taken that it is removed from the carcass within 24 h of the death of the pig (Jyantilakan *et al.*, 2012).

2.4.1 Gelatinextraction from Hides and Skins

Gelatin is made from fresh edible raw materials (hides or bone). This is a water soluble protein produced by the controlled hydrolysis of a water-insoluble collagen. The gelatin from hide is processed by three major steps. Firstly, non-collagenous material is removed from the raw material, followed by controlled hydrolysis of collagen to gelatin. Finally, the gelatin is recovered and dried.Gelatin has high amount of glycine and proline but lower level of tryptophan and methionine.

2.4.2 Gelatin in the Food and Pharmaceutical Industries

Gelatinhas good gel forming capacity making its potential use in dessert, bakery, candies, icecream, and dairy products(Choa *et al.*, 2005; Jamilah and Harvinder, 2002). Because of its "melt in the mouth" properties; it is mainly used in jellied deserts but is also added to a range of meat products such as meat pies. Gelatin is also widely to stabilize ice cream and other frozen desserts because it is thought to inhibit recrystallization of lactose and formation of ice crystals during the storage. High-bloom gelatin is mainly added as a protective colloid to ice cream, yoghurt and other frozen desserts. Collagen extracted from cattle hides can be used in the meat industry to make the collagen sausage. Collagen from hides and skins is also be used as emulsifier as it can bind large quantities of fat which makes it a useful additive or filler for meat products (Jyantilakan*et al.*, 2012).

Approximately 6.5% of the total production of gelatin is used as a binding and compounding agent in medicated tablets and pastillesmanufacturing in the pharmaceutical industry. It is used as an important ingredient in zinc gelatine; a protective ointment used for the treatment of ulcerated varicose veins (Hidaka and Liu, 2003). By whipping gelatin into a foam, treating with formaldehyde and drying, it can be converted into a sterile sponge used in surgery for implantation of a drug or antibiotic directly into a specific area(Estaca *et al.*, 2009). Being proteinaceous in nature, gelatine is used as a plasma expander for blood in cases of very severe shock and injury. Blood clotting can be stimulated during surgery by a product made from extracted collagen (Jyantilakan *et al.*, 2012). Properties like emulsifying and stabilizing makes its utility in cosmetic products, silk screen printing and photogravure printing etc. (Arvanitoyannis, 2008).

2.5 Uses of Bones

Bones constitute a major part of the carcasses such as 15% of beef carcasses,11% of pork carcasses, and 16% of lamb carcasses. Bones are also used to make soups and gelatine. In recent years, new techniques have been employed by meat industry to get more meat from bones. The mechanical deboning of beef, pork or lamb produces tissue that is termed as "mechanically separated", "mechanically removed" or "mechanically deboned". Many countries had now approved these meats either mixed or alone for use in meat products (Field, 1981). For example the United Statesin 1978, approved mechanically separated red meat to be use as red meat. But the flavour and quality of the final products are reduced if a high percentage of mechanically separated red meat is incorporated. Mechanically separated meat contains high water content and darker colour so makes the final product darker and softer and therefore used in limited amount. Commercially, mechanically separated meat is added in range of 5.0–20.0% in hamburger and ground beef, and 10.0–40.0% in sausages. Mechanically recovered meat has a bad consumer perception due to Health concerns linked with Bovine Spongiform Encephalopathy (BSE) contamination in some countries (Arvanitoyannis and Ladas, 2008. The marrow present inside some of the bones constitutes 4.0–6.0% of the carcass weight (West and Shaw, 1975) is also used as food.

2.6 Glands and Organs

2.6.1 Glands and Organs As a Food

Animal organs and glands are often nutritionally rich and provide a wide range of flavours and textures (Jayathilakan *et al.,* 2012). Organs such as brain, heart, kidneys, liver, lungs and spleenare commonly used as human foods. Other organs like rumen, reticulum, omasum and abomasum of sheep and cattle, tongue, the stomach and uterus, the bovine pancreas and udder of pigs and the testes and thymus of pigs and sheep can be used (Liu, 2002). The glands are properly cleaned and surrounding fat and connective tissue trimmed off. Then glands are packed in waxed paper and rapid freezing (-18°C or less) is done to stop tissue breakdown from bacterial growth. Different organs are treated differently to make them suitable for consumption. The brain, nervous system and spinal cord are softer in texture, so blanched to make them firm before cooking and then peeled off. Heart is used as a table meat and is tough because of cardiac muscles. Whole hearts can be roasted or braised while sliced heart meat is grilled or braised. Heart meat is often also used as an ingredient in processed meats. After removing from the fatty cushion which holds the kidney in place, the ureter and blood vessels are trimmed. Then kidney is cooked whole or in slices, and is generally broiled, grilled, or braised. Most widely used edible organ liver is used as liver paste and sausages (Devatkal *et al.*, 2004a). Livers from lambs, veal calves and young cattle are preferred for the table use, due to their lighter flavor and texture. Braised or broiled livers are preferably consumed. Lungs of pig, calf and lamb are mainly used to make some stuffing and sausages and processed meats (Darine *et al.*, 2010). Intestines after boiling are used as food meat meal, tallow, pet foodor fertilizer. However, the main use of the intestines is in making of sausage casings (Bhaskar *et al.*, 2007). When removed from the carcass, animal intestines are very fragile and heavily contaminated with microorganisms. Therefore, they are cleaned immediately after the animal slaughtering. To prepare sausage casing, intestines are removed from the abdomen, the ruffle fat is removed and the faeces are stripped out. Sometimes fermentation may be done. Then the inner mucosa membrane is separated from the casing, all strings and blood residue are removed. Finally, the intestines are soaked, salted and packaged for further use as sausage casings (Jyantilakan *et al.*, 2012: Rahman *et al.,* 2014).

2.6.2 Medicinal and Pharmaceutical uses of Glands and Organs

Animal glands and organs have been used traditionally as medicine in many countries, including India,China and Japan. The pharmaceutical and medicinal uses of glands and organs are as following:

i. **Glands:** The hormonal secretion from endocrine glands consists of several enzymes which regulates of the body metabolism. These glands include the thyroid, parathyroid, liver, lungs, pancreas, pituitary, stomach, kidney, adrenal, corpus luteum, ovary and follicle. The glands of healthy animals are collected only. Generally, locating a gland needs some experience because they are small and encased in other tissues. Function and importance of different glands of different animals vary depending on their species, age and sex of the animal. After slaughtering, breakdown of the gland tissue is started from bacterial growth, so rapid freezing is required. Before freezing, the glands are cleaned, and the surrounding fat and connective tissue is trimmed off, packed in waxed paper and stored at "18 °C or less. In pharmaceutical industry, glands are inspected, sliced and mixed with different solutions for extraction, or placed in a vacuum drier. Excess of fat is removed using organic solutions such as gasoline, light petroleum, ethylene or acetone. After drying and defatting of the glands or extracts, they are milled into a powder and made into capsules, or used in a liquid form. Safety and potency test are done before they are sold (Jayathilakan *et al.,* 2012).

ii. **Organs:** Brain, nervous systems and spinal cords are natural source of 70-cholesterol which is involved in vitamin D_3 synthesis and as an emulsifier in cosmetics (Ejike and Emmanuel, 2009). Some other materials are also extracted from the hypothalamus of the brain for the same purpose. The hormonal secretion of the pineal gland named melatonin is being used to cure the problems related to brain like schizophrenia, insomnia and mental retardation (Devatkal *et al*., 2004; Jayathilakan *et al*., 2012).

The liver is the largest gland in the animal body. The liver of mature cattle usually weighs 5 kg and 1.4 kg for pig approximately. Raw ground liver is mixed with slightly acidified hot water to produce liver extract. The liver extract is concentrated into a paste in a vacuum at a low temperature to be used as stock for the pharmaceutical industries. Liver extract has been used as a source of vitamin B_{12}, and also as a nutritional supplement used to treat pernicious anaemia (Colmenero and Cassens, 1987; Devatkal *et al.*, 2004a,b). Heparine extracted from the liver, lungs and the lining of the small intestines, is used as an anticoagulant to prolong the clotting time of blood and as blood thinner during surgery and organ transplants.

Bile juice is a mixture of acids, proteins, pigments, cholesterol etc., and can be extracted from the gall bladder. It is mainly used to improve liver functioning and for the treatment of indigestion, constipation and bile tract disorders. Both dry extract as well as liquid form of bile from cattle or pigs are available. Some ingredients of bile, such as prednisone and cortisone are used as medicines, can be isolated separately. Gallstones from gall bladder, having aphrodisiac properties, are used as ornaments to make necklaces and pendants (Jyantilakan *et al.*, 2012: Rahman *et al.,* 2014).

Insulin obtained from pancreas regulates sugar metabolism in body cells and is used in the treatment of diabetes. Glucagon, hormone from pancreas is used to increase blood sugar, and to treat insulin overdoses or low blood sugar caused by alcoholism. Chymotrypsin and trypsin are used to improve healing of wounds after surgery or injury (Jyantilakan *et al.*, 2012).

Ovaries of animals can be extracted for progesterone and oestrogen hormones which are used in treatment of reproductive system problems. Relaxin hormone often used during childbirth, is taken from the ovaries of pregnant cows (Jyantilakan *et al.*, 2012).

The intestines of sheep and calves are used for the manufacture of catgut, threads which are used to make internal surgical sutures. The lining of the small intestines of pigs and cattle is collected and processed into a dry powder for heparin preparation.

2.7 Edible Tallow and Lard

Animal fats (lard and tallow) are an important by-product of the meat processing industry. Tallow, lard and grease are separated from animal fatty tissue by rendering, which separate the fat from the bone and protein using either continuous flow or batch cooking vessels (Thimjos *et al.*, 2014). Lard is the fat rendered from the clean tissues of healthy pigs while tallow is hard fat from cattle. Wet rendering process involves heating of the fatty tissues in the presence of water, gently at a low temperature. The quality of the lard or tallow from wet rendering is better than that of products from dry rendering. Inedible tallow and greases and low-quality lard are produced by dry rendering. Incineration, composting, anaerobic fermentation and oleochemical processes can also be employed to obtain tallow and lard. Rendered lard can be used directly as an edible fat, but usually subjected to bleaching and deodorizing treatment to enhance the consumer acceptance. Traditionally, lard and tallow are used for deep frying (Weiss, 1983). Tallow and lard are also used for production of margarine and shortening (Ghotra *et al.,* 2002). Edible lard is utilized in emulsified products and sausages (Chrysam, 1985). However, due to consumer health concerns, their use in the fast-food industry is decreasing.

3. Poultry Industry

Poultry industry produces diverse range of products, including eggs, chicken and turkey. Chicken meat is suggested more nutritious compared with other meats, which had greatly increased its consumption and hence broiler production. Also a range of easy to prepare processed products supplied by the poultry industry further increased poultry products consumption. USA, Brazil and China are largest producers accounting for more than 40 million tons per year production (USDA, 2014). Poultry processing plants produce feathers, soft meat, blood, deboning residue, and dead on arrival as their major waste materials. Thus it is necessary to deal with this waste efficiently as the growth and profit of poultry industry largely depends on waste management.

There are three primary waste products: dissolved air flotation sludge from poultry, compost from dead birds and hatchery waste many litter and manure from production facilities. Animal excreta, hair, feathers, mortalities and processing wastes are main waste produced which can be convertible to useful resources. The intensive and large scale production of litter and manure resulted in excessive waste application on crop land or incautious stockpiling and deposit of waste nearby waterways (Simpson, 1991; Salminen and Rintala, 2002). Utilization of such waste as soil fertilizer is also limited due to its high oxygen demand, physical clogging of soil by fat accumulation, and presence of diseases causing microflora in dead, hatchery and litter compost. The poultry edible wastes are converted into different valuable products like blood meal, meat and bone meal, feather meal and fats/oils (Salminen, and Rintala, 2002; Lasekan *et al.,* 2013). Although these meals are rich in protein, but due to lack of essential amino acids (Onifade *et al.*, 1998), and high calcium, phosphorous and lysine content of the meat and bonemeal (Batal and Dale, 2011), their nutritional utilisation is limited. Feathers are made up of 90% protein and account for approximately 8% of the adult chicken weight; representing an enormous waste of poultry industry (Onifade *et al.*, 1998). Feather waste has been also utilised as fertilizers, bedding material, and for decorative purpose (Jayathilakan *et al.*, 2012). They are mainly composed of a highly recalcitrant insoluble structural protein keratin. Keratin is made up of tightly packed protein chains strongly stabilized by several hydrogen bonds and hydrophobic interactions, therefore difficult to decompose. Mechanical resistance and inertness to conventional proteolytic enzymes is also extended by cross-linking of polypeptide chains by several disulfide bonds (Brandelli, 2008; Kornillowicz-Kowalska and Bohacz, 2011). However, hydrolysis of insoluble feather keratins can be done by somemicrobial enzymes converting them into feedstuffs, fertilizers and films (Onifade *et al.*, 1998; Gupta and Ramnani, 2006). In addition, applications of these enzymes are also demonstrated for pharmaceutical and cosmetic purposes (Brandelli, 2008). Proteolytic enzymes can be also utilised to improve the nutritional value of poultry by-products such as mechanically deboned meat (Rossi *et al.*, 2009) and feather meals (Odetallah *et al.*, 2003; Pedersen *et al.*, 2012). Thus, by-products produced during poultry processing can be converted into added-value materials using enzymatic catalysis as an interesting alternative. Biotechnological approaches using microbial enzymes have been extensively studied to develop suitable processes for conversion of feathers into digestible proteins and amino acids (Kornillowicz-Kowalskaand Bohacz, 2011; Gupta *et al.*, 2013). Properties of a bacterium *Bacillus licheniformis*, which ferment and convert feathers to feather lysate, a digestible protein source for animal feed use, was explored. Another enzyme secreted by this bacterium i.e. keratinase, a potent proteinase that hydrolyses collagen, elastin and feather keratin; was purified and characterized.

3.1 Bio-conversion of Chicken Waste into Value Added Products

Feather hydrolysates can be converted into useful energy sources such as methane gas, fuel pellets for heating (Ichida *et al.*, 2001; Dudynski *et al.*, 2012), and bio-hydrogen production (Balint *et al.*, 2005). The development of an effective conversion method of feather waste into fuels and energy resources may address the increasing interest in energy conservation and recycling. Conversion of animal manure to methane in an efficient thermophilic anaerobic digester system was reported by Shih (1993). Chicken waste contains sufficient carbon substrate(s) (37%) and high nitrogen content (more than 4%) suitable for bioconversion into value added products (Barik *et al.*, 1991). Mainly, two value added products Methane and Organic acids (Shih, 1993; Jones and Ogden, 1984) can be obtained from chicken waste. The bioconversion of chicken waste can be done through two mechanisms. In one approach, methane is produced by fermenting the chicken waste with selected microbial cultures under anaerobic conditions. In a second approach, the anaerobic fermentation of the chicken waste is carried out in the presence of methane inhibitor. It prevent the production of methane, thus force the accumulation of organic acids or alcohols (Fig. 2).

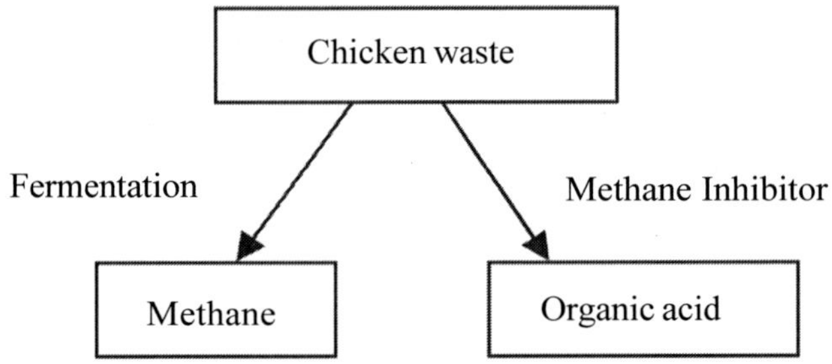

Fig. 2: Production of methane and organic acids from chicken waste

3.2 Biofuel production from meat effluents

Meat industry generates a huge amount of strong pollutant solidand liquid wastes resulting in serious environmental damage (Francisco *et al.*, 2011). Power plant operators are emphasizing on the use of this waste as a secondary fuel by thermal recycling (Arvanitoyannis and Ladas, 2008). Poultry with 9% moisture content can be burnt without the usage of extra fuel. Therefore electrical power can be efficiently generated using poultry litter. Organic solid waste arising from the meat industry can also be used as a fuel in the cyclonic combustor for energy generation (Elaine *et al.*, 2011). The biodegradable residues originating from meat processing industries can also be used for power generation which can be further used as an energy source in different food processing plants for their energy requirements (Cosmin and Florin, 2014). A large amount of sludge is generated when organic matter from the meat industrial effluent is removed by physiochemical treatment. Commercially, for removal of organic matter from the waste water, ferric sulfate is used as a coagulant which produces 0.83 to 0.87 kg biomass/m^2 of treated waste water (De Sena *et al.*, 2008). Biomass fuel has high boiling temperature seems to be a significant source of energy production. To technically characterize this fuel, combustion of biofuel with saw dust in ratio 4:1 is carried out. Also, to limit the emission of SO_2 and NO_2 below local or international limits, operational conditions are standardized. Biofuel obtained from meat fats and fish oil can be a substitute for diesel fuels. Cattle manure, wastes from aquaculture and pig waste isused for biogas production. Biogas production from animal waste is studied extensively in last decade (Arvanitoyannis and Kassaveti, 2008; Francisco *et al.*, 2011).

4. Fish Industry

4.1 Fish waste Utilization

Fish waste is abundant in minerals, proteins and fat. By-products such as heads, belly flaps, frames and parts of the viscera like liver and roe are of high nutritional value, containing high quality proteins and lipids with long chain ω-3 fatty acids. In addition, they were also found rich in micronutrients like vitamins A, D, niacin and riboflavin as well as minerals such as zinc, iron, selenium and iodine (Olsen *et al.*, 2014).The use of by-products as fishmeal or fish protein hydrolysates and fish oil from by-products can be indirectly helpful in providing healthy food since the expanding aquaculture sector is byfar the largest user of these products (FAO, 2012). Fish protein hydrolysate produced by enzymatic treatment of waste fish scraps from 5 marine species (white croaker, horse mackerel, flying fish, chub mackerel and sardine) was studied (Khan *et al.*, 2003) and used as a cryoprotectant to suppress proteins degradation of fish during frozen storage. Protein hydrolysate and peptide from yellow tail fish bone and swine skin wastes can be used as food ingredients (Morimura *et al.*, 2002). Protein hydrolysates can also be used to produce peptone hydrolysate which is growth media for lactic acid bacteria in bacterioc in production (Vanquez *et al.,* 2004; Tahajod and Rand, 1996). Generally for microbiological media, peptones are obtained from good quality pork, beef or horse meat), but fish and high-protein fish wasteis far better (Skorupa and Sikorski, 1993). By-products of fish and crustaceans processing can be used in producing high-value products like chitin, chitosan, collagen, gelatin, enzymes, bioactive peptides, specific proteins and pigments (Kim and Mendis, 2006; Blanco *et al.*, 2007; Arvanitoyannis and Kassaveti, 2008; Gomez-Guillen *et al.*, 2009; Ferraro *et al.*, 2010; Rustad *et al.*, 2011; Kandra *et al.*, 2012). Collagen or keratin from livestock and fish waste can be converted to new physiologically functional food materials by enzymic hydrolysis (Ohba *et al.*, 2003). Moreover, unsaturated fatty acids can be extracted from the waste different fish varieties including Indian mackerel, Indian oil sardine and Pink perch (Amit *et al.*, 2012). Aidos *et al.* (2001) extracted fish oil from by-products of salted matjes to study its stability and quality characteristics.Long-chain ω-3 fatty acids (eicosapentaenoic acid and docosahexaenoic acid) obtained from marine wastesare sold either as ethyl esters (EE) or triacylglycerols (Dyerberg *et al.,* 2010; Sears *et al.*, 2010).

Similarly, bioactive peptides and enzymes extracted from fish waste can be used in fish sauce preparation and fish feed (Gildberg, 2004). Catfish frames and miscut fillets can be utilized in production of smoked catfish sausage (Rust, 1995). It has been suggested different flavouring such as shrimp sauce can be prepared from shrimp by-products. Characteristics of salt-fermented sauces from shrimp by-products wasstudied by Kim *et al.*, (2003) and reported that good quality salt-fermented sauces can be prepared using shrimp processing by-products. Fish waste can be used as animal and poultry feed (Hammoumi *et al.,* 1998) by fermentation using microbial culture of *Lactobacillus plantarium* and *Saccharomyces* species. Use of mixed fermentation by pure culture of yeasts and lactic acid bacteria strains pure culture resulted in better transformation, preservation and quality of final product (Faid *et al.,* 1997). Generally, fish waste either unsuitable for edible purposes or having high oil content or excessive bones are converted to valuable feed and industrial products (Bimbo and Crowther, 1992). Also, restructured fish products can be prepared from discarded fish waste and under-exploited fish species (Borderias and Mateos, 1996). There are several alternative uses of fish processing waste, like utilization of fish mince, fishmeal production, fish as a source of nutraceutical ingredients, applications of fish gelatin, the possible use of fish and protein concentrate as a food source etc. (Table 5).

A good yield of protein from fish waste products from lake waste can be recovered by alkaline extraction (Batista, 1999). Organic acids and amino acids can be recovered from organic waste such as fish meat and waste discovered from fish markets by sub-critical water hydrolysis (Yoshida *et al.*, 1999).

4.2 Preparation of Chitin and Chitosan from Fish Waste

The chemical compositions of fisheries waste depends on the varieties of raw materials and bodies parts. For example, in terms of the types of raw materials, chitin content is higher in shrimp shells than crab shells. Regarding the different parts of crabs, highest proportion of protein is present in ventral, the highest chitin is available in the feet shells, while highest mineral salts are found in dorsal shell and claws clamp. Crab shells are rich in chitin (25–35%), protein (20–30%), and calcium carbonate-based mineral salts (40–50%), therefore, mainly used in the production of chitin and chitosan (Abdou *et al.*, 2008; Brine and Austin, 1981). But demineralized and deproteinized of shrimp and crab shell waste is necessary to obtain chitin and chitosan (Gagne and Simpson, 1993; Jung *et al.*, 2007; Oh *et al.*, 2007; Sini *et al.*, 2007; Chen *et al.*, 2008; Jo *et al.,* 2008; Zhao and Xia, 2009). In recent years, not only the research on basic analysis of chitin and chitosan is going but their utilization value and industrial potential is also investigated. The major areas of application include food ingredients, biomedical applications (Jayakumar *et al.*, 2010; Murakami *et al.*, 2010; Muzzarelli *et al.*, 2007; Senel and McClure, 2004; Khor and Lim, 2003; Okamoto *et al.*, 2003), water treatment (Bhatnagar and Sillanpaa, 2009; Kartal and Imamura, 2005; Prado *et al.*, 2004), and personal-care products (Rinaudo, 2006; Krajewska, 2004; Twu *et al.*, 2003; Yen *et al.*, 2002; Perugini *et al.*, 2000).

4.2.1 Chitin

Chitin and chitosan can be produced by chemical/biological methods from shrimp and crab shell. Demineralization and deproteinization of marine waste material was done using strong acids or bases in chemical method ofchitin preparation. But, partial deacetylation of chitin and hydrolysis may occur resulting in final inconsistent physiological properties. Also, chemical treatments create waste water which require neutralization and detoxification for efficient waste management. Further more, because of the presence of sodium hydroxide, the value of the deproteinized liquid is diminished (Wang *et al.*, 2010; Oh *et al.*, 2000; Yang *et al.*, 2000; Brine *et al.*, 1993). In biological methods, enzymatic treatment (protease) (Oh *et al.*, 2000; Wang and Chio, 1998), and microbial fermentation using protease-producing bacteria (Wang *et al.*, 2010a, 2010b; Wang *et al.*, 2008a, 2008b, 2008c; Jo *et al.*, 2008; Jung *et al.*, 2007; Oh *et al.*, 2000; Sini *et al.*, 2007; Yang *et al.*, 2000) are commonly used. Currently,

Table 5: Potential uses of fish waste

Final waste	Treatment	Physiochemical characteristics
Fish waste mainly head, skin, bones, viscera and sometimes whole fish	Heat treatments at 65, 80, 105 and 150 °C for 12 h, moisture content reduced to 10–12%	Rich source of minerals, protein (58%), fat (19%), detection of toxic substances such as As, Pb, Hg and Cd upto non-problematic concentrations, waste digestibility decreased with temperature
Raw fish oil	Filtration pre-treatment with or without the presence of two catalysts (iron oxide and calcium phosphate monobasic) and ozone treatment (5 g/h, 16 g/m^3) (about 8000 ppm) at room temperature for 1 h and 30 min, respectively	Almost identical HHV (10700 kcal/kg) and lower flash and pour points (37 °C and –16 °C, respectively) compared to commercial diesel fuel, no production of sulfur oxides, lowered or no soot, polyaromatic and carbon dioxide emissions
Fish skin, bone and fin	Collagen isolation	collagen recovery (36–54%) and denaturation temperatures of skin collagen (25.0 – 26.5 °C), bone collagen (29.5 – 30.0 °C) and fin collagen (28.0 – 29.1 °C)
Fish bone waste	Heat treatment of raw bone (600 °C/24 h or 900 °C/12 h)	Better removal capacity and well-crystallized hydroxyapatite at 600 °C, raw bone showed lower activity and crystallinity, bone sample heated at 900 °C showed similar activity with raw bone and developed crystallinity of hydroxyapatite

Source: Arvanitoyannis (2008) in Jayathilakan *et al.,* (2012)

microbial proteolytic enzymes are used for deproteinization of marine crustacean wastes to convert it into useful biomass. Several researchers reported microbial methods to be a simple and in expensive alternative to chemical methods for preparation of chitin (Wang *et al.*, 2010b; Oh *et al.*, 2000; Wang and Chio, 1998). The deproteinization of chitin wastes of crab, shrimp, and squid pen results in enzymatic hydrolysates or culture broth which are richin protein hydrolysates (amino acids and peptides). These could be used as growth media to incubate other useful microorganisms. As a result, waste water treatment cost could be reduced. Due to these niches, both the enzymatic methods using proteolytic enzymes and the microbial methods using protease-producing microbes become more and more significant (Table 6).

Table 6: Biological methods for the preparation of chitin from biowaste of shrimp and crab

Microbes/enzymes	Biowaste of crab/shrimp shell
Microbial fermentation	
Bacillus subtilis, Euarotiumrepens, Monascuspurpureus, Pseudomonas aeruginosa,	Crab and shrimp shell
Bacillus sp., *P. aeruginosa*	Squid pen
Serratiamarcescens	Squid pen, Crab shell
S. ureilytica	Squid pen
L. paracasei/S. marcescens	Crab shell, Squid pen
Chryseobacteriumtaeanense, C. indologenes, Aspergillus niger	Shrimp shell
Enzymatic treatment	
Chymotrypsin	Demineralized shrimp shell
Papain	Demineralized shrimp shell, Shrimp and crab shell
Bromelain	Crab and shrimp shell
P. aeruginosa protease	Crab and shrimp shell

Source: Wang *et al.*, (2011)

4.2.2 Chitosan

Chitosan can be prepared from chitin by deacetylization. These methods include:

i. Heat-alkali method

ii. Enzymatic method (enzyme hydrolysis using chitin deacetylase)

iii. Microbiological method (fermentation using chitin deacetylase-producing microbes).

The heat-alkali method is used most frequently as chitosan with higher degree of deacetylation (DD) is produced (Rinaudo, 2006). However, the alkali concentration, amount ratio, temperature and reaction time may affect the degree of deacetylation and the degree of depolymerization (DP) of the chitosan produced. However, in the enzymatic and microbiological methods, although without the problems of degradation of chitosan molecular chain and waste alkali treatment, main disadvantage is long reaction time and less resultant deacetylation degree (DD) (Kim *et al.*, 2008).

5. Conclusion

A number of food, medicinal, pharmaceutical and many other uses can be described for recovered molecules and products from meat, poultry and fish industry waste. Animal glands and organs such as thyroid, parathyroid, liver, lungs, pituitary, pancreas, corpus luteum, stomach, adrenal, kidney, ovary, and follicle can beutilised as food, medicine or for extraction of valued biomolecules. Brains, nervous systems and spinal cords are a good source of cholesterol, a raw material for vitamin D_3 synthesis while melatonin, extracted from the pineal gland, is used for the treatment of schizophrenia, insomnia, and other mental diseases. Purified bovine albumin is used in testing for the Rh factor, in antibiotic sensitivity tests, and as a stabilizer for vaccines. Proteolytic enzymes can be also utilized to improve the nutritional value of some of the poultry by-products such as mechanically deboned meat and feather. Thus, by-products produced during poultry processing can be converted into added-value materials using enzymatic catalysis as an interesting alternative. Waste products from the meat, poultry and fish processing must be efficiently dealt with as the growth of these industries depends largely on waste management. However, feedstuffs, fertilizers, and films can be produced by hydrolysis of insoluble feather keratins using microbial enzymes. Treated fish waste has found many applications among such as animal feed, dietectic products (chitosan), biodiesel/biogas, cosmetics (collagen) and natural pigments (after extraction). The most practical uses of fish processing by-products are as food or indirectly in producing feed ingredients. Worldwide, demand for fish products is high and it is increasing, especially for meat products containing land-based fish processing by-products. But the up-gradation of these by-products to so-called co-products produced for human consumption requires, however, that implementation of quality assurance systemssuch as GMP and HACCP. But, sometimes, this may not be possible in all existing processing facilities. Also, with the increased concerns over health, more efficient utilization of these byproducts can be practiced utilizing new developed technologies. In India, slaughterhouse waste is not managed properly and several efforts are being taken for the effective management of these wastes. Competition among the industries has also been proven as a strong incentive for better utilization of meat by-products. This is again important for the meat industries because to remain viable in future, increased profits and lower production costs are also necessary.

References

Abdou, E. S., Nagy, K. S. A. and Elsabee, M. Z., 2008. Extraction and characterization of chitin and chitosan from local sources. *Bioresource Technology*, 99:1359-1367.

Aidos, I., A-van-der, P., Boom, R. M., Luten, J. B., 2001. Upgrading of maatjes herring byproducts: production of crude fish oil. *J Agric Food Chem.*, 49(8): 3697–3704.

Amit, K. R., Swapna, H. C., Bhaskar, N., and Baskaran, V., 2012. Potential of seafood industry byproducts as sources of recoverable lipids: Fatty acid composition of meat and nonmeat component of selected Indian marine fishes. *Journal of Food Biochemistry*, 36: 441–448.

Anon, 1995. Making valuable products out of animal waste. *Misset World Poultry* 11(6): 31.

Arvanitoyannis, I. S. and Kassaveti, A., 2008. Fish industry waste: Treatments, environmental impacts, current and potential uses. *International Journal of Food Science and Technology*, 43: 726–745.

Arvanitoyannis, I. S. and Ladas, D., 2008. Meat waste treatment methods and potential uses. *Int J Food Sci Technol.*, 43(3): 543–559.

Arvanitoyannis, I. S., 2008.Waste management for the food industries. London: Academic Press an imprint of Elsevier, 1100.

Autio, K., Lyytikainen, H., Malkki, Y. and Kanko, S., 1985. Penetration studies of blood globin gels. *J Food Sci.*, 50(3): 615–617.

AVEC, 2014. *Annual Report 2014*. Association of Poultry Processors and Poultry Trade in the EU Countries: Brussels.

Baiano, A., 2014. Food waste. Recovery of Biomolecules from food waste- A Review, 19,14822, doi: 10.3390/molecules 190914821

Balint, B., Bagi, Z., Toth, A., Rakhely, G., Perei, K. and Kovacs, K. L., 2005. Utilization of keratin-containing biowaste to produce biohydrogen. *Applied Microbiology and Biotechnology*, 69: 404-410.

Barik, S., Forgacs, T. and Isbister, J., 1991. Bioconversion of Chicken Wastes to Value-added Products. *Bioresour. Technol*, 36(3): 229-234.

Batal, A. and Dale, N., 2011. *Feedstuffs. Ingredient Analysis Tables*. Athens: University of Georgia.

Batista, I., 1999. Recovery of proteins from fish waste products by alkaline extraction. *European Food Research Technol.*, 210(2): 84–89.

Benjakul, S., Oungbho, K., Visessanguan, W., Thiansilakul, Y. and Roytrakul, S., 2009. Characteristics of gelatin from the skins of big eye snapper, *Priacanthustayenus* and *Priacanthusmacracanthus*. *Food Chem.* 116(5): 445–451.

Bhaskar, N., Modi, V.K., Govindaraju, K., Radha, C., Lalitha, R.G., 2007. Utilization of meat industry by products: protein hydrolysate from sheep visceral mass. *BioresourceTechnol* 98(2): 388–394

Bhatnagar, A. and Sillanpaa, M., 2009. Applications of chitin- and chitosan-derivatives for the detoxification of water and waste water—A short review. *Advances in Colloid and Interface Science*, 152: 26–38.

Bimbo, A. P. and Crowther, J. B., 1992. Fish meal and oil: current uses. *J Am Oil ChemSoc.*, 69(3): 221–227.

Blanco, M., Sotelo, C. G., Chapela, M. J. and Perez-Martýn, R. I., 2007. Towards sustainable and efficient use of fishery resources: present and future trends. *Trends in Food Science & Technology*, 18: 29-36.

Borderias, J. A. and Mateos, P. M., 1996. Restructured fish products. *Alimentaria*, 269, 53–62.

Brandelli, A., 2008. Bacterial keratinases: useful enzymes for bioprocessing agroindustrial wastes and beyond. *Food and Bioprocess Technology,* 1: 105-116.

Brine, C. J. and Austin, P. R., 1981. Chitin variability with species and method of preparation. *Comparative Biochemistry and Physiology*, 69B: 283–286.

Brine, C. J., Sandford, P. A. and Zikakis, J. P., 1993. Advances in chitin and chitosan. Elsevier Science Publishers, London, pp. xxii + 685, ISBN 1-85166-899-3

Burch, J. E., Lipinsky, E.S. and Litchfield, J.H., 1963. Technical and economic factors in the utilization of waste products. *Food Technol.* 17:1266.

Chatli, M.K., Padda, G.S. and Devatkal, S.K., 2005. Augmentation of animal by-products processing for the sustainability of meat industry. *Ind. Food Ind.* 24(5): 69-73.

Chatterjee, A.K., Dempster, I.F. and Sharma, N. ,1991. Review of meat industry in India. FAO/ UNDP Project No.TCP/IND/8955.

Chen, X., Li, C., Ji, X., Zhong, Z. and Li, P., 2008. Recovery of protein from dischargedwastewater during the production of chitin. *Bioresource Technology*, 99: 570–574.

Choa, S. M., Gub, Y. S. and Kima, S.B., 2005. Extracting optimization and physical properties of yellow fin tuna (*Thunnusalbacares*) skin gelatin compared to mammalian gelatins. *Food Hydrocolloids*., 19(2): 221-229.

Chrysam, M. M., 1985. Table spreads and shortenings. In: Applewhite TH, editor. Bailey's industrial oil and fat products, 3, New York: John Wiley and Sons, 41–125.

Colmenero, F. J., Cassens, R. G., 1987. Influence of an extract of liver on color and shelf stability of sliced bologna. *Meat Sci.*, 21(3): 219–230.

Cosmin, M. and Florin, A., 2014. Assessing the power generation solution by thermalchemical conversion of meat processing industry waste. *Energy Procedia*, 50: 738–743.

Darine, S., Christophe, V. and Gholamreza, D., 2010. Production and functional properties of beef lung protein concentrates. *Meat Sci.,* 84(4): 315–322.

De Sena, R. F., Claudino, A., Moretti, K., Bonfanti, I. C. P., Moreira, R. F. P. M. and Jose, H. J., 2008. Biofuel application of biomass obtained fromameat industry wastewater plant through the flotation process — a case study. *Resources, Conservation and Recycling*, 52: 557–569.

Del, P. H., Rendueles, M. and Díaz, M., 2008. Effect of processing on functional properties of animal blood plasma. *Meat Sci.,* 78(3): 522–528.

Devatkal, S., Mendiratta S.K., Kondaiah, N., 2004a. Quality characteristics of loaves from buffalo meat, liver and vegetables. *Meat Sci,* 67(2):377–383

Devatkal, S., Mendiratta, S. K., Kondaiah, N., Sharma, M. C., and Anjaneyulu ASR., 2004b. Physicochemical, functional and microbiological quality of buffalo liver. *Meat Sci.,* 68(5): 79–86.

Dudynski, M., Kwiatkowski, K, & Bajer, K., 2012. From feathers to syngas – technologies and devices. *Waste Management*, 32: 685-691.

Dyerberg, J., Madsen, P., Moller, J. M., Aardestrup, I. and Schmidt, E. B., 2010. Bioavailability of marine n-3 fatty acid formulations. *Prostaglandins, Leukotrienes and Essential Fatty Acids*, 83: 137-141.

Ejike, C.E.C.C. and Emmanuel, T.N., 2009. Cholesterol concentration in different parts of bovine meat sold in Nsukka, Nigeria: implications for cardiovascular disease risk. *African J of Biochem Res*., 3(4): 095–097.

Elaine, V., Robson, L.S., Waldir, A., Chtistine, A.A., Maurício de, S., Regina, F.P.M. *etal*., 2011. Organic solid waste originating from the meat processing industry as an alternative energy source. *Energy*, 36: 3897–3906.

Estaca, J. G., Montero, P. F., Martin, F. and Gomez-Guillen, M. C., 2009. Physico-chemical and film-forming properties of bovine-hide and tuna-skin gelatin: a comparative study. *JFood Eng*., 90(3): 480–486.

Faid, M., Zouiten, A., Elmarrakchi, A., Achkari-Begdouri, A., 1997. Biotransformation of fish waste into a stable feed ingredient. *Food Chem*., 60(1): 13-18.

FAO, 2008. www.taostat.org

FAO, 2012. The state of the world fisheries and aquaculture 2012. Rome: FAO, Available at http://www.fao.org/docrep/016/i2727e/i2727e.pdf Accessed 30.05.13.

Ferraro, V., Cruz, I. B., Jorge, R. F., Malcata, F. X., Pintado, M. E. and Castro, P. M. L., 2010. Valorisation of natural extracts from marine source focused on marine by-products: a review. *Food Research International*, 43: 2221-2233.

Field, R.A., 1981.Mechanically deboned red meat. *Adv Food Res.*, 27(1): 23–107.

Francisco, C., Lopez-Rodriguez, F., Ruiz-Celma, A., Fernando, R., and Gonzalez-Gonzalez, A., 2011. Recycling, reuse and energetic valuation of meat industry wastes in Extremadura (Spain). *Resources, Conservation and Recycling,* 55: 393–399.

Gagne, N. and Simpson, B. K., 1993. Use of proteolytic enzymes to facilitate recoveryof chitin from shrimp wastes. *Food Biotechnology*, 7: 253-263.

Ghost, R., 2001. Fractionating of biological macromolecules using carrier phase ultrafiltration. *Biotechnol Bioeng*., 74, 1–11, doi:10.1002/bit.1089.

Ghotra, B. S., Dyal, S. D., Narine, S.S., 2002. Lipid shortenings: a review. *Food ResIntl.*, 35(2): 1015–1048.

Gildberg, A., 2004. Enzymes and bioactive peptides from fish waste related to fish silage, fish feed and fish sauce production. *J Aquatic Foods Product Technol*, 13(2): 3-11

Gomez-Guillen, M. C., Gimenez, B., Lopez-Caballero, M. E. and Montero, M. P., 2011. Functional and bioactive properties of collagen and gelatin from alternative sources: a review. *Food Hydrocolloids*, 25: 1813-1827.

Grosse, C., 1984. Absatz und Vermarktungsmoglichkeiten fur Schlachtneben-produkte und Schlachtabfalle in der Bundesrepublik Deutschland. Dissertation, Universitat Bonn, Institute fur Agrarpolitik, Marktforschung und Wirstschaftssoziologie, Marz.

Gupta, R., Sharma, R., Beg, Q. K., 2013. Revisiting microbial keratinases: next generation proteases for sustainable biotechnology. *Crit Rev Biotechnol*, 33:216–228.

Gustavsson, J., Cederberg, C., Sonesson, U., van Otterdijk, R. and Meybeck A., 2011. Global food losses and food waste: extent, causes and prevention. Rome: Food and Agriculture Organisation of the United Nations (FAO); p. 29.

Hammoumi, A., Faid. M., El-Yachioui, M. and Amarouch, H., 1998. Characterization of fermented fish waste used in feeding trials with broilers. *Process Biochem.*,33(4): 423-427.

Hidaka, S. and Liu, S.Y., 2003. Effects of gelatins on calcium phosphate precipitation: a possible application for distinguishing bovine bone gelatin from porcine skin gelatin. *JFood Compos Anal.*, 16(3): 477–483.

Irshad, A., Sureshkumar, S., Shalima S.A. and Sutha, M.,2015. Slaughter house by-product utilization for sustainable meat industry- a review.*Int. J. Develop. Res.*5(6): 4725-4734.

Ichida, J. M., Krizova, L., LeFevre, C. A., Keener, H. M., Elwell, D. L., and Burtt, E. H., 2001. Bacterial inoculum enhances keratin degradation and biofilm formation in poultry compost. *J. Microbiol. Methods*, 47: 199–208.

Jack, A.O. and Yun-Hwa, P.H., 2011. Blood-derived products for human consumption. *Revelation and Science*, 1: 14–21.

Jamilah, B. and Harvinder, K.G., 2002. Properties of gelatins from skins of fish-black tilapia (*Oreochromismossambicus)* and red tilapia (*Oreochromisnilotica*). *FoodChem*., 77(3): 81–84.

Jayakumar, R., Prabaharan, M., Nair, S. V. and Tamura, H., 2010. Novel chitin and chitosan nanofibers in biomedical applications. *Biotechnology Advance*, 28: 142–150.

Jayathilakan, K., Sultana, K., Radhakrishna, K. and Bawa, A.S., 2012. Utilization of by products and waste materials from meat, poultry and fish processing industries: a review, *J Food SciTechnol,*49(3): 278-293.

Jo, G. H., Jung, W. J., Kuk, J. H., Oh, K. T., Kim, Y. J. and Park, R. D., 2008. Screening of protease-producing *Serratiamarcescens* FS-3 and its application to deproteinization of crab shell waste for chitin extraction. *Carbohydrate Polymers*, 74: 504–508.

Jones, H. B. and Ogden, E. A., 1984. Energy potential from livestock and poultry wastes in the South. USDA Agric. Econ. Rep. 522.

Jung, W. J., Jo, G. H., Kuk, J. H., Kim, Y. J., Oh, K. T. and Park, R. D., 2007. Production of chitin from red crab shell waste by successive fermentation with *Lactobacillus paracasei*KCTC-3074 and *Serratiamarcescens* FS-3. *Carbohydrate Polymers*, 68: 746-750.

Kandra, P., Challa, M. and Kalangi Padma Jyothi, H., 2012. Efficient use of shrimp waste: present and future trends. *Applied Microbiology and Biotechnology*, 93: 17-29.

Kartal, S. N. and Imamura, Y., 2005. Removal of copper, chromium, and arsenic from CCA-treated wood onto chitin and chitosan. *Bioresource Technology*, 96: 389–392.

Khan, M. A. A., Hossain, M. A., Hara, K., Ostomi, K., Ishihara, T. and Nozaki, Y., 2003. Effect of enzymatic fish-scrap protein hydrolysate on gelforming ability and denaturation of lizard fish Sauridawanieso surimi during frozen storage. *Fisheries Sci.*, 69(6): 1271-1280.

Khor, E. and Lim, L. Y., 2003. Implantable applications of chitin and chitosan. *Biomaterials*, 24: 2339–2349.

Kim, J.S., Shahidi, F., Heu, M.S., 2003. Characteristics of salt-fermented sauces from shrimp processing by-products. *J Agric Food Chem.,* 51(3): 784–792.

Kim, S. K. and Mendis, E., 2006. Bioactive compounds from marine processing byproducts e a review. *Food Research International*, 39: 383-393.

Kim, Y. J., Zhao, Y., Oh, K. T., Nguyen, V. N. and Park, R. D., 2008. Enzymatic deacetylation of chitin by extracellular chitin deacetylase from a newly screened *Mortierella* sp. DY-52. *Journal of Microbiology and Biotechnology*, 18: 759–766.

Kornillowicz-Kowalska, T. and Bohacz, J., 2011. Biodegradation of keratin waste: theory and practical aspects. *Waste Management*, 31:1689-1701.

Krajewska, B., 2004. Application of chitin and chitosan-based materials for enzyme immobilizations: A review. *Enzyme and Microbial Technology*, 35: 126–139.

Kurbanoglu, E.B. and Kurbanoglu, N.I., 2004. Utilization as peptone for glycerol production of ram horn waste with a new process. *Energy Convers Manage*, 45(2): 225-234.

Lasekan, A., Bakar, A., and Hashim, D., 2013. Potential of chicken by-products as sources of useful biological resources. *Waste Management*, 33: 552-565.

Laufenberg, G., Kunz, B. and Nystroem, M., 2003. Transformation of vegetable waste into value added products: (A) the upgrading concept, (B) practical implementation. *Bioresour. Technol.*, 87: 167–198.

Liu, D.C., 2002. Better utilization of by-products from the meat industry 2002-10-01. Extension Bulletins. Food and fertilizer Technology Center for the Asian and Pacific region (FFTC publication database).

Morimura, S., Nagata, H., Uemura, Y., Fahmi, A., Shigematsu, T. and Kida, K., 2002. Development of an effective process for utilization of collagen from livestock and fish waste. *Process Biochem,* 37(12): 1403–1412.

Murakami, K., Aoki, H., Nakamura, S., Nakamura, S., Takikawa, M., Hanzawa, M., *et al*., 2010. Hydrogel blends of chitin/chitosan, fucoidan and alginate as healingimpared wound dressings. *Biomaterials*, 31: 83–90.

Muzzarelli, R. A. A., Morganti, P., Morganti, G., Palombo, P., Palombo, M., Biagini, G., *et al.,* 2007. Chitin nanofibrils/chitosan glycolate composites as wound medicaments. *Carbohydrate Polymers*, 70: 274–284.

Odetallah, N. H., Wang, J. J., Garlich, J. D. and Shih, J. C. H., 2003. Keratinase in starter diets improves growth of broiler chicks. *Poultry Science*, 82: 664-670.

Oh, Y. S., Shih, I. L., Tzeng, Y. M. and Wang, S. L., 2000. Protease produced by *Pseudomonas aeruginosa* K-187 and its application in the deproteinization of shrimp and crab shell wastes. *Enzyme and Microbial Technology*, 27:3–10.

Oh, K. T., Kim, Y. J., Nguyen, V. N., Jung, W. J. and Park, R. D., 2007. Demineralization of crab shell waste by *Pseudomonas aeruginosa* F722. *Process Biochemistry*, 42: 1069-1074.

Ohba, R., Deguchi, T., Kishikawa, M., Arayad, F., Morimura, S. and Kida, K., 2003. Physiological functions of enzymatic hydrolysates of collagen or keratin contained in livestock and fish waste. *Food SciTechnol Res*, 9(1): 91-93.

Okamoto, Y., Yano, R., Miyatake, K., Tomohiro, I., Shigemasa, Y. and Minami, S., 2003. Effects of chitin and chitosan on blood coagulation. *Carbohydrate Polymers*, 53: 337–342.

Olsen, R. L., Toppe, J. and Karunasagar, I., 2014. Challenges and realistic opportunities in the use of by-products from processing of fish and shellfish. *Trends in Food Science & Technology*, 36(2):144-151.

Onifade, A. A., Al-Sane, N. A., Al-Musallam, A. A. and Al-Zarban, S., 1998. A review: Potentials for biotechnological applications of keratin-degrading microorganisms and their enzymes for nutritional improvement of feathers and other keratins as livestock feed resources. *Bioresource Technology,* 66: 1-11.

Oreopoulou, V. and Russ, W., 2007. Utilization of By-Products and Treatment of Waste in the Food Industry. Springer: New York, NY, USA.

Pedersen, M. B., Yu, S., Plumstead, P. and Dalsgaard, S., 2012. Comparison of four feed proteases for improvement of nutritive value of poultry feather meal. *Journal of Animal Science*, 90: 350-352.

Perugini, P., Genta, I., Pavanetto, F., Conti, B., Scalia, S. and Baruffini, A., 2000. Study on glycolic acid delivery by liposomes and microspheres. *International Journal of Pharmaceutics*, 196: 51-61.

Prado, A. G. S., Torres, J. D., Faria, E. A. and Dias, S. C. L., 2004. Comparative adsorption studies of indigo carmine dye on chitin and chitosan. *Journal of Colloid and Interface Sciences*, 277: 43–47.

Rahman, U., Sahar, A. and Khan, M. A., 2014. Recovery and utilization of effluents from meat processing industries, *Food Research International*, http://dx.doi.org/10.1016/j.foodres.2014.09.026

Rinaudo, M., 2006. Chitin and chitosan: Properties and applications. *Progress Polymer Science*, 31: 603–632.

Rivera, J. A., Sebranek, J. G., Rust, R. E. and Tabatabai, L. B., 2000. Composition and protein fractions of different meat by-products used for petfood compared with mechanically separated chicken (MSC). *Meat Sci.*, 55(5): 53-59.

Rossi, D. M., Flores, S. H., Venzke, J. G. and Ayub, M.A.Z., 2009. Biological evaluation of mechanically deboned chicken meat protein hydrolysate. *Brazilian Journal of Nutrition*, *22*: 879-885.

Rust, K., 1995. Smoked catfish sausage: adding value to by-products. *Aquaculture-magazine*, 21(2): 22, 24, 26, 28.

Rustad, T., Storro, I. and Slizyte, R., 2011. Possibilities for the utilization of marine by-products. *International Journal of Food Science & Technology*, 46: 2001-2014.

Salminen, E. and Rintala, J., 2002.Anaerobic digestion of organic solid poultry slaughterhouse waste – a review. *Bioresource Technology*, 83: 13-26.

Sears, A. V., Ho, C. K. M. and Walker, S. W., 2010. Omacor (omega-3- acid ethyl esters). *Practical Diabetes International*, 27: 38-39.

Segree, A. and Falasconi, L., 2011. *IlLibro Nero DelloSpreco in Italia: Il Cibo*, EdizioniAmbiente: Milano, Italy. (In Italian)

Senel, S. and McClure, S. J., 2004. Potential applications of chitosan in veterinary medicine. *Advances in Drug Delivery Reviews*, 56: 1467-1480.

Sharma, B.D. and Sharma, K., 2011. Outlines of Meat Science and Technology, Jaypee Brothers Medical Pub (p) Ltd., 360.

Shih, J. C. H., 1993. Recent development in poultry waste digestion and feather utilization – a review. *Poult Sci*., 72(9): 1617–1620.

Sielaff, H., 1996. Fleischtechnologie. Behr's Verlag, Hamburg.

Silva,V.D.M. and Silvestre, M.P.C., 2003. Functional properties of bovine blood plasma intended for use as a functional ingredient in human food. *LWT- Food Sci Technol.* 36(5), 709–718.

Simpson, T.W., 1991. Agronomic use of poultry industry waste. *Poultry Science*, 70:1126-1131.

Sini, T. K., Santhosh, S. and Mathew, P. T., 2007. Study on the production of chitin and chitosan from shrimp shell by using *Bacillus subtilis* fermentation. *Carbohydrate Research*, 342: 2423-2429.

Skorupa, K., Sikorski, Z. E., 1993. Potential for utilization of low-grade fish material for production of microbiological peptones. *Przem Spoz*, 47(6):159–161.

Tahajod, A. S., Rand, A. G., 1996. Seafood waste potential to support antimicrobial compound production by lactic acid bacteria. IFT Annual meeting: Book of abstracts, ISSN 1082–1236: 31-32.

Thimjos, N., Janne, L., Hannu, K., and Fredriksson-Ahomaa, M., 2014. Meat by-products. In P. Miguel, & L.G. Maria (Eds.), Meat Inspection and Control in the Slaughterhouse. John Wiley and Sons, Ltd.

Toldrá, F., Aristoy, M.C., Mora, L.,Reig, M., 2012. Innovations in value-addition of edible meat by-products.*Meat Sci.* 92: 290–296

Twu, Y. K., Huang, H. I., Chang, S. Y. and Wang, S. L., 2003. Preparation and sorption activity of chitosan/cellulose blend beads. *Carbohydrate Polymers*, 54: 425–430.

Unsal, M. and Aktas, N., 2003. Fractionation and characterization of edible sheep tail fat. *MeatSci*.2003, 63(4): 235–239.

USDA, (2014). Livestock and poultry: World markets and trade. Foreign Agricultural Service USDA. Available at http://apps.fas.usda.gov

Vanquez, J. A., Gonzalez, M. P. and Murado, M. A., 2004. Peptones from autohydrolyzed fish vicera for nisin and pediocin production. *J Biotechnol*, 112(3): 299-311.

Wan, Y., Ghost, R. and Cui, Z., 2002. High resolution plasma protein fractionation using ultrafiltration. *Desalination*. 144, 301–306 ,doi: 10.1016/S0011-9164(02):00332-6.

Wang, S. L. and Chio, S. H., 1998. Deproteinization of shrimp and crab shell with the protease of *Pseudomonas aeruginosa* K-187. *Enzyme and Microbial Technology*, 22: 629–633.

Wang, S. L., Chen, S. J. and Wang, C. L., 2008a. Purification and characterization of chitinases and chitosanases from a new species strain *Pseudomonas* sp. TKU015 using shrimp shells as a substrate. *Carbohydrate Research*, 343: 1171–1179.

Wang, S. L., Pen, J. H., Liang, T. W. and Liu, K. C., 2008b. Purification and characterization of a chitosanase from *Serratiamarcescens* TKU011. *Carbohydrate Research*, 343:1316–1323.

Wang, S. L., Lin, H. T., Liang, T. W., Chen, Y. J., Yen, Y. H. and Guo, S. P., 2008c. Reclamation of chitinous materials by bromelain for the preparation of antitumor and antifungal materials. *Bioresource Technology*, 99:4386–4393.

Wang, S. L., Liu, K. C., Liang, T. W., Kuo, Y. H. and Wang, J. Y., 2010a. In vitro antioxidant activity of liquor and semi-purified fractions from squid pen biowaste by *Serratiaureilytica* TKU013. *Food Chemistry*, 119:1380–1385.

Wang, S. L., Chang, T. J. and Liang, T. W., 2010b. Conversion and degradation of shellfish wastes by *Serratia sp*., TKU016 fermentation for the production of enzymes and bioactive materials. *Biodegradation*, 21:321–333.

Yang, J. K., Shih, I. L., Tzeng, Y. M. and Wang, S. L. 2000. Production and purification of protease from a *Bacillus subtilis* that can deproteinize crustacean wastes. *Enzyme and Microbial Technology*, 26:406–413.

Weiss, T. J., 1983. Bakery shortenings and frying shortenings. In food oils and their uses. Connecticut: The AVI Publishing Company, Inc, 153-165.

West, G. C. and Shaw, D. L., 1975.Fatty acid composition of dall sheep bone marrow. *Comp BiochemPhysiol B BiochemMol Biol.*, 50(4): 599–601.

Yen, Y. H., Ho, Y. S., Lee, C. C., Chang, W. T., Twu, Y. K. and Chang, A. C., 2002. Microbial reclamation of tea lees and chitinous materials for the preparation of deodorants and ethylene removing agents. *Food Science and Agricultural Chemistry (Taiwan)*, 4:136–141.

Yoshida, H., Terashima, M. and Takahashi, Y., 1999. Production of organic acids and amino acids from fish meat by sub-critical water hydrolysis. *Biotechnol Prog.*, 15(60):1090–1094.

Young, R.H. and Lawrie, R.A., 2007. Utilization of edible protein from meat industry by-products and waste. *Intl J Food Sc Technol.* 9(2):171–177.

Zhao, L. and Xia, W., 2009. Stainless steel membrane UF coupled with NF process for the recovery of sodium hydroxide from alkaline wastewater in chitin processing. *Desalination*, 249:774-780.

4

Status of Agro-industrial Byproducts and Wastes: Special Emphasis on Deoiled Rice Bran, Paddy Husk, Potato Peel and Banana Peel

Kulsum Jan, Khalid Bashir, Shumaila Jan and D.C. Saxena

Abstract

Agro-food industries generate a large amount of by-products and wastes. These byproducts and wastes have a negative impact in terms of the environmental concern due to the increase of pollutant disposal, and industrial sustainability because of high costs related to their management. These byproducts and wastes are rich in minerals, sugars and proteins. The composition and characteristics of wastes from different food processing industries vary and rely upon the production technique and the nature of the product. India is the second largest producer of rice/paddy in the world and the utilization of rice bran is gaining importance. However, a small fraction of these have been utilized. In case of fruits and vegetables, industrial processing of potato generates between 70 and 140 thousand tons of peels worldwide annually. Moreover, 37% of world's total annual production of banana is shared by India. Hence, to minimize the disposal fees and trash collection new policies and methods have been developed for handling and treatment of wastes and byproducts. This chapter envisages the status of different agro-food industrial byproducts and wastes for the development of different food and non-food products.

Keywords: Agro-industries, byproducts, banana, deoiled rice bran, potato, peel, wastes

1. Food Industry byproducts

1.1 De-oiled Rice Bran

1.1.1. Structure and composition of rice

Rough rice/paddy is covered by husk, and removal of it by de-husking results in brown rice.Brown rice is covered by bran layers, namely, pericarp, testa, and aleurone layers obtained by the removal of 5–10% of brown rice by de-branning or polishing (Jayadeep *et al.*, 2009). Bran is a hard outer layer of rice grain and consists of combined aleurone and pericarp as shown in Fig. 1. Along with germ, it is an integral part of whole grain and is often produced as a by-product of milling in the production of refined grains. It constitutes 8% of the weight of the whole grain (Rabbani and Ali, 2009). When bran is removed from grains, it loses a portion of nutritional value. Bran should not be confused with chaff, which is a coarser scaly material surrounding the grain, but not forming part of the grain itself.

The utilization of rice bran is gaining importance in many studies due to the fact that, during the processing of whole rice, large amounts of the grain's outer layers are removed, raising the concentration of nutrients in the bran and rendering it an important source of nutrients for industry and human consumption (Imsanguan *et al.,* 2008; Lilitchan *et al.,* 2008).

The lysine content of rice bran is 3–4%, which is higher than present in the rice endosperm. Rice bran contains 22–29% crude fat which includes approximately 1.8% gum and 0.4% wax. The full fat rice bran contains 18–22% oil including bio-active phytochemicals such as oryzanols, phytosterols, tocotrienols, squalene, polycosanols, phytic acid, ferulic acid, inositol hexaphosphate respectively (Ardiansyah *et al.,* 2006).

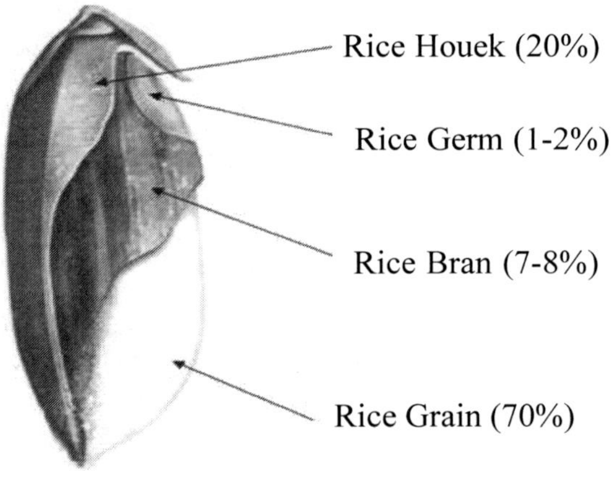

Fig. 1: Structure of rice with different layers

The total dietary fiber (TDF) content of rice bran ranges from 20 to 27% with less than 2% as soluble dietary fiber. Ambashankar and Chandrasekaran (1998) reported that full fat rice bran contains a good content of protein (13.20 to 17.13%), fat (14.00 to 22.90%), carbohydrate (16.10%), fiber (9.50 to 13.20%), and vitamins and minerals. It also contains considerable amount of oil (15–25%) (Lakkakula *et al.,* 2004). For this reason, special attention is being given to the extraction of edible oil from rice bran (Danielski *et al.,*2005). Navam *et al.* (2014) also stated that rice bran should be defatted and heat treated to prevent lipid oxidation.

Kaewboonnum *et al.*(2008) hydrolyzed the deoiled bran after oil extraction and described deoiled rice bran as rich source of proteins and amino acid. The extraction of oil leaves behind the deoiled rice bran which can be utilized for various food and non-food industrial applications.

1.1.2 Status of deoiled rice bran (DRB)

India is the second largest producer of rice/paddy in the world next to China. Approximately 1692 million tons are harvested worldwide annually (FAO, 2014), out of which India produces 159 million MT of paddy and 127 million MT of rice. The Indian production of rice bran is 5 MT/yr and 70% of the total production is sold cheaply as animal feed (FAO, 2014). About half of rice bran produced per year is solvent extracted for rice bran oil leaving deoiled meal as the byproduct (Lee *et al.*, 2005). Deoiled bran is used as animal feed (Pannu *et al.,* 2002; Katiha *et al.,*2005). The effect of incorporation of deoiled rice bran at varying levels (5, 10 and 15%) on the quality characteristics of bread including physical, rheological and sensory attributes showed that DRB can be incorporated in breads upto 10 and 15% (Sairam *et al.,* 2011). Deoiled rice bran can be used as adhesives in composites (Pan *et al.,* 2005) and as a substrate for production of enzymes (Nizamudddin *et al*., 2008). Sunphorka *et al.* (2012) observed that deoiled rice bran despite being high in protein content is typically disposed off as agricultural waste or sold as a low-cost animal feed after recovery of the rice bran oil, and so are cheap waste products. Besides being readily and cheaply available throughout the year, the utilization of deoiled rice bran is limited for the development of biodegradable composites or products.

1.1.3 Components of deoiled rice bran

Sairam *et al.* (2011) reported that commercial defatted rice bran contains 17g/100g of protein, 11.44 g/100g fiber, 0.66% fat, 14.65 g/100g ash, calcium 255ppm, 166 phosphorous and 290 ppm iron. The components of deoiled rice bran are starch and dextrin (46.7%), cellulose and hemicelluloses (11.3%), protein (18.4%), lipid (1.4%), ash (10.4%) and others (11.8%) (Tanaka *et al.,* 2006). Wang *et al.* (2015) also reported that deoiled rice bran contains good amount of protein (14–16%). Protein has attracted much attention in the field of packaging due to its biodegradability and binding properties (Cuq *et al.,* 1998). Protein reactions in deoiled rice bran include formation of both non-covalent and disulfide bonds after extrusion. Protein–protein interactions may be enhanced by decreased temperature and macromolecular alignment. Moreover, the presence of fiber results in crystalline aggregation leading to parallel fiber formation of varying length and thickness. Hence, a wide range of interaction energy is possible for protein cross-linking with protein and other molecules. Therefore, hydrophobic, cation–mediated electrostatic interactions and covalent bonds also contribute to the stabilization of the three dimensional network formed after extrusion (Areas, 1992). Earlier research also claimed that new peptide bonds are responsible for extrudate structure (Burgess and Stanley, 1976). Deoiled rice bran is a cheap protein source and hence, could be utilized for the development of extrudates which can be further utilized for development of biodegradable pots/composites. Hitherto, the deoiled rice bran containing relatively high level of protein (as well as complex polysaccharides) could not be utilized to its full potential. Hence, a valid alternative may also be its utilization in various non-food applications such as planting containers/composites used for transplantation etc.

2 Food Industry Wastes

2.1 Types

Food industry produces large amount of both solids and liquid wastes, resulting from the preparation, processing and consumption of food. These wastes cause severe disposal and potential pollution problems and represent a loss of valuable biomass and nutrients. Beside their pollution and hazard aspects, in many cases, food processing wastes might have a potential for conversion into useful products of higher value as by-product, or even as raw material for other industries, or for use as food or feed after biological treatment (Litchfield, 1987). The composition and characteristics of wastes produced from different food processing industries vary and extremely rely upon the production technique and the nature of the product. For example, wastes from meat processing plants will contain a high fat and protein content, horticulture and cereal industry produces wastes rich in cellulosic material, waste from the canning industry will contain high concentrations of sugar and starches etc (Kosseva and Webb, 2013). The waste may not only differ from location to location but also vary from one time of the year to another.

2.1.1 Paddy husk

Paddy husk is an agro-waste which is produced in about 100 million of tons. Paddy husk accounts for approximately one-fifth of the annual gross rice production in the world. The rice production in Asia produces about 770 million tons of husk annually. India, one of the biggest rice producers in the world, not surprisingly, also produces vast amounts of rice husk. Bihar alone is estimated to produce 1.8 billion kilograms of rice husk every year. The rice milling process usually generates about 20-30% husk, bran between 8-12% and milled rice from 50 to 63.5% (Marlina *et al.,*2014). Presently, having no commercial value in itself, paddy husk usually ends up being burned in open spaces, thus causing environmental pollution and disposal problems. Paddy husk offers great opportunities for their production of convenient products with reduced expenses (Singh *et al.,*2008). Due to the need to conserve energy and resources, efforts have been made to burn the husk under controlled conditions and to utilize the resultant ash in building, semiconductor, composite, and abrasive materials (Siqueira *et al.,*2009). The chemical constituents vary from sample to sample which may be due to the different type of paddy, geographical conditions, soil chemistry, climatic variation and fertilizers used in the paddy growth (Chaudhary *et al.,*2004). Ndazi *et al.* (2007) investigated that the rice husk is a cellulose-based fibre, and could be utilized for the development of composite panels. However, rice husks have not been successfully exploited like other cellulose fibers due to poor interaction between rice husks and the binding materials and therefore results in weak particle–matrix adhesion. The rice husk is available in plenty in rice producing countries, which can be used for value addition, hence, economic benefits to the producers and to the nation as well.

2.1.2 Banana peel

In recent years, production of banana juice, banana wine, banana powder, banana chips etc is established on a larger scale and subsequently, their peels are obtained in excess amount (Lokeswari, 2010). These gets accumulated in bulk at hotels, houses and food industries posing serious environmental problems (Shobhana *et al.,*2013). Banana (*Musa sapientum*) is grown extensively in tropical and subtropical countries and is the largest produced fruit contributing about 27% of the world's banana production, 37% of which is shared by India (Mohapatra *et al.,*2010). Peels are the major by-products of banana crop obtained during the processing of various products such as chips, flours, pulps, dried, and jam, spirits distilled from wine or beer (Lokeswari, 2010). The main banana residue is the fruit peel which accounts for 30–40% of the total fruit weight (Benjamin *et al.,*2014). Banana peel flour can potentially offer new products with standardized compositions for various industrial and domestic uses (Emaga *et al.,* 2007).

Banana peels are not being used for any other purposes and are mostly dumped as solid waste at large expense. Hence, it is essential to find valid applications; otherwise it can cause a real environmental problem (Zhang *et al.,*2005). Banana peels are used for the production of alcohol (Tewari *et al.,*1986), methane (Bardiya and Somayaji, 1996), food for livestock (Onwuka *et al.,*1997) or adsorbents for water purification (Annadurai *et al.,* 2002). However, till date, banana peels have not been used for the development of biodegradable molded products.

2.1.3 Potato peel

Another agro industrial waste is potato peel obtained from the potato processing industry which also has become an environmental concern worldwide (Mushimiyimana and Tallapragada, 2015). Potato peel is a zero value waste from potato processing plants. The problem of the improper management of potato peel waste causes considerable concern to the potato industries thus implying the need to identify an integrated, environment-friendly solution (bio composite) (Arapoglou *et al*., 2010). Therefore, processing potato peels into a higher valuable product is not only an environmentally viable solution to waste disposal issues but also creates a non-food based economy for potato processing industries.

After corn, rice, and wheat, potatoes are the world's fourth largest crop and have experienced a steady growth over the last two decades (FAO, 2014) with production of 376 million tons. Potato peel waste is a zero value by-product, which occurs in big amounts after industrial potato processing and can range from 15 to 40% of initial product mass, depending on the peeling method and other defect removal, trimming, and cutting processes can generate an additional 15% waste (Mader *et al.,*2009;Sepelev and Galoburda, 2015). Industrial processing generates between 70 and 140 thousand tons of peels worldwide annually (Chang, 2011).

A large amount of potato peels are discarded during processing for chips by many industries and the major limitation in the use of potato peels for livestock feeding is its low protein content (Akintomide and Antai, 2012). Potato peels have been widely used for biogas production, lactic acid extraction, phenolic acids extraction and ultrasonic extraction of steroidal alkaloids (Wu, 2016).

3 Conclusion

Accumulation of agro-industrial by-products and wastes in bulk is posing serious environmental problems. Hence, to prevent this, it has become necessary to develop alternative commercial application of these agro industrial wastes.In order to recycle, recover and convert the by-products and wastes into value added products different technologies have been involved. These by-products and wastes from agro-food industries, such as natural fibres and proteins could be converted to value added innovative food and non food products (extruded snacks, biscuits, biodegradable films, trays, and containers etc). Paddy husk having no commercial value in itself usually ends up being burned hence, offers great opportunities for their production of convenient products. Similarly, banana and potato peel possessing least market values could also be utilized for the development of products with reduced expenses.

References

Akintomide, M., Antai, S. 2012. Protein Enrichment of Irish potato (Solanium tuberosium) peels through Solid Substrate Fermentation by Saccharomyces cerevisiae and Aspergillus Niger. *J. Environmental Science Toxicology and Food Technology*, 1(5): 15-19.

Ambashankar, K., Chandrasekaran, D. 1998. Chemical composition and metabolizable energy value of rice waste for chicken. *Ind. Vet. J.* 75: 475–476.

Annadurai, G., Juang, R.S., Lee, D.J. 2002. Use of cellulose-based wastes for adsorption of dyes from aqueous solutions. *J. Hazardous Materials*. 92(3): 263-274.

Arapoglou, D., Varzakas, T., Vlyssides, A., Israilides. C. 2010. Ethanol production from potato peel waste (PPW). *Waste Manage*. 30: 1898–1902

Ardiansyah, S.H., Koseki, T., Ohinata, K., Hazhizume, K., Komai, M. 2006. Rice bran fractions improve blood pressure, lipid profle, and glucose metabolism in stroke-prone spontaneously hypertensive rats. *J. Agric. Food. Chem.* 54: 1914-1920.

Areas, J.A.G. 1992. Extrusion of proteins. *Crit. Rev. Food Sci. Nutr.* 32: 365–392.

Bardiya, N., Somayaji, D. and Khanna, S. 1996. Biomethanation of banana peel and pineapple waste. *Bioresour Technol.* 58(1): 73-76.

Benjamin, C., Singh, P.K., Dipuraj, P.S. 2014. Bio-ethanol production from banana peel by simultaneous saccharification and fermentation process using cocultures Aspergillus niger and Saccharomyces cerevisiae. *Int. J. Curr. Microbiol. App. Sci.* 3(5): 84-96.

Burgess, G.D., Stanley, D.W. 1976. A possible mechanism for thermal texturization of soybean protein. *Canadian Institute of Food Science and Technology*. 9: 228–230.

Chang, K.C. 2011. Polyphenol antioxidants from potato peels: Extraction optimization and application to stabilizing lipid oxidation in foods. *Polyphenol Antioxidants From Potato Peels: Extraction Optimization and Application to Stabilizing Lipid Oxidation in Foods.* 1-8.

Chaudhery, D.S., Jokands, M.C. Cser, F. 2004. Recycling Rice Husk Ash: Filler Material Polymeric Composites. *J. Advance in Polymer Technol.* 23(2): 147-155.

Cuq, B., Gontard, N., Guilbert, S. 1998. Proteins as agricultural polymers for packaging production. *Cereal Chem*. 75(1): 1-9.

Danielskia, L., Carsten, Z., Haiko, H., Gerd B. 2005. A process line for the production of raffinated rice oil from rice bran. *J. of Supercritical Fluids.* 34: 133–141.

Emaga, T. H., Andrianaivo, R. H., Wathelet, B., Tchango J. T., Paquot, M. 2007. Effects of the stage of maturation and varieties on the chemical composition of banana and plantain peels. *Food Chem.* 103: 590–600.

FAO. 2014. FAOSTAT Agricultural Data. Food and Agricultural Commodities Production. http://faostat.fao.org/site/339/

Imsanguan, P., Roaysubtawee, A., Borirak, R., Pongamphai, S., Douglas, S., Douglas, P.L. 2008. Extraction of á-tocopherol and y-oryzanol from rice bran. *LWT - Food Sci. Technol*. 41(8): 1417-1424.

Jayadeep, A., Vasudeva, S., Sathyendra, R.B.V., Srinivas, A., Ali, S.Z. 2009. Effect of Physical Processing of Commercial De-oiled Rice Bran on Particle Size Distribution, and Content of Chemical and Bio-functional Components. *Food Bioprocess Technol.* 2: 57–67.

Kaewboonnum, W., Wachararuji, K., Shotipruk, A. 2008. Value added products from by-products of rice bran oil processing. *Chiang Mai J Sci.* 35(1): 116-122.

Katiha, P.K., Jena, J.K., Pillai, N.G.K., Chakraborty, C., Dey, M.M. 2005. Inland aquaculture in India: past trend, present status and future prospects. *Aquaculture Economics & Management*, 9(1): 237-264.

Kosseva, M.R., Webb, C. 2013. Concluding remarks and future prospects. Food industry wastes, Academic press. 295-303 Litchfield, J.H. 1987. Microbiological and enzymatic treatments for utilizing agricultural and food processing wastes. *Food Biotechnol.* 1(1): 29-57.

Lakkakula, N., Rao, M.L., Terry, W. 2004. Rice bran stabilization and rice bran oil extraction using ohmic heating. *Bior Technol.* 92: 157–161.

Lee, J.W., Lee, S.W., Kim, M.K., Rhee, C., Kim, I.H., Lee, K.W. 2005. Beneficial effect of the unsaponifable matter from rice bran on oxidative stress in vitro compared with α-tocopherol. *J. Scie Food Agr.* 85: 493–498.

Lilitchan, S., Tangprawat, C., Aryusuk, K., Krisnangkura, S., Chokmoh, S., Krisnangkura, K. 2008. Partial extraction method for the rapid analysis of total lipids and y-oryzanol contents in rice bran. *Food Chem.* 106(2): 752-759.

Lokeswari, N. 2010. Statistical optimization of experimental variables associated with production of alpha amylases by bacillus subtilis using banana agroresidual wastes in solid-state fermentation. *Rasayan J. Chem.* 3(1): 172-178.

Mader, J., Rawel, H., Kroh, L. 2009. Composition of phenolic compounds and glycoalkaloids α-solanine and α-chaconine during commercial potato processing. *J. Agric. Food Chem.* 57: 6292" 6297.

Marlina, G.E., Wirjosentono, B., Bukit, N., Agusnar, H. 2014. Preparation and Characterization of Rice Husk Ash as Filler Material in to Nanoparticles on Hdpe Thermoplastic Composites. *Chemistry and Materials Research.* 6(7): 14-24.

Mohapatra, D., Mishra, S. and Sutar, N. 2010. Banana and its by-product utilization: an overview. *J Sci Ind Res*, 69(5): 323-329.

Mushimiyimana, I., Tallapragada, P. 2015. Agro wastes residues as strategy to produce cellulase. *Int J ChemTech Res.* 8(1): 89-97.

Navam, S., Hettiarachchy. 2014. Heat-stabilized defatted rice bran (HDRB) as an alternative growth medium for Saccharomyces cerevisiae. *J Food Nutr.* 1: 1- 6.

Ndazi B.S., S. Karlsson., J.V. Tesha, C.W. 2007. Nyahumwa. Chemical and physical modifications of rice husks for use as composite panels. *Composites: Part A.* 38: 925–935.

Nizamuddin, S., Sridevi, A., Narasimha, G. 2008. Production of -galactosidase by Aspergillus oryzae in solid-state fermentation. *African Journal of Biotechnology*. 7 (8): 1096-1100.

Onwuka, C.F.I., Adetiloye, P.O. Afolami, C.A. 1997. Use of household wastes and crop residues in small ruminant feeding in Nigeria. *Small Ruminant Research*, 24(3): 233-237.

Pannu, M.S., Kaushal, J.R., Wadhwa, M., Bakshi, M.P.S. 2002. Effect of Naturally Fermented Wheat Straw Based Complete Feeds on the Growth of Buffalo Calves. *Asian-Aust. J. Anim. Sci.* 15(11): 1568-1572.

Rabbani, G.H., Ali, M. 2009. New ideas and concepts Rice bran: A nutrient-dense mill-waste for human nutrition. *The Orion Medical Journal.* 32(3): 694-701.

Sairam, S., Gopala, A. G., Krishna, Asna, U. 2011. Physico-chemical characteristics of defatted rice bran and its utilization in a bakery product. *J Food Sci Technol.* 48(4): 478–483.

Sepelev, I., Galoburda, R., 2015. Industrial potato peels waste application in food production: a review. In Research for Rural Development. International Scientific Conference Proceedings (Latvia). Latvia University of Agriculture. 1: 130-136.

Shobhana, J., Dhanashree, C., Shirish, R. 2013. Lipase production from banana peel extract and potato peel extract. *Int. J. Res. Pure. Appl. Microbiol.* 3(1): 11-13.

Singh, D., Kumar, R., Kumar, A., Rai, K.N. 2008. Synthesis and characterization of rice husk silica, silica-carbon composite and H_3PO_4 activated silica. *Cerâmica*, 54(330): 203-212.

Siqueira, E.J., Yoshida, I.V.P., Pardini, L.C., Schiavon, M.A. 2009. Preparation and characterization of ceramic composites derived from rice husk ash and polysiloxane. *Ceramics International*, 35(1): 213-220.

Sunphorka, S., Warinthorn, C., Yoshito, O., Somkiat, N. 2012. Protein and Sugar Extraction from Rice Bran and De-Oiled Rice Bran using Subcritical Water in a Semi-Continuous Reactor: Optimization by Response Surface Methodology. *Int. J. Food Eng.* 8(3): 1-22.

Tanaka, T., Hoshina, M., Tanabe, S., Sakai, K., Ohtsubo, S., Taniguchi, M. 2006. Production of D-lactic acid from defatted rice bran by simultaneous saccharification and fermentation. *Bioresour Technol.* 97(2): 211–217.

Tewari, H.K., Marwaha, S.S., Rupal, K. 1986. Ethanol from banana peels. *Agricultural wastes*. 16(2): 135-146.

Wang, C., Feng, X., Dan, L., Min, Z. 2015. Physico-chemical and Structural Properties of Four Rice Bran Protein Fractions Based on the Multiple Solvent Extraction Method. *Czech J. Food Sci.* 33(3): 283–291.

Wu, D. 2016. Recycle Technology for Potato Peel Waste Processing: A Review. *Procedia Environmental Sciences*, 31: 103-107.

Zhang, P., Whistler, R. L., BeMiller, J. N. Hamaker, B. R. 2005. Banana starch production, physicochemical properties and digestibility. A review. *Carbohydr Polym.* 59: 443–458.

5

Role of Essential Oils in Meat and Meat Products

Heena Sharma, Sudheer Kumar, Tarun Pal Singh, Arvind, Anupama Sharma

Abstract

Meat is considered to be a highly perishable food commodity because of its biological composition. Thus, to extend its shelf life and maintain its nutritive value, there is an urgent need to find out alternatives for synthetic anti-microbial and anti-oxidants. This will not only serve the purpose of meat product manufacturer's but will also satisfy the consumers' demand for minimally processed meat products devoid of synthetic preservatives. This review discusses the natural antimicrobial and anti-oxidants sources viz., *various essential oils, their composition and application in different meat and meat products. Essential oils from basil, rosemary, thyme, oregano, ginger, basilica, balm, coriander, rosemary and clove have exhibited a better potential to be used as an antimicrobial agent in meat and meat products. They owe their anti-microbial properties to the phenolic compounds present in them. They dislocate cell membrane and disrupt functionality of bacterial cell membrane and eventually leading to the release of intracellular components. However, essential oils are not widely used due to the pungent and intense aroma imparted to the food, thus there is still need to work out on the novel technologies which can not only increase food shelf life but at the same time, are sensorially acceptable to the consumers.*

Keywords: Essential oils, meat products; anti-microbial, anti-oxidant; shelf life; food safety and quality

1. Introduction

Meat is a highly perishable food commodity due to its biological composition. Now a day's, consumers demand for minimally processed, ready to eat meat products devoid of any synthetic preservative. Thus, minimally processed meat product industries have dramatically gained popularity over the previous few years. As a result, major concern for meat industry is to extend the shelf life of perishable meat and meat products. The time period between product packaging and its end use, while the product's organoleptic properties remain acceptable for the consumer is defined as shelf life and it depends mainly on the initial microbial load of the product.

Main factor associated with chemical deterioration in food is lipid oxidation. Rancid flavour is produced due to oxidation of lipids and which reduces the sensory along with nutritional quality of the products making them unacceptable to consumers. During lipid oxidation reactions, free radicals are generated in food matrix which is responsible for many health problems including cancers, diabetes and cardiovascular diseases and soon effective anti-oxidants are usually added in meat and meat products in order to minimize their oxidative deterioration and extending their shelf life. Synthetic antioxidants *viz*., butylated hydroxyanisole (BHA), butylated hydroxitoluene (BHT) and propyl gallate are commonly used in many foods to reduce or delay the oxidation process. Increasing concern are growing among the consumers regarding the potential consequence of the addition of synthetics compounds to food has paved the way to identify innovative and natural antioxidants that would deliver as an alternative to the synthetic compounds. This would give a clear and natural image to meat and meat products and one such possibility is the use of essential oils.

Several studies have been done regarding the use of essential oils as natural compounds because they show antioxidant as well as antimicrobial activity. Natural antioxidants from food plants have an upper edge over the synthetic preservatives as they are easily accepted by the consumers; safe to use; no need of any safety tests; belong to natural resources; and have acceptable sensory properties. The above mentioned properties of essential oils have posed immense interest among the researchers to find a novel alternative to synthetic anti-oxidants and thus, satisfying the consumer demands for the use of natural additives in foods.

2. Essential Oils (EOs)

Essential oils (also called ethereal oils) are complex mixtures of volatile lipophilic substances. According to International Organization for Standardization (ISO), Essential oils are defined as products obtained from plant parts by steam drag distillation. They have been certified with Generally Recognised as Safe (GRAS) status by USFDA, and can also be recognised as the possible alternative to artificial additives, which are otherwise harmful to the human beings. Approximately 300 EOs are commercially important in the flavour and fragrance market. These oils have been broadly used in food products due to their biological properties and flavor attributes. Essential oils are considered as safe food additives at concentrations < 2 mg/kg body wt/day. They possess antioxidant, antibacterial, antiviral and antifungal properties. Essential oils owe their antimicrobial activity to a number of small terpenoid and phenolic compounds, and in their pure form also, exhibit antibacterial or antifungal activity. They are effective against both Gram negative and Gram positive microorganisms, although, Gram positive are less resistant than Gram negative bacteria. Before their use as "natural preservatives", careful assessment is needed, so that when added to the food product, they are sensorially acceptable to the consumer.

Table 1: Different essential oils, active components and their composition

Essential oil	Active components	Composition
Clove oil (*Syzigium aromaticum* L.)	Eugenol	Eugenol (21-83.73%) Eugenyl acetate (0.2-11.37%) β-caryophyllene (0-3.47%)
Thyme (*Thymus vulgaris* L.)	Thymol	Thymol (15-50%) p-cymene (9-25%) Carvacrol (2-15%) γ-terpinene (7-15%)
Holy basil (*Ocimum sanctum* L.)	Eugenol	Eugenol (2-60.2%) Mehtyl eugenol (0.87-82.98%) β-caryophyllene (4.13-44.60%) β-elemene (0.76-32.41%)
Oregano (*Origanum vulgare* L)	Carvacrol	Carvacrol (3-60%) Thymol (0.48-17.98%) α-terpinene (0-10%) p-cymene (1-17%)
Cinnamon (*Cinnamomum cassia)*	(E)-cinnamaldehyde	(E)-cinnamaldehyde (65-72.45%) Benzoic acid, 2-O H-methyl ester (15-21%) Cinnamaldehyde (5-21%)
Coriander (*Coriandrum sativum* L)	Linalool	Linalool (40.9-79.9%) Meryl acetate (2.3-14.2%) γ-terpinene (0.1-13.6%)
Rosemary officinalis (*Rosmarinus ofûcinalis* L.)	1,8-cineole, α-pinene	1,8-cineole (18.7-29.36%) α-pinene (2-31.23%) Camphor (7-15.4%)
Lemon grass oil (*Cympopogon citratus* L.)	Geranial	Geranial (40-47%) β-citral/Neral (32%)

2.1 Oregano Oil

Oregano is a distinct spice of the Mediterranean cuisine which is obtained by drying leaves and flowers of *Origanum vulgare*. It is distinguished for its antioxidative and antimicrobial activity. Carvacrol and thymol are two main phenols responsible for this activity and comprises about 78-82% of the oregano essential. Furthermore, it also contains other minor constituents such as g-terpinene and p-cymene, two monoterpene hydrocarbons which also contribute to anti- microbial activity. Oregano essential oil has tremendously achieved the interest and significance of researchers as a possible "natural" antimicrobial to be used in food during the past few years. The inclusion of oregano oil in films is considered as an appealing opportunity by manufacturers to delay microbial food spoilage.

2.2 Coriander Oil

Coriandrum sativum L. belongs to the family *Apiaceae* and steam distillation of its dried seeds yields coriander essential oil. It is commonly used as a flavouring agent and adjuvant in the food industry. Coriander oil is certified for incorporation in food by FDA, FEMA and the Council of Europe. 70% of oil is present as linalool, which is the principal component of coriander oil. It comprises of approximately 30% terpene hydrocarbons and 70% oxygenated compounds and outlined to own antimicrobial properties.

2.3 Cinnamon Oil

Cinnamon belongs to the *Lauraceae* family and is a significant traditional herbal medicine that is widely distributed in China, Vietnam, Sri Lanka, Madagascar and India. Essential oils are paramount constituents of cinnamon bark, and these oils encompass considerable quantities of terpenes and aromatic compounds. Cinnamaldehyde is the prime component of cinnamon essential oil. It has been known to bear tremendous anti-inflammatory, antioxidant, anticancer and antibacterial properties. Cinnamaldehyde is recognised as a flavouring agent by FDA and is permitted to be incorporated in food.

2.4 Lemon Grass Oil

Lemon grass, *scientifically known as Cymbopogon citrates*, is a broadly used herb in tropical countries, chiefly in Southeast Asia. Lemongrass essential oil constitutes mainly, citral, which is a mixture of two stereo-isomeric monterpene aldehydes *viz*., the Transisomer, geranial (40–62%) and the cis isomer, neral (25–38%). Caffeic acid, catecol, chlorogenic acid, hydroquinone and elimicin are common phenolic compounds isolated from the plant. The chromatographic fraction of the essential oil has shown antibacterial activity against *Staphylococus aureus*, *Bacillus subtilis, Escherichia coli, Shigella flexneri* and *Salmonella Paratyphi*. Individually, α-citral (geranial) and β-citral (neral) components exhibit an antibacterial action on Gram-negative as well as gram-positive organisms.

2.5 Thyme Oil

Thyme essential oil is obtained from an aromatic plant *Thymus vulgaris L.*, which belongs to *Labiateae* family and is utilized for its various properties in foods. Thyme oil comprises of more than 60 ingredients. Most of the components of thyme oil possess considerable antioxidant and antimicrobial properties. Phenols i.e thymol and carvacrol, and monoterpene hydrocarbons i.e p-cymene (18.5–23.5%) and c-terpinene (16.1–18.9%) are the more active and chief constituents of thyme oil. In addition to this, *in vitro* studies revealed that these phenolic compounds acquire antimicrobial activity against a broad spectrum of Gram negative or positive bacteria.

2.6 Ajowan Oil

The major phenolic compound present in Ajowan (*Trachyspermum ammi* or *Carum copticum)* is thymol. It has been reported to be a antispasmodic, germicide, and antifungal agent. Ethanol and acetone extracts of ajowan oil also has inhibitory activity against many bacteria viz., *Bacillus subtilis, E. coli, Pseudomonas* spp and *S. aureus*. Ajowan is considered as among the best essential oils when studied on basis of total phenolic contents and trolox equivalent antioxidant capacity assays. The volatile constituents of ajowan (*Trachyspermum ammi*) seeds are found to have inhibitory action on fungi (*Myrothecium roridum, Acrophialophora fusispora, Drechslera tetramera, Curvularia lunata, F. poae, Papulaspora* sp., *Alternaria grisea, A. tenuissima, Fusarium chlamydosporum* and *Rhizoctonia solani*).

2.7 Garlic Oil

Garlic *(Allium sativum)* is one of the most generally used ingredients as a flavour enhancer for most of the food products. Garlic has not only antifungal, antiviral, antiprotozoal and antibacterial action, but also has beneficial effects on the immune systems and cardiovascular system. The antibacterial activity of garlic resulted from thiosulfinates (mainly allicin), which contributes for most of the antimicrobial activity, in addition to its flavour and aroma. The compound Allicin is highly unstable and further disintegrates to produce some organosulfur compounds such as diallyl disulfide, methyl allyl di- and trisulfides, diallyl trisulfide, ajoenes, diallyl sulphide, vinyl dithiins etc, depending on how the garlic is prepared.

2.8 Beetal Oil

Beetal (*Piper betle)* are popularly known as *Paan* in India. The betel leaves are also reported to possess antioxidant activity in addition to anticarcinogenic and antimutagenic properties. Beetal oil has strong antimicrobial activity against *Proteus vulgaris, S. pyrogenes, E. coli, Pseudomonas aeruginosa,*

Staphylococcus aureus etc., beside this, the leaf extract also exhibits the bactericidal activity against the urinary tract inhabiting pathogenic bacteria such as *Citrobacter koseri, Enterococcus faecalis, Klebsiella pnemoniae, Citrobacter fruendi* etc.

2.9 Ginger Oil

Ginger plant (*Zingiber officinale*), belonging to the family *Zingiberaceae*, has been widely used as spice and flavouring agent in foods since ancient times. The ginger oil mainly contains polyphenol compounds, namely 6-gingerol and its derivatives, which exhibits high antioxidant activity. Ginger was reported to have medicinal properties which includes antiviral, antifungal, antioxidant, antimicrobial, anticancer activities and anti-inflammatory, and exhibits characteristic odours and flavours with a pungent taste. The homologous series of phenols called gingerols are responsible for pungency and odour in fresh ginger. Extracts of ginger rhizome contain characteristic phenolic compounds gingerol and gingero derived compounds with various biological activities specifically; anti-cancerous and anti-oxidant activity. Curcumin is another active component present in ginger having wide range of activities including antibacterial, anticancer, antioxidant and anti-inflammatory activity. In addition to this, it also activates the heme oxygenase-1 activity and helps in protection of endothelial cells against oxidative stress arisen due to free radicals.

2.10 Citrus Oil

The genus Citrus has approximately 16 species in the family *Rutaceae* and is mainly cultivated in subtropical regions. Citrus EOs makes up the largest sector of the world production of essential oils. Monoterpenes make up 97% of the citrus oil composition with alcohols, however among monoterpenes, aldehydes and esters (1.8 to 2.2%) constitute the lowest percentage components. The main chemical element of citrus oils is limonene (32 to 98%) , and contains the various components such as sweet orange containing 68-98%, lemon 45-76% and bergamot 32-45%. Lemon and bergamot contains 0.015% and 10.231% (v/v) concentration, respectively, of Linalool. Citrus EOs is categorized as GRAS and their scent and flavours led themselves to be used in food. Lemon, sweet orange and bergamot and their components, linalool and citral, not limonene, were reported to reveal antimicrobial effects both in direct oil and vapour form against *E. coli* O157, *Bacillus cereus, L. monocytogenes, S. aureus* and *Campylobacter jejuni* . Citrus limonum was found to be effective against *E. coli* with a MIC of 2.5 ml/100 ml and a minimum bactericidal concentration (MBC) of 2.8 ml/100 ml in brain heart infusion broth at 37°C.

2.11 Nutmeg Oil

Nutmeg (*Myristica fragrans*) is a broadly used spice and aromatic component in the food industry, because it contains flavour enhancing compounds such as carotenoids, vitamins, flavonoids and phenols. The main component of nutmeg essential oil consists of hydrocarbon monoterpenes which includes 61-88% as α-pinene, β-pinene, sabinene. Besides this, nutmeg oil also contains monoterpenes acid (5-15%), and aromatic ether (2-18%) such as safrole, myristicin, elemicin. Nutmeg has been reported to have excellent free radical scavenging activity, chelation of metallic ions and lipid oxidation inhibition. In addition to this, it also possesses anti-inflammatory, anti fungal and antibacterial activities.

2.12 Rosemary Oil

Rosmarinus officinalis L., belongs to the family *Labiatae* is extensively established as one of the herb spices with the strong aroma and good antioxidant activity. It has been reported to possess effective antimicrobial activity. Oil owes its antimicrobial properties to major components such as 1,8-cineole, bornyl acetate, camphor, and a-pinene. Rosemary essential oil has been revealed to have free radical-scavenging antioxidant and antibacterial activities. Carnosol rosmanol, epirosmanol, rosmadiphenol are the major phenolic compounds present in this essential oil and possess valuable anti-oxidants.

2.13 Clove Oil

Clove is a commonly occurring spice, which not only possess antioxidant properties, but also exhibits antimicrobial activity in food products. The inhibitory action of clove oil on microorganisms is due to the presence of the terpenoids which exert their action by membrane disruption. Eugenol is a 2-methoxy phenolic derivative which comprises 90% of the antioxidant activity of BHA thus, acting as a principal constituent of clove oil. Clove is found to be the strongest antioxidant in an oil/water emulsion, although, inhibitory effect on pathogenic microorganisms will be more effective by higher level of clove oil.

2.14 Holy Basil

Basil is herbaceous, white-purple ûowering plant of the family *Lamiaceae* and grown mainly in India and Iran. More than 150 basil species are present which belongs to the genus *Ocimum*. Among these, holy basil (*Ocimum sanctum* L.) and sweet basil (*Ocimum basilicum* L.) are the two most extensively grown species for essential oil production. Holy basil oil possesses antimicrobial; insecticidal activity in addition to anti-oxidant activity. Basil oil contain mainly monoterpene derivatives such as 1,8-cineole, camphor, linalool, geraniol and limonene. The minor constituents contain primarily phenol derivatives, such as eugenol, methyl-cinnamate, estragole, chavicol methyleugenol.

3. Mode of Action of Essential Oils

Essential oils are hydrophobic in nature and thus interact well with lipid membrane of bacterial pathogens. Since, essential oils are hydrophobic in nature, thus it allows them to partition in the lipids of the bacterial and mitochondria cell membrane, which disturbs the structures and makes them further permeable in nature. Due to the increase in permeability of membrane, leakage of the inner cell components of the cell occurs, resulting in potassium ion reflux, and ultimately leading to cell death. Cell can remain alive all the way through a definite amount of leakage without loss of viability; however, huge deficit of cell contents or exit of essential molecules and ions will lead to death. Cell death might occur before lysis with tea tree oil. Anti-bacterial activity of essential oils is attributed to the presence of phenols in them. The phenolic compounds cause the dislocation of cell membrane and disrupt its functionality and eventually leading to the release of intracellular components.

4. Essential Oils in Meat and Meat Products

Essential oils have inhibitory activity against pathogens and food spoilage microorganisms, but their effect in food is achieved with a higher concentration as compared to the minimum inhibitory concentration (MIC) obtained in conventional nutrient media. Thus, because of the higher concentration of oil in the food, there occurs an increase in the flavour intensity of the food products leading to unacceptability of the product. Essential oils from basil, rosemary, thyme, oregano, ginger, basilica, balm, coriander, rosemary and clove have exhibited a better potential to be used as an antimicrobial agent in meat and meat products

Oregano oil is a scientifically viable alternative in fine paste meat products to improve acceptance, delay oxidative stability and reduced microbial growth in bologna sausages. Coriander oil has been reported to have higher DPPH radical scavenging activity when compared to other oils. The usual and maximum usage levels of coriander oil in meat products approved by FEMA are 43 ppm and 68.47 ppm respectively. Coriander leaves showed stronger antioxidant activity than the seed. During last decade, the antimicrobial activity of garlic and organosulfur compounds from garlic was evaluated thoroughly against food spoilage bacteria and food-borne pathogens. The antimicrobial activity of garlic oil (undiluted form) is 200 times more efficacious than garlic powder and 900 times the strength of fresh garlic. Moreover, the oil and extract of garlic have been generally recognized as safe (GRAS) for use in food by the FDA. Rohani and others (2011) studied anti listerial activity of nisin and garlic oil separately and in combination and found significant reduction on its growth. Besides its antimicrobial effect, garlic also showed effective antioxidant activity *in-vivo*

Table 2: Source and mode of action of different essential oils

Essential oil	Source	Active component	Mode of action	References
Clove oil and Holybasil	Clove- Bud Holybasil- Herb	Eugenol	Changes in cell permeability, Rapid potassium loss, release of cellular components, increase in free cytosolic Ca^{2+}	Walsh and others (2003), Wang and others (2010) Cui and others (2015)
Thyme	Herb	Thymol	Telomerase inhibition (anti-fungal action), Membrane perforation, Decline in intracellular ATP, Efflux of H^+ and K^+ and influx of nucleic acid stains	Shapiro and Guggenheim, (1995) Darvishi and others (2013)
Oregano	Herb	Carvacrol	Depletes intracellular ATP pool, transportation of ions across cytoplasmic membrane, suppress enterotoxin production	Ultee and others (2000) Chavan and Tupe, (2014) Lambert and others (2001)
Cinnamon	Bark	Cinnamaldehyde	Leekage of cellular components, Reduced intracellular pH, affected membrane integrity,inhibition of cell division (non-competitive inhibitor of β-(1,3)-glucan synthase)-antifungal action	Shen and others (2015) Oussalah and others (2006) Bang and others (2000)
Coriander oil	Seed	Linalool	Damage cytoplasmic membrane,increased cell permeability, DNA leakage from cell	Silva and others (2015) Hyldgaard and others (2012)
Lemon grass oil	Leaf	Citral	Change in cell permeability, releasing cellular components	Nguefack and others (2004) Leite and others (2014)
Rosemary oil	Herb	p-cymene	Membrane expansion, affecting membrane potential of intact cells, decreased cell motility, decrease in enthalpy and melting temperature of membranes	Ultee and others(2002) Cristani and others (2007)

and *in vitro*. Inclusion of ginger or basilica EOs in beef patties provides improved safety properties with significantly lower standard plate counts, lactic acid bacteria, and *E. coli* numbers compared with those for the control group (no lipids and EOs) and products containing animal fats. Citral (0.5-3% w/v) has also been shown to possess inhibitory activity against *S. Typhimurium* in fish cubes with reduction in the final population of up to 1.5 log colony forming units (cfu)/g . A study investigating orange and lemon dry powder at 5% (w/w) for their potential use as antimicrobials in beef meatballs found these to be very effective against LAB over a 12-day period, both reducing the lactic acid bacteria load to under the detection limit of <1.69 log cfu/g. Nutmeg essential oil was able to inhibit fat oxidation in egg yolk lipids and chicken tissue homogenates. It has 37 components of which 31.3% was terpinen 4 oil having antifungal activity.

5. Limitations and Future Perspectives

The major limitation associated with the use of essential oils in food products is pungent and intense aroma imparted to the product which decreases the overall acceptability of the product. Thus, further investigations are inevitable to find out the most active molecules of essential oils and the conditions which increase their efficiency without having any negative impact on the sensory quality of product. However, Lanciotti and others (2004) had stated the potential ways by which the impact can be reduced to a certain extent:

1. Food formulation should be optimized in such a way that perception of essential oils is minimized.
2. The concept of 'Hurdle Technology' can also be applied i.e essential oils or their most active bioactive components can be combined with other preservation methods.
3. Novel methodology should be devised in order to strengthen the interaction between essential oils and bacterial cell membrane.

Besides these, other potential utilization of essential oils includes their incorporation in the dietary regimen of animals: In case of ruminants, methane and ammonia emissions can be lessened by modifying their metabolism and in case of non-ruminants/ monogastrics, essential oils can be successfully used as alternatives to antibiotic growth promoters which provides beneficial results in relation to their growth performance and gut microflora. However, their mode of action in animal growth has not been studied in detail and still needs thorough investigation.

Table 3: Potential application of different essential oils in meat and meat products

Type of meat and meat products	Concentration applied	Results	References
Oregano oil			
Minced meat	0, 0.05, 0.5 and 1% v/w	0.5% and 1% of oregano oil were effective, delayed glucose and lactate consumption aerobically, proteolysis was significantly inhibited	Skandamis & Nychas, (2001)
Raw chicken meat fillets	1 g/100 ml N,O-carboxymethyl chitosan (NOCC) and 1% oregano essential oil (OEO) dip	1.2 and 2.8 log cfu/g reduction in L. *monocytogenes* was achieved for the OEO and NOCC treated samples, respectively after 14 day of storage, Complete inhibition of *L. monocytogenes* was reported for the combination of OEO and NOCC on day 2 and 4 of storage	Khanjari *et al.* (2013)
Beef meatballs	0.5%, 1%, or 2% (v/w)	0.5% of oil suppressed concentrations of <10^2 CFU/g of S. aureus	Pesavento *et al.* (2015)
Rabbit meat	Dietary supplementation of 100 and 200 mg/kg of feed	Inhibitory effect on total viable count, Lactic acid bacteria during refrigerated storage	Soultos *et al.* (2009)
Thyme oil			
Beef burger	0.02%,0.04 and 0.06%	Shelf life of 0.02% oil treated samples was extended for three days more than control during refrigerated storage. While beef burger treated with0.04 and 0.06% oil showed five days more than control.	Kassem *et al.* (2011)
Minced fish meat	0.4%, 0.8% and 1.2% level	0.8% and 1.2% oil reduced *L. monocytogenes* viable count below 2 log cfu/g after 6 days	Abdollahzadeh *et al.* (2014)
Minced beef meat	0.3%, 0.6% and 0.9%	oil at 0.6% showedinhibitory activity against *E. coli* O157:H7 during storage at 10^0 C.	Solomakos *et al.* (2008)
Chicken breast meat	0.5%	Inhibition of growth of *E. coli* and lactic acid bacteria, lowered total microbial count	Fratianni *et al.* (2010)

Contd.

Type of meat and meat products	Concentration applied	Results	References
Holy basil oil			
Fresh cut-lettuce	0.01, 0.032 and 0.08 ml/L (in combination with Mint)	Oils at concentration of 0.08 ml/L were most effective antimicrobial treatment against *E. coli* O157: H7 and S. *typhimurium*	Karagözlü *et al.* (2011)
Beef patties	0.2%	Lower total plate count and *E. coli* when compared to control	Dzudie *et al.* (2004)
Clove oil			
Cooked beef, pork and mutton	250mg/100g	Controlled TBARS formation till6 days at 5 °C storage	Jayathilakan *et al.* (2007)
Ground chicken meat (packaging film)	1, 2 and 3% (in combination with CMC and PVOH)	Control samples spoiled within 4 days of storage whereas, samples packed in active films containing 3% clove oil, CMC and PVOH had shelf life of 12 days	Muppalla *et al.* (2014)
Buffalo meat	0.1% clove in combination with 2% lactic acid v/v	Reduced TBARS value, Aerobic Plate Count, psychrophillic count and coliforms	Naveena *et al.* (2006)
Chicken frankfurters	1 and 2%	Inhibited the growth of *L. monocytogenes* at 5^0 and 15^0C	Mytle *et al.* (2006)
Coriander oil			
Ground beef	0.2% v/w	Extended acceptability by 3 days and inhibited the growth of Enterobacteriaceae by 1–2 log cycles as compared to control.	Michalczyk *et al.* (2012)
Meat and bone meal protein film (edible)	0.1 % w/v	useful for antimicrobial food packaging	Lee *et al.* (2015)
Lemon grass oil			
Sea bass slices	Gelatin film incorporated with 2.5% (w/w) lemongrass essential oil (LEO)	Retarded growth of lactic acid bacteria (LAB), psychrophilic bacteria and Enterobacteriaceae during 12 days of storage, lower K value, total volatile base nitrogen (TVB) and TBARS valuein LEO film wrapped samples	Ahmad *et al.* (2011)
Ground beef	3.90, 7.80 and 15.60 µl/g	Inhibited the growth of *Salmonella enterica* serotype Enteritidis during storage period at refrigeration temperature	De Oliveira *et al.* (2012)

Contd.

Type of meat and meat products	Concentration applied	Results	References
Rosemary oil			
Lamb meat	0.06% with EDTA-Lysozyme (1.5%)	Reduced TBARS value at refrigeration temperature compared to control	Smeti *et al.* (2013)
Pork liver sausages	1 and 5%	Inhibited the growth of *L. monocytogenes*	Pandit &Shelef, (1994)
Chicken fillets	0.2% in combination	Shelf extension of 7-8 days under vacuum packaging when compared to control	Ntzimani *et al.*(2010)
Cinnamon oil			
Liquid whole egg	7000ppm	2 log CFU/ml reduction in Salmonella count	Valverde *et al.* (2010)
Broiler meat	100 and 200ppm (in feed)	Significantly affected feed conversion ratio and reduction in cholesterol and H/L ratio in meat	Hengel *et al.* (2011)
Ground beef	2.5 and 5.0% of crude and commercial cinnamon EOs and stored at refrigeration (8°C), chilling (0°C) temperatures for 7 days	3.5-4.0 log CFU/g reduction of *L. monocytogenes* was reported within 7 days of storage by 5% commercial cinnamon oil.	Khaleque *et al.* (2016)
Chilled shrimp	2g/100ml (in polysachharide bilayer film)	Significantly reduced microbial growth including *L. monocytogenes*	Arancibia *et al.* (2014)
Beef	500 mg/kg DM (dietary supplementation)	Useful as a rumen fermentation modifier in beef production systems	Khorrami *et al.* (2014)
Garlic oil			
Chicken sausages	0.06g/kg	Reduced TBARS value and lipid oxidation in products compared to control	Sallam *et al.* (2004)
Ginger oil			
Chicken meat	1:150, 1:250 and 1:500	Significant decrease in bacterial count was obtained with 1:150 and 1:250 concentrations as compared to 1:500.	Sudarshan *et al.* (2010)

6. Conclusion

Meat is a nutrient dense food item, providing an optimum environment for proliferation of microorganisms and often leads to the spoilage of valuable protein source. Therefore, it is essential that adequate safety measures are applied to maintain its quality. It will definitely ascertain the consumers' satisfaction from the view point of healthier food. In this context, essential oils provide a new, promising and natural alternative for safety of food against pathogens and micro-organisms. Phenolic compounds in the essential oil are mainly responsible for their anti-microbial activity. However, their use is still limited because they contribute pungent and intense aroma to the food, thus there is need to work out on the novel technologies which can not only increase the food stability but at the same time, are sensorially acceptable to the consumers.

References

Abdollahzadeh, E., Rezaei, M. and Hosseini, H. 2014. Antibacterial activity of plant essential oils and extracts: The role of thyme essential oil, nisin, and their combination to control *Listeria monocytogenes* inoculated in minced fish meat. *Food Cont*, 35(1):177-183.

Ahmad, A., Khan, A., Akhtar, F., Yousuf, S., Xess, I., Khan, L. and Manzoor, N. 2011. Fungicidal activity of thymol and carvacrol by disrupting ergosterol biosynthesis and membrane integrity against Candida. *Eur J Clin Microbiol Infect Dis:* 41–50.

Arancibia, M., Gimenez, B., López-Caballero, M.E. and Montero, P. 2014. Release of cinnamon essential oil from polysaccharide bilayer films and its use for microbial growth inhibition in chilled shrimps. *LWT- Food Sci Tech*, 59(2): 989-995.

Chavan, P.S. and Tupe, S. G., 2014. Antifungal activity and mechanism of action of carvacrol and thymol against vineyard and wine spoilage yeast. *Food Cont,* 46*:* 115-120.

Cristani, M., D'Arrigo, M., Mandalari, G., Castelli, F., Sarpietro, M. G., Micieli, D., Venuti, V., Bisignano, G., Saija, A. and Trombetta, D., 2007. Interaction of four monoterpenes contained in essential oils with model membranes: implications for their antibacterial activity. *J Agric Food Chem,* 55:6300-6308.

Cui, H., Zhao, C. and Lin, L. 2015. The specific antibacterial activity of liposome-encapsulated Clove oil and its application in tofu. *Food Cont*, 56:128-134.

Darvishi, E., Omidi, M., Bushehri, A.A., Golshani, A. and Smith, M.L., 2013. Thymol antifungal mode of action involves telomerase inhibition. *Med Mycol,* 51(8): 826-34.

Dzudie, T., Kouebou, C., Essia-Ngang, J. and Mbofung, C., 2004. Lipid sources and essential oils effects on quality and stability of beef patties. *J Food Engg,* 65: 67-72.

Fratianni, F., De Martino, L., Melone, A., De Feo, V., Coppola, R. and Nazzaro, F., 2010. Preservation of chicken breast meat treated with thyme and balm essential oils. *J Food Sci,* 75: 528-535.

Hyldgaard, M., Mygind, T. and Meyer, R.L. 2012. Essential oils in food preservation: mode of action, synergies, and interactions with food matrix components. *Front Microbiol,* 3: 12.

Jayathilakan, K., Sharma, G., Radhakrishna, K. and Bawa, A. 2007. Antioxidant potential of synthetic and natural antioxidants and its effect on warmed over flavour in different species of meat. *Food Chem,* 105: 908–916

Karagozlu, N., Ergönül, B. and Özcan, D., 2011. Determination of antimicrobial effect of mint and basil essential oils on survival of E. coli O157: H7 and *S. typhimurium* in fresh-cut lettuce and purslane. *Food Cont,* 22*:* 1851-5.

Kassem, G.M., Atta-Alla, O.A., and Ali, F.H.M., *2011*. Improving the quality of beef burger by adding thyme *essential oil* and *jojoba oil*. *Arch. Zootec,* 60*:* 787–795.

Khaleque, M.A., Keya, C.A., Hasan, K.N., Hoque, M.M., Inatsu, Y. and Bari, M.L., 2016. Use of cloves and cinnamon essential oil to inactivate *Listeria monocytogenes* in ground beef at freezing and refrigeration temperatures. *LWT - Food Sci Technol,* 74*:* 219-223.

Khanjari, A., Karabagias, I. and Kontominas, M., 2013. Combined effect of N, O-carboxymethyl chitosan and oregano essential oil to extend shelf life and control *Listeria monocytogenes* in raw chicken meat fillets. *LWT-Food Sci Technol,* 53*:* 94-99.

Khorrami, B., Vakili, A.R., Mesgarana, M.D. and Klevenhusen, F., 2015. Thyme and cinnamon essential oils: Potential alternatives for monensin as a rumen modifier in beef production systems. *Ani Feed Sci Technol,* 200: 8-16.

Lanciotti, R., Gianotti, A., Patrignani, F., Belletti, N., Guerzoni, M.E. and Gardini, F., 2004. Use of natural aroma compounds to improve shelf-life and safety of minimally processed fruits. *Trends Food Sci Technol,* 15(3-4): 201-208.

Lee, J. and Song, K.B., 2015. Application of an Antimicrobial Protein Film in Beef Patties Packaging. *Korean J. Food Sci. An*, 35(5): 611-614.

Leite, M.C.A., de Brito Bezerra, A.P., de Sousa, J.P., Guerra, F.Q.S. and de Oliveira Lima, E., 2014. Evaluation of Antifungal Activity and Mechanism of Action of Citral against Candida albicans. *Evi Compl Alt Med, Article ID 378280,* doi:10.1155/2014/378280

Michalczyk, M., Macura, R., Tesarowicz, I. and Banas, J. 2012. Effect of adding essential oils of coriander (*Coriandrum sativum* L.) and hyssop (*Hyssopus officinalis* L.) on the shelf life of ground beef. *Meat Sci,* 90: 842-850.

Muppalla, S.R., Kanatt, S.R., Chawla, S.P. and Sharma, A. 2014. Carboxymethyl cellulose-polyvinyl alcohol films with clove oil for active packaging of ground chicken meat. *Food Packag Shelf Life*, 2(2): 51-58

Mytle, N., Anderson, G.L., Doyle, M.P. and Smith, M.A., 2006. Antimicrobial activity of clove (*Syzgium aromaticum*) oil in inhibiting *Listeria monocytogenes* on chicken frankfurters. *Food Cont,* 17*:* 102-107.

Naveena, B.M., Muthukumar, M., Sen, A.R., Babji, Y. and Murthy, T.R., 2006. Improvement of shelf-life of buffalo meat using lactic acid, clove oil and vitamin C during retail display. *Meat Sci,* 74*:* 409-415.

Ntzimani, A.G., Giatrakou, V.I. and Savvaidis, I.N., 2010. Combined natural antimicrobial treatments (EDTA, lysozyme, rosemary and oregano oil) on semi cooked coated chicken meat stored in vacuum packages at 4 °C: Microbiological and sensory evaluation. *Innov Food Sci Emerg Technol* 1*:* 187–196.

Oussalah, M., Caillet, S., Saucier, L. and Lacroix, M., 2006. Antimicrobial effects of selected plant essential oils on the growth of a *Pseudomonas putida* strain isolated from meat. *Meat Sci, 73:* 236-244.

Pandit, V.A. and Shelef, L.A., 1994. Sensitivity of Listeria monocytogenes to rosemary (*Rosmarinus officinalis* L.). *Food Microbiol,* 11: 57–63.

Pesavento, G., Calonico, C., Bilia, A., Barnabei, M., Calesini, F., Addona, R., Mencarelli, L., Carmagnini, L., Di Martino, M. and Nostro, A.L., 2015. Antibacterial activity of Oregano, Rosmarinus and Thymus essential oils against *Staphylococcus aureus* and *Listeria monocytogenes* in beef meatballs. *Food Cont,* 54:188-199.

Sallam, K.I., Ishioroshi, M. and Samejima, K., 2004. Antioxidant and antimicrobial effects of garlic in chicken sausage. *LWT-Food Sci Technol* 37: 849-855.

Silva, F. and Domingues, F.C., 2015. Antimicrobial Activity of Coriander Oil and Its Effectiveness as Food Preservative. *Cr Rev Food Sc Nutr*, 57(1):35-47

Skandamis, P.N. and Nychas, G.J., 2001. Effect of oregano essential oil on microbiological and physico-chemical attributes of minced meat stored in air and modified atmospheres. *J Appl Microbiol*, 91: 1011-1022.

Smeti, S., Atti, N. and Mahouachi, M., 2013. Effects of rosemary extracts incorporation on Barbarine lamb's growth and carcass characteristics. In: Ben Salem H. ed.), López-Francos A. (Ed.). Feeding and management strategies to improve livestock productivity, welfare and product quality under climate change. *Zaragoza: CIHEAM / INRAT / OEP / IRESA / FAO:* 219-222.

Solomakos, N., Govaris, A., Koidis, P. and Botsoglou, N., 2008. The antimicrobial effect of thyme essential oil, nisin and their combination against *Escherichia coli* O157:H7 in minced beef during refrigerated storage. *Meat Sci,* 80: 159-166.

Soultos, N., Tzikas, Z., Christaki, E., Papageorgiou, K. and Steris, V., 2009. The effect of dietary oregano essential oil on microbial growth of rabbit carcasses during refrigerated storage. *Meat Sci,* 81: 474-478.

Sudarshan, S., Fairoze, N., Wilfred-Ruban, S., Badhe, R. and Raghunath, B.V., 2010. Effect of aqueous extract and essential oils of ginger and garlic as decontaminant in chicken meat. *Res J Poult Sc*i, 3(3): 58-61.

Valverde, M.T., Iniesta, F.M., Garrido, L.C., Rodríguez, A.T., García-García, I. and Macanas, H., 2010. Inactivation of Salmonella spp in refrigerated liquid egg products using essential oils and their active compounds. Proceedings in *International Conference on Food Innovation "Food Innova".*

Wang, W., Zhang, L., Li, N. and Zu, Y., 2010. Chemical composition and in vitro antioxidant, cytotoxicity activities of *Zingiber officinale* Roscoe essential oil. *Afri J Biochem Res* 6(6): 75-80.

6

Chitosan and its Application in Dairy Industry

Priyanka Singh Rao, Heena Sharma, Richa Singh
Karuna Meghawal and Diwas Pradhan

Abstract

Chitin has been ranked at second position after cellulose as the most abundant natural biopolymer. Chitin has similar chemical structure to that of cellulose with 2-acetamido-2-deoxy-b-d-glucose (NAG) monomers attached via ß (1–>4) linkages. Chitosan is the deacetylated (to varying degrees) form of chitin, which, unlike chitin, is soluble in acidic solutions. Therefore, Chitosan, a copolymer of glucosamine and N-acetyl glucosamine, is amongst the most copious biopolymers on earth and finds wide range of biomedical and industrial applications. It has been approved in 1983 by USDA as a feed additive. Chitin basically is obtained from prawn/crab shells and chemical treatment of chitin produces chitosan. Since supplies of seafood waste are seasonable and variable, so fungi can be used as alternative source for chitosan. The unique physicochemical properties of chitosan provide great potential of its utilization in food industry especially dairy industry such as production of dairy products, dairy waste water treatment, extension of shelf life of dairy products etc. In recent years, exotic synthetic compounds are losing their appeal, thus application of chitinous products in dairy as well as processing aids has received considerable attention. The modified chitosan with greater functional properties has increased application in different dairy foods. This chapter focuses on the fundamental uses of chitosan and their derivatives in a variety of dairy industry applications.

Keywords: Chitosan, Dairy Products, Milk Proteins, Lactose, Dairy Waste Water

1.Introduction

Evolution of name 'Chitin' has its roots in the Greek word 'chiton', which means a coat of mail, and it is believed that word 'chitin' was first used by Bradconnot in 1811. It is basically a glycan, which is linked by ß (1–>4) linkage and comprises of 2-acet-amido-2-deoxy- ß-D-glucose (N-acetylglucosamine) (Fig 1). However, Chitosan is the low acetyl substituted derivative of chitin and comprises primarily of glucosamine, 2- amino-2-deoxy-b-d-glucose, known as (1—>4)-2-amino- 2-deoxy-D-glucose. Chitosan owe its unique physico-chemical properties to the presence of three reactive functional groups in its chemical structure, an amino group ($-NH_2$) as well as both primary and secondary hydroxyl groups (-OH) at the C-2, C-3 and C-6 positions, respectively (Fig 2). Modification of these reactive groups in processing industry has made possible the utilization of its untapped potential in varying fields of application. Chitosan has not only been reported to possess biodegradable, biocompatible non-toxic, biofunctional *etc.* but also has been reported to possess strong antimicrobial and antifungal activities.

Chitin is the chief structural module of the exoskeleton of invertebrates and the cell wall of fungi. Now days, the major concern of sea food processing industry is related to disposal of large quantities of crustaceans processed waste and this is mainly because of slow rate of biodegradation of chitin in crustacean shell waste. Disposal of shellfish processing discards has, thus, been a challenge for most of the shellfish-producing countries. Therefore, production of value-added products viz., chitin, chitosan and their derivatives and application of products in diverse fields is of paramount significance. The economical feasibility and profitability of this industry is also possible with further extraction of proteins, carotene, pigments *etc.* from discards of processed shrimp and crab. Therefore, chitin and its deacetylated form, chitosan, have been receiving regular attention and infact, are of significance from past few decades due to their prospective extensive array of industrial applications.

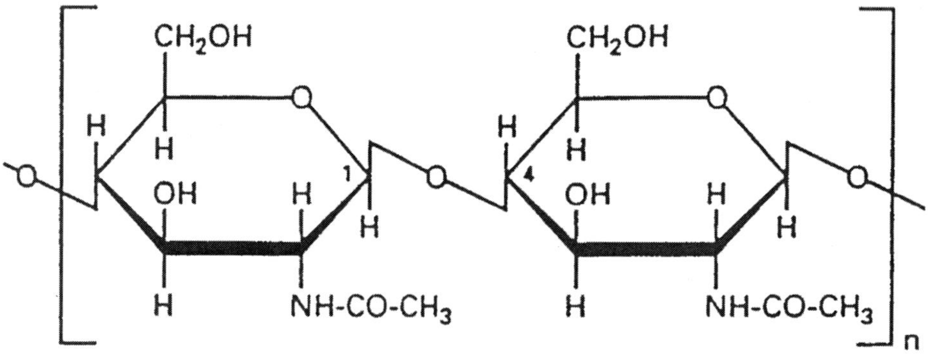

N-Acetyiglucosamine N-Acetyiglucosamine

Fig. 1: Chemical Structure of chitin (Lertsutthiwong *et al.*, 2002)

2. Source of Chitin and Chitosan

Chitin is chiefly present as a structural constituent in exoskeleton of invertebrates and fungal cell walls. Among various species of crustaceans, shrimp and crab shell wastes are broadly used for chitin isolation. Chitin is abundantly and majorily found in fungi and the classes namely, *Basidiomycetes* and *Phycometes*. In fungi, it is mostly found in cell wall and structural membranes of other parts of fungi such as mycelia, stalks and spores. The amounts vary between traces and up to 45% of the organic fraction, the rest being mostly proteins, glucans and mannans. The quantum of chitin varies depending on physiological parameters either of natural environment or artificial conditions such as fermentation conditions in fungi culturing. Natural form of chitin is present in the Mucorales, namely, Mucor, Absidia and Rhizopus species. However, few reports cite the presence of Chitosan in *Lentinus edodes,* which is a shitake mushroom of *Basidiomycete* family. However, slime mold (Myxomycetes) and bacteria (Schizomycetes) lack chitin.

Among various constituents, chitin is one of the major and chief components present in hyaline outer walls of spores of Glomus species and is abundantly found in primary septa present between daughter and mother cells of fungi, *S.crevisiae*. Oomycete *Pythium ultimum* contains both cellulose and chitin in its hyphal walls, however *Phythophthora parasitica* contains only cellulose and on the other hand, *Fusarium oxysporum* (Ascomycete) and *Rhizoctonia solani* (Basidiomycete) contain only chitin. *Cryptococcus neoformans*, a zoopathogenic fungi contains chitin but do not contain ß (1,3)-glucan. Four edible mushrooms, *Lycophyllum shimeji*, *Lentinus edodes*, *Volvariella volvacea* and *Pleuro- tussajor-caju* comprises of chitin as a minor component in mycelia and fruits and caps of fruiting bodies, whereas, chitin is absent in fungal sheaths of *Phellinus noxius*, a white-rot fungus.

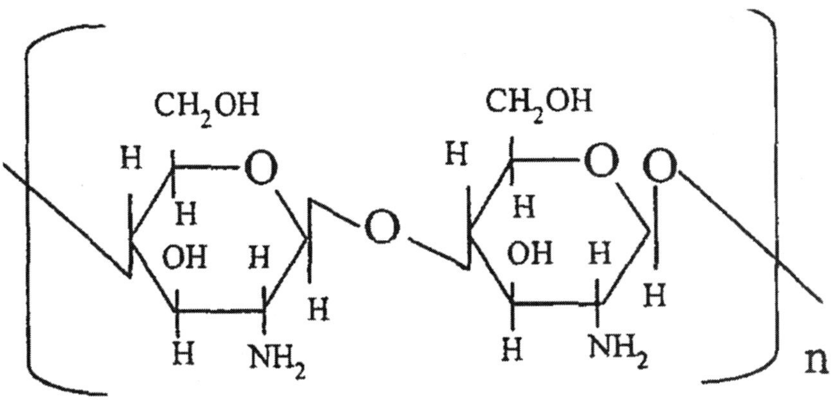

Fig. 2: Structure of Chitosan (Lertsutthiwong *et al.*, 2002)

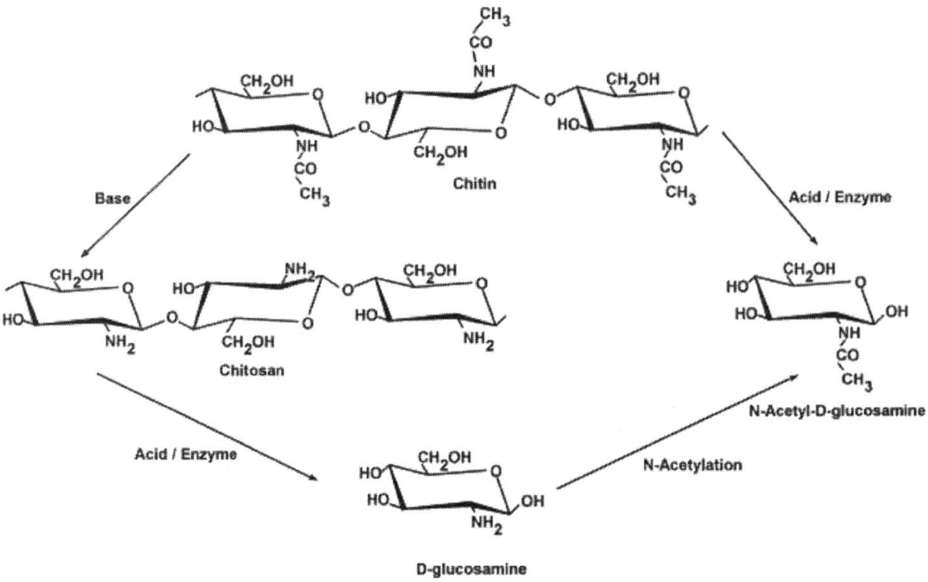

Fig. 3: Various derivatives from chitin (Mourya and Inamdar, 2008)

Chitin and its derivative chitosan, deacetylated form, (Fig 3) have been of significance in the past few decades due to their prospective expansive variety of industrialized applications. Nonetheless, very few considerations have been diverted towards dairy application of these versatile biopolymers. Processing discards can be successfully converted to valuable by products and other useful materials and this can be recognized as an appropriate challenge for research and development in dairy industry including chitin and chitosan applications.

3. Isolation

The most abundant organic compound of nitrogen is chitin. It is reported that 10 gigabytes (approximately 1.10^{13}kg) of chitin is recycled in the biosphere each and every year. Crab or shrimp shells, in addition to fungal mycelia are by far the most easily available source of chitin. Production of chitin is mainly coupled with food industry processing and manufacturing such as shrimp canning. Although the molecular mass of chitin has not been indentified yet, however synthesis of chitin by baker's yeast produces homogeneous chains containing 120± 170 GlcNAc monomer units corresponding to ca. 24,000 ± 34,500 Daltons.

Chitosan-glucan complex is produced by fermentation process in a similar fashion as citric acid is produced from *Aspergillus niger*. The processing of the fungal waste from *A. niger* and *Mucor rouxii* involves an alkali treatment which produces chitosan–glucan complexes. The role of alkali in this step is removal of proteins and decetylation of chitin simultaneously. A few alkali- soluble glucans also gets detached, depending on the alkali concentration. Processing of crustacean shells principally involves protein removal and calcium carbonate dissolution as calcium carbonate is found abundantly in crab shells. Thus, chitin so obtained, is deactylated in 40% NaOH at higher temperature (120°C) for 1-3 h. This step leads to the production of deactylated chitin, Chitosan. However, repeating the above steps sequentially yield the complete deacteylation.

Due to the seasonal availability and variability in the supply of sea food, researchers have diverted their attention towards utilization of alternative sources of Chitosan. Studies were further focused on fungi as the alternative and feasible source of Chitosan. As mentioned earlier, chitosan can be produced and isolated from the cells walls of fungi which provide an immense potential for more uniform products.

4. Application of Chitosan in Dairy Sector

4.1. Isolation of milk proteins

Polysaccharides have a unique property of interacting with proteins and forming gels, emulsions, acting as an antioxidant/ stabilizer. Interactions between chitosan and milk protein are of great importance in the design of dairy formulations such as milk. Milk provides a good source of biologically active components, in particular protein. Major protein fraction in bovine milk is casein and whey proteins which are further divided into six major groups' αS1-, αS2-, β- or κ-CN, α-lactalbumin (α-LA) and *β*- lactoglobulin. In addition to this, incorporation of chitosan to milk causes coacervation of milk protein due to protein polysaccharide interaction. Milk proteins can be processed into different dairy products, most important of which, is cheese and whey is a valuable by product of cheese industry, which is composed of 0.4-.0.6% protein, 0.5-0.7% minerals and 0.03-.0.6% fat.

Removal of proteins from whey is utmost important processing step during products preparation in dairy processing industries. Here, chitosan can be successfully employed for coagulating the proteins and the mechanism by which chitosan forms complexes with whey proteins is determined by the physical and chemical properties of chitosan. The cationic property of chitosan can be utilized to adsorb glycomacropeptide (GMP) molecules from milk whey proteins. GMP is the C-terminal part of κ-casein which is released into the whey during cheese making. Immobilization of β-cyclodextrin was performed to native chitosan beads by cross-linking with 1,6-hexamethylene diisocyanate. Results of the desorption experiments showed that the regeneration and utilization of modified beads could be done in many cycles without significant decrease in the capacity and selectivity.

Harvesting of fungal mycelia

↓

Addition of 50 ml of 1N NaOH/g of mycelia

↓

Homogenization

↓

Sterilization of contents is done at 121°C for 20 minutes (alkali treatment).

↓

Centrifugation at 6000 rpm for 20 min

↓

Washing with distilled water for neutralization (pH 7)

↓

Collection of Alkali Insoluble Material (AIM)

↓

Treatment with 2% acetic acid at 95OC for 6 h and Centrifugation at 6000 rpm for 15-20 min

↓

Separation of acid insoluble fraction

↓

Isolation of supernatant containing Chitosan

↓

Adjustment of pH with 2N NaOH

↓

Precipitation of fungal Chitosan

↓

Centrifugation at 6000 rpm, for 15 min

↓

Washing with distilled water for 4-5 times

↓

96% ethanol and acetone to rinse the Chitosan

↓

Drying in vacuum oven dryer at 60°C

Fig. 4: Isolation of chitin from fungal cell wall (Kannan *et al.*, 2011; Abdulkarim *et al.*, 2013).

Presence of electronic pair on nitrogen atom provides chitosan the ability to form complex and in some cases, chelate linkages are also established with metals. These linkages are formed under all the conditions with metals but alkali and alkaline earth ones. Introduction of raw milk with colloidal solution of chitosan results in separation of raw milk into protein rich and protein free fractions, where chitosan acts as an active whey protein cationic completing agent. These types of interactions between protonated chitosan and negatively charged ions of milk serum proteins occur at a very narrow range of pH 5.0-6.5. The β- lactoglobulin, α- lactalbumin and bovine serum albumin has an isoelectric point of 4.9-5.4, 4.6 and 4.8, respectively. Ionic interaction between these whey proteins and chitosan is possible because of negative charge of whey proteins at pH above 5.0 and positive charge of chitosan upto pH of 6.5.

Therefore, the major proteins which interact with chitosan are β- lactoglobulin, α- lactalbumin and bovine serum albumin, however, lactoferrin and other minor whey proteins do not interact with whey and get involved in complex formation. Chitosan reacts with whey at pH above their iso-electric points resulting in the formation of an insoluble complex.

4.2. Isolation of Lactose

Now days, the largest by product of dairy industry is whey, which contains high concentrations of dissolved organic substances. These substances are chiefly responsible for environmental pollution and Biological Oxygen Demand (BOD) of whey ranges from 30-50g/l. It is assumed that lactose content of milk is main factor responsible for high BOD value. Therefore, lactose isolation is necessary for reduction in BOD of whey to maximum extent and this isolated lactose will be utilized in numerous ways in dairy industry owing to its unique physico-chemical and functional properties.

Chitosan (mol. Wt. 430 kDa) with 87% degree of deacetylation is mainly used for lactose isolation. The concentration of lactose in both crude and deproteinized whey remains almost similar before and after the treatment. However, protein, lactose and ash content decreases significantly to 62-85%,

Whey (pH 6.0) + Chitosan
↓
Kept at RT/2hr/stirring
↓
Concentrate B (7 fold v/v)
↓
Cooled at RT
↓
Seeded with crystalline lactose
↓
Kept overnight at 15°C
↓
Centrifuge
↓
Vacuum dried at 60 °C

Fig. 5: Flow diagram for the method of isolation of lactose (Mukhopadhyay *et al.*, 2003)

70-80% and 50-75%, respectively. Whey proteins are negatively charged at pH 6.0. Thus, coagulation results due to the electrostatic interaction between proteins and chitosan which is the major reason behind the decreased concentration of protein in chitosan treated whey. Significant decrease in ash content also indicates that bulk of minerals present in whey is removed by chitosan treatment.

During deproteinization, calcium and magnesium present in whey are removed out thus; ash content in deproteinized whey is always lower than crude whey. Floculation and precipitation of chitosan-fat globule membrane complex also results in reduced concentration of fat. Lactose prepared from chitosan gel treated crude or deproteinized whey by crystallization procedure contained 2.25 and 1.57% ash, respectively. In addition to this, deproteinization by chitosan treatment also resulted in reduction of BOD by almost 13% and after isolation of lactose, BOD was further reduced to 5620 ppm, which was the reduction of 87% of its original value. Being non - toxic and biodegradable polymer, chitosan can be successfully and safely used by the dairy processing industries.

4.3. Anti-microbial Packaging Film

In recent years, there has been a particular focus on film forming packaging material having antimicrobial property which will improve the shelf life of food. Comparing chitosan with other active films used as packaging materials, it has been found that chitosan is more advantageous than other biomolecule based active films and owe its uniqueness to its antibacterial activity and chelating ability (bivalent ions). Successful utilization of chitosan has been reported in the form of films as a packaging material for preservation of different kinds of dairy foods. Various organic acids and essential oils are also used along with chitosan matrix for the preparation of anti-microbial films and these films have been investigated for their ability to inhibit the growth of commonly encountered food spoilage and pathogenic organisms.

Anti-microbial activity of chitosan against various target organisms, however, depends on the properties of chitosan, such as extent of deacetylation, molecular weight, pH of medium, type of target organism and reaction of solute with chitosan (electrostatic interaction or covalent bonding). It has been reported that fungi are more sensitive to chitin than bacteria and among bacteria, gram positive are more sensitive than gram negative bacteria. Besides bacteria, chitosan strongly affects the growth of the yeast namely, *Saccharomyces cerevisiae*, *Zygosaccharomyces bailii*, *Candida albicans* and *Candida glabrata.* Several researchers have cited the significance of molecular weight of chitosan in exhibiting its anti-microbial activity and it is reported that chitosan with low molecular weight/ average molecular weight possesses stronger antimicrobial activity than high molecular weight. This can be explained with a fact that the size and conformation appears to be elementary to comprehend the efficacy of low molecular weight chitosan. Small chains in low molecular weight molecules are more mobile and get easily attracted than big chains which aid the embracement of a comprehensive conformation and successful binding to membrane surface. The anti-microbial activity of chitosan also depends on the deacetylation degree. It is believed that as the degree of deacteylation decreases, efficacy of antimicrobial activity of chitosan increases. Various studies were carried out to investigate antimicrobial activity against fungi (*Aspergillus fumigatus, Aspergillus parasiticus, Fusarium oxysporum, Candida albicans)* and bacteria; both gram negative and gram positive bacteria *(Staphylococcus aureus, Staphylococcus saprophyticus, Samonella tiphymurium, Pseudomonas aeruginosa, Enterococcus faecailis, Aeromonas hydrophila)* and it was observed that antimicrobial activity increased with decreased deacetylation. The (-amino (NH_2) and hydroxyl (-OH) groups are two main dominant reactive sites in chitosan molecule, whereas, solubility and protonation determine the degree of deactylation. Therefore, as deacetylation is decreased, more quantum of free -NH_2 group is present which yields stronger antimicrobial activity against target organisms.

The other factor which affects antimicrobial activity of chitosan is temperature. It has been proven scientifically that antimicrobial activity of chitosan is significantly higher at 37^{0}C than refrigeration temperature. Ability of chitosan to bind with various food components such as proteins, electrolytes (inorganic), pectins, alginates etc, has provided them with unique cationic character which makes its activity to be temperature dependent. Different types of films used in dairy industry:

1. Chitosan – polysaccharide based film –
    - Chitosan-topioca starch based edible film and coatings
    - Hydroxypropyl methylcellulose edible films with chitosan
    - Chitosan/pectin laminated films with lactic acid
2. Chitosan-protein based film –
    - Round scad protein chitosan based film
    - Chitosan whey protein films
    - Fish gelatin Chitosan film

Coating of ricotta cheese surface with chitosan - whey protein edible film prevents the growth of microbial contaminants and extended shelf life of packaged product. Additionally, bioactive chitosan films can also be used as a vehicle to incorporate and improve the nutritive value of food along with other ingredients like flavouring agents, colorants, antimicrobial and anti-oxidant agents.

5. Utilization in Dairy Products

5.1. Cheese

Chitosan has been broadly utilized in food and processing industry; especially in dairy products production. Production of cheese, mainly cottage cheese is increasing day by day in dairy processing industries. Chitosan can be used to improve the preservation of a very perishable mozzarella cheese. Normal shelf life of mozzarella cheese is around 4-5 days. Use of chitosan/lactic acid solution in starter culture, inhibits the growth of spoilage microflora up to 10 days during refrigerated storage. Mycological quality and shelf-life of Kareish cheese treated with different concentrations of chitosan can be improved with less growth of yeast and mold. Thus, it can be concluded that improvement in the mycological quality and extension of shelf life has been possible by treating Kareish cheese with chitosan.

5.2. Fermented and Frozen milk and milk products

Yoghurt is popular fermented milk product in the world with numerous health benefits as it contains various beneficial viable micro-organisms that compete with pathogenic bacteria for nutrients. Different food ingredients have been added to yoghurt formulation to enhance its nutritive value. Fortification of chitosan in yoghurt can enhance its nutraceutical property. Ausar *et al.* (2002) observed that *molecular weight and concentration of chitosan affect the* growth of three representative milk fermentative bacteria (*Propionibacterium freudenreichii, Streptococcus thermophilus and Lactobacillus delbrueckii* ssp. *bulgaricus*). *However, incubation of chitosan with milk before interaction with bacteria resulted in reversal of inhibition effects. Thus, milk fermentation process was also affected by the presence of milk fat or casein micelles.* Use of chitosan in dairy products is limited because of its low solubility and in these regard, use of nanosized chitosan could be helpful in better solubility and bioavailability. Another form of chitosan, nano-powdered chitosan (NPC), can be effectively used in cholesterol-reduced yoghurt and lowering of lactic acid bacteria counts of NPC-added yoghurt is observed when stored at 4°C for 20 days, thus representing a likelihood of prolonging the shelf life of yogurt. In addition to this, concentrations (0.3-0.5%) of NPC can be utilized to make NPC-added cholesterol-reduced yogurt exclusive of significantly affecting sensory properties. Another frozen dairy product, where chitosan can be exploited successfully, is ice cream. Replacement of gelatin by chitosan to the extent of 60% in ice-cream has also been made possible since it increases the viscosity and over run of ice cream.

5.3. Dairy beverages

Modified chitosan can be used in milk beverages to create a functional product, in which the polysaccharide will function as a technological, functional, bactericidal, or bacteriostatic agent. Besides this, addition of ascorbic acid-soluble nano-chitosan into the milk increases amount of L-ascorbic acid, thus indicating an augmentation in health benefits. 1-3% of nano chitosan (v/v) is usually added to develop nano powdered chitosan added milk without any adverse effects on sensory attributes. Property of chitosan to form gels was utilized to develop chocolate milk using modified chitosan (hydrogel) as a thickening agent. The hydrogel chitosan is not only effective as a thickening agent but also furnishes a good acceptability of the beverage.

6. Treatment of Dairy Waste Water

Importance of pre treatment of dairy waste water has been realized due to the increasing load to municipal waste water treatment plants. Thus, it not only shares the load but also leads to the production of sludge which can act as a source of food additive. Organic biopolymers which are non toxic are found to be appropriate for this purpose. Some reports have suggested the use of anionic polymers such as sodium Carboxy methylcellulose (CMC) for treatment of waste water, however the lacunae associated with this is that the process is pH dependent and consumes both acid and bases. Thus, the disadvantages associated with anionic polymers have paved the way to find out the novel approach for treatment of dairy waste water. In this regard, non toxic cationic biopolymer, chitosan has been evaluated as a substitute for CMC. The use of chitosan in water purification applications generally has been comprehensively reviewed, in respect of its utilization in decolorizing dye house effluents, the treatment of food-processing wastes, metal ion removal and sludge conditioning. Chitosan can also be used as an effective coagulant which can reduce COD by 79%, turbidity by 93% and TSS by 73% in dairy industry waste water.

7. Encapsulation of Milk Protein and Peptides

Chitosan, as the only natural positive polysaccharide, has advantage of forming stable complex with negative compounds, which makes chitosan a good candidate for the encapsulation and controlled release. Bovine β-lactoglobulin (β-Lg) is the major milk whey protein with isoelectric point of 4.9. Chitosan can be used for encapsulation of β-Lg on the basis of electrostatic attraction between protein and polysaccharide; however, the formation of complexes depends mainly on ionic strength, pH and protein concentration.

Milk derived bioactive peptides have also been in trend to formulate functional foods. Microencapsulation of these peptides further improves the stability of the peptides. Chitosan (CS) can be used to encapsulate bioactive peptide, namely caseinophosphopeptides (CPPs) in the form of nanocomplexes. Caseinophosphopeptides are phosphoseryl residues rich dietary antioxidant with the ability to sequester metal ion and inhibit lipid oxidation by chelation with non-chelating mechanisms such as free radical scavenging. At low CS/CPP mass ratio, negatively charged CPP gets absorbed on positively charged chitosan molecule chains to form intramolecular nanocomplexes saturated with CPPs (CPPNP). Subsequently, the negatively charged CPPNP are bridged by the addition of positively charged CS, resulting in the formation of neutral biopolymer complexes. Further addition of excess chitosan breaks down the bridges of associative complexes and cause formation of positively charged spherical nanocomplexes. Phosphorylated groups in the CPP's might be dominant site for interaction with $-NH_3+$ groups on the chitosan molecular chains. Thus, it is a simple and efficient way to prepare biopolymer nanocomplexes that can be used for the encapsulation and delivery of peptides and enzyme.

8. Conclusions

Nowadays, milk processing industry is focusing towards the development of functional foods and advanced process treatments. Chitosan and their derivatives have been considered as versatile biopolymers in various dairy applications. Unique cationic character and versatile properties makes it useful as active antimicrobial packaging materials, preserving and extending the shelf life of milk products. The ability to form complex with milk protein, makes it suitable for recycling of dairy waste water, whey treatment and also for encapsulation of milk protein and peptides. Chitosan, in its native stage as well as in modified form has application in various functional dairy products like cheeses, ice cream, yoghurt and beverages. Overall chitosan and its derivatives have novel application in dairy sector, but their potential uses as functional ingredient need to be studied in detail. Basically, the molecular weight, chain length and ionic strength of chitosan influences it functional property. Further, the impact of this biopolymer on human physiology and their mechanism of action need to be established.

References

Andres,Y., Giraud,L., Gerente,C. and Le Cloirec, P., 2007. Antibacterial Effects of Chitosan Powder: Mechanisms of Action. *Environmental Technology,* 28(12):1357-1363.

Ausar, S.F., Landa, C.A., Bianco, I.D., Castagna, L.F. and Beltramo, D.M., 2001. Hydrolysis of a chitosan-induced milk aggregate by pepsin, trypsin and pancreatic lipase. *Biosci. Biotechnol. Biochem,* 65: 2412–2418.

Ausar, S.F., Passalacqua, N., Castagna, L. F., Bianco, I.D. and Beltramo, D.M., 2002. Growth of milk fermentative bacteria in the presence of chitosan for potential use in cheese making. *International Dairy Journal*, 12(11): 899–906.

Baker, L. G., Specht, C. A., and Lodge, J. K., 2011. Cell Wall Chitosan Is Necessary for Virulence in the Opportunistic Pathogen Cryptococcus neoformans. *Eukaryotic Cell*, 10(9): 1264–1268.

Benhamou, N., and Bélanger, R. R., 1998. Induction of systemic resistance to *Pythium* damping-off in cucumber plants by benzothiadiazole: ultrastructure and cytochemistry of the host response. *The Plant Journal*, 14: 13–21.

Chen, C., Chen, S., and Hsieh, J., 2015. Proteomic Analysis of Polysaccharide-Milk Protein Interactions Induced by Chitosan. *Molecules*, 20: 7737-7749.

Cheung, P.C.K., 2013. Mini-review on edible mushrooms as source of dietary fiber: Preparation and health benefits. *Food Science and Human Wellness*, 2 (3–4):162–166.

Chollangi, A. and Hossain, M.M., 2007. Separation of proteins and lactose from dairy wastewater. *Chemical Engineering and Processing: Process Intensification,* 46(5):398-404.

Cuartas-Uribe, B., Alcaina-Miranda, M.I., Soriano-Costa, E., Mendoza-Roca, J.A., Iborra-Clar, M.I. and Lora-García, J., 2009. A study of the separation of lactose from whey ultrafiltration permeate using nanofiltration. *Desalination,* 241(1-3): 244-255.

Darmadji, P. and Izumimoto, M., 1994. Effect of chitosan in meat preservation. *Meat Science*, 38(2): 243–254.

Dao, V.H., Cameron, N.R., and Saito, K., 2016. Synthesis, properties and performance of organic polymers employed in flocculation applications. *Polym. Chem.*, **7**: 11-25.

Del Carpio-Perochena, A., Bramante, C. M., Duarte, M. A. H., de Moura, M. R., Aouada, F. A. and Kishen, A., 2015. Chelating and antibacterial properties of chitosan nanoparticles on dentin. *Restorative Dentistry and Endodontics*, 40(3): 195–201.

Eduardo, M.F., Mello, K.G.P.C.D., Polakiewicz, B. and Lannes, S.C.D.S., 2014. Evaluation of Chocolate Milk Beverage Formulated with Modified Chitosan. *Journal of Agricultural Science and Technology*, 16(6): 1301-1312.

El-Diasty, E.M., Eleiwa, N.Z. and Aideia, H.A.M., 2012. Using Of Chitosan as Antifungal Agent in Kariesh Cheese. *New York Science Journal*, 5(9): 5-10.

Ganzle, M.G., Haase, G. and Jelen, P., 2008. Lactose: Crystallization, hydrolysis and value-added derivatives. *International Dairy Journal*, 18 (7): 685-694.

Hammond, M.D. and Skonberg, I., 2012. Anti-oxidant properties of Chitosan coatings on frozen atlantic salmon fillet portions. *Journal of Aquatic Food Product Technology*, 21: 351-361.

Hongpattarakere, T. and Riyaphan, O., 2008. Effect of deacetylation conditions on antimicrobial activity of chitosans prepared from carapace of black tiger shrimp (*Penaeus monodon*). *Songklanakarin J. Sci. Technol*, 30 (1): 1-9.

Khalaf S, A., 2004. Production and Characterization of Fungal Chitosan under Solid-State Fermentation Conditions. *International Journal of Agriculture and Biology*, 6(6):1033-1036.

Kim,H., Jeong, Y., Bae, I. and Kwak, H., 2014. Physicochemical and Sensory Properties of Nanopowder Chitosan Added Maribo Cheese during Ripening. *Korean J. Food Sci. An*, 34(1): 57-64

Kitts, D. D., 2005. Antioxidant properties of casein phosphopeptides. *Trends Food Sci Technol*, 16: 549-554.

Kumar, M.N.V.R., 2000. A review of chitin and chitosan applications. *React. Funct. Polym*, 46: 1-27.

Lower, S.E., 1984. Polymers from the Sea Chitin and Chitosan. *Manufacturing Chemist*, 55: 73-75.

Moeini, H., Nahvi, I. and Tavassoli, M., 2004. Improvement of SCP production and BOD removal of whey with mixed yeast culture. *Electronic Journal of Biotechnology,* 7(3): 252-258.

Mourya, V.K. and Inamdar, N.N., 2008. Chitosan-modifications and applications: Opportunities galore. *Reactive and Functional Polymers,* 68(6):1013-1051.

Mukhopadhyay, R., Talukdar, D., Chatterjee, B. P. and Guha, A. K., 2003. Whey processing with chitosan and isolation of lactose. *Process Biochemistry*, 39: 381- 385.

Puvvada, Y.S., Vankayalapati, S. and Sukhavasi, S., 2012. Extraction of chitin from chitosan from exoskeleton of shrimp for application in the pharmaceutical industry. *International Current Pharmaceutical Journal*, 1(9):258-263.

Raafat, D. and Sahl, H., 2009. Chitosan and its antimicrobial potential – a critical literature survey. *Microbial Biotechnology*, 2(2):186–201.

Rabea, E.I., Badawy, M.E., Stevens, C.V., Smagghe, G. and Steurbaut, W., 2003. Chitosan as antimicrobial agent: applications and mode of action. *Biomacromolecules*, 4:1457–1465

Rinaudo, M., 2006. Chitin and chitosan: Properties and applications. *Progress in Polymer Science*, 31(7): 603-632.

Selmer-Olsen, E., Ratnawera, H.C. and Pehrson, R., 1996. A novel treatment process for dairy wastewater with chitosan produced from shrimp-shell waste. Water Science and Technology, 34(11):33-40.

Seo, M.H., Lee, S.Y., Chang, Y.H. and Kwak, H.S., 2009. Physicochemical, microbial, and sensory properties of yogurt supplemented with nanopowdered chitosan during storage. *J Dairy Sci*, 92(12): 5907-5916.

Tharanathan, R.N., 2003. Biodegradable films and composite coatings: Past, present and future. *Trends in Food Science and Technology*, 14 (3):71–78.

Tsai G.J., SU H., Chen H.C. and Pan C.L., 2002. Antimicrobial activity of shrimp chitin and chitosan from different treatments and applications of fish preservation. *Fisheries Sci*, 68(1):170-177.

Tsai, G.J., Zhang, S.L. and Shieh, P.L., 2004. Antimicrobial activity of a low-molecular-weight chitosan obtained from cellulase digestion of chitosan. *Journal of Food Protection*, 67: 396–398.

Uryash, V.F., Larina, V.N., Kokurina, N.Y., Bakulin, A.V., Kashtanov, E.A. and Varlamov, V.P. 2012. Chitin and chitosan orderliness degree and thermochemical characteristics dependence form biological origin. *Russian Journal of Physical Chemistry* A, 86(1):5–12.

7

Non-Conventional Probiotics for Human Use

Sudheendra CH. V.K., Gopikrishna G., Madhavi T.V. and Tanmay Hazra

Abstract

Probiosis has emerged in the early 20th century after Ellie Metchnikoff proposed his hypothesis that organisms were reponsible for longivity of ethnic people of Balkan region of Russia and ever since it has grow into a major scientific field which has its applications extending into farming, aquaculture and prophylactics in humans. Vast research was carried out on this topic and Lactobacillus sp. *and Bifidobacterium* sp, *are the two important genus that are highly studied and widely recognized universally as conventional probiotics. Apart from these two genus there exists many other bacterial species which have shown promising probiotic potential. Such non conventional probiotics are widely used in some parts of world as commercial food products with health beneficial effects, pharmaceutical products or being tested for their safe utilization in human beings. The present chapter tries to covers some genera and their potential and application in prophylactics.*

Keywords: *Bacillus*, probiotic, enterococcus, *E. coli Nissle*, propionibacterium, yeast, *clostridium* sp.

1. Introduction

Foods with health beneficial effects are called functional foods and are achieving prominance in the present day health conscious world. Among these functional foods, Probiotic foods segement is considered as an important segment (Shah, 2007). Inexhaustible research is being carried out on probiotics after Ellie Metchnik off published his findings "Prolongation of Life". The term "probiotics" was first coined by Lilly and Stillwell (1965) and defined " microorganisms promoting the growth of other microorganisms". Later on many definitions were given by scientists in due course of time. Food and Agricultural Organisation has defined "Probiotics are live microorganisms, which when administered in adequate amounts confer a health benefit on the host" (FAO, 2002). International Dairy Fedaration (2003) defined "Oral probiotics" as "living micro-organisms,which upon ingestion in certain numbers, exert health benefits beyond inherent basic nutrition".

The field of probiosis has emerged as a new field of science with applications in farming and aqaculture as alternatives to antibiotics as well as prophylactics in humans. *Lactobacillus* sp. and *Bifidobacterium* sp. enjoy a special status as probiotics. They aremost widely documented and universally usedspecies of probiotics (Sullivan and Nord, 2002; Nira *et al*., 2007; Vasiljevic and Shah, 2008; Gogineni *et al.,* 2013). Apart from these two genera there are numerous other bacterial species with probiotic potential, that are presently used or being tested for their safe utilization. In this present chapter we try to cover some potentials and applications of these non conventional probiotic.

1.1. ***Bacillus*** **species**

Bacillus species are allochthonous,saprophytic Gram-positive microorganisms commonlyfound in soil, water, dust and air (Nicholson, 2002).Under adverse conditions these organismscan form endospores which are highly resistant to different physico-chemical elements (Krajcikova *et al*., 2009; Nicholson *et al*., 2002). This capability allows them to survive unfavourable conditions like acidic conditions and bile present in the human digestive system, food manufacturing processes and during storage (Clavel *et al*., 2004).

There are nearly 318 recognized species of the genus *Bacillus* (www. bacterio. net), among them bonafide species being used as probiotics are*B. subtilis*, *B.cereus*, *B.licheniformis*, *B. pumilus*, *B. clausii* and *B. coagulans*. *Bacillus* sp. areadministered in spore form as they can resist the unfavorable conditions during gastrointestinal transit (GIT) in human as well as in animals(Hoa *et al*., 2000; Guo *et al*., 2006). Some animal studies have indicated that the ingested spores could Germinate and survive in GIT (Angert and Losick, 1998; Biourge *et al.*,1998; Hoa *et al*., 2001; Casula and Cutting, 2002; Duc *et al*., 2004; Leser *et al.,* 2008;). The products manufactured using *bacillus* spores can be classified into two major groups, those for prophylactic use and those sold as health food supplements or novel foods. Present chapter we stress in prophylactic products sold throughout the world.

1.2. Bacillus subtilis

This organismisfound to be highly safe for human usage (Osipova *et al*., 1998;) and has displayed antagonistic effect both *in vitro* and *in vivo* against different human bacterial pathogens such as *Campylobacter* sp., *Escherichia coli*,

Staphylococcus aureus and *Helicobacter pylori* (Sorokulova *et al.*, 1997; Agarry *et al.*, 2005). Substances similar to antibiotics were found to be secreted because of which this anti pathogenic activity could be observed (Pinchuk *et al.*,2001; Naclerio *et al.,* 1993). It also plays an important role as an immune-stimulatory agent in a variety of diseases (Sato *et al.*,1992; Duc *et al.*, 2004). It can be given as food suppliment indifferent forms *viz*., powdered, through frozen milk or by fermented soya based product (Hong *et al.,* 2008; Kitamura *et al.*, 2010; Wongputtis in *et al.,* 2012). Many commercial products are available in market around the world containing strains *Bacillus subtilis* which are used for various health benefits (Table 1).

1.3. B. cereus

Another spore forming organism that is widely used as anelementin different drug formulations prepared for humans. It secretes bacteriocin type products which inhibits the growth, of *B. licheniformis, B. subtilis, Enterococcus faecalis, E. coli, S. aureus, Lactobacillus helveticus* and *L. casei* (Torkar and Matijašic, 2003). Cen Biot, a commercial product sold in Brazil contains *B. cereus* which in hibited *E. coli* and *Yersinia pseudotuberculosis* which were not inhibited by antibiotics at low concentrations (Turnes *et al.,*1999). Bactosubtil French product contains *Bacillus cereus* IP5832.

1.4. B. clausii

Strains were found to be microaerophilic, but only few were able to grow anaerobically in a nitrate medium. The spores showed the ability to germinate and grow in the presence of conjugated bile salts (up to 1%, w/v) or free bile salts (0.2%). Theyalso demonstrated tolerance for the combined acid-bile challenge (Cenci *et al.*, 2006). Common side-effects related to anti *H. pylori* antibiotic therapy were found to be reduced in *B. clausii* bacteriotherapy (Nista *et al.*, 2004). Immunomodulatory effect was observed in allergic children with recurrent respiratory infections when they were treated with *Bacillus clausii.* Many commercial products can be found throughout the globe especially for treatment of gut microbial imbalance and other problems like diarrhea. The list of some products is given in Table 1.

1.5. Bacillus polyfermenticus

It was first isolated from aerial samples by Terakado in 1933. Since then this organism is used for treating intestinal disorders particularly in East Asia. It was later manufactured commercially and is available in markets of Japan and Korea (Lee *et al.*, 2001). This organisms prolonged survival in the gastrointestinal tract was due to its characteristic endospore that showed resistantance to all the intestinal enzymes and fluids (Lee *et al.*, 2001).

Some strains also produce bacteriocins that possess antimicrobial property and also had anti listerial propeties (Lee *et al.*, 2001,). Oral administration of *Bacillus polyfermenticus* inhumans,stimulated Immunoglobulin (IgG) production that helps in alleviation of gasterointestinal disorders (Kim *et al.*, 2006). It also displayed anti tumour properties and anticancer effect against colon cancer (Ma *et al.*, 2010),. This organism was also found to have capability of healing wounds in human intestines Im *et al.* (2009).

1.6. Bacillus indicus

This was found to produce caroteniods (Duc *et al.*, 2006) and also can be used as a food supplement (Hong *et al.*, 2008).

1.6. Bacillus amyloliquefaciens

This organism is well known for its production of á-amylase and proteases. It is phenotypically similar to *Bacillus subtilis*. It survives low pH conditions *i.e.* 2.0 to 3.0 and was found to be resistant to bile salts at a concentration of 0.3 % (w/v). Strains belonging to this organism were able to produce antimicrobial compounds which possess antibacterial properties against food borne pathogens such as *Escherichia coli* and *Pseudomonas aeruginosa* and fungi like *Aspergillus clavatus, A. fumigates, A. niger* and *Gibberella moniliformis*. This organism is used in many drug formulations through out the world which can be seen in Table-1.

Oral Dosage of *Bacillus oligonitrophilus* have shown to prolong the life of cancer patients and stabilized the cancer growth (Malkov *et al.*, 2005).

Bactisubtil (Merrell, Neuilly-sur-Seine, France) a drug approved in France in the 1950s also contains *Bacillus* CIP 5832 as an active ingredient and recommended in infants against antibiotic-induced diarrhoea (Lestradet, 1995).

Table 1 : List of *Bacillus* containing products marketed around the world region wise

Product Name	Organism(s) Present
Bacillus subtilis	
Lactipan Plus (Italy)	*Bacillus subtilis* (Capsule)
Bee juvit subtilis(Vietnam)	*Bacillus subtilis*
Mega Sporebiotic(USA)	*Bacillus subtilis*
Vetom 1.1 (capsules & powder)(Russia)	*Bacillus subtilis* VKPM B strain 7048
Komarova Powder (Russia)	*Bacillus subtilis* strain VKPM B-10641 (DSM 24613)
Vetom 1.23(Russia)	*Bacillus subtilis* recombinant strain VKPM B-10641 (DSM 24613)
Pastylbio (Vietnam)	*B. subtilis* (Sachets (1g))
Primal Defense	*B. subtilis* and *B. licheniformis* and other 12 bacterial strains
Bibactyl (Vietnam)	*B. subtilis*
Bidisubtilis(Vietnam)	of *B. subtilis*
Biosubtyl DL (Vietnam)	*B. subtilis&L. Acidophilus*
Medilac Human(China)	*B. subtilis* strain RO179 plus *E. faecium.*
Biosporin (Ukraine)	A mixture of two strains of living antagonistic bacteria *B. subtilis* 2335 (sometimes referred to as *B. subtilis* 3) and *B. licheniformis* 2336 (ratio is 3:1)
Garars (Russia)	Originally isolated from animal fodder There are a number of versions of this product produced in different countries including a recombinant form, Subalin
Nature's First Food (USA)	42 species listed as probiotics including: *B. subtilis, B.polymyxa, B. pumilus* and *B. Laterosporus*
Thrive	*Bacillus Subtilis* HU58*Bacillus Indicus* HU36*Bacillus ClausiiBacillus Coagulans*
Nutri Commit 30 Billion Probiotics	*Bacillussubtilis*, *Bacillus coagulans*
Bacillus clausii	
Enterogermina (Italy)	At least 4 different strains of *B. clausii* (suspension)
Domuvar (Italy)	*Bacillus clausii* in Vials (suspension), No longer marketed
Progermila (Vietnam)	*B. clausii*
Spobio® Cl (Vietnam)	*B. clausii*
Bacillus cereus	
Bactisubtil (Germany)	*Bacillus cereus* strain IP 5832b(ATCC 14893) (Capsule)
Biovicerin (Brazil)	*B. cereus* strain GM (Suspension)
Subtyl (Vietnam)	*B. cereus* species termed *B. cereus* var vietnami (Capsule)
Biosubtyl (Vietnam)	*B. cereus* mixed with tapioca (Sachet (1 g))
Bacillus amyloliquefaciens	
Vetom 2 (Russia)	*Bacillus amyloliquefaciens* strain VKPM B-10642 (DSM 24614) *Bacillus amyloliquefaciens* strain VKPM B-10643 (DSM 24615)

Contd.

NOZDRIN Nasal Drops(Russia)	*Bacillus amyloliquefaciens* strain VKPM B-10642
BIOSEPTIN GELSkin Gel (Russia)	*Bacillus amyloliquefaciens* strain VKPM B-10642 (DSM 24614) and *Bacillus amyloliquefaciens* strain VKPM B-10643 (DSM 24615).
Sporolac(India)	*Bacillus coagulans*
FIVELAC(USA)	*Bacillus coagulans, Bacillus subtilis, Enterococcus faecalis, Lactobacillus acidophilus, Bifidobacterium longum*
Other *Bacillus* species	
Flora-Balance (USA)	*Brevobacillus laterosporus* BOD. (Capsules)
Biosubtyl (Vietnam)	*B. pumilus* spores mixed with tapioca. Sachet (1 g)
Bispan(S. Korea)	*B. polyfermenticus* SCD (Tablet)
Vetom 3(Russia)	Bacillus licheniformis VKPM B 7038

2. Enterococci

Thiercelin and Jouhaud (1903) first described and proposed *Enterococci* as a new genera. *Enterococcus faecium* and *Enterococcus faecalis* are two organisms which can be used as a probiotics for both humans and animals, however *E. faecalis* is used mostly for animals.

2.1. Enterococcus faecium

This is a natural inhabitant of the human oral cavity, gut flora (10^5–10^7 CFU /g of stool) and upper genital tract. It can also be found in different habitats like in plants, birds, reptiles, insects, soil and water. Spherical to ovoid cells predominantly ound in pairs and short chains which can also be found as elongated cells. Non motile and motile strains can be found. They are strictly anaerobic strains. They can adopt to grow aerobically and such strains were isolated from bovine alimentary track.

Diseases caused by *E. coli, salmonellae* or *Clostridia E. faecium* strains in animals can be efficiently treated using this organism (Maia *et al.*, 2001; Bujnáková *et al.*, 2004). Ability to withstand the harsh conditions existing in the GIT and colonising the human GIT was observed (Pimental *et al.,* 2012). Enterococcus strains were found to alliviate different types of diarrhoea, cholesterol lowering effect, and immune regulation. Among enterococci, only *E. faecium* of human origin is used as a commercial probiotic (e.g., Probican paste; Medipharm Ltd.) (Belicová *et al.,* 2004; Mego *et al.*, 2005), other commercial products are *E. faecium* SF68® (NCIMB 10415, produced by Cerbios-Pharma SA, Barbengo, Switzerland) and *E. faecalis* Symbioflor 1 (Symbio Pharm, Herborn, Germany).

Vitacanis commercial probiotic preparation (composed of *L. acidophilus, E. faecium* and *Saccharomyces cerevisiae*) show best effectivity against *Salmonella enterica serovar typhimurium* in the GIT of gnotobiotic mice.

Originally isolated from a healthy Swedish baby also known as *E. faecium* SF68. It is an active ingredient of some probiotic products intended for humans (Cremonini *et al.,* 2002). *E. faecium* NCIMB 10415 was authorized as a probiotic strain in European Union. *E. faecium* strain SF68 can effectively treat chronic hepatic encephalopathy, acute diarrhoea as well as antibiotic associated diarrhoea in humans (Wun-derlich *et al.*, 1989). It also exerts inhibitory effects against important enteropathogens (Ranjan *et al.*, 2004). It was found very effective in treatment of *Giardia* infection and eliminates Trophozoites in the small intestines (Benyacoub *et al.*,2005).This organism has its impact on many illnesses like antibiotic associated diarrhoea, irritable bowl syndrome and immune regulation (Wunderlich *et al.*, 1989; Chen *et al.*, 2010;). *E. faecium* SF68 is one of the best documented and effective probiotics for diarrhoea.

Another probiotic strain which is important in this genus is M-74, which has demonstrated on effectiveeliminatation of pathogenic bacteria in the case of inflammatory bowel disease and reduce colon cancer in humans (Mego *et al.*, 2005).Enhancement of nonspecific immunity was observed both in *in vitro and in vivo* tests (Ebringer *et al.,*1995). Cultivation of this strain in mediumenriched by selenium, has amplified its immunostimulatory and antimutagenic activity in both *in vitro* and *in vivo* tests (Ebringer *et al.,* 1995; Belicová *et al.*, 2004). It showed inhibitory action against important enteropathogens, including enterotoxigenic *E. coli*, *Salmonellae*, *Shigellae*, and clostridia.

E. faecium containing fermented milk product Gaio® (Yoghurt) (MD Foods, Denmark) has been sold in Denmark and in the United Kingdom since several years. The manufacturer claims that the product has a hypocholesterolemic effect on individuals (Bertolami *et al.*, 1999). However, 2 long-term studies, which lasted 12 weeks and 6 months, respectively, unsuccessful in showing any reduction in cholesterol levels of individuals who received Gaio yogurt, compared with that in control subjects at the end of treatment (Agerbaek *et al.*, 1995; Richelsen *et al.*, 1996).

Belicová *et al.* (1999) demonstrated that milk fermented through *E. faecium* M-74 exhibited dose-dependent inhibition of selected mutagens and UV-irradiation in the *Salmonella* and *Euglena* assays.

Another probiotic product Walthers ECOFLOR (Walthers Health Care, Den Haag, The Netherlands) is available in the market that contains an *E. faecium* strain, claims the efficacy against diarrhoea. It possesses anti-carcinogenic effect, and enterocins active towards *L. monocytogenes* were produced, the possible reduction of the LDL-cholesterol level could be observed.

Another strain *E.faecium* WB 2000 has expressed probiotic character by inhibiting cariogenic streptococcal biofilm formation (Suzuki *et al.*, 2011).

Ability to attach on the intestinal epithelium and barring pathogenic bacteria such as *Listeria monocytogenes in vitro* could be observed when strain *E. faecium SE906* was administered. This strain was also safe to be used as it has low aminogenic potential, antibiotic resistance pattern and virulence determinants. It can be considered as a potential probiotic meat starter culture suitable formanufacture of dry-fermented Iberian sausages (Moyano *et al.*, 2009).

Table 2: Some commercial products sold around world containing *E. faecium.*

Product Name	Organism(s) Present
E.faecium	
Walthers ECOFLOR(Netherlands)	*Enterococcus faecium*
SF68®(Swizerland)	*Enterococcus faecium*
Symbioflor 1(Germany)	*Enterococcus faecium*
Vitacanis(France)	*Enterococcus faecium*
ProbiMax 8 (Finland)	*Enterococcus faecium, Bifidobacterium bifidum, Lactobacillus acidophilus, Lactobacillus casei, Lactobacillus plantarum, Lactobacillus rhamnosus, Streptococcus thermophilus, Bifidobacterium longum*
Health Bac (USA)	*Enterococcus faecium along with 8 other probitic organisms.*
Probiotic blends	*Enterococcus faecium M 74*
Diaflor(Canada)	*Enterococcus faecium SF68*
Bioflorin®(Swizerland)	*Enterococcus faecium SF68*

2.2. Escherichia coli Nisslestrain 1917 (EcN)

During World War I, this strain was originally isolated from a soldier who escaped a severe outbreak of diarrhoea affecting his detachment from troops. Nissle 1917, alias SK22 or DSM6601 (Blaser and Reller, 1981; Oda, 1995) have beneficial effect on several types of intestinal disorders. Since early 1920s this organism was being sold as a probiotic. EcN (O6:K5:H1) was used as medicine in treatment of chronic inflammatory and infectious diseases of the intestine (Araki *et al.*, 2004; Guzy *et al.*, 2008). Patients with IBD can be treated with EcN (Boudeau *et al.*, 2003,). EcN ameliorates colitis (Kruis *et al.,* 1997; Schultz *et al.*, 2004; Schultz, 2008; Tromm *et al.*, 2004, Gionchetti *et al.*,2005; Matthes *et al.*, 2010, Petersen *et al.,* 2014, Scaldaferri *et al.*, 2016) exhibited an inhibitory effect on the adhesion and invasion of intestinal epithelial cells by AIEC *in vitro* (Stentebjerg-Olesen *et al.*, 1999; Mego *et al.,* 2005; Schlee *et al.*, 2007*)*, it stimulates immune response system and inhibit *Salmonella typhimurium in vivo* (Lima-Filho *et al.,* 2004). *E. coli* Nissle 1917 has capability to effect directly on the imune response mechanism (Cukrowska *et al.*, 2002; Sturm *et al.*, 2005, 2008; Helwig *et al.*, 2006; Wehkamp *et al.*, 2004). It can be used in treating chronic constipation without any side effects (Möllenbrink and Bruckschen,1994). This strain had a superior alleviating effect on diarrhoea caused by viral effect in infant and toddlers (Henker *et al.,* 2007). Ec Nmeets all requirements and is recognized as a safe organism for human use (Sun *et al.,* 2005). In a recent study conducted in *ex vivo* mouse ileal tissues when exposed to EcN elevated the production of seretonin level, which contributes in feeling happy (Nzakizwanayo *et al.,* 2015). Despite its successful therapeutic application, only little is known about the beneficial traits contributing to the strains probiotic character. The mechanisms principal to the probiotic nature, specifically at the molecular level, still have to be elucidated.

3. Clostridium butyricum

Clostridium butyricum Miyairi (CBM) was first isolated by Dr. Miyairi from human feces in 1933 at the department of Hygiene at Chiba Medical College, Japan. Since many years this organism was also used clinically to treat intractable diarrhoea and antibiotic-induced colitis patients in Japan, Korea and China. It is stable against adverse conditions in stomach, and successively enters colon. It germinates, proliferates there ultimately producing Short Chain Fatty Acids (SCFA).The mechanism behind CBM's effectiveness against diarrhoea may be due to properties like inhibiting putrefying bacteria and creating conditions for the proliferation to beneficial bacteria (especially bifidobacteria and lactobacilli). Antagonistic interaction against *Candida albicans*, *Clostridium difficile*, entero toxigenic *Escherichia coli*, *Klebsiella* sp., *Salmonella* sp. and *Vibriosp*. has been shown by CBM. (http://www.miyarisan.com/english_main.htm).

For both non-antimicrobial induced diarrhoea and antimicrobial associated diarrhoea (AAD) conditions in humans, *Clostridium butyricum* MIYAIRI 588 strain has been used as a probiotic. Oral administration of CBM588 alleviated dextron sulfate sodium (DSS)-induced colitis in rats as well as in humans. So CBM588 administration can be carried out as an alternative to butyrate enema (Okamoto *et al.*, 2000). Use of CBM along side antibiotics has reduced the changes in the intestinal flora and decreased the incidence of gastrointestinal side effects (Shimbo *et al.*, 2005; Fujii *et al.*, 2006). Cure to *H. pylori* infection in the mice was demonstrated following treatment with spores of *C. butyricum* (Takahashi *et al.*, 2000; Kamiya *et al.*, 2006). The probiotic bacterium CBM strain 588 has preventive and therapeutic effects on Enterohemorrhagic *Escherichia coli* (EHEC) O157:H7 (Takahashi *et al.,* 2004). CBMis effectively normalizes the intestinal flora disturbed by antibiotics for both the treatment and the prophylaxis of AAD in children (Seki *et al*., 2003). Bio-Three drug containing *Clostridium butyricum* was found effect immune response system and helps in better digestion of food along with free bowl movement in humans (Hua *et al*., 2010).

4. Yeasts

Widely distributed species of yeast, *Saccharomyces boulardii* has been described as a bio-therapeutic agent. It was discovered by French researcher Boulard in 1923, isolated from a tropical fruit (lychee fruit) which grows in Southeast Asia. It belongs to Saccharomycetaceae family and is Gram positive in nature. It is in elliptical or spherical shape and has a size of 4-8 µm. *S. boulardii* forms ascospore and grows in standard yeast mediums with an optimal growth temperature of 37°C and has the capability to assimilate and ferment carbohydrates and can prevent microbial pathogen growth. This yeast species has displayed no pathogenic properties and was used for the treatment of diarrhoea, prevention and the treatment of intestinal infections and in the maintenance of inflammatory bowel disease in the south Asian countries. In 1962, lyophilised commercial preparation of *S. boulardii* was introduced in France, which was used as a cure for diarrhea. Lyophilised *S. boulardii* is being used clinically in Europe, Asia, Africa and South America. Anti-inflammatory, antimicrobial, enzymatic, metabolic and antitoxic activities has been shown by *S. boulardii* in Preclinical and experimental studies (Ertor, 2003; Billoo *et al.,* 2006; Szajewska, 2012). Some of the commercial products that are being sold around the world presented in Table 3.

Investigational studies revealed partially the molecular mechanisms triggered to improve the host health (Zanello *et al*., 2009). *S. boulardii* is one of the first and currently the only one commercialized yeast for human medicine (Martins *et al*., 2005). *S. boulardii* survived the gastrointestinal tract's harsh conditions carried out using *in vitro* systems simulating human gastric/small intestinal (TIM) and large intestinal (ARCOL) environments (Diot *et al*., 2012) .

Oral administration of *S. boulardii* could treat or prevent gastrointestinal diseases such as AAD, recurrent *Clostridium difficile*-associated diseases, traveller's diarrhoea, children acute diarrhoea, enteral tube feeding-associated diarrhoea, AIDS-associated diarrhoea, rotavirus diarrhoea intestinal bowel disease such as Crohn's disease and ulcerative colitis and irritable bowel syndrome (Corthier *et al.,* 1986; Castex *et al.,* 1990; Czerucka *et al*., 1991; Elmer and Corthier, 1991; Pothoulakis *et al.,* 1993; Zanello *et al*., 2009, Grandy *et al*., 2010). Its also has beneficial effects in promoting iron absorption (Mai *et al.,* 2002) and effective prevention of recurrent Clostridium difficile-induced pseudomembranous colitis, as well as the antagonistic action of *E. coli* (Czerucka *et al.,* 2000;Czerucka and Rampal, 2002). *H. pylori* infected asymptomatic patients can be treated with triple therapy combined with *Lactobacillus GG, S. boulardii*, or *Lactobacillus / Bifidobacterium* (Kamiya *et al.*, 2006).

S. boulardii prevents the degradation of intestinal layers from toxins (Agawane and Lonkar, 2004) and also stimulates the immune response (Qamar *et al.*, 2001; Agawane and Lonkar, 2004). Enteropathogenic *E. coli*(EPEC) mediated apoptosis of epithelial cells was delayed in the presence of *S. boulardii* and it exerted a protective effect on epithelial cells after EPEC adhesion by modulating the signaling pathway induced by bacterial infection (Czerucka *et al.*, 2000). Fermentation of soymilk with probiotic *S. boulardii* improves the biological functionality by making isoflavones biologically available, increased calcium content and easily digestible protein, reduction of glycosides and increasing in aglycones (Rekha and Vijayalakshmi, 2008, 2010).

Martins and associates (2005), demonstrated that *S. cerevisiae* showed negligible adhesion ability; however, it could survive acidic conditions and grow in the presence of bile.salts. *S. cerevisiae* 905, from "aguardente" (cachaça) production, showed viable intestinal populations with fecal levels that never fell below 10^6 cfu/g. It inhibited the proliferation of *S. typhimurium* in ileum and *C. difficile*in the colon and cecum of gnotobiotic mice (Martins *et al.*, 2005). *S. cerevisiae* 832, *S. Cerevisiae* KK1 were of human origin possess characteristics such as assimilation of cholesterol *in vitro* and tolerance to low pH levels, gastric juice, and bile indicate that they may be promising candidate strains which can be used as probiotics (Psomas *et al.*, 2003).

Three strains of yeasts isolated from human gastrointestinal tract and feta cheese *viz., S. cerevisiae* 982, *S.boulardii* KK1 *and Kluyveromyces lactis* 630 strains exhibited increased polymorpho nuclear cell influx and phagocytic activity as well as cytokine production in the air pouch which at par with potency as the probiotics Ultra levure *S. boulardii* and *Lactobacillus acidophilus* NCFB 1748 (Kouralis *et al.*, 2010).

Kluyveromyces lactis was most adhesive to Caco-2 cells. *K.lactis* proliferated under anaerobic conditions, and showed acid and bile tolerance; however, growth was moderate at 37°C. Thus, it was concluded that *K. lactis* as a probiotic agent could be expected to enhance immune modulation rather than improve the intestinal flora (Kumara *et al.*, 2004).

The yeast strains namely *Pichia fermentans* BY5, *Pichia. kudriavzevii* BY10, *P. kudriavzevii* BY15 and *Yarrowia lipolytica* HY4 isolated from raw milk showed basic probiotic characteristics such as survival to gastric juices and adhesion to HT-29 cells and may serve as potential probiotics in assimilating cholesterol in the human intestine (Chen *et al.*, 2010).

Table 3: List of some commercial products containing *Saccharomyces boulardii* sold thorough out the world.

Sr.No	Product Name	Sr.No	Product Name
1.	Jarrow Formulas,	12.	Macflora
2.	Walgreens Saccharomyces Boulardii Probiotic Capsules	13.	Bolardi
3.	Econorm	14.	Florastor
4.	Delponorm	15.	Enzobioz
5.	Entrolac-Z	16.	Reequre Plus
6.	Hitic – SB	17.	Recepro- SB
7.	Actiflor	18.	Delflora- R
8.	Sacnorm	19.	Dia Flora
9.	Sacro-250	20.	Enteric Ecol
10.	Biflor	21.	Florafix
11.	Unisac	22.	Enterol

5. Conclusion

The utilization of spores as probiotics is expanding, which can be proved by number of products that are commercially available. In many countries, products sold as pharmaceuticals must meet pre market criteria for efficacy and safety. Current government legislation does not provide impeccable definitions concerning the appropriateness of various bacteria forits usage infood and as supplement in developed countries as well as in India.

Further experimental studies should better elucidate the mechanisms of action of probiotic organisms and suggest their new therapeutic applications. Gene technology is playing major role in studying new strains. Gene sequencing is allowing us to understand mechanisms and functionality of probiotics. Barry Goldin, Ph.D., Professor at Tufts University School of Medicine, has opined "The full potential of probiotics can only be realized when their benefits can be established scientifically. It is highly likely that benefits from current and future probiotics have gone undetected and, therefore, full utilization of these organisms has not been achieved".

References

Agarry, O.O., Akinyosoye, F.A. and Adetuyi, F.C., 2005. Antagonistic properties of microogranisms associated with cassava (Manihot esculenta Crantz) products. *African Journal of Biotechnology*, 4:627-632.

Agawane, S.B. and Lonkar, P.S., 2004. Effect of probiotic containing Saccharomyces boulardii on experimental ochratoxicosis in broilers: hematobiochemical studies. *Journal of Veterinary Science*, 5:359–367.

Agerbaek, M., Gerdes, L.U. and Richelsen, B.,1995.Hypocholesterolaemic effect of a new fermented milk product in healthy middle-aged men. *European Journal of Clinical Nutrition*, 49: 346–352.

Angert, E.R. and Losick, R.M., 1998.Propagation by sporulation in the guinea pig symbiont Metabacterium polyspora. *Proceedings of the National Academy of Sciences of United States of America*, 95:10218–10223.

Araki, Y., Andoh, A., Takizawa, J., Takizawa, W. and Fujiyama, Y., 2004. Clostridium butyricum, a probiotic derivative, suppresses dextran sulfate sodium-induced experimental colitis in rats. *International Journal of Molecular Medicine*, 13:577–580.

Belicova, A., Krajcovic, J., Dobias, J. and Ebringer, L., 1999. Antimutagenicity of Milk Fermented by Enterococcus fcecium. *Folia Microbiologia,*44:513–518.

Belicova, A., Krizkova, L., Dobias, J., Krajcovic, J. and Ebringer, L., 2004.Synergic activity of selenium and probiotic bacterium *Enterococcus faecium* M-74 against selected mutagens in Salmonella assay. *Folia Microbiologia*, 49:301–305.

Benyacoub, J., Perez, P.F., Rochat, F., Saudan, K.Y., Reuteler, G., Antille, N., Humen,M., De Antoni, G. L., Cavadini, C., Blum, S. and Schiffrin, E. J., 2005. *Enterococcus faecium* SF68 Enhances the Immune Response to *Giardia intestinalis* in Mice. *Journal of Nutrition*, 135:1171–1176.

Beric, T., Stankovic, S.,, Draganic, V., Kojic, M., Lozo, J. and Fira, D., 2013. Novel antilisterial bacteriocin licheniocin 50.2 from *Bacilluslicheniformis* VPS50.2 isolated from soil sample. *Journal of Applied Microbiology*, 116:502—510.

Bertolami, M.C., Faludi, A.A. and Batlouni, M., 1999.Evaluation of the effects of a new fermented milk product (Gaio) on primary hypercholesterolemia. *European Journal of Clinical Nutrition*, 53:97-101.

Billoo, A. G., Memon, M. A., Khaskheli, S. A., Murtaza, G., Iqbal, K., Saeed Shekhani, M., & Iddiqi, A. Q. (2006). Role of a probiotic (Saccharomyces boulardii) in management and prevention diarrhoea. *World Journal of Gastrology*, 12(28):4557-4560.

Biourge, V., Vallet, C., Levesque, A., Sergheraert, R., Chevalier, S. and Roberton, J.L., 1998. The use of probiotics in the diet of dogs. *Journal of Nutrition* 128:2730S–2732S.

Blaser, M. J., and L. B. Reller., 1981.Campylobacter enteritis. *New England Journal of Medicine*, 305:1444–1452.

Boudeau, J., Glasser, A.L., Julie, S., Colombel, J.F. and Michaud, A.D., 2003. Inhibitory effect of probiotic *Escherichiacoli* strain Nissle 1917 on adhesion to and invasion of intestinal epithelial cells by adherent–invasive *E. coli* strains isolated from patients with Crohn's disease. *Alimentary Pharmacology Therapy*, 18:45–56.

Bujnáková, D., Vlková, E., Rada, V. and Kmet, V., 2004.Aggregation of Lactobacilli and Bifidobacteria with *Escherichia coli* O157. *Folia Microbiologia*, 49:143-146.

Castex, F., Corthier,G., Jouvert, S., Elmer, G.W., Lucas, F. and Bastide, M., 1990.Prevention of *Clostridium difficile*-induced experimental pseudomembranous colitis by *Saccharomyces boulardii*: a scanning electron microscopic and microbiological study. *Journal of General Microbiology*, 136:1085-1089.

Casula, G., Cutting, S.M., 2002. Bacillus probiotics: spore germination in the gastrointestinal tract. *Applied Environmental Microbiology*, 68:2344–2352.

Cenci, G., Trotta, F.and Caldini, G., 2006. Tolerance to challenges miming gastrointestinal transit by spores and vegetative cells of *Bacillus clausii*. *JournalAppliedMicrobiology*,101: 1208–1215.

Chen, L.S., Ying, M.A., Maubois, J.L., He, S.H., Chen, L.J. and Li, H.M., 2010. Screening for the potential probiotic yeast strains from raw milk to assimilate cholesterol. Dairy Science Technology, 90:537–548.

Clavel, T., Carlin, F., Lairon, D., Nguyen-The, C. and Schmitt, P., 2004. Survival of *Bacilluscereus* spores and vegetative cells in acid media simulating human stomach. *Journal of Applied Microbiology*, 97: 214-219.

Corthier, G., Dubos, F. and Ducluzeau, R., 1986.Prevention of *Clostridium difficile* induced mortality in gnotobiotic mice by *Saccharomyces boulardii. Canadian Journal of Microbiology*, 32:894–896.

Cremonini, F., di Caro, S., Santarelli, L., Gabrielli, M., Candelli, M., Nista, E.C., Lupascu, A., Gasbarrini, G. and Gasbarrini, A., 2002. Probiotics in antibiotic-associated diarrhoea. *Digestive Liver Disease*,34:S78–S80.

Cukrowska, B., LodInova-ZadnIkova, R., Enders, C., Sonnenborn, U., Schulze, J. and Tlaskalova-Hogenova, H. 2002. Specific proliferative and antibody responses of premature infants to intestinal colonization with nonpathogenic probiotic *E. coli* strain Nissle 1917. *Scand J Immunol.*, 55 pp. 204–209.

Czerucka, D. and Rampal, P. (2002).Experimental effects of *Saccharomycesboulardii* on diarrheal pathogens. *Microbes and Infection*, 4:733–739.

Czerucka, D., Dahan, S., Mograbi, B., Rossi, B. and RampaL, P. (2000). *Saccharomycesboulardii* preserves the barrier function and modulates the transduction pathway induced in enteropathogenic *Escherichiacoli*-infected T84 cells. *Infection and Immunity*, 68:5998–6004.

Czerucka, D., Nano, J.L., Bernasconi, P. and Rampal, P., 1991. Response of the IRD intestinal epithelial cell line to *Clostridium difficile* toxins A and B in rats. Effect of *Saccharomyces boulardii. Gastroentérologie clinique et biologique*, 15:22 - 27.

Diot, S. B., Denis, S., Chalancon, S., Chaira, F., Cardot, J.M. and Alric, M., 2012. Use of Artificial Digestive Systems to Investigate the Biopharmaceutical Factors Influencing the Survival of Probiotic Yeast During Gastrointestinal Transit in Humans. *Pharmaceutical Research*, 29, pp.1444–1453.

Duc, L. H., Hong, H.A., Barbosa, T. M., Henriques, A. O. and Cutting, S. M., 2004.Characterization of Bacillus probiotics available for human use. *Applied Environmental Microbiology*, 70:2161–2171.

Duc, L.H., Fraser, P. and Cutting, S.M., 2006. Carotenoids present in halotolerant Bacillus spore formers. *FEMS Microbiology Letters*, 255:215–224.

Ebringer, L., Ferenίk, M., Lahitová, N., Kaèáni, L. and Michálková, D., 1995.Anti-mutagenic and immuno-stimulatory properties of lactic acid bacteria. *World Journal of microbiology and Biotechnology*, 11:294-298.

Elmer, G.W. and Corthier, G., 1991. Modulation of *Clostridiumdifficile* induced mortality as a function of the dose and the viability of the *Saccharomycesboulardii* used as a preventative agent in gnotobiotic mice. *Canadian Journal Microbiology*, 37:315-317 .

Ertor, O. (2003). Saccharomyces boulardii: infeksiyöz ishal tedavisinde yeni bir seçenek mi? *Klimik Dergisi*, 16:3-7.

Food and Agriculture Organization/World Health Organization. 2002. Report of a Joint FAO/WHO Working Group on Drafting Guidelines for the Evaluation of Probiotics in Food. Available at: http://www.fda.gov/ohrms/dockets/dockets/95s0316/95s-0316-rpt0282-tab-03-ref-19-joint-faowho-vol219.pdf . Accessed on 31/3/14.

Fujii, H., Maruyama, K., Moriguti, M., Sato, Y., Takahashi,T., Ito, K., Yokoyama, H., 2006.Effect of *Clostridiumbutyricum* when Combined with Vancomycin in Treatment of *Clostridiumdifficile*-Associated Diarrhea. *Japan Journal of Pharmaceutical and Health Care Science*, 32:1009-1013.

Gionchetti, P., Rizzello, F., Morselli, C., Sollazzi, L., Davies, S.,Tambasco, R., Bernabini, C.and Campieri, M. (2005).Probiotics in Inflammatory Bowel Disease *Business Briefing : European Gastroenterology Reviews:*86-88.

Gogineni VK, Morrow LE, Malesker MA (2013) Probiotics: Mechanisms of Action and Clinical Applications. *J Prob Health* 1: 101. doi:10.4172/ jph.1000101

Grandy, G., Medina, M., Soria, R., Terán, C.G. and Araya, M., 2010. Probiotics in the treatment of acute rotavirus diarrhoea. A randomized, double-blind, controlled trial using two different probiotic preparations in Bolivian children. *BMC Infectious Diseases*, 10: 253:1-7.

Guo, X., Li, D., Lu, W., Piao, X. and Chen, X., 2006. Screening of Bacillus strains as potential probiotics and subsequent confirmation of the in vivo effectiveness of *Bacillus subtilis* MA139 in pigs.*Antonie vanLeeuwenhoek*, 90:139–146.

Guzy, C., Paclik, D., Schirbel, A., Sonnenborn, U., Wiedenmann, B. and Henker, J., Laass, M., Blokhin, B.M., Bolbot, Y.K., Maydannik, V.G., Elze, M. and Schulze, C.W.J., 2007. The probiotic *Escherichia coli* strain Nissle 1917 (EcN) stops diarrhoea in infants and toddlers. *European Journal of Pediatrics*,166:311-318.

Helwig, U., Lammers, K.M., Rizzello, F., Brigidi, P., Rohleder, V., Caramelli, E., Gionchetti, P., Schrezenmeir, J., Foelsch, U.R., Schreiber, S. and Campieri, M. 2006. Lactobacilli, bifidobacteria and E. coli nissle induce pro- and anti-inflammatory cytokines in peripheral blood mononuclear cells. *World Journal of Gastroenterology*, 12:5978-86.

Henker, J., Laass, M., Blokhin, B.M., Bolbot, Y.K., Maydannik, V.G,, Elze, M., Wolff, C. and Schulze, J. 2007. The probiotic *Escherichia coli* strain Nissle 1917 (EcN) stops acute diarrhoea in infants and toddlers. *European Journal of Pediatrics*,166: 311–318

Hoa, N.T., Baccigalupi, L., Huxham, A., Smertenko, A., Van, P.H., Ammendola, S., Ricca, E. and Cutting, S.M., 2000. Characterization of Bacillus species used for oral bacteriotherapy and bacterioprophylaxis of gastrointestinal disorders. *Applied Environmental Microbiology*, 66:5241–5247.

Hoa, T.T., Duc, L.H., Isticato, R., Baccigalupi, L., Ricca, E., Van, P.H. and Cutting, S.M., 2001.Fate and dissemination of Bacillus subtilis spores in a murine model. *Applied Environmental Microbiology*, 67:3819–3823.

Hong, H.A., Duc, L.H. and Cutting, S.M., 2005.The use of bacterial spore formers as probiotics. *FEMS Microbiology Reviews*, 29:813-835.

Hong, H.A., Huang, J.M., Khaneja, R., Hiep, L.V., Urdaci, M.C. and Cutting, S.M., 2008. The safety of *Bacillus subtilis* and *Bacillus indicus* as food probiotics. *Journal of Applied Microbiology*, 105:510–520.

Hua, M.C., Lin, T.Y., Lai, M.W., Kong, M.S., Chang, H.J. and Chen, C.C., 2010. Probiotic Bio-Three induces Th1 and anti-inflammatory effects in PBMC and dendritic cells. *World Journal of Gastroenterology*, 16:3529-3540

Im, E., Choi, Y.J., Kim, C.H., Fiocchi, C., Pothoulakis, C. and Rhee, S.H., 2009a. The angiogenic effect of probiotic *Bacilluspolyfermenticus* on human intestinal microvascular endothelial cells is mediated by IL-8. *American Journal of Physiology - Gastrointestinal Liver Physiology*, 297:G999-G1008.

International Dairy Federation 2003. Health effects of probiotics and culture-containing dairy products in humans. *Bulletin* 380/2003:1-17.

Kamiya, S., Takahashi, M., Manzoku, T., Oka, K., Osaki, T., Hanawa, T., Kurata S. and Taguchi, H., 2006.Probiotics and *Helicobacterpylori* infection. *Microbial Ecology in Health and Disease*, 18:177-180.

Kim, H.S., Park, H., Cho, I.Y., Paik, H.D. and Park, E., 2006. Dietary supplementation of probiotic *Bacillus polyfermenticus*, Bispan strain, modulates natural killer cell and T cell subset populations and immunoglobulin G levels in human subjects. *Journal of Medicinal Food*, 9:321-327.

Kitamura, Y., Sun, J.F., Takahashi, S. and Hansen, C. L., 2010.Growth characteristics of *Bacillussubtilis* (Natto) in milk. *International Journal of Dairy Technology,* 63:418-422.

Kourelis, A., Kotzamanidis, C., Tzanetaki, E. L., Papaconstantinou, J., Tzanetakis, N., and Yiangou, M., 2010. Immunostimulatory activity of potential probiotic yeast strains in the dorsal air pouch system and the gut mucosa. *Journal of Applied Microbiology*, 109: 260–271.

Krajcikova, D., Lukacova, M., Mullerova, D., Cutting, S.M. and Barak, I., 2009. Searching for protein-protein interactions within the *Bacillussubtilis* spore coat. *Journal of Bacteriology*, 191:3212-3219.

Kruis, W., Schutz, E., Fric, P., Fixa, B., Judmaier, G. and Stolte, M., 1997. Double-blind comparison of an oral *Escherichia coli* preparation and mesalazine in maintaining remission of ulcerative colitis. *Alimentary Pharmacology Therapy*, 11:853-858.

Kumura, H., Tanoue, Y., Tsukahara, M., Tanaka, T. and Shimazaki, K., 2004.Screening of Dairy Yeast Strains for Probiotic Applications. *Journal of Dairy Science*, 87:4050–4056.

Lee, K.H., Jun, K.D., Kim, W.S. and Paik, H.D., 2001.Partial characterization of polyfermenticin SCD, a newly identified bacteriocin of *Bacilluspolyfermenticus*. *Letters in Applied Microbiology*, 32:146-51.

Leser, T.D., Knarreborg, A. and Worm, J. 2008. Germination and outgrowth of *Bacillus subtilis* and *Bacillus licheniformis* spores in the gastrointestinal tract of pigs. *Journal of Applied Microbiology*, 104:1025–1033.

Lestradet, H., 1995.Probiotiques: le Bacillus CIP 5832 chez l'homme et l'animal. Medecine Et Chirurgie Digestives, 24:37–39.

Lilly, D.M.and Stillwell, R.H., 1965.Probiotics: Growth-promoting factors produced by microorganisms. *Science*, 147:747–748.

Lima-Filho, J.V.M., Vieira, L.Q., Arantes, R.M.E.and Nicoli, J.R., 2004. Effect of the *Escherichiacoli* EMO strain on experimental infection by *Salmonellaenterica* serovar *Typhimurium* in gnotobiotic mice. *Brazilian Journal of Medical and Biological Research*, 37:1005-1013.

List of prokaryotic names with standing in nomenclature (1997). Genus Bacillus available at: http://www.bacterio.net/bacillus.html accessed on 31/03/14.

Ma, E.L., Choi, Y.J., Choi, J., Pothoulakis, C., Rhee, S.H. and Im, E., 2010. The anticancer effect of probiotic *Bacilluspolyfermenticus* on human colon cancer cells is mediated through ErbB2 and ErbB3 inhibition. *International Journal of Cancer*, 127:780–790.

Mai, T. T., Igarashi, K., Hirunuma, R., Takasaki, S., Yasue, M., Enomoto, S., Kimura, S. and Nguyen, C.V., 2002.Iron absorption in rats increased by yeast glucan. *Bioscience Biotechnology Biochemistry*, 66:1744–1747.

Maia O.B., Duarte R., Silva A.M., Cara D.C. and Nicoli J.R., 2001.Evaluation of the components of a commercial probiotic in gnotobiotic mice experimentally challenged with *Salmonellaenterica* subsp. *enterica* ser. *Typhimurium*. *Veterinary Microbiology*, 79: 183-189.

Malkov, S.V., Markelov, V.V., Polozov, G.Y., Sobchuk, L.I., Zakharova, N.G., Barabanschikov, B.I., Kozhevnikov, A.Y., Vaphin, R.A., Trushin, M.V., 2005.Antitumor features of *Bacillusoligonitrophilus* KU-1 strain. *Journal of Microbiology Immunology and Infection*, 38:96 -104.

Martins, F. S., Nardi, R. M. D., Arantes, R. M. E., Rosa, C. A., Neves, M. J. and Nicoli, J. R., 2005.Screening of yeasts as probiotic based on capacities to colonize the gastrointestinal tract and to protect against enteropathogen challenge in mice. *Journal of General and Applied Microbiology*, 51:83–92.

Matthes, H., Krummenerl, T., Giensch, M., Wolff, C., Schulze, J. 2010. Clinical trial: probiotic treatment of acute distal ulcerative colitis with rectally administered *Escherichia coli* Nissle 1917 (EcN). BMC Complement Altern Med. 10:13. doi: 10.1186/1472-6882-10-13.

Mego, M., Májek, J., Konèeková, R., Ebringer, L., Èierniková, S., Rauko, P., Kováè, M., Trupl, J., Slezák, P., Zajac, V., 2005. Intramucosal bacteria in colon cancer and their elimination by probiotic strain *Enterococcusfaecium* M-74 with organic selenium. *Folia Microbiologia*, 50:443–447.

Miyarisan Pharmaceutical CO., Ltd., *Clostridiumbutyricum* MIYAIRI strain, Available at : http://www.miyarisan.com/english_main.html. accessed on 31/03/2014.

Möllenbrink. M. and Bruckschen, E., 1994. Treatment of chronic constipation with physiologic *Escherichia coli* bacteria. Results of a clinical study of the effectiveness and tolerance of microbiological therapy with the *E. coli* Nissle 1917 strain (Mutaflor). *Medizinische Klinik - Intensivmedizin und Notfallmedizin*, 89:587-593

Moyano, S.R., Martin, A., Benito, M.J., Aranda, E., Casquete, R., and Cordoba, M.D.G., 2009. Safety and Functional Aspects of Preselected Enterococci for Probiotic Use in Iberian Dry-Fermented Sausages. *Journal of Food science*, 74:399-404.

Naclerio, G., Ricca, E., Sacco, M.and De Felice, M., 1993.Antimicrobial activity of a newly identified bacteriocin of *Bacilluscereus*. *Applied Environmental Microbiology*, 59:4313–4316.

Nicholson, W.L., 2002 a.Roles of Bacillus endospores in the environment. *Cellular and Molecular Life Sciences*, 59:410–416.

Nicholson, W.L., Fajardo-Cavazos, P., Rebeil, R., Slieman, T.A., Riesenman, P.J., Law, J.F. and Xue, Y., 2002 b. Bacterial endospores and their significance in stress resistance. *Antonie Van Leeuwenhoek*, 81:27-32.

Nira, H.K., Mizumachi, K., Nomura, M., Kobayashi, M., Fujita, Y., Okamoto, T., Suzuki, I., Tsuji, N.M., Kurisaki, J. and Ohmomo, S., 2007.Lactococcus sp. as Potential Probiotic Lactic Acid Bacteria. *Japan Agricultural Research Quarterly*, 41:181 – 189.

Nista, E.C., Candelli, M., Cremonini, F., Cazzato, I.A., Zocco, M.A., Franceschi, F., Cammarota, G., Gasbarrini ,G. and Gasbarrini, A., 2004.*Bacillusclausii* therapy to reduce side-effects of anti-*Helicobacterpylori* treatment: randomized, double-blind, placebo controlled trial. *Alimentary Pharmacology Therapeutics*, 20:1181–1188.

Nzakizwanayo, J., Dedi, C., Standen, G., Macfarlane, W.M., Patel, B.A. and Jones, B.V. 2015. *Escherichia coli* Nissle 1917 enhances bioavailability of serotonin in gut tissues through modulation of synthesis and clearance. Sci Rep., 30, 5 pp.17324. doi: 10.1038/srep17324.

Oda, T., 1995.Role of mast cells in dextran sulfate sodium-induced experimental colitis in rats. *Journal of Kyoto Prefectural University of Medicine*, 104:1069–1082.

Okamoto, T., Sasaki, M., Tsujikawa, T., Fujiyama, Y., Bamba, T. and Kusunoki. M., 2000. Preventive efficacy of butyrate enemas and oral administration of *Clostridiumbutyricum* M588 in dextran sodium sulphate induces colitis in rats. *Journal of Gasteroenterology*, 35:341-356.

Osipova, I.G., Sorokulova, I.B., Tereshkina, N.V. and Grigoreva, L.V., 1998. Safety of bacteria of the genus Bacillus, forming the base of some probiotics. *Zhurnal Mikrobiologii, Epidemiologii Immunobiologii*, 6:68–70.

Petersen, A.M., Mirsepasi, H., Halkjær, S.I., Mortensen, E.M., Nordgaard-Lassen, I., and Krogfelt, K.A. 2014.Ciprofloxacin and probiotic *Escherichia coli* Nissle add-on treatment in active ulcerative colitis: a double-blind randomized placebo controlled clinical trial. *Journal of Crohns Colitis.* 8(11):1498-505

Pimentel, L. L., Mättö , J., Malcata, F. X., Pintado, M.E. and Saarela, M. (2012). Survival of potentially probiotic enterococci in dairy matrices and in the human gastrointestinal tract. *International Dairy Journal*, 27:53-57.

Pinchuk, I.V., Bressollier, P., Verneuil, B., Fenet, B., Sorokulova, I.B., Me´Graud, F. and Urdaci, M.C., 2001.*Invitro* anti-*Helicobacterpylori* activity of the probiotic strain *Bacillussubtilis* 3 is due to secretion of antibiotics. *Antimicrobial Agents Chemotherapy*, 45:3156–3161.

Pothoulakis, C., Kelly, C.P., Joshi, M.A., Gao, N., O'Keane, C.J., Castagliuolo, I. and Lamont, J.T., 1993. *Saccharomycesboulardii* inhibits Clostridium difficile toxin A binding and enterotoxicity in rat ileum. *Gastroenterology*,104:1108-1115.

Psomas, E. I., Fletouris, D. J., Tzanetaki, E. L, and Tzanetakis, N., 2003. Assimilation of cholesterol by yeast strains isolated from infant feces and Feta cheese. *Journal of Dairy Science*, 86:3416–3422.

Qamar, A., Aboudola, S., Warny, M., Michetti, P., Pothoulakis, C., Lamont, J.T. and Kelly, C.P., 2001. *Saccharomycesboulardii* stimulates intestinal immunoglobulin A immune response to *Clostridiumdifficile* toxin A in mice. *Infection and Immunity*, 69:2762–2765.

Ranjan, A., Malik, R.K., Naresh, K., 2004.Newly Emerging Applications of Enterococci in Dairy Foods. *Indian Dairyman* 56, 67-74.

Rekha, C. R. and Vijayalakshmi, G., 2008. Biomolecules and Nutritional Quality of Soymilk Fermented with Probiotic Yeast and Bacteria. *Applied Biochemistry and Biotechnology,* 151:452–463

Rekha, C.R., and Vijayalakshmi, G., 2010. Bioconversion of isoflavone glycosides to aglycones, mineral bioavailability and vitamin B complex in fermented soymilk by probiotic bacteria and yeast. *Journal of Applied Microbiology*, 109:1198–1208.

Richelsen, B., Kristensen, K. and Pedersen, S.B., 1996.Long-term (6 months) effect of a new fermented milk product on the level of plasma lipoproteins—a placebo-controlled and double blind study. *European Journal of Clinical Nutrition*, 50:811–815.

Sato, T., Nagal, K., Suzuki, K., Morioka, M. and Saito. T., Nohara, C., Susaki, K. and Takebayashi, Y., 1992.A new isocoumarin antibiotic, Y-05460M-A. *Journal of Antibiotics*, 45:1949–1952.

Scaldaferri, F., Gerardi, V., Mangiola, F., Lopetuso, L.R., Pizzoferrato, M., Petito, V., Papa, A., Stojanovic, J., Poscia, A., Cammarota, G. and Gasbarrini, A. 2016. Role and mechanisms of action of Escherichia coli Nissle 1917 in the maintenance of remission in ulcerative colitis patients: An update. *World Journal of Gastroenterology*. 22(24) pp.5505-11.

Schlee, M., Wehkamp, J., Altenhoefer, A., Oelschlaeger, T.A., Stange, E.F. and Fellermann, K., 2007. Induction of human beta-defensin 2 by the probiotic *Escherichiacoli* Nissle 1917 is mediated through flagellin. *Infection and Immunity*, 75:2399–2407.

Schultz, M. 2008. Clinical Use of *E. coli* Nissle 1917 in inflammatory Bowel Disease. *Inflammatory Bowel Diseases*, 14:1012–1018.

Schultz, M., Strauch, U.G., Linde, H.J., Watzl, S., Obermeier, F., Gottl, C., Dunger, N., Grunwald, N., Scholmerich, J. and Rath, H.C., 2004.Preventive effects of *Escherichiacoli* strain Nissle 1917 on acute and chronic intestinal inflammation in two different murine models of colitis. *Clinical and Diagnostic Laboratory Immunology*, 11:372–378.

Seki, H., Shiohara, M., Matsumura, T., Miyagawa, N., Tanaka, M., Komiyama, A.and Kurata, S., 2003. Prevention of antibiotic-associated diarrhea in children by *Clostridiumbutyricum* MIYAIRI. *Pediatrics International*,45:86-90.

Shah, N. P., 2007.Functional cultures and health benefits *Int. Dairy J.* 17, 1262–1277.

Shimbo, I., Yamaguchi, T., Odaka, T., Nakajima, K., Koide, A., Koyama, H., Saisho, H., 2005. Effect of *Clostridiumbutyricum* on fecal flora in *Helicobacterpylori* eradication therapy. *World Journal of Gastroenterology*, 11:7520-7524.

Sorokulova, I. B., Kirik, D. K. and Pinchuk, I.V., 1997.Probiotics against Campylobacter Pathogens. *Journal of Travel Medicine*, 4:167–170.

Stentebjerg-Olesen,B.,Chakraborty,T. and Klemm,P., 1999.Type 1 fimbriation and phase switching in a natural *Escherichiacoli* fimB null strain, Nissle 1917. *Journal of Bacteriology*, 181:7470–7478.

Sturm, A., 2008. The probiotic *Escherichia coli* strain Nissle 1917 induces gd T cell apoptosis via caspase- and FasL-dependent pathways. *International Immunology*, 20:829–840.

Sturm, A.L., Rilling, K., Baumgart, D.C., Gargas, K., Abou-Ghazalé, T., Raupach, B., Eckert, J., Schumann, R.R., Enders, C., Sonnenborn, U., Wiedenmann, B. and Dignass, A.U., 2005. *Escherichia coli* Nissle 1917 distinctively modulates T-cell cycling and expansion via toll-like receptor 2 signaling. *Infection and Immunity*, 73:1452-1465.

Sullivan, Å. and Nord, C. E. 2002.Probiotics in human infections. *Journal of Antimicrobial Chemotherapy,* 50:625–627.

Sun, J., Gunzer, F., Westendorf, A.M., Buer, J., Scharfe, M., Jarek, M., Gobling, F., Blocker, H. and Zenga, A.P., 2005.Genomic peculiarity of coding sequences and metabolic potential of probiotic *Escherichiacoli* strain Nissle 1917 inferred from raw genome data. *Journal of Biotecnology*, 117:147–161.

Suzuki, N., Yoneda, M., Hatano, Y., Iwamoto, T., Masuo, Y. and Hirofuji, T. (2011). *Enterococcusfaecium* WB2000 inhibits biofilm formation by oral cariogenic Streptococci. *International Journal of Dentistry*:1-5.

Szajewska, H. (2012). An update on Saccharomyces boulardii. *Przeglad Gastroentorogiczny*, 7(6):351-358.

Takahashi, M., Taguchi, H., Yamaguchi, H., osaki, T. and Kamiya, S., 2000.Studies of the effect of *Clostridiumbutyricum* on *Helicobacterpylori* in several test models including gnotobiotic mice. *Journal of Medical Microbiology*, 49:635-642.

Takahashi, M., Taguchi, H., Yamaguchi, H., Osaki, T., Komatsu, A. and Kamiya, S., 2004. The effect of probiotic treatment with *Clostridiumbutyricum* on enterohemorrhagic *Escherichiacoli* O157: H7 infection in mice. FEMS Immunology and. *Medical Microbiology*, 41:219–226.

Thiercelin, M. E. and Jouhaud, L. (1903). Reproduction de l'entérocoque; taches centrales; granulations péripheriques et microblastes. *Comptes rendus des séances de la Société de biologie et de ses filiales*, 55:686–688.

Torkar K. G. and Matijašc, B. B., 2003.Partial Characterisation of Bacteriocins Produced by *Bacilluscereus* isolates from Milk and Milk Products. *Food Technology and Biotechnology*, 41:121–129.

Tromm, A., Niewerth, U., Khoury, M., Baestlein, E., Wilhelms, G., Schulze, J., Stolte, M., 2004. The Probiotic *E. coli* strain nissle 1917 for the treatment of collagenous colitis: first results of an open-label trial. *Zhurnal of Gastroenterology*, 42:365-369.

Turnes, C.G., dos Santos, F. A., da Cruz, W.F. and Monteiro, A.V., 1999.Properties of the *BacillusCereus* strain used in probiotic CenBiot. *Revista de Microbiologia*, 30:11-14.

Vasiljevic, T. and Shah, N.P., 2008.Probiotics—From Metchnikoff to bioactives. *International Dairy Journal*, 18:714– 728.

Wehkamp, J., Harder, J., Wehkamp, K., Meissner, B. W., Schlee, M., Enders, C., Sonnenborn, U., Nuding, S., Bengmark, S., Fellermann, K., Schröder J. M. and Stange, E.F., 2004. NF-êB- and AP-1-mediated induction of human beta defensin-2 in intestinal epithelial cells by *Escherichiacoli* Nissle 1917: a Novel Effect of a Probiotic Bacterium. *Infection and Immunity*, 72:5750-5758.

Wongputtisin, P., Khanongnuch, C., Khongbantad, W., Niamsup, P. and Lumyong, S., 2012. Screening and selection of *Bacillus* spp. for fermented corticate soybean meal production. *Journal of Applied Microbiology*, 113:798-806.

Wunderlich, P.F., Braun, L., Fumagalli, I., D'Apuzzo, V., Heim, F., Karly, M., Lodi, R., Politta, G., Vonbank, F. and Zeltner, L., 1989. Double-blind report on the efficacy of lactic acid-producing Enterococcus SF68 in the prevention of antibiotic-associated diarrhoea and in the treatment of acute diarrhoea. *Journal of International Medical Research,* 17: 333–338.

Zanello, G., Meurens, F., Berri, M. and Salmon, H., 2009. *Saccharomycesboulardii* effects on gastrointestinal diseases. *Current Issues in Molecular Biology,* 11:47-58.

8

Nutrigenomics in Food Technology

Kamal Gandhi, Tanmay Hazra, Seema Rana and Ravinder Kaushik

Abstract

Nutrition and genetics both have very crucial role in human health and in development of chronic diseases such as cancer, osteoporosis, diabetes and cardiovascular diseases. Difference between individuals in response to dietary intervention is a well-known phenomenon in nutrition research (Ordovas, 2008).The effect of dietary changes on phenotypes such as blood cholesterol, body weight and blood pressure can differ significantly between individuals (Ordovas et al.*, 2007). Various bioprocess i.e. ingestion, absorption, digestion, transport, metabolism and excretion of nutrients and food bioactive components in human body is carried out through proteins such as enzymes, receptors, transporters, ion channels and hormones. Genetic variation leads to altered production and affect functional properties of these proteins. Furthermore nutritional efficacy is also different among different individuals which might be affected by nutritional status. Thus diet and gene expression are interrelated and have a mutual effect on physiology of human body.*

Keywords: Nutrigenomics, Diet, Genes, Genetic, Disease

1. Introduction

The science that provide a molecular understanding, how nutrition affects mammalian metabolism and health by altering gene on basis of an individual's genetic makeup (Ordovas and Corella, 2004). The study of relationship between diet and its affect on genes is called nutrigenomics (or nutritional genomics). It is a linking term between two complimentary approaches: how nutrient affects gene function and how genetic variation affects nutrient response. Nutrigenomics explains how individual DNA and genetic code affect his specific need for certain nutrients and maintain optimal health throughout life. Beneficial and detrimental health effects of diet are identified. It establishes diet-gene interactions through application of genomic principles in nutritional research and formulate associations between specific nutrients and genetic factors (German, 2005). Thus nutrigenomics facilitate greater understanding of how nutrition affects metabolic pathways and how this process is related to diet-related diseases (Chadwick, 2004).

Genetic level differences either at level of single nucleotide polymorphism or at gene level, influence individual response to diet. Nutrigenetics reveals how genetic makeup of individual respond to various dietary nutrients (Muller and Kersten, 2003). Different individuals respond to same nutrient differently by virtue of their genetic make-up. Genetic variation effects the interaction between diet and disease and also required nutrition recommendations. Diet-gene interactions refer to the dietary modification of the effect of a genetic variant on phenotype or health outcome measure (Ordovas, 2008).

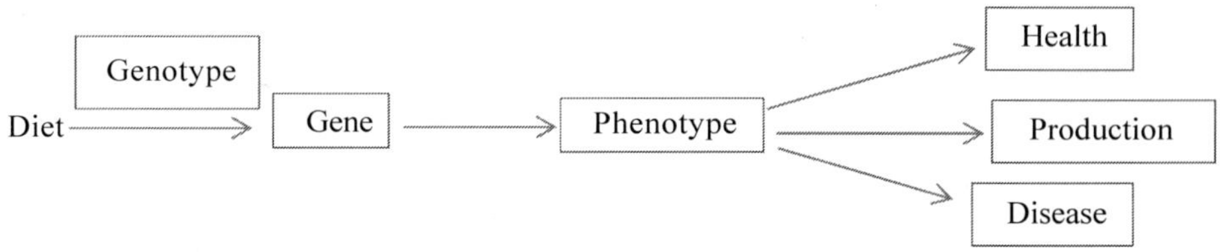

Fig. 1: Diet-gene interaction

2. Diet and Disease Interaction

Diet supplies both energy and building blocks for growth and development of organism. Different nutrients have their own biological activity. Few nutrients act as radical scavengers known as antioxidants and provide protection against oxidation causing cardiovascular disease, damage to nucleic acid etc. Other nutrients have shown to be potent signalling molecules and act as nutritional hormones (Muller and Kersten, 2003). Many diseases and disorders are well co-related with nutrition in terms of essential nutrients, imbalance of macronutrients, or event toxic concentrations of certain food components. There are multietiological diseases caused by interaction of different nutrients with several genes (Mariman, 2006).

3. Genetic Base of Disease

Effect of diet at gene level intervened on phenotypes such as body weight, blood pressure and blood cholesterol levels and results in significant interpersonal differences (Ordovas, 2008). Several other factors like gender difference, age, physical activity, genetic composition, smoking etc. can also influence dietary responses. Lactose intolerance is an example of effect of genetic variant on phenotype as genetic variation in the lactase gene results in inadequate production of lactase in the small intestine. Affected individuals are unable to efficiently break down the primary milk sugar (lactose) from dairy products which limits the consumption of milk and dairy foods (Swallow, 2003). Another condition phenylketonuria exist due to mutation in corresponding gene for enzyme phenylalanine hydroxylase (PAH) renders it non functional. Affected person is not able to metabolize the amino acid phenylalanine to the amino acid tyrosine and not able to consume phenylalanine containing foods such as eggs, fish, chicken, milk, cheese etc (Lokitnov, 2003).

4. Effect of Nutrients on Gene Expression (Siddique *et al.,* 2009)

The expression of specific genes and proteins is influenced by a number of intrinsic factors like transcription, translation and post transcriptional modifications, stage of cell cycling. Genomes are exposed to many types of environmental stimuli during lifetime including nutrition. Therefore, the genetic expression is modified by different nutrients like carbohydrate, fat, proteins and phytochemicals etc. Large number of nutrients with different concentrations may bind to different target depending on their affinities and affect gene expression in different ways. Nutrient may bind to transcriptional receptor or may affect metabolic pathway or at cellular level through cell signaling affect gene expression as shown in figure 2.

4.1 Direct Interactions

After interacting with a receptor, nutrients behave as transcription factor that is able to bind with DNA and induce gene expression. Nuclear hormone receptor is a family of transcription group act as nutrient sensor which binds nutrients and their metabolites eg, retinoic acid receptor, Fatty acid receptor etc, in the promoter region of genes by undergoing a conformational change. This change results in coordinated dissociation of co-repressor and association of co-activator proteins for transcriptional modification (Garg *et al.*, 2014).

4.2 Epigenetic Interactions

Nutrients are able to change the structure of DNA (or of histone proteins in chromatin) by inducing changes in DNA methylation pattern and modification of histone protein that chronically alter gene expression. Through action of repressor protein that attach to silencer region of DNA gene expression is also affected. These changes last through cell divisions for full cell life duration (Bird, 2007).

4.3 Genetic variations

Common genetic variations such as single-nucleotide polymorphisms (SNPs) can alter the expression or functionality of genes.

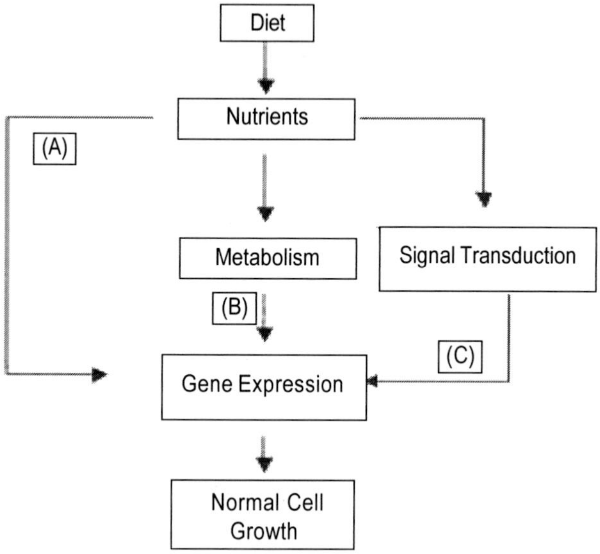

Fig. 2: (Pathway A) Directly as ligands for transcription factor receptors, (Pathway B) Metabolic pathways, (Pathway C) Gene regulation or cell-signaling (Kaput, 2004)

5. Effect of Carbohydrates on Gene Expression

Extent of variation in gene expression by virtue of nutrients is dependent upon type and amount of nutrient present in diet. Carbohydrates are the main energy source among which glucose provide instant energy for various metabolic activities of body. Feeding high-energy diet to rats leads to early development of obesity and metabolic syndrome, apparently through an inability to cope with energy density of the diet (Archer *et al.*, 2004). Obesity is associated with decrease in mRNA levels for the oxygenic neuropeptides, NPY (neuropeptides Y), Ag RP (Agouti Related Peptide) *etc* (Archer *et al.*, 2004b)

Gabriely *et al.*, 2001 checked the effect of hyperglycemia on liver angiotensinogen (AGT) gene expression and observed approximately three fold increase in AGT gene expression in liver. In mammals the response to dietary glucose is complex because it combines primary effects of glucose metabolism itself and secondary effects to glucose-dependent hormonal modifications, mainly pancreatic stimulation of insulin secretion and inhibition of glucagon secretion (Siddique *et al.*, 2009). In the pancreatic - cells, glucose is the primary physiological stimulus for the regulation of insulin synthesis and secretion.

In liver, in the presence of insulin, glucose induces expression of genes encoding glucose transporters and glycolytic and lipogenic enzymes, e.g. L-type pyruvate kinase (L-PK), acetyl-CoA carboxylase (ACC), and fatty acid synthase, and represses genes of the gluconeogenic pathway, such as the phosphoenolpyruvate carboxykinase gene (Ferre *et al*., 1996). Although insulin and glucagon were long known as critical in regulating gene expression, recently glucose also has been shown to play a key role in transcriptional regulation.

6. Effect of Fat on Gene Expression

Dietary fat in addition to its role as an energy source and component of membrane lipids, has profound effects on gene expression, leading to changes in metabolism, growth, and cell differentiation. The effects of dietary fat on gene expression reflect an adaptive response to changes in the quantity and type of fat ingested. In mammals, fatty acid regulated transcription factors include peroxisome proliferator–activated receptors (PPARα, -β, and -γ), HNF4α, NFκB, and SREBP1c (Sessler and Natambi, 1998).These factors are regulated by direct binding of fatty acids, fatty acyl coenzyme A, or oxidized fatty acids to receptors. Oxidized fatty acid regulation of G-protein–linked cell surface receptors and intracellular calcium levels and activation of signaling cascades target the nucleus and affect cell signaling (Siddique *et al.*, 2009).

At cellular level, the physiological response to fatty acids depend on quantity, chemistry, and duration of the fat ingested; cell-specific fatty acid metabolism (oxidative pathways, kinetics, and competing reactions); cellular abundance of specific nuclear and membrane receptors and involvement of specific transcription factors in gene expression. (Sessler and Natambi, 1998). These mechanisms are involved in the control of carbohydrate and lipid metabolism, cell differentiation and growth.

6.1. Effect of PUFA on Gene Expression

PUFA decreases the gene transcription and impair mRNA stability and thus suppress several hepatic genes like decreased the activity of enzyme Ä9 Desaturase. PUFA regulated genes have PUFA –RE in promoter region and hereby binds and may blocks or enhance transcription. PUFA activates perioxisome proliferator activated receptor (PPAR) which suppresses fatty acid synthesis (Sessler and Natambi, 1998). Lipogenic enzymes in liver decreased as result of feeding a diet containing 60% linoleic acid (Jeffcoat and James., 1978). Fatty acids stimulated the expression of adipocyte fatty acid binding protein (ap2) mRNA. In the 3T3–L1 adipocyte cell line, arachidonic acid (n-6) decreased SCD1 m RNA stability in a dose dependent manner (80% maximum repression), in the same way as linoleic and eicosapentanoicacids (Sessler *et al*., 1996).

Mechanism

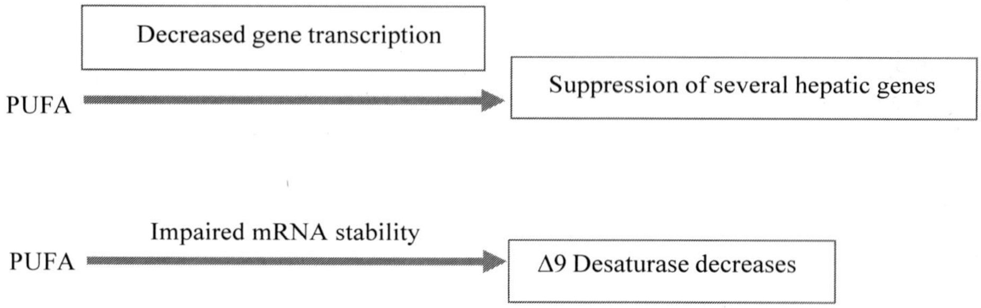

Fig. 3: Effect of PUFA on gene expression

6.2. Effect of Protein on Gene Expression

Protein is very essential for growth, reproduction, immunity and for normal maintenance of body function. In many developing countries protein insufficiency is still remains a major and serious problem. The function of protein in body is not only at macro level but it also function at gene level. A variety or number of genes responds to dietary protein. Concentration and quality of protein influences gene expression. Insulin secretion was reduced in rats, which are fed with low protein diet due to reduction in pancreatic b-cell mass lower response of remaining b-cells to nutrients and lowered protein kinase activity (PKA) (Lee *et al.*,1993). PKA is involved in potentiation of glucose induced insulin secretion by gastrointestinal hormones such as GIP and GLP-Low protein diet feeding to rats altered the gene expression, which are responsible for proteins related to insulin biosynthesis, secretion and cellular remodeling. Normal insulin secretion is influenced by level of Protein Kinase C (PKC), K+ channel protein, calcium ion (Ca^{2+}) and PKAa. Increased ATP to ADP ratio achieved through glucose metabolism, close the K+ ATP channel, which leads to depolarization of b-cells. Depolarized b-cells opens the voltage dependent Ca^{2+} channels which results in influx of calcium and led to exocytosis of insulin granules. Feeding low protein di*et al*so increased expression of PFK in islets (teramers M, P, L, and C) and results in defective glucose metabolism; it further leads to deceased glucose induced insulin secretion. Feeding low protein diet decreases insulin level, it also acts through decreased movement of intracellular calcium. (Siddique *et al.*, 2009)

6.3. Effect of Amino acids on Gene Expression

The first step of protein translation is the formation of the 43s pre-initiation complex containing methionyl tRNA, eIF2, GTP. This is followed by the association of methionyl tRNA and eIF2 – GTP that bind to the 40s ribosomal sub unit. The GTP is hydrolyzed late in the initiation process, and eIF2 is released from the ribosome as an inactive eIF2-GTP complex. Formation of eIF2-GTP is mediated by the guanine–nucleotide exchange factor eIF2B. The mechanism to regulate eIF2B activity may be at the level of the ribosomal protein S6 and eukaroyotic elongation factor 2 (elF-2) which is phosphorylated in response to many agents, including growth factors and hormones initiation process.

6.4. Effect of Vitamins on Gene Expression

PEPCK (Phospho Enol Pyruvate Kinase) is vitamin A dependent enzyme involved in one of the important step of gluconeogenesis i.e. conversion of oxaloacetate to phosphoenol pyruvate. Vitamin A deficiency condition leads to change in chromosomal structure of RARE (Retinoic Acid Responsive Element), which further affect coregulator binding and activity (Antras-Ferry, 1994). PEPCK–RARE and pre initiation complex interaction leads to reduced RNA polymerase II association with PEPCK promote and finally results in insufficient PEPCK (Hall *et al.*, 1992). With adequate level of vitamin A sufficient mice PEPCK gene expression is highly induced in the food deprived state, when blood glucose levels are reduced.

Biotin (Vitamin B2) is involved in gluconeogenesis, fatty Acid Synthesis and Amino acid catabolism. Biotin act as prosthetic group in 4 carboxylase enzymes, i.e. Pyruvate carboxylase, Acetyl CoA carboxylase, ProponylcoA carboxylase,b-methyl crotonyl CoA carboxylase. Defect in Biotin utilisation causes hyperammonemia, acidosis, Coma, Seizures, Skin Rash & Alopecia (Charles *et al.*, 1979). Biotin deficiency alters hepatic urea genesis by altering gene expression of urea cycle enzymes and induces glucokinase mRNA in starved rats (Bonjour, 1981).

Ascorbic acid is a signaling molecule that regulates expression of a battery of genes. It plays a potential role in embryonic development and cell differentiation (Belino *et al.*, 2010). Ascorbic acid deficiency changes hepatic gene expression in scurvy prone individual (Siddique *et al.*, 2009). In an another study Canali *et al.*, (2014) reported vitamin C supplementation modulated gene expression differently upon the inflammatory stimulus and synthesis of anti-inflammatory cytokine IL-10.

6.5. Effect of Minerals on Gene Expression

Zn controls gene of small intestine, thymus and hepatocytes. MTF-I, Zn dependent transcriptional activator regulates metallothionin I & II through MRE (Metal Responsive Element Factor- I). For protein preparation of HT-29 cells, involve Zn dependent KLF4 transcription factor, which directly interferes in cell cycle. ATP synthatase, Cytochrome c, cytochrome a, NADP Dehydrogenase-I &II are regulated by Zn. Thus Zn depletion results in Impaired Energy

Metabolism (Vallee and Alud 1993, Siddique *et al.*, 2009). Hasse *et al.*, 2015 reported that zinc regulates many protein involved in signal transduction and has extensive impact on leukocyte gene expression. Thus Zinc has a significant impact on the immune system of organism, and zinc deficiency, as well as supplementation, modulates immune function.

7. Benefits from Nutrigenomics

Nutrigenomics can be used to improve our understanding of how nutrition affects various health outcomes. Current trends in personalized nutrition have focussed on the role of genetic variation to understand why some individuals respond differently to the same nutrients consumed.

7.1. New Biomarkers for Nutrition-related Diseases

The comparison of biopsy material between patients and matched controls will reveal genes that are specifically up- or down regulated during disease progression. Some of those genes or their combined expression profile can be used as biomarkers for different stages of disease. They can be incorporated into diagnostic protocols for determining the right moment for disease-stage-specific nutritional intervention or therapy (Mariman, 2006).

7.2. To monitor the Efficacy of Nutritional Intervention

Similar comparative studies before, during and after an intervention will reveal genes and expression profiles indicative of the progress and the success of treatment by nutrition.

7.3. Genes and Molecular Pathways as Targets for Prevention

Knowledge about genes and the molecular pathways that are part of cell cycle with their specific role in the pathogenesis will bring forth novel strategies for prevention of disease or progress of disease.

7.4. Knowledge-based Functional Foods

A pathogenic gene expression profile can be pursued by using mixtures of specific nutrients as nutraceuticals. Because nutrition can be employed in a natural way, it is expected that the general public will accept it more easily than remedies for the actual prevention of disease. In the pre-symptomatic phase, expression profiles may serve as early biomarkers and also knowledge on the molecular pathogenesis, will be of importance for designing novel functional foods.

8. Applications of Nutrigenomics in Animal Science

8.1. To develop Animal Feed/Food Matching to its Genotype

Nutrigenomics is a great boon for development of new foods and feeds that can be matched to genotypes of animals for benefit of health and enhance normal physiological processes.

8.2. To select Nutrients Fine-tuned with Genes of Animal

Aim of nutrigenomics is to nurture good genes and bad ones to be switched down. Nutrigenomics helps for selection of nutrients for increasing efficacy of health beneficiary genes and DNA- present in every cell and every tissue of an animal (Ghormade *et al.*, 2011).

8.3. To Understand the Aging Process in Animals

A nutrigenomic approach can be applied to understand the aging process in companion animals. Healthy adult animals provided with the same foods can be studied to identify the gene expression and biochemical differences characteristic of the aging process. Foods for senior animals can then be rationally designed and evaluated for their ability to modify gene expression profiles in animals to more closely reflect those found in healthy adult animals, which has the potential to improve health and quality of life.

8.4. Nutrigenomics and Reproduction

The science of nutrigenomics has begun to use information obtained from basic studies of the genome to evaluate the effects of diet and nutrient management schemes on gene expression. While the effects of nutrition on fertility are only partially understood, modern nutrigenomics will undoubtedly play a key role in developing strategies for addressing some of the limitations in reproductive performance. Oligo based and cDNA microarray techniques make it possible to understand many of the factors which control the regulation of gene transcription and globally evaluate gene expression profiles by looking at the relative abundance of gene-specific mRNA in tissues. These techniques provide an unprecedented amount of information and are only now being used to examine key reproductive, developmental, and performance characteristics in cattle.

8.5. Nutrigenomics and Immune System

The concept underlying nutrigenomics is that nutrition is the key element of health maintenance, particularly for the immune system, so that an optimum level of nutrition will ensure optimum animal health. A deficiency of an essential nutrient will eventually affect the body performance.

9. Difference Between Nutrigenomics and Nutrigenetics

Nutrigenomics aims to determine the influence of common dietary ingredients on the genome, and helps to relate the resulting different phenotypes to differences in the cellular and/or genetic response of the biological system. Nutrigenetics, on the other hand, aims to understand how the genetic makeup of an individual coordinates their response to diet, and thus considers underlying genetic polymorphisms. It embodies the science of identifying and characterizing gene variants associated with differential responses to nutrients, and relate this variation to states of disease (Mutch *et al.*, 2005). Both disciplines are dependent on diet/genome interactions; however, their approaches and immediate goals are different. Nutrigenomics will unreveal the optimal diet within a series of nutritional alternatives, whereas nutrigenetics will yield critically important information that will assist clinicians in identifying the optimal diet for a given individual, i.e. personalized nutrition.

9.1. Challenges

A major challenge of nutrigenomics is to identify gene-nutrient interactions that affect complex diseases such as obesity, diabetes, cancer and cardiovascular disease that take several years or even decades to develop and have multifactorial etiologist. It is often difficult to determine the role of specific dietary factors and gene variants in development of these diseases. The concept of diet-gene interactions involves a genetic variant which modulate the effect of dietary factor on a specific phenotype or health outcome measure such as serum lipid concentrations, high blood glucose or obesity.

10. Conclusion

A major goal of nutrigenomics is prevention of the onset and progression of chronic disease. Findings of nutrigenomics are able to correlate nutrients to metabolic pathways that affect disease outcomes. The incorporation of genetics into nutritional epidemiologic studies aims to improve their consistency. Current research could lead to the development of personalized nutrition guidelines for individuals and specific sub-populations which could decrease the risk of chronic diseases.

References

Antras-Ferry, J., Franckhause, S., Robin, D., Robin, P., Granner, D. K., Claude, F. 1994. Expression of the phosphoenolpyruvatecarboxykinase gene in 3T3-F442 A adipose cells: Effects of retinoic acid and differentiation. *Biochem J.* 302:943–948.

Archer, Z.A. Findlay, P.A. McMillen, S.R. Rhind, S.M. and Adam, C. L. 2004b. Effects of nutritional status and gonadal steroids on expression of appetite-regulatory genes in the hypothalamic arcuate, nucleus of sheep. *J. Endocrinol.* 182:409–419.

Archer, Z. A., Rayner, D.V., Mercer, J.G. 2004a. Hypothalamic gene expression is altered in underweight but obese juvenile male Sprague-Dawley rats fed a high-energy diet. *J. Nutr.* 134:1369-1374.

Belin, S., Kaya, F., Burtey, S. and Fontes, M. 2010. Ascorbic acid and gene expression: another example of regulation of gene expression by small molecules. *Current Genomics*. 11:52-57.

Bird A. 2007. "Perceptions of epigenetics". Nature. 447 (7143): 396–8. *Bibcode*: *Natur*.447.396B. doi:10.1038/nature05913. PMID 17522671.

Bonjour, J. P. 1981. Biotin dependent enzymes in inborn errors of metabolism in humans. Karger. Basel. *Wld. Rev. Nutr. Diet.* 38:1-88.

Canali, R., Natarelli, L., Leoni, G., Azzini, E., Comitato, R., Sancak, O., Barella, L. and Virgili, F. 2014. Vitamin C supplementation modulates gene expression in peripheral blood mononuclear cells specifically upon an inflammatory stimulus: a pilot study in healthy subjects. 9(3):390. doi: 10.1007/s12263-014-0390-x. Epub 2014 Mar 7.

Chadwick, R. 2004. *Proceedings of the Nutrition Society.* 63:161-166.

Charles, B.M. Hosking, G.; Green, A. Pollit, R. Bartlett, K. Taitz, L.S. 1979. Biotin responsive alopecia and development regression. *Lancet*. 1:118–120.

DiLella, A. G. S. C. Kwok, F. D. Ledley, J. Marvit, and Woo, S. L. 1986. Molecular structure and polymorphic map of the human phenylalanine hydroxylase gene.*Biochemistry.* 25 (4):743-749.

Ferre, T., Riu, E., Bosch, F., Valera, A. 1996. Evidence from transgenic mice that glucokinase is rate limiting for glucose utilization in the liver. *FASEB J.* 10:1213–1218.

Gabriely, I. Yang, X.M. Cases, J.A. Ma, X.H.Rossetti, L.and Barzilai. N. 2001. Hyperglycemia modulates angiotensinogen gene expression. Am. J. Physiol. Regulatory Integrative Comp. *Physiol*. 281: 795–802.

Garg, R., Sharma, N. and Jain, S. 2014. Nutrigenomics and Nutrigenetics: Concepts and Applications in Nutrition Research and Practice. *Acta Medica International*. 124-130.

Ghormade,V., Khare, A. and Baghel, R. 2011. Nutrigenomics and its Applications in Animal Science. *Vet. Research Forum.* 2:147-155.

Hall, R.K. Scott, D.K. Noisin, E.L. Lucas, P.C. and Granner, D.K. 1995. Activation of the phosphoenolpyruvate. *Proc Natl Acad Sci*. 92(2):412-416.

Jeffcoat, R. and James, A.T. 1978. The control of stearoyl-CoA desaturase by dietary linoleic acid. *FEBS Lett.* 85:114–118.

Kaput, J. 2004. Diet-disease gene interactions. *Nutrition*, 20(1):26-31.

Lee, P.D., Conover, C.A., Powell, D.R. 1997. Regulation and function of insulin-like growth factor binding. *Proc Soc Exp Biol Med.* 216(3):319-57.

Loktionov, A. 2003. Common gene polymorphisms and nutrition: emerging links with pathogenesis of multifactorial chronic diseases. *J. Nutr. Biochem.;* 14:426–51.

Mariman, C.M. 2006. Nutrigenomics and nutrigenetics: the revolution in nutritional science. Biotechnol. *Appl. Biochem*. 44:119-128.

Muller, M. and Kersten, S. 2003. Nutrigenomics: Goals and strategies. *Nat. Rev. Genet*. 4: 315-322.

Mutch, D. M., Wahli, W. and Williamson, G. 2005. Nutrigenomics and nutrigenetics: the emerging faces of nutrition. *FASEB J.* 19:1602-1616.

Ordovas, J. M. 2008. Genotype-phenotype associations: modulation by diet and obesity. Obesity (Silver Spring) *16 Suppl*. 3:40-46.

Ordovas, J. M. and Corella, D. 2004. Nutritional genomics. *Annu. Rev. Genomics Hum. Genet.* 5:71–118.

Ordovas, J. M., J. Kaput, and D. Corella. 2007. Nutrition in the genomics era: cardiovascular disease risk and the Mediterranean diet. *Mol. Nutr. Food Res.* 51 (10):1293-1299.

Protein-1. *Proc. Soc. Exp. Biol. Med.* 1993; 204: 4–29.

Sessler, A.M. and Natambi, J.M. 1998. Polyunsaturated Fatty Acid Regulation of Gene Expression. *J. Nutr.* 128:123–926.

Sessler, A.M. Kaur, N.Palta, J.P. and Natambi, J.M. 1996. Regulation of stear-oyl-CoA desaturase 1 mRNA stability by polyunsaturated fatty acids in 3T3-L1 adipocytes. *J. Biol. Chem.* 271: 29854–29858.

Siddique, R. A. Tandon, M. Ambwani, T. Rai, S.N. and Atreja, S. K. 2009. Nutrigenomics: Nutrient-Gene Interactions.. *Food Reviews International* 25:326–345,

Swallow, D. M. 2003. Genetics of lactase persistence and lactose intolerance. *Annu. Rev. Genet.* 37:197-219.

Vallee, B. and Alud, D. 1990. Zinc coordination, function, and structure of zinc enzymes and other proteins. *Biochem.*, 29:5647–5659.

9

Micronutrient Fortification in Milk and Milk Products

Sumit Arora, Apurva Sharma, Shilpa Shree and Chitra Gupta

Abstract

Micronutrient (vitamin and mineral) deficiencies affect more than 2 billion people worldwide and are especially prevalent in developing countries including India. Conditions due to vitamin mineral deficiencies account for 7.3 percent of the global disease burden.Iron deficiency (anemia), vitamin A and iodine deficiency disorders continue to be a grim public health problem. Thus, elimination of vitamin and mineral deficiencies is essential to improve the overall health of the masses as well as to sustain economic growth and national development. Food fortification is an effective intervention to deliver vitamin and mineral rich foods to large populations. In addition to the prevention of vitamin and mineral deficiencies, food fortification is an effective measure to raise vitamin and mineral levels by moving the population towards consuming recommended dietary allowances for most micronutrients-making it a long–term and a sustainable strategy. India is the largest producer of milk in the world with 146.3 million tonnes and the consumption rate of milk and milk products by all age groups of people are high.Therefore, fortification of milk with mineral and vitamins could be a safe and effective strategy to fight these micronutrient deficiencies.

Keywords: Food fortification, Vitamins, Minerals, Micronutrient deficiency

1. Micronutrient Malnutrition

Nutrition and national development are closely related and are interdependent. The consequences of malnutrition and also micronutrient malnutrition setting early in life, reach beyond the individual and the families involved. Society suffers as a whole when children cannot learn; poor health restricts productivity and young malnourished mothers give birth to the next generation of malnourished children. Micronutrients are essential vitamins and minerals required on a daily basis to ensure good health and to enable the body to fight diseases. They are referred to as micronutrients because individual need them in small quantities. Micronutrient malnutrition is a severe and widespread problem that threatens the health and development of India's population. Lack of essential vitamins and minerals compromises the immune system, affects physical and cognitive development and significantly contributes to the global burden of diseases. From a public health view point, malnutrition, including micronutrient malnutrition, also contributes to the diet-related non-communicable degenerative diseases like diabetes mellitus, hypertension, cardiovascular diseases, obesity and concerned contribution to high rates of morbidity and mortality.

Vitamin and mineral deficiencies affect more than 2 billion people worldwide and are especially prevalent in developing countries including India (Ezzati *et al.,*2004). Conditions arising due to vitamin and mineral deficiencies account for 11 percent of the global burden of the disease and vitamin A deficiency ranks among the 15 leading causes of global burden (Black *et al.,*2008). Out of the world population of seven billion, two billion suffer from micronutrient deficiencies (Global nutrition report, 2016). Globally, micronutrient deficiencies of greatest public health significance are those of iron, vitamin A, iodine and vitamin D. Insufficient dietary intake of these essential nutrients result in long lasting effects on physical growth, cognitive development, immune response and productivity. In our country more than half the population across any age group consume less than 50% of their daily needs of iron, zinc, vitamin A, folate and other B-vitamins (NNMB 2012). About one third of the world's population was reported to be deficient in one or more micronutrients. Consumption of fruits, vegetables, meat and eggs which are considered as richest sources of vitamin and minerals is very low among the Indian population. Vitamins and minerals deficiencies often go unnoticed, hence called "hidden hunger" (NSSO2011).

2. The Biological Significance of Key Micronutrients

a. Iron

Iron is an essential micronutrient because it plays a vital role in many metabolic processes including oxygen transport, oxidative metabolism, cellular proliferation and growth (Allen *et al.*, 2006). Iron deficiency has earned distinction as the most common nutritional deficiency in the world today. It affects more than 20% of world's population because iron imparts an important role in the formation of blood (Walter *et al.*, 1998; Navarrete *et al.*, 2002). Anemia is one of the World Health Organization's top 10 target disease for cure and prevention (WHO 2008). Despite all attempts to eradicate or even reduce iron deficiency anemia (IDA), it remains the most prevalent nutritional deficiency disorder in the world affecting around 1 billion people of which nearly 400 million are children (Powell *et al.*, 2014). In developing countries every second pregnant woman and about 40% of preschool children are estimated to be anaemic (Ezzati *et al.*, 2004). The incidence of iron deficiency anaemia (IDA) is high among infants, teenagers and women of child bearing age, in both developing and industrialized countries. Global prevalence of anaemia is 47.4% in preschool aged children, 41.8% in pregnant women and 30.2% in non-pregnant women (Badham *et al.*, 2007). In India, prevalence of anaemia is 79% in children of 6-35 months age, 55% in women of 15-49 years and 24% in men of 15-49 years of age (NNP1993; NFHS 2007).

b. Zinc

It is the second most abundant transition metal in organisms after iron and it is the only metal which appears in all enzyme classes (Broadley *et al.*, 2007). It is involved in numerous aspects of cellular metabolism (Classen *et al.*,2011). Zinc is an ion that is required by 10% of the eukaryotic proteome and plays a vital role in >300 cellular functions including proliferation, apoptosis, cell signaling, and differentiation (Bostanci *et al.*, 2014). Zinc is involved in gene expression, DNA and protein synthesis and development of the immune, reproductive and skeletal systems, and antioxidant processes (Jarosz *et al.*, 2017). It supports normal growth and development during pregnancy, childhood, and adolescence (Maret, 2006). It is also believed to possess antioxidant properties, which may protect against accelerated aging and helps speed up the healing process after an injury; however, studies differ as to its effectiveness (Milbury and Richer, 2008). Zinc ions are effective antimicrobial agents even at low concentrations. Gastroenteritis is strongly attenuated by ingestion of zinc and this effect could be due to direct antimicrobial action of the zinc ions in the gastrointestinal tract, or to the absorption of the zinc and re-release from immune cells (Rink and Gabriel, 2000). In the brain, zinc is stored in specific synaptic vesicles by glutamatergic neurons and can modulate brain excitability (Bitanihirwe and Cunningham, 2009).

c. Calcium

Calcium is a major component of mineralized tissues and is required for normal growth and skeletal development (Kaushik *et al.*, 2015). Calcium alone constitutes about 2 percent of the total body weight and most of this is distributed in bones (National Dairy Council, 1992). The majority of calcium (~99%) is found in the bones and teeth. The remaining 1% is contained in the serum, extravascular fluid, muscles, and other tissues (Committee of Nutrition, 1999). Therefore, obtaining sufficient amounts of calcium helps in increasing bone metabolism and improves overall bone health (Cashman, 2002).

Dietary calcium deficiency has been linked epidemiologically to several chronic diseases including osteoporosis, osteomalacia, hypertension, colon cancer, and obesity (Zemel *et al.,* 2004). Low intake of calcium from foods and other sources is the major cause of deficiency in children and adolescents because of increased demand for minerals during development. Main causes of calcium deficiency are intake of diets low in calcium; inability to absorb and metabolize calcium; or kidney, intestinal and liver diseases. Oxalate and phytate are two common examples of substances that are generally believed to interfere with calcium absorption (Wasserman and Comer, 1959; Lengemann and Allen, 1959). According to National Institute of Health (2000), only about 25% of boys and 10% of girls get enough calcium in their diets. Inadequate intake of calcium, Low consumption of vitamin D, age, kidney disorders, abnormal parathyroid glands, decrease in levels of hormones and anti-nutrients are the conditions which may lead to calcium deficiency.

d. Vitamin A

Vitamin A and its derivatives are essential for biological processes such as vision, immune function, reproduction, maintenance of epithelial tissue, and differentiation. Vitamin A deficiency (VAD) causes different pathological consequences such as night blindness, loss of vision, retardation, shortening and thickening of bones, atrophy of the testes, foetal reabsorption, and immunodeficiency (Doldo *et al.,* 2015). Among micronutrients, vitamin A deficiency is most lethal. The major cause of VAD is inadequate dietary intake of the preformed retinol or precursors of vitamin A. Increased vitamin A requirement in certain physiological or pathological conditions, inadequate absorption or loss of intestinal contents in diarrhea are often contributory factors in establishing VAD. An estimated 250 million preschool children are vitamin A deficient and this deficiency is the leading cause of preventable blindness in children and increases the risk of disease and death from severe infections. An estimated 250000 to 500000 vitamin A deficient children become blind every year, half of them dying within 12 months of losing their sight (Allen *et al.*, 2006).The risks become less in older children, but VAD reduces overall immunity and makes children susceptible to diseases like measles and diarrhea. United Nations Children's Fund (UNICEF) estimated that VAD is a public health concern in 75 countries of Asia and Africa. Horton *et al.* (2008) reported that VAD is a public health concern if the mortality rate of children below five years is greater than 70/1,000. This means that the death of more than 70 children among 1,000 indicates VAD. In 1970, the mortality rate of children under five years in India was 130/1000, thereby making VAD a public health concern was important (Hindu Health, December 8, 2001). In pregnant women, VAD causes night blindness and may increase the risk of maternal mortality (Allen *et al.,*

2006). Clinical symptoms of VAD such as night blindness are seen among women of reproductive age and in pregnant women (Gragnolati *et al.*, 2005). This clearly shows that all age groups are at risk of VAD and there are no specific interventions to cover various population groups, specifically, the children above 5 years, pregnant women and women in post-partum phase.

e. Folic acid

Folates represent an essential nutrition component (important B vitamin) in the human diet, involved in many metabolic pathways, mainly in carbon transfer reactions such as purine and pyrimidine biosynthesis and amino acid interconversions (Kim *et al.*, 2004). Health authorities recommend that all women who plan to become pregnant should take a daily dose of 400 μg folic acid supplementation (FAS) and appropriate dietary folate intake from before conception to the third month of pregnancy to reduce the risk of neural tube defects, while not exceeding the tolerable upper intake level of 1000 μg/day (Navarrete-Muñoz *et al.*, 2015). A low folate intake has also been associated with the risk of cardiovascular diseases due to elevated levels of homocysteine, a risk factor in the coronary heart disease (Morrison *et al.,* 1995) and the incidence of certain forms of cancer (Ames, 1999). Besides, a number of health disorders viz. Alzheimer's and coronary heart diseases; osteoporosis, increased risk of breast and colorectal cancer, poor cognitive performance, hearing loss, neural tube defects etc. have been attributed to the folate deficiency (Le Blanc *et al.*, 2007). The interest in the health implications of taking FAS has increased recently. Regarding pregnancy, several studies have suggested that FAS use may be an important protective factor for some birth outcomes such as placental abruption, spontaneous abortion, stillbirth, preterm delivery, adverse fetal growth and preeclampsia (Mantovani, *et al.*, 2014). Therefore, an exogenous supply of folic acid appears inevitable to prevent nutritional deficiency especially in view of the inability of mammalian cells to synthesize this vital biomolecule (Sarma and Duttagupta, 1995). Mammalian cells cannot synthesize folate; therefore, an exogenous supply of this vitamin is necessary to prevent nutritional deficiency. Although folate is omnipresent in a normal human diet, folate deficiencies still occur frequently, even in well-developed countries (Konings *et al.*, 2001; O'Brien *et al.*, 2001) Secondary folate deficiency (also giving rise to megaloblastic anemia) may be due to vitamin B_{12} deficiency (Fishman *et al.*, 2000). Hence folate deficiency in humans is associated with several health problems, such as anemia, cancer, cardiovascular diseases as well as neural tube defects in newborns.

f. Vitamin D

Vitamin D has long been known to play an important role in bone development by promoting calcium absorption in the gut and bone mineralization (Bilodeau*et al.*, 2011). It has been estimated that 1 billion people worldwide have vitamin D deficiency or insufficiency (Holick and Garabedian, 2006). The chief biological function of vitamin D_3 in the human body is to control the absorption, transport and deposition of calcium and to lesser extent phosphorous (Van den Berge, 1997). Vitamin D_3 has been shown to aid the functioning of the pancreas, foetal development, immunity, muscle contraction and nerve conduction in all the body cells (Kaushik *et al.*, 2014).Vitamin D_3 has been shown to aid the functioning of the pancreas, fetal development, and immunity (Feldman *et al.,* 2005). Without vitamin D, only 10 to 15% of dietary calcium and about 60% of phosphorus is absorbed (Deluca, 2004). The interaction of 1, 25 dihydroxy vitamin D with the vitamin D receptor increases the efficiency of intestinal calcium absorption to 30 to 40 % and phosphorous absorption to approximately 80 % (Holick and Garabedian, 2006). Skeletal muscles have a Vitamin D receptor and many require vitamin D for maximum function (Bischoff-ferrari, 2006). Men and women with 25-hydroxyvitamin D levels above 35ng/ml had a 176 ml increase in the forced expiratory volume in 1 second (Black and Scragg, 2005). Vitamin D deficiency causes inadequate calcium and phosphorus in the blood for proper bone mineralization, resulting in bone weakening and bowing under pressure. When these occur in a child, it is called rickets; in adults and elders, it is called osteomalacia and ospeoporosis. Signs of rickets include enlarged head, joints, and rib cage; a deformed pelvis and bowed legs. Osteomalacia can cause fractures in the hip, spine and other bones (Leboff *et al.*, 1999). There are limited dietary sources of vitamin D, including cod liver oil, fatty fish such as salmon, as well as small amounts found in egg yolks (Kaushik *et al.*, 2013).

3. Strategies for Control of Micronutrient Malnutrition

The control of micronutrient deficiencies is an essential part of the overall effort to fight hunger and malnutrition. Pharmaceutical supplementation involves the administration of supplements to individuals diagnosed with a certain micronutrient deficiency. However, it fails owing to poor compliance, poor coverage, absence of commitment at the national and community levels and poorly designed communications (Gibson *et al.,*1998). The International Conference on Nutrition (ICN) held in Rome (1992) emphasized the importance of food based activities in their plan of action geared at addressing the issue of micronutrient malnutrition (FAO/WHO 1992).

Micronutrient deficiencies can be prevented and even eliminated if optimal quantities of the micronutrients are consumed by populations on a regular basis.

The 11th five year plan (2007-2012), report of the working group on integrating nutrition with health and the draft of National Health Research Policy (NHRP 2010) identified micronutrient malnutrition as a major concern. Countries may lose two to three percent of their Gross Domestic Product (GDP) as a result of iron, iodine, and zinc deficiencies (http://www.gainhealth.org/knowledge-centre/fast-facts-malnutrition/, 2016). In India, loss due to micronutrient deficiencies costs 1% of its GDP which is ultimately a loss of Rs. 27,720 crores per annum in terms of productivity, illness, increased health care costs and death (Kotecha, 2008). "Providing micronutrients" has been recognized as having the best cost/benefit ratio to achieve a major impact in the developing world as stated by more than fifty economists in the Copenhagen Consensus (Hoddinott *et al.,*2012). Food fortification, the addition of specific nutrients to food or water, has been shown to be an effective strategy to combat micronutrient malnutrition (Cook and Reusser, 1983; Stekel *et al.,*1988).

Policy and programme responses include food-based strategies that can be used to improve micronutrient malnutrition management:

a) Supplementation with pharmaceuticals dispensed in adequate forms

b) Fortification of food or water with nutrients

c) Consumer education and dietary change through the expansion of the demand for, and supply of, nutrient rich food. (Salgueiro *et al.,* 2007)

3.1 Food Fortification

Food fortification is the public health policy of adding micronutrients (essential trace elements and vitamins) to foodstuffs to ensure that minimum dietary requirements are met. The Codex *General Principles for the Addition of Essential Nutrients to Foods* (Codex1987) defines "fortification" as "the addition of one or more essential nutrients to a food whether or not it is normally contained in the food, for the purpose of preventing or correcting a demonstrated deficiency of one or more nutrients in the population or specific population groups". Fortification refers to addition of vitamins and minerals to commonly consumed foods in order to prevent nutritional deficiencies. Minute quantities of missing nutrients in the daily diet such as vitamin A, iron and iodine are added to commonly consumed foods e.g. milk, wheat flour, rice and oil to enhance the nutrient quantity of food (FSSAI 2016). Food fortification differs from other programmes as it involves the addition of nutrients to foods in respect to its nutritional intervention with a specifically defined target and fortified food products are expected to become a main source of the specifically added nutrient. Consequently, food fortification is expected to help in preventing nutritional inadequacy in targeted populations in which a risk of nutrient deficiency has been identified. A realistic level of fortification is to provide the equivalent of 20-40% of the daily requirements of target nutrient through a single food item (Huma *et al,* 2007).

The public health benefits of fortification may either be demonstrable, or indicated as potential or plausible by generally accepted scientific research. This may include:

- Prevention or minimisation of the risk of occurrence of micronutrient deficiency in a population or specific population groups.
- Contribution to the correction of a demonstrated micronutrient deficiency in a population or specific population groups.
- Potential for improvement in nutritional status and dietary intakes that may be, or may become, suboptimal as a result of changes in dietary habits or lifestyles.
- Plausible beneficial effects of micronutrients consistent with maintaining or improving health (e.g. there is some evidence to suggest that a diet rich in selected antioxidants might help to prevent cancer and other diseases). (Allen *et al.,* 2006)
- Fortification technology is simple to use and easy to implement
- Cost of fortification is minimal
- Nutrients regularly used in staple food fortification prevent diseases, strengthen the immune system and improve productivity and cognitive development. (FSSAI 2016)

3.1.1 Types of food fortification

Food fortification can take several forms. It is possible to fortify foods that are widely consumed by the general population (mass fortification); foods designed for specific population subgroups, such as complementary foods for young children or rations for displaced populations (targeted fortification); allow food manufacturers to voluntarily fortify foods available in the market place (market-driven fortification); fortify foods at household level (household fortification) and/or fortification of the staple foods by breeding and genetic modification of the plants (bio fortification). Mass fortification is nearly always mandatory, while targeted fortification can be either mandatory or voluntary depending on the public health significance of the problem it is seeking to address. Market-driven fortification is always voluntary. However, it is governed by regulatory limits (Allen *et al.,* 2006). Household and bio fortification are also gaining importance (Nestel, 2003).

a. Mass fortification

Mass fortification is the term used to describe the addition of one or more micronutrients to foods commonly consumed by the general public, such as cereals, condiments and milk. It is usually instigated, mandated and regulated by the government sector. Mass fortification is generally the best option when the majority of the population has an unacceptable risk, in terms of public health, of being or becoming deficient in specific micronutrients. Mass food fortification is being promoted as the nutritional intervention to prevent the physiological and clinical consequences associated with micronutrient deficiencies and has the most favourable cost to benefit ratio (Allen *et al.,* 2006). Although this statement may be true in many cases, it depends on the existence of several pre conditions. These include:

- Accessibility of the food fortification vchicle by the target population.
- Adequate manufacturing and industrial settings which ensure cost effective production and supervision.
- Compatibility of fortificants (the source of micronutrients) with the nature and use of the food vehicle.
- Affordability of additional costs resulting from the fortification process for consumers and manufacturers.
- Confirmation of the quality of the product at the production site.
- Reliable enforcement actions by government authorities to assure compliance of standards and regulations.
- Legitimate and justifiable food labeling
- Nutrition and health claims that promote healthy practices.

b. Targeted fortification

In targeted food fortification programmes, foods aimed at specific subgroups of the population are fortified, thereby increasing the intake of that particular group rather than that of the population as a whole. Examples include complementary foods for infants and young children, foods developed for school feeding programmes, special biscuits for children and pregnant women and rations (blended foods) for emergency feeding and displaced persons. In some cases, such foods may be required to provide a substantial proportion of daily micronutrient requirements of the target group (Allen *et al.,*2006).

c. Market-driven fortification

The term "market-driven fortification" is applied to situations whereby a food manufacturer takes a business-oriented initiative to add specific amounts of one or more micronutrients to processed foods. Although voluntary, this type of food fortification usually takes place within government-set regulatory limits (Allen *et al.,* 2006).

d. Household fortification

Efforts are underway in a number of countries to developand test practical ways of adding micronutrients to foods at the household level, in particular, to complementary foods for young children. In effect, this approach is a combination of supplementation and fortification, and has also been referred to as "complementary food supplementation" (Nestel, 2003).

e. Bio fortification of staple foods

It involves the breeding and genetic modification ofplants so as to improve their nutrient content and absorption. Certain cereals (maize, millet and sorghum) and legumes (lentils, chickpeas, peas and soybeans) are known for their high iron content, various varieties of carrot and sweet potatoes for their favourable â-carotene levels, and maize for their low phytate content, these can be used as vehicles for fortification (Beyer, 2002; Lucca *et al.,* 2002).

4. Milk as a Vehicle for Micronutrient Fortification

India is the largest producer of milk with 146.3 million tonnes of production and per capita availability of 322g/ day (NDDB 2016). Fortification of processed milk has potential for high coverage in India. Milk in its natural form is almost unique as a balanced source of man's dietary needs. Milk and milk products provide a convenient and useful vehicle for fortification with micronutrients and has following benefits:

- Since milk is centrally processed, hence quality control can be effectively implemented
- Milk and milk products are widely consumed regularly in predictable amounts by people of all age groups
- Cost is affordable by target population
- Stability and bioavailability of the added micronutrients in milk remains high (Nair *et al.,* 2003)

5. History and Successful Interventions

Fortification of milk with vitamins commenced in early nineties. USA, UK, Malaysia, Thailand and Mexico initiated fortification of milk with vitamin A in 1923, 1923, 1985, 1993 and 2002, respectively (FSSAI 2016). Vitamin D fortification of milk in the UK is reported to have started in 1923. Several countries have established mandatory fortification of milk, since early in this century (Argentina, Brazil, Malaysia, Mexico, USA etc.). Additionally, several other countries add micronutrients to milk voluntarily, particularly low-fat or fat-free liquid and dried milks (Raunhardt and Bowley, 1996). Dried milk and flavoured milk powders are often fortified with vitamin A, vitamin D, calcium and iron. Milk-based infant formula and weaning foods are fortified with a range of vitamins, minerals and other nutrients such as polyunsaturated fatty acids. In 2005, US regulation (Pasteurized Milk Ordinance) stipulated vitamin A fortification in all reduced fat milk products. During 1980s, the Department of Food, Government of India introduced a scheme of fortifying milk with vitamin A at 2000IU/L for toned/double toned milk to prevent nutrition blindness. The government reimbursed the cost of vitamin A premix to the dairies for fortifying milk for three years, after which dairies were asked to reabsorb the cost. In 1988-89, total quantity of milk fortified with vitamin A was 3.2 million litres per day (NNP 1993). Today, Mother Dairy continues to fortify vitamin A and D in its 9 lakh litres of bulk vended milk per day. Rajasthan Cooperative Dairy Federation started fortifying milk in the year 2013 with vitamin A and D and has demonstrated a successful model of providing these essential vitamins to millions of people in Rajasthan.

Recently, Food Safety and Standards Authority of India (FSSAI) has formulated a comprehensive regulation on fortification of foods namely "Food Safety and Standards (Fortification of Foods) Regulations (FSSR), 2016". These regulations have set the standards for food fortification and encourage the production, manufacture, distribution, sale and consumption of fortified foods. The regulations also provide for specific role of FSSAI in promotion of food fortification and to make fortification mandatory. Five categories of food are covered under this regulation i.e. wheat flour, rice, milk, oil and salt. FSSAI approved the fortification of wheat flour and rice with iron, folic acid, vitamin B_{12}, zinc, vitamin A, thiamin, riboflavin, niacin and pyridoxine, fortification of milk and oil with vitamin A and D and fortification of salt with iodine or double fortified with iron and iodine. Vitamin A fortified in milk, vegetable oil, *atta* and *maida* should be in the form of retinylpalmitate, retinyl acetate and retinyl propionate. In rice, vitamin A has to be fortified as retinylpalmitate (FSSR 2016).

6. Technology of Liquid Milk Fortification

The technology of milk fortification is relatively simple and no additional equipments are needed or can be practiced with minor modifications in the existing plant. Vitamins that can be added to milk are available in dry powder form. The fat soluble vitamins are also available in an oily form. Mineral/vitamin fortification can be practiced at several stages in the production. However, liquid milk is usually fortified prior to pasteurisation or ultra-high temperature treatment. Homogenisation is especially crucial for oily preparations of vitamins. A model flow chart of liquid milk fortification (O'Brien and Robertson 1993) is presented in figure 1.

Aliquot of cold milk
↓
Oily vitamins premix
↓
Homogenisation
↓
Bulk milk (with any added dry vitamins/minerals)
↓
Mix by stirring
↓
Bulk agitation (minimal aeration)
↓
Pasteurisation
↓
Homogenisation
↓
UHT treatment
↓
Cooling
↓
Packaging

Fig. 1: Process flow chart of liquid milk fortification

7. Fortification of Milk and Milk Products with Minerals and Vitamins

7.1 Mineral Fortification

Selection of an appropriate mineral fortificant (iron, calcium etc) is based on its organoleptic considerations, bioavailability, cost and safety. The colour of iron compounds is often a critical factor during fortifying milk and milk products. The use of more soluble iron compounds often leads to the development of off-colours and off-flavours due to reactions with other components of the food material. Infant cereals have been found to turn grey or green on addition of ferrous sulphate. Off-flavours can be the result of lipid oxidation catalysed by iron. The iron compounds themselves may contribute to a metallic flavour. Some of these undesirable interactions with the food matrix can be avoided by coating the fortificant with hydrogenated oils or ethyl cellulose (Jackson and Lee, 1991). Bioavailability of iron compounds is normally stated relative to a ferrous sulphate standard. The highly water soluble iron compounds have superior bioavailability (Richardson, 1990). Bioavailability of the insoluble or very poorly soluble iron compounds can be improved by reducing particle size. Unfortunately this is accompanied by increased reactivity in deteriorative processes. The problem of low bioavailability of some of the less reactive forms of iron is often circumvented by the use of absorption enhancers like, ascorbic acid, sodium acid sulphate and orthophosphoric acid, added along with the fortificant.

a) ***Iron fortification*:** Iron fortification of infant formula has been associated with a fall in the prevalence of anaemia in children aged less than 5 years in the United States (Fomon, 2001). Encapsulated iron and Vitamin C in cheese led to a product of comparable quality with control unfortified cheese, a recovery of 72% and 94% of iron and Vitamin C was obtained on using polyglycerol monostearate as coating material (Kwak *et al.*, 2003). Iron and zinc fortified buffalo milk yoghurt was prepared. The results of this study showed that no effect on components of milk but zinc salts caused increase in acidity as compared to iron salts (El-Behairy and Mohamed, 2010). Iron fortification using ferrous sulphate and whey protein chelated iron had a significant effect on physico-chemical and sensory attributes on Gouda cheese but during maturity, the metallic flavour of the cheese was masked by lipolytic, glycolytic and proteolytic products thereby leading to an acceptable iron fortified Gouda cheese (Indumathi *et al.*, 2013). Milk fortified with soluble ferric pyrophosphate (FPP) (25 mg/L iron) and vitamin A (2500 IU) showed comparable sensory and physico-chemical attributes with unfortified control samples. The bioaccessibility of fortified milk was found to be slightly higher than that of milk fortified with iron alone (Sachdeva *et al.*, 2015). A study showed that the iron microcapsules prepared with blend of gum Arabic, maltodextrin and modified starch could be used for the milk fortification purpose with better sensory and storage stability (Chitra *et al.*, 2015).

b) ***Zinc fortification*:**Among the first row transition metals, zinc is second only to iron in terms of abundance and importance in biological systems. Abd-Rabou *et al.* (2010) studied the effect of fortification of cheese curd with zinc on the properties of the Edam cheese. Both fresh and stored (2 to 12 weeks at 5±1°C) Edam cheese was fortified by different sources of dietary zinc such as zinc acetate, zinc chloride and zinc sulphate at a level of 150 mg zinc / kg cheese curd. They found that Edam cheese fortified with zinc was higher in acidity, acid value and protein fractions during storage period than control. Whereas, cheese fortified with zinc acetate recorded the highest organoleptical scores, which were more pronounced and preferable compared to control and other treatments. Zinc-fortified cheddar cheese containing 228 mg of zinc/kg of cheese was manufactured from milk that had 16 mg/kg food grade zinc sulphate added. Cheese were aged for 2 months, culture activity during cheese making and ripening and compositional, chemical, texture and sensory characteristics were compared with control cheese with no zinc sulfate added to the cheese milk. Fortification of 16mg/kg zinc sulphate in cheese milk was a suitable approach to fortify cheddar cheese without changing the quality of cheddar cheese (Kahraman and Ustunol, 2012). Lactose-zinc complex fortified milk containing 30 mg of zinc/ L of milk was evaluated for sensory and physico-chemical properties and it was reported that the fortified milk did not affect the sensory and physicochemical properties of milk during storage. Milk fortified with lactose-zinc complex showed higher bioavailability of zinc than milk fortified with zinc salt (Sharma *et al*., 2015).

c) ***Calcium fortification***:Calcium fortified food products or milk is a convenient option to increase dietary calcium intake (Kruger *et al.,* 2003). Calcium in milk is easily absorbed by the intestine and is considered to have a higher bioavailability than calcium in vegetables or cereals. Two factors in milk i.e. lactose and casein have been suggested to be responsible for promoting calcium absorption and leading to an apparent higher bioavailability (Miller and Berner, 1989). Fortification of buffalo milk with calcium at the rate of 50mg/100ml using three calcium salts (gluconate, lactate and chloride) resulted in decrease of pH, which was restored to its original value with the addition of disodium phosphate. Out of 3 salts, Calcium gluconate fortified milk had highest heat stability and bioavailability (Arora *et al.,* 2005). Milk was fortified with four different calcium salts – calcium chloride, calcium acetate, calcium hydroxide, and calcium citrate. Upon the addition of calcium salts, there was a marked change in milk pH and acidity except when calcium citrate was added. The heat stability of calcium citrate fortified milk was higher in comparison to the control milk and other calcium fortified milks (Kaushik *et al*., 2014).

7.2 Vitamins

The fat soluble vitamins which include vitamin A, D, E and K, however, exist either as oil or as crystals, which may cause processing difficulties during the production of certain type of dairy products. One of the problem encountered with the vitamins, is their limited stability in presence of heat, humidity and oxygen. Among the water soluble vitamins, vitamin C, folic acid, vitamin B_6 and vitamin B_{12} are the less stable. However, in the case of fat soluble vitamins vitamin A, D and E are least stable (Mortensen and Gotfredson, 1996).

In order to improve the stability of these vitamins, a number of different coating technologies have been developed. One of the most important methods to protect the fat soluble vitamins is microencapsulation, which results in a highly sophisticated powder, where the vitamin is kept protected from degradation by the coating material used for the encapsulation. During microencapsulation, the fat soluble vitamins are brought from the form of oil or a crystal – which in some processes would be difficult to handle – to the form of a free flowing powder much easier to handle and mix with other dry ingredients. When two or more vitamins are added to a food product at the same manufacturing stage, this is commonly done in the form of premix or as blend. Premix is a homogenous mixture of desired vitamins in a dry powder form, whereas a blend is the same for the fat soluble vitamins, but in an oily form. A premix can consist of both water soluble and fat soluble vitamins and carotenoids, in which case the fat soluble vitamins have to be microencapsulated.

a) ***Vitamin D fortification***: Feasibility of vitamin D fortification (250IU per 240ml serving) in HTST milk (2% fat) was studied and reported that vitamin D fortification of HTST milk (2% fat) was feasible and stable (upto 21 days) and had no impact on sensory characteristics of product (Hanson and Metzger, 1984). Stability of vitamin D in fortified skim milk during storage and effect of different packaging materials, HTST and UHT on shelf life of product was determined and found that vitamin D_3 was relatively stable in all milks during 4 weeks of shelf life (Liu, 2003). Kazmi *et al.* (2007) studied fortification and quantification of vitamin D_3 in cheese, yoghurt and ice cream and concluded that vitamin D_3 was stable in these products. Stability of vitamin D_2 in milk was examined in vitamin D_2 fortified milk during different heat treatments like pasteurization, boiling and sterilization. Fortified milk was stored for seven days in both glass and plastic bottles under refrigerated temperature, non-significant loss of vitamin D_2 was observed, whereas, on storage in polyethylene pouches significant loss was reported, as vitamin D_2 decreased from 596.66 to 548.04 IU (Kaushik *et al.*, 2013).

b) ***Vitamin A fortification***: Maguer and Jackson (1983) examined the stability of vitamin A in fortified fluid milks and reported less destruction of vitamin A by pasteurisation or direct ultra-high temperature treatment. The vitamin remained relatively stable up until and beyond the coded pull dates of the pasteurised (12 days) and ultra-high temperature processed (3 months) milk samples stored at 4 and 20°C, respectively. Storage of 2% ultra-high temperature processed milk at 35°C adversely affected its vitamin stability, notably after 12 weeks of storage. Cartons of the 2% ultra-high temperature processed white and chocolate milks that had been stored either at 20 or 35°C for varying periods, once opened, may be kept for 12 days at 4°C without appreciable decline in vitamin A content. The effect of microwave heating for 2-4 minutes on retinol content of milk was studied and found that in whole milk, retinol content was not modified after microwave heating for 2-4 minutes, in low fat milk, microwave heating for 2 minutes lowered retinol content (91.7% retention) and in skim milk, retinol was not detected before or after microwave heating (Medrano *et al.*, 1994). Effect of package light transmittance on the vitamin content of fortified UHT low-fat milk was evaluated. Milk was stored under light with an intensity of 700 lux in polyethylene terephthalate (PET) bottles with varying light transmittance to monitor the changes in the vitamin A content over a storage period of 12 weeks at 23°C. In clear PET bottles, a reduction of 93% of the initial content was observed. In all pigmented PET bottles, the vitamin retention was only slightly higher; the losses ranged between 70 and 90% for vitamin A. In the control sample stored in dark, a 16% loss could be observed for vitamin A (Saffert *et al.*, 2008). Bioavailability of iron in milk fortified with ferric pyrophosphate (FPP) soluble and vitamin A acetate was evaluated by Sachdeva *et al.* (2015). The results of in vivo study showed that feeding of rats with lyophilates of milk fortified with FPP soluble and FPP soluble + vitamin A acetate had a significant effect on the balance indices of the iron as well as on the haematological parameters and iron liver status. Results suggested that Vitamin A plays a significant role in enhancement of iron absorption and utilization in body.

c) ***Folic acid fortification***: Folic acid and 5-methyltetrahydrofolate bioaccessibility in fortified milk was studied by dynamic *in vitro* gastrointestinal model. It was reported that milk was a suitable carrier for folate, because both folic acid and 5-CH(3)-H(4) folate were easily released from the matrix and available for absorption (Verwei, *et al.*, 2003). Effect of different concentration and stage of addition of folic acid on the physico-chemical and sensory characteristics of strawberry yogurt was studied and no difference was observed in sensory analysis and physico-chemical properties of product after fortification (Boenka and Aryana, 2007).

8. Considerations During Fortification of Micronutrient into Milk & Milk Products

- *Bioavailability of commercial preparations:* Bioavailability of different compounds facilitates the selection of the optimal compound.
- *Nutrient–nutrient reaction:* Interaction among the nutrients and other food components is a key factor in nutrient addition. For example, vitamin C will improve the absorption of iron (Kiran *et al*, 1977). On the other hand, the iron will accelerate vitamin degradation. Fortification of calcium in milk may interfere with absorption of iron or zinc (Weaver, 1998).
- *Nutrient-matrix reaction:* The added nutrient must not react with any component of the milk. For example, iron is a pro-oxidant and can accelerate the development of fat rancidity, destroy some of the vitamins and form coloured products.
- *Shelf-life and packaging:* Many of the fortified milk and milk products may have limited shelf life and thus may need different types of packaging which can be either oxygen impermeable or opaque to light. This is particularly true for the fortification of liquid milk with vitamin A as vitamin A fortified milk develops off flavour within 6 h when exposed to light, compared to 12 h for control (Fellman *et al.*, 1991). All the fortified products require proper labelling on the pack.
- *Process considerations:* The stability of vitamins is well known during various processing conditions and the same knowledge can be applied while processing the vitamin fortified milk.
- *Cost factor:* Cost may not be a crucial factor in the manufacture and marketing of fortified milk and milk products.
- *Safety factor:* There should be sufficient insurance against excessive intake of the fortificant. Unlike water soluble vitamins, fat soluble vitamins exhibited toxicity at higher concentrations.

9. Conclusion

Fortification has many benefits for the health of populations around the world. It is one of the best strategies for reducing the prevalence of micronutrient malnutrition in both developed and developing countries around the world. It poses no risk for the normal individual as food consumption is self-limiting and the micronutrient absorption falls, as their stores increase. This prevents excessive micronutrient accumulation. Food fortification is an attractive option for reducing the health care costs related to nutritional disorders. There are many vehicles for the fortification of micronutrients but it must be carried out in such a way that the bioavailability of the micronutrients is the maximum. The food product in which the fortification is done is also of utmost importance e.g. wheat flour is suitable for iron fortification while full cream milk for vitamin D due to the complex nature of the two foods. Milk is also considered as a very good fortification vehicle owing to the fact that it is centrally processed, widely distributed and regularly consumed by all sections of the society in predictable amounts and bioavailability of the added nutrients remains high. It is time to fast track our progress and move in a direction where fortified food is available and easily accessible to all.

References

Abd-Rabou, N., Zaghloul, A. N., Seleet, F. L. and El–Hofi, M. A., 2010. Properties of Edam cheese fortified by dietary zinc salts, *Journal of American Science*, 6(10):441-446.

Allen, L., Benoist, B. D., Dary, O. and Hurrell, R., 2006. Guidelines on food fortification with micronutrients. World Health Organization and Food and Agriculture Organization of the United Nations (WHO/FAO).

Ames, B.N., 1999. Micronutrient deficiencies cause DNA damage and cancer. *Food Science and Agricultural Chemistry*, 1, pp.1–15.

Arora, S., Ranjan, P., Sharma, G. S., Sindhu, J. S., Singh, G., Singh, A.K. and Kansal, V. K., 2005. Effect of calcium fortification on heat stability and physico-chemical properties of mixed (cow and buffalo 1:1) milk. *Indian Journal of Dairy Science*, 58(4):242-246.

Badham, J., Zimmermann, M. B. and Kraemer, K., 2007. The Guidebook: Nutritional Anaemia. Sight and Life Press, Basel, Switzerland.

Beyer, P., 2002. Golden Rice: Introducing the beta-carotene biosynthesis pathway into rice endosperm by genetic engineering to defeat vitamin A deficiency. *Journal of Nutrition*, 132:506S–510S.

Bilodeau, L., Dufresne, G., Deeks, J., Clement, G., Bertrand, J., Turcotte, S., Robichaud, A., Beraldin, F. and Fouquet, A., 2011. Determination of vitamin D_3 and 25-hydroxyvitamin D_3 in foodstuffs by HPLC UV-DAD and LC–MS/MS. *Journal of Food Composition and Analysis*, 24:441-448.

Bischoff-Ferrari, H.A., Giovannucci, E., Willett, W.C., Dietrich, T. and Dowson-Hughes, B., 2006. Estimation of optical serum concentrations of 25-hydroxyvitamin D for multiple health outcomes. *The American Journal of Clinical Nutrition*, 84:18-28.

Bitanihirwe, B.K. and Cunningham, M.G., 2009. Zinc: The brain's dark horse. *Synapse,* 63: 1029-1049.

Black, P. N. and Scragg, R., 2005. Relationship between serum 25-hydroxyvitamin D and pulmonary function in the Third National Health and Nutrition Examination Survey. *Chest*, 128:3792-3798.

Black, R. E., Allen, L. H., Bhutta, Z. A., Caulfield, L. E., De Onis, M., Ezzati, M., Mathers, C. and Rivera, J., 2008. Maternal and child undernutrition: global and regional exposures and health consequences. *The lancet*, 371(9608):243-260.

Boeneke, C.A. and Aryana K. J., 2007. Effect of folic acid fortification on the characteristics of strawberry yoghurt. *Journal of Food Technology*, 5(4):271-278.

Bostanci, Z., Mack, R. P. J., Lee, S., Soybel, D. I. and Kelleher, S. L., 2014. Paradoxical zinc toxicity and oxidative stress in the mammary gland during marginal dietary zinc deficiency. *Reproductive Toxicology,* 54:*84-92.*

Broadley, M., White, P.J., Hammond, J.P., Zelko, I. and Lux, A., 2007. Zinc in plants. *New Phytologist*, 173:677-702.

Cashman, K. D., 2002. Calcium intake, calcium bioavailability and bone health. *British Journal of Nutrition,* 87(2):169S–177S.

Classen, H. G., Grober, U., Low, D., Schmidt, J. and Stracke, H., 2011. Zinc deficiency: Symptoms,causes, diagnosis and therapy. *Medizinische Monatsschriftfur Pharmazeuten,* 34, pp.87-95.

Codex Alimentarius Commission 1987. Codex Standard Follow-up Formula CODEX STAN 156-1987 (amended 1989). Joint FAO/WHO Food Standards Programme.

Committee of Nutrition 1999. Calcium requirements of infants, children and adolescents. *Pediatrics,* 104:1152-1157.

Cook, J. D. and Reusser, M. E., 1983. Iron fortification: an update. *American Journal of Clinical Nutrition*, 38 (4):648-659.

DeLuca, H. F., 2004. Overview of general physiologic features and functions of vitamin D. *American Journal of Clinical Nutrition*, 80:1689S-1696S.

Doldo, E., Costanza, G., Agostinelli, S., Tarquini, C., Ferlosio, A., Arcuri, G., Passeri, D., Scioli, G. M. and Orlandi, A., 2015. Vitamin A-Cancer treatment and prevention: The New Role of Cellular Retinol Binding Proteins. Hindawi Publishing Corporation, BioMedical Research International.

El-Behairy, S. A. and Mohamed, E. A., 2010. Properties of yoghurt made from fortified buffalo's milk with iron and zinc salts. *World Journal of Dairy and Food Sciences,* 5(2):207-213.

Ezzati, M., Lopez, A. D., Rodgers, A. and Murray, C. J., 2004. Comparative quantification of health risks: The global and regional burden of disease attributable to selected major risk factors. World Health organization. Geneva, Switzerland.

FAO/WHO 1992. International Conference on Nutrition World Declaration and Plan of Action for Nutrition.

Feldman, D., Zhao, X. Y. and Krishnan, A.V., 2000. Editorial/mini-review: Vitamin D and prostate cancer. *Endocrinology,* 141:5–9.

Fellman, R. L., Dimick, P. S. and Hollender, R., 1991. Photooxidative stability of vitamin A fortified 2% low fat milk and skim milk. *Journal of Food Protection*, 54:113-116.

Fishman, S. M., Christian, P. and West, K. P., 2000. The role of vitamins in the prevention and control of anemia. *Public Health Nutrition*, 3:125–150.

Fomon, J.S., 2001. Infant Feeding in the 20th Century: Formula and Beikost. *Journal of Nutrition,* 131(2):409-420.

FSSAI 2016. Journey of food fortification. Fighting malnutrition improving lives. Food Safety and Standards Authority of India. New Delhi, India.

FSSR 2016. Food Safety and Standards (Fortification of Foods) Regulations.Food Safety and Standards Authority of India. Ministry of Health and Family Welfare, Government of India, New Delhi, India.

Gibson, R. S., Ferguson, E. L. and Lehrfeld, J., 1998. Complementary foods for infant feeding in developing countries: their nutrient adequacy and improvement. *European Journal of Clinical Nutrition,* 52(10):764-770.

Global Nutrition Report 2016. http://www.globalnutritionreport.org, accessed on 23rd September 2016.

Gragnolati, M., Shekar, M., Das Gupta, M., Bredenkamp, C. and Lee, Y. K., 2005. India's undernourished children. A call for reform and action, World Bank Report.

Gupta, C., Chawla, P., Arora, S., Tomar, S. K. and Singh, A. K., 2015. Iron microencapsulation with blend of gum arabic, maltodextrin and modified starch using modified solvent evaporation method-Milk fortification. *Food Hydrocolloids*, 43:622-628.

Hanson, A. and Metzger, L. E., 1984. Vitamin D fortification and stability in dairy products. Midwest Dairy Foods Research Center Department of Food Science and Nutrition University of Minnesota, St. Paul, MN.

Hindu Health, December 8, 2001.

Hoddinott, J., Rosegrant, M. and Torero, M., 2012. 'Challenge Paper: Hunger and Malnutrition' Copenhagen consensus center.

Holick, M.F. and Garabedian, M., 2006. Vitamin D: photobiology, metabolism, mechanism of action, and clinical applications. *American Society for Bone and Mineral Research*, pp.129-137.

Horton, S., Begin, F., Greig, A. and Lakshman, A., 2008. Micronutrient supplements for child survival (vitamin A and zinc). *Copenhagen consensus center*.

Huma, N., Rehman, S.U., Anjum, F. M., Murtaza, M. A. and Sheikh, M. A., 2007. Food fortification strategy-preventing iron deficiency anemia: a review. *Critical Reviews in Food Science and Nutrition*, 47 (3):259-265.

Indumathi, K. P., Kaushik, R., Arora, S. and Wadhwa, B. K., 2013. Evaluation of iron fortified Gouda cheese for sensory and physicochemical attributes. *Journal of Food Science and Technology*, 52, pp.493-499.

Jackson, L. and Lee, K., 1991. Microencapsulated iron for food fortification. *Journal of Food Science,* 56:1047-1050.

Jarosz, L., Agnieszka, M., Gradzki, Z., Kwiecien, M and Kalinowski, M., 2017. The effect of feed supplementation with zinc chelate and zinc supplementation with zinc sulphate on selected humoral and cell mediated immune parameter & cytokine concentration in broiler chickens. *Research in Veterinary Science*, 112: 59-65.

Kahraman, O. and Ustunol, Z., 2012. Effect of Zinc fortification on cheddar cheese quality, *Journal of Dairy Science*, 95(6):2840-2847.

Kaushik, R., Sachdeva, B. and Arora, S., 2013. Vitamin D2 stability in milk during processing, packaging and storage. *LWT - Food Science and Technology*:1-6.

Kaushik, R., Sachdeva, B. and Arora, S., 2015. Heat stability and thermal properties of calcium fortified milk. *CyTA - Journal of Food*, 13:305-311.

Kaushik, R., Sachdeva, B., Arora, S., Kapila, S. and Wadhwa, B. K., 2014. Bioavailability of vitamin D_2 and calcium from fortified milk. *Food Chemistry*, 147:307-311.

Kazmi, S. A., Vieth, R. and Rousseau, D., 2007. Vitamin D fortification and quantification in processed dairy products. *International Dairy Journal*, 17(7):753-759.

Kim, Y.I., 2004. Will mandatory folic acid fortification prevent or promote cancer. *American Journal of Clinical Nutrition,* 80(5):1123–1128.

Kiran, R., Amma. M.K.P. and Sareen, K.N., 1977. Milk fortification with a system containing both iron and ascorbic acid. *The Indian Journal of Nutrition and Dietetics*.14:260-266.

Konings, E.J.M., Roomans, H.H., Dorant, E., Goldbohm, R. A., Saris, W. H. and Van Den Brandt, P. A., 2001. Folate intake of the Dutch population according to newly established liquid chromatography data for foods. *American Journal of Clinical Nutrition*, 73:765–776.

Kotecha, P. V., 2008. Micronutrient malnutrition in India: Let us say "no" to it now. *Indian Journal of Community Medicine*, 33(1):9-10.

Kruger, M.C., Brown, K.E., Collett, G., Layton, L. and Schollum, L.M., 2003. The Effect of fructooligosaccharides with various degrees of polymerization on calcium bioavailability in the growing rat. *Experimental Biological Medicine*, 228(6), pp.683-688.

Kwak, H.S., Yang, K. M. and Ahn, S., 2003. Microencapsulated iron for milk fortification. *Journal of Food Chemistry*, 51 (26):7770-7774.

LeBlanc, J.G., Giori, G.S.D., Smid, E. J., Hugenholtz, J. and Sesma, F., 2007. Folate production by lactic acid bacteria and other food-grade microorganisms. *Communicating Current Research and Education Topics: Trends Applied in Microbiology*, 1:329–339.

Leboff, M. S., Kohlmeier, L. and Hurwitz, S., 1999. Occult vitamin D deficiency in postmenopausal US women with acute hip fracture. *Journal of American Medical Association*, 281: 1505–1511.

Lengemann, F. W. and Allen, N. N., 1959. Development of rumen function in the dairy calf. II. Effect of diet upon characteristics of the rumen flora and fauna of young calves. *Journal of Dairy Science*, 42(7):1171-1181.

Liu, Y., 2003. Beta lactoglobulin complexed vitamin A and vitamin D in skim milk: Shelf life and bioavailability. Ph.D Thesis, North Carolina State University, Raleigh, N. C.

Lucca, P., Hurrell, R. and Potrykus, I., 2002. Fighting iron deficiency anemia with iron-rich rice. *Journal of the American College of Nutrition*, 21 (3):184S–190S.

Maguer, I. L. and Jackson, H., 1983. Stability of vitamin A in pasteurized and ultra-high temperature processed milks. *Journal of Dairy Science*, 66 (12):2452-2458.

Mantovani, E., Filippini, F., Bortolus, R. and Franchi, M., 2014. Folic acid supplementation and preterm birth: results from observational studies. *Biomedical Research International*, 481914, doi:10.1155/2014/481914.

Maret, W. and Sandstead, H. H., 2006. Zinc requirements and the risks and benefits of zinc supplementation. *Journal of Trace Elements in Medicine and Biology*, 20:3-18.

Medrano, A., Hernandez, A., Prodanov, M. and Vidal-Valverde, C., 1994. Riboflavin, tocopherol and retinol retention in milk after microwave heating. *Lait*, 74 (2):153-159.

Michael, F. H., Neil C. B., Heike, A. B., Catherine, M. G., David, A. H., Robert, P. H., Hassan, M. and Connie, M. W., 2011. Evaluation, Treatment, and Prevention of Vitamin D Deficiency: an Endocrine Society Clinical Practice Guideline. *The Journal of Clinical Endocrinology and Metabolism*, 96 (7):1911-1930.

Milbury, P.E. and Richer, A.C., 2008. Understanding the Antioxidant Controversy: Scrutinizing the "fountain of Youth". Greenwood Publishing Group.

Miller, D.D. and Berner, L.A., 1989. Is solubility *in-vitro* a relative predictor of iron bioavailability?.*Biological Trace Element Research*, 19:11-17.

Morrison, H. I., Schaubel, D., Desmeules, M. and Wigle, D.T. 1995. Serum folate and risk of fatal coronary heart disease. *The Journal of the American Medical Association*, 275:1893–1896.

Mortensen, B.L. and Gotfredsen, P. 1996. Fortification- nutritional improvement of dairy products. *Danish Dairy Food Industry worldwide:* 64-65.

Nair, P.K., Sharma, R. and Arora, S. 2003. Milk and milk products as a vehicle for fortification. *Indian Food Industry*, 23(1):48-51

National Dairy Council 1992. Calcium and Health. Fact file no 1. Nutrition service, 5-7 John Princes street, London.

National dairy development board 2016. http://www.nddb.org/sites/default/files/pdfs/milk%20prod.pdf (accessed on 4 December, 2016).

National Family Health Survey (NFHS-3) 2007. National Report (2005-2006), Ministry of Health and Family Welfare, Government of India.

National Institute of Health 2000. Milk matters-for your child's health. National Institute of Child Health and Human Development, 1-16.

National Nutrition Policy (NNP) 1993. Government of India, Department of Women and Child development, Ministry of Human Resource Development, New Delhi, (www.wed.nic.in/nnp.pdf).

Navarrete, N. M., Camacho, M. M., Lahuerta, J. M., Monzo, J. M. and Fito, P., 2002. Iron deficiency and iron fortified foods - a review. *Food Research International*, 35(2-3): 225-231.

Navarrete-Munoz, E. M., Valera-Gran, D., Hera, M. G., Gimenez-Monzo, D., Morales, E.,Julvez, J., Riano, I., Tardon, A., Ibarluzea, J., Santa-Marina, L., Murcia, M., Rebagliato, M. and Vioque, J., 2015.Use of high doses of folic acid supplements in pregnant women in Spain: an INMA cohort study. *BMJ open*, 5:e009202. doi:10.1136.

Nestel, P., 2003. Complementary food supplements to achieve micronutrient adequacy for infants and young children. *Journal of Pediatric Gastroenterology and Nutrition*, 36:316–328

NNMB 2003. National Nutrition Monitoring Bureau Reports, National Institute of Nutrition, Hyderabad.

NSSO Report 2011. Household Consumer Expenditure (HCE) Survey in India. National Sample Survey Office. Ministry of Statistics & Programme Implementation, Government of India.

O'Brien, A. and Robertson, D., 1993. Vitamin Fortification of Foods (Specific applications). In: Ottaway, P. B., Efitor. The Technology of Vitamins in Food. (1st ed.). Blackie Academic & Professional, London. pp. 114-142.

O'Brien, M. M., Kiely, M., Harrington, K. E., Robson, P. J., Strain, J. J. and Flynn, A. 2001. The North/South Ireland Food Consumption Survey: Vitamin intakes in 18-64-year-old adults. *Public Health Nutrition,* 4(5A):1069–1079.

Powell, J.J., Bruggraber, S., Faria, N., Poots, L. K., Hondow, N., Pennycook, T. J., Latunde-Dada, G. O., Simpson, R. J., Brown, A. P. and Pereira, D. I., 2014. A nano disperse ferritin-core mimetic that efficiency corrects anemia without luminal iron redox activity. *Nanomedicine: Nanotechnology, Biology and Medicine,* 10:1529-1538.

Raunhardt, O. and Bowley, A., 1996. Mandatory food enrichment. Nutriview Supplement 1, Vitamin Division, F. Hoffmann-La Roche Ltd., Basel, Switzerland.

Richardson, D. P., 1990. Food fortification. *Proceedings of the Nutrition Society*.49:39-50.

Rink, L. and Gabriel, P., 2000. *Zinc and the immune system. Proceedings of the Nutrition Society*, 59:541-542.

Sachdeva, B., Kaushik, R., Arora S. and Kapila, S., 2015. Bioavailability of iron in multiple fortified milk. *Journal of Food Science and Technology*, 52(9):6017-6023.

Saffert, A., Pieper, G. and Jetten, J., 2008. Effect of package light transmittance on the vitamin content of milk, Part 3: Fortified UHT low-fat milk. *Packaging Technology and Science*, 22 (1):31-37.

Salguiero, J., Torti, H., Meseri, E., Furno, J., Zubillaga, M., Janjetic, M., Barrado, A. and Boccio, J., 2007. Bioavailability studies of stabilized iron (II) sulphate by means of the prophylactic-preventive method. *Biological Trace Element Research*, 120(1-3):110-113.

Sarma, J. D. and Duttagupta, C., 1995. Improved microbiological assay for folic acid based on microtiter plating with *Streptococcus faecalis*. *Journal of AOAC International*,78:1173–77.

Sekel, A., Olivares, M., Cayazzo, M., Chadud, P., Claguno, S. and Pizaro, F., 1988. Prevention of iron deficiency by milk fortification. II. A field trial with a full fat acidified milk. *American Journal of Clinical Nutrition*, 47:265-269.

Sharma, A., Shilpashree, B.G., Arora, S. and Tomar, S. K., 2015. Lactose – zinc complex preparation and evaluation of acceptability of complex in milk. *LWT-Food Science and Technology*, 64:275-281.

UNICEF. 2011. Levels and Trends in Child Mortality, Report 2011, UN Inter-agency Group for Child Mortality Estimation New York.

Van den Berge, H., 1997. Bioavailability of vitamin D. *European Journal of Clinical Nutrition,* 51(Suppl 1):S76–S79.

Verwei, M., Arkbage, K., Havenaar, R., Berg, H., Witthoft, C. and Schaafsma, G., 2003. Folic acid and 5-methyltetrahydrofolate in fortified milk are bioaccessible as determined in a dynamic *in- vitro* gastrointestinal model. *Journal of Nutrition*, 133(7):2377-2383.

Walter, T., Pino, P., Pizarro, F. and Lozoff, B., 1998. Preventing of iron deficiency anemia: comparison of high and low iron formulas in term healthy infants after six months of life. *Journal of Pediatrics*, 132 (4):635-640.

Wasserman, R.H. and Comer, C.L., 1959. Carbohydrates and gastrointestinal absorption of radiostrontium and radiocalcium in the rat. *Experimental Biology and Medicine,* 1(2): 314-317.

Weaver, C.M., 1998. Calcium in food fortification strategies. *International Dairy Journal*, 8: 443-449.

WHO. The global burden of disease: 2004. update. Geneva: WHO; 2008.

Zemel, M. B. and Miller, S.L., 2004. Dietary calcium and dairy modulation of adiposity and obesity risk. *Nutrition Reviews*, 62(4):125–131.

10

Hygienic Design of the Food Processing Equipments

Subhash Prasad, Tanmay Hazra and Sudheendra CH.V.K

Abstracts

To ensure safe food and adequate sanitation programs, the equipment used for processing of food products must be designed, fabricated, constructed, and installed according to sound hygienic design principles. This ensures the equipment can be adequately cleaned and sanitized, and that surfaces are resistant to daily exposure to corrosive food products and cleaning/sanitizing chemicals. This chapter focuses primarily on fundamental principles of hygienic design, which protect the product from microbial, chemical, and foreign-body contamination. This is followed by a discussion of general aspects of hygienic construction and design of food equipments, the selection of materials of construction and specification of surface finishes, fabrication, installation and cleaning and sanitization. Quality of raw materials or foods ingredients, proper processing, packaging and storage of finished products decides the quality of the food products. Planning for plant and equipment layout, its design, services (water, air, refrigeration, steam), waste disposal etc. are some of the critical factors, which contributes to quality. In addition, the food processing equipment must comply with strict standards and regulations, which are necessary for securing the quality and safety of the food products to the consumers.

Keywords: Food contact materials, hygienic design, materials of construction, sanitizing protocols, legislation

1. Introduction

The criteria for the hygienic design of equipment intended for the processing of foods. Its fundamental objective is the prevention of the microbial contamination of food products. Such contamination may, of course, originate from the raw materials, but the product may also be contaminated with micro-organisms during processing and packaging. If equipment is of poor hygienic design, it will be difficult to clean. Residues (soil) may be retained in crevices and dead areas, allowing the micro-organisms which they harbour to survive and multiply. These may cross-contaminate subsequent batches of product. Although a primary objective of design remains that the equipment is able to fulfil its engineering function, sometimes the requirements of hygiene will conflict with this. In seeking an acceptable compromise it is imperative that food safety is never put at risk.

Upgrading an existing design to meet hygiene requirements can be prohibitively expensive and may be unsuccessful and so these are most effectively incorporated into the initial design stage. The long term benefits of doing so are not only product safety but also the potential to increase the life expectancy of equipment, reduce maintenance and consequently lower operating costs.

For sanitary/ hygienic design of food processing equipment's it is necessary to consider the following points.

- Basic principles of hygienic design.
- Selection of the raw material for the process materials.
- Surface finish.
- General design features.
- Details of constructions.
- Protection of the product from microbial or other contaminations.
- Effectiveness of cleaning and sanitation.

2. Fundamental Principles of Hygienic Design

Principle 1. Cleanable to a Micro-biological Level

Food equipment must be constructed and be maintainable to ensure that the equipment can be effectively and efficiently cleaned and sanitized over the lifetime of the equipment. The removal of all food materials is critical. This means preventing bacterial ingress, survival, growth and reproduction. This includes product and non-product contact surfaces of the equipment.

While a piece of equipment may be visually clean, absent of soil or organic matter, it does not necessarily mean that it is microbiologically clean. What food processors would like to see is a piece of equipment that can be cleaned to a microbiological level, as well as clean to the eye. This principle refers to any kind of unwanted microorganisms, including pathogens and spoilage organisms.

Principle 2. Made of Compatible Materials

Construction materials used for equipment must be completely compatible with the product, environment, cleaning and sanitizing chemicals, and the methods of cleaning and sanitation. Equipment materials of construction must be inert, corrosion resistant, nonporous and nonabsorbent.

This principle emphasizes the importance of making sure that a product surface is impervious to the materials to which it is exposed. This is very important because the use of incompatible construction materials may cause corrosion or pitting on a material such as aluminum, for example, that would create a harborage area where microorganisms, water, soil or food can collect. Essentially, the processor wants to minimize areas where microorganisms can hide, live and survive. By eliminating incompatible materials in the construction of the processing equipment, the processor reduces the likelihood of creating a hospitable environment where bugs can grow.

Principle 3. Accessible for Inspection, Maintenance, Cleaning and Sanitation

All parts of the equipment shall be readily accessible for inspection, maintenance, cleaning and/or sanitation. Accessibility should be easily accomplished by an individual without tools. Disassembly and assembly should be facilitated by the equipment design to optimize sanitary conditions.

Dave Kramer's quote applies here: "If you can't see it and you can't touch it, then you can't clean it." In other words, in a non-CIP environment you need to be able to get everything clean. There are four elements of cleaning that processors use: mechanical action, temperature, a chemical that will break up fats and proteins, and time. With these, the processor should be able to remove any food soil from equipment, as long as he gets the mechanical action and chemicals in the right amount of time and in the right concentration into those places where there are soils. Designing equipment to increase accessibility for cleaning ensures the success of this four-pronged protocol, since the soil will be more visible.

Principle 4. No Product or Liquid Collection

Equipment shall be self-draining to assure that food product, water, or product liquid does not accumulate, pool or condense on the equipment or product zone areas.

The processor does not want to have any areas in the system where water can collect, or where product can collect and later develop into a foreign material as it dries out, crusts and hardens. Standing water can serve as a harborage or growth point for microorganisms, and any time moisture is introduced into an environment there is an increased chance for microbial growth.

Principle 5. Hollow Areas Hermetically Sealed.

Hollow areas of equipment (e.g., frames, rollers) must be eliminated where possible or permanently sealed (caulking not acceptable). Bolts, studs, mounting plates, brackets, junction boxes, name plates, end caps, sleeves and other such items must be continuously welded to the surface of the equipment and not attached via drilled and tapped holes.

In most food processing plants, there is a lot of framework used on pieces of equipment, and we want to make sure that there are no penetrations that would allow moisture and/or food materials or organic matter to get inside or under the surface of equipment. If this occurs, microorganisms will grow, leak out and recontamination the environment. Eliminating or sealing hollow areas is easily addressed by equipment designers.

Principle 6. No Niches.

All parts of the equipment shall be free of niches such as pits, cracks, corrosion, recesses, open seams, gaps, lap seams, protruding ledges, inside threads, bolt rivets and dead ends. All welds must be continuous and fully penetrating.

This principle means just what it says: Food processing equipment should not have harborage points. Not only should equipment be evaluated to ensure that the original welding by the manufacturer is continuous and niche-free, but processors also should take care when modifying equipment in the plant environment. Often equipment is modified by the processor to make it fit into a room or to make it consistent with other designs or product lines existing in the plant, and during such modification activities a hollow framework might be penetrated and create a microbial growth niche.

Principle 7. Sanitary Operational Performance

During normal operations, the equipment must perform so it does not contribute to unsanitary conditions or the harborage and growth of bacteria.

This principle is linked to Principle 4: A processor doesn't want anything on the production line that is going to cause microbial counts to increase throughout the course of the day. During operation, you want to make sure that you have minimal moisture and product buildup in different product zones. In an ideal world, the processor wants to increase productivity and run the lines as efficiently and safely within the regulated timeframe. If, for example, the processor operates a wet process that adds moisture all the time, there likely will be increased microbial counts on the conveyor. Designing the conveyor or other equipment parts to minimize product buildup and moisture allows the production run to be increased to the extent allowed by regulation and to maximize the benefit of the operation during that time while minimizing any type of quality defect.

Principle 8. Hygienic Design of Maintenance Enclosures.

Maintenance enclosures (e.g., electrical control panels, chain guards, belt guards, gear enclosures, junction boxes, pneumatic/hydraulic enclosures) and human machine interfaces (e.g., pushbuttons, valve handles, switches, touch screens) must be designed, constructed and be maintainable to ensure food product, water, or product liquid does not penetrate into, or accumulate in or on the enclosure and interface. The physical design of the enclosures should be sloped or pitched to avoid use as a storage area.

Engineers involved with the EDTF stressed the importance of this principle, noting that there are many equipment installations whereby an ideally designed piece of equipment is placed adjacent to an electrical box (a perfect harborage place for water leakage) and/or pushbuttons that are not cleanable. This principle not only addresses product contact surfaces, but the entire asset represented by the piece of equipment. This moves the consideration beyond the surface to ensure that all of the maintenance enclosures and other connections to the equipment are appropriately designed and also can be cleaned and sanitized.

Principle 9. Hygienic Compatibility with Other Plant Systems.

Design of equipment must ensure hygienic compatibility with other equipment and systems (e.g., electrical, hydraulics, steam, air, water).

Ensuring the hygienic compatibility of the equipment with other systems is both a processor responsibility to the equipment manufacturer as well as an equipment manufacturer responsibility to the processor. The processor wants to make sure that equipment introduced into a facility is designed and built to be usable with the plant systems. Processors can communicate to equipment manufacturers the established electrical, hydraulic, steam, compressed air and oil filtration and water systems information to assist in improved design strategies prior to the equipment being built and arriving at the plant.

Principle 10. Validate Cleaning and Sanitizing Protocols.

The procedures prescribed for cleaning and sanitation must be clearly written, designed and proven to be effective and efficient. Chemicals recommended for cleaning and sanitation must be compatible with the equipment, as well as compatible with the manufacturing environment.

Equipment manufacturers are not cleaning procedure experts; their manufacturing facilities resemble machine shops teeming with lathes and metal shaping equipment. It is a rare equipment manufacturing operation that would have the ability to wash a piece of equipment, much less sanitize it. However, food processors utilize cleaning and sanitizing systems every day, and can provide useful insight as to the best way to clean and sanitize equipment in given plant environments. This principle recommends that the equipment manufacturer work with the individual processor during the equipment design stage, so that by the time the equipment is being constructed, the equipment company will have a fairly good vision of how the equipment can be cleaned and sanitized in a processing plant. When it is delivered to the processing plant, the processor also will have a clear vision of what needs to be done to successfully clean it.

3. General Aspects of Hygienic Construction and Design of Food Equipment

The surfaces of food equipment can be subdivided into two categories: (i) food product contact surfaces, and (ii) non-product contact surfaces.

A food product contact surface is defined as a surface in "direct contact with food residue, or where food residue can drip, drain, diffuse, or be drawn" (FDA, 2004b). Because these surfaces, if contaminated, can directly result in food product contamination, rigid sanitary design criteria must be met. Non-product contact surfaces are those that are part of the equipment (e.g., legs, supports, housings) that do not directly contact food. As contamination of non-product contact surfaces can cause indirect contamination of the food product, these surfaces cannot be ignored with regard to sanitary design.

3.1 Food Product Contact Surfaces

In terms of sanitary design, all *food contact surfaces* should be: smooth; impervious; free of cracks and crevices; nonporous; nonabsorbent; non-contaminating; nonreactive; corrosion resistant; durable and maintenance free; nontoxic; and cleanable.

If the surface is coated with metal alloy or non-metal (e.g. ceramics, plastic, rubber) in any way, the final surface must meet the above requirements. 3A Standards require that such coatings maintain corrosion resistance, and be free of surface delamination, pitting, flaking, chipping, blistering, and distortion under conditions of intended use. Similarly, if any other modification or process is used in fabrication (e.g., welded, bonded, or soldered) it should be done using appropriate materials and in a manner that ensures the final surface meets the sanitary design criteria.

3.2 Material of Construction

Materials of construction are usually selected based on their strength, elasticity, hardness, toughness, sensitivity to wear, corrosion and fatigue resistance, ease of fabrication, availability and price. However, in the construction of food processing equipment and services, the hygienic properties of materials of construction, such as sensitivity to fouling, cleanability and inertness in contact with the food produced, are as important. To select the most appropriate materials of construction for use in either the food contact, either the non-food contact area, the equipment manufacturer must have knowledge of the physical, chemical and thermal behaviour of an as large as possible range of market available materials of construction, must be familiar with their hygiene characteristics, and must have insight in the laws, regulations, standards and guidelines applicable to the materials of construction used in the design and manufacturing of his food processing equipment.

A variety of materials are used in the construction and fabrication for different applications in food equipment. These materials vary in their properties with regard to workability, compatibility, and sanitary design features. Depending upon the application, various metals as well as non-metals (e.g., plastics, rubber) are used. Some materials are not recommended and should be avoided.

- **Stainless steel** is the preferred general use metal for food contact surfaces because of its corrosion resistance and durability in most food applications. However, not all stainless steel is equal. In general, the properties of the stainless steel alloy are related to its relative composition with regard to chromium and nickel level. Corrosion resistance varies with chromium level, and structural strength varies with nickel level. The relative levels of these components are often given as a ratio. For example, the American Iron and Steel Institute (AISI) 300 Series Stainless Steel, commonly recommended for food contact surfaces is also termed 18/8 indicating that it is 18% Cr and 8% Ni. 3A Sanitary Standards require 316 (or 18/10) stainless steel for most surfaces. They allow the use of 304 stainless steel only for utility usage (e.g. pipes), and restrict the use of 303 stainless steel.

  The properties of stainless steel can change with continued use, especially under conditions where the chromium oxide layer is altered (e.g. incompatible cleaners, abrasive cleaners, abrasive cleaning pads, or chlorine and related sanitizers). Therefore, it is recommended that surfaces be passivated (using nitric acid or other strong oxidizing agents) initially and on a regular frequency thereafter, to maintain a passive (nonreactive) oxide film on the surface. Passivation of stainless steel food contact surfaces is recommended after any surface repair, polishing, or working.

- **Titanium** has excellent durability and corrosion resistance (especially in an acidic environment). However, its use is limited by high cost. Titanium is used in stainless steel alloys for food equipment used in the processing of food products with high acid and/or salt content (e.g., citrus juice, tomato products).
- **Platinum,** another excellent corrosion resistant material, would also be highly desirable, but, obviously, the cost of this rare material would prohibit its use.
- **Gold** has been approved as a food contact surface in certain 3-A Sanitary Standards. In some cases, gold is used for soldering optical sensors (e.g., fiber optics) into stainless steel fittings. Gold is desirable in these applications for its resistance to abrasion and compatibility with glass.

Other metals are limited by application as follows:

- **Copper** is primarily used for equipment used in the brewing industry, with some use for cheese vats in Swiss cheese manufacture, due to tradition. Care should be used with copper equipment when processing acid products, as copper residues can leach into the product.
- **Aluminum** is used in certain parts and components where lighter weight is desired. However, aluminum has poor corrosion resistance and can become pitted and cracked with continued use. Care should taken when cleaning and sanitizing aluminum components as oxidizing chemicals can accelerate the pitting of the metal. In most food contact applications, aluminum must be coated with an acceptable material. Plastic coatings such as polytetrafluorethylene (PTFE or Teflon®) are common.
- **Carbonized metal and cast iron** are only used for frying and cooking surfaces, and similar applications in food service.
- **Galvanized iron** should be avoided as a food contact surface because it is highly reactive with acids. A variety of non-metal materials are used as food contact surfaces in specific applications of food equipment (e.g., probes, gaskets, membranes). These materials should meet the same sanitary design and cleanability requirements as metals when used in these applications as described in 3 A Sanitary Standards and other standards. Non-metal surfaces, in general, lack the corrosion resistance and durability of metal surfaces, therefore, maintenance programs should include frequent examination for wear and deterioration under continued use, and replacement as appropriate.

Non-metal materials used in food contact surfaces include:

- Plastics, rubber, and rubber-like materials that should be food grade and should meet the requirements designated under 3A Sanitary Standards (18-03 and 20-20).
- Multi-use plastics, rubber, and rubber-like materials may also be considered as indirect food additives under FDA regulations.
- Ceramics are used primarily in membrane filtration systems. They may also be used in other limited applications if wear resistance is necessary.
- Glass may be used as a food contact surface. These applications are limited due to the potential for breakage. Specially formulated glass materials such as Pyrex® have proven successful. When glass is used, it must be durable, break resistant or heat resistant glass. Some applications where glass is used are light and sight openings into vessels and in very limited glass piping applications.
- Paper has been used over the years as a gasket material in piping systems designed for daily disassembly. Paper is considered a single use material.
- Wood, which is highly porous and difficult to clean, should be avoided as a food contact surface. Wood is restricted in food service applications by most regulatory agencies, with the exception of hardwood cutting boards and tight grain butcher blocks.

3.3 Construction and Fabrication

Food equipment should be designed and fabricated in such a way that all food contact surfaces are free of sharp corners and crevices. All mating surfaces must also be continuous (*e.g.*, substantially flush). Construction of all food handling or processing equipment should allow for easy disassembly for cleaning and inspection. Where appropriate (*e.g.*, vessels, chambers, tanks), equipment should be self-draining and pitched to a drainable port with no potential hold up of food materials or solutions (Fig. 1).

Piping systems not designed for routine disassembly must be sloped to drain (Fig. 2). Piping systems installed in modern food processing systems designed for cleaning in- place (CIP), require special consideration and close monitoring with regard to drainage.

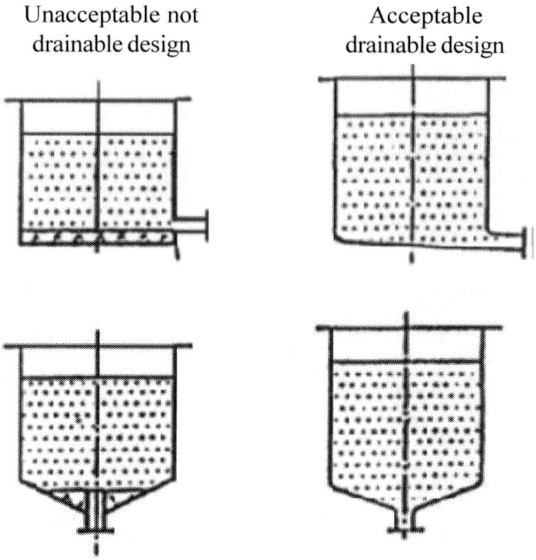

Fig. 1: Examples of acceptable vs. unacceptable self-drainage design for tanks and vessels (EHEDG, 1995)

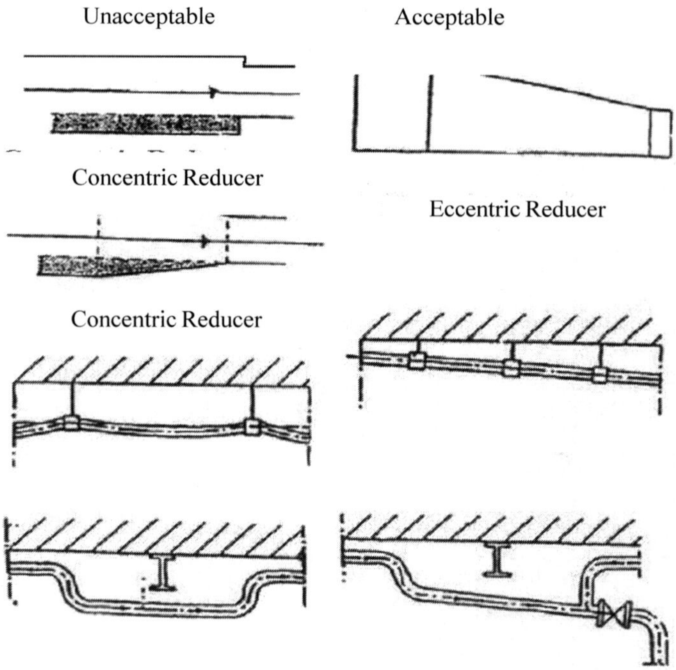

Fig. 2: Drainage of pipes (Graham, 1992)

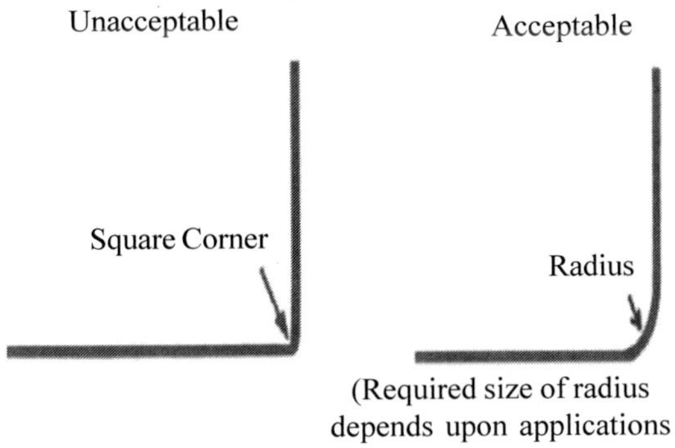

Fig. 3: Acceptable vs. unacceptable internal angles of food equipment (FDA, 2000)

(a) Internal angles should be coved or rounded with defined radii as shown in Fig. 3. Equipment standards specify appropriate radii for specific equipment applications and components. For example, radii requirements stated in the 3A Sanitary Standards indicate that "all internal angles 135degrees or less should have a minimum radii of 1/4 inch(6.35 mm)." The standards allow for smaller radii whereneeded for function within certain specifications.

(b) **Permanent joints**: Should be smooth, durable, and meet all sanitary design criteria. Equipment standards generally require that welded joints on stainless steel surfaces be continuous, butt-type joints (Fig. 4) and ground to at least as smooth as a No. 4 finish. If the welded joint is at a corner, it must be coved to the appropriate radius and ground smooth (Fig. 5). Use of soldered joints should be limited by application with use of only non-toxic materials. Press fits and shrink fits are generally discouraged and should be limited only to applications where welded joints are not possible (e.g. bushings).

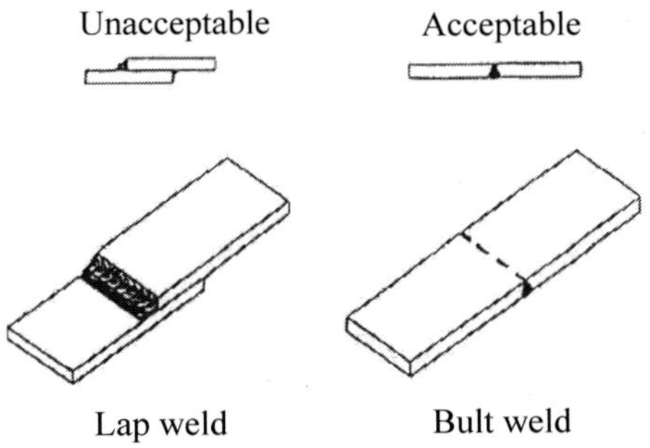

Fig. 4: Permanent welded joints showing butt weld vs. lap weld (Adapted from EHEDG, 1995)

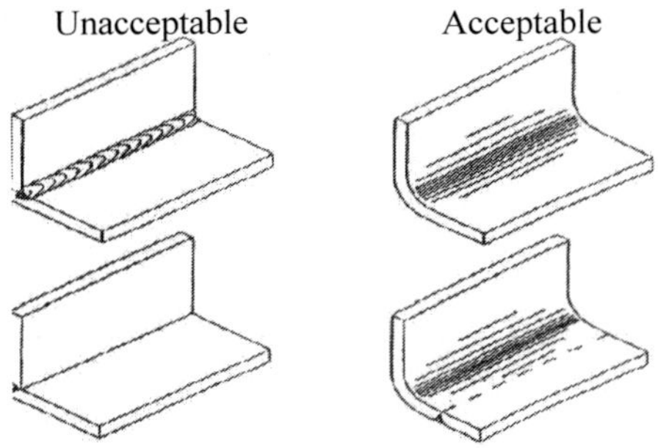

Fig. 5: Corner welds in food equipment(FDA, 2000)

(c) **Connections, attachments, and ancillary equipment**: Care should be taken when connecting pipes, gauges, thermometers, probes, or other equipment to food contact surfaces. It is necessary to ensure the connection does not create a dead end or an area where food product can accumulate and is not accessible to cleaning solutions. Such connections should be close coupled (e.g., pipe connection should not be of length greater than one pipe diameter) as shown in Fig. 6. Examples of an acceptable and an unacceptable gauge connection are shown in Fig. 7. Shafts, bearings, agitators, and other attachments or ancillary components should be attached to food equipment in such a way that the food contact zone is sealed from contamination caused by leakage of lubricants or other contaminants into the product zone. Such components should be accessible and removable for cleaning. Threads of food equipment are to be avoided in or over the food product zone.

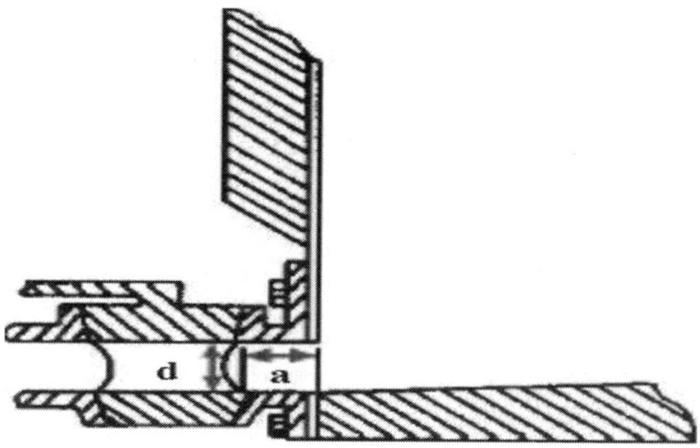

Fig. 6: Closed connection length (a) no greater than the pipe diameter (d)

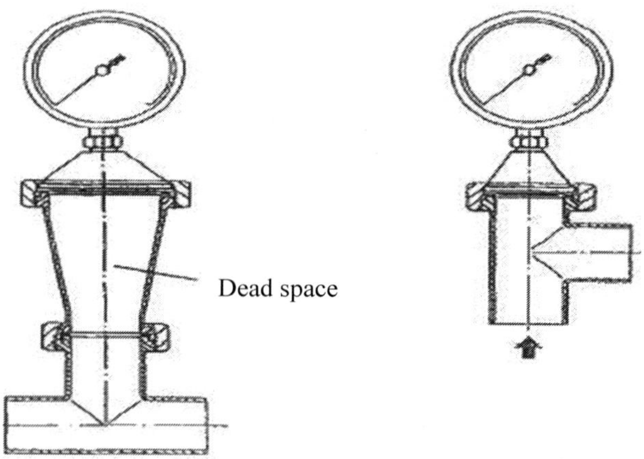

Fig. 7: Acceptable vs. unacceptable gauge connection

(d) Openings, covers, and top rims:-Any opening or cover should be designed, fabricated, and constructed in such a manner as to adequately protect food products from contamination and to divert potential contamination away from the food product zone. Openings should be lipped and covered with a shoe box type design (Fig. 8). And the top rims of equipment should be constructed and fabricated to avoid the collection of water droplets or dust (Fig. 9).

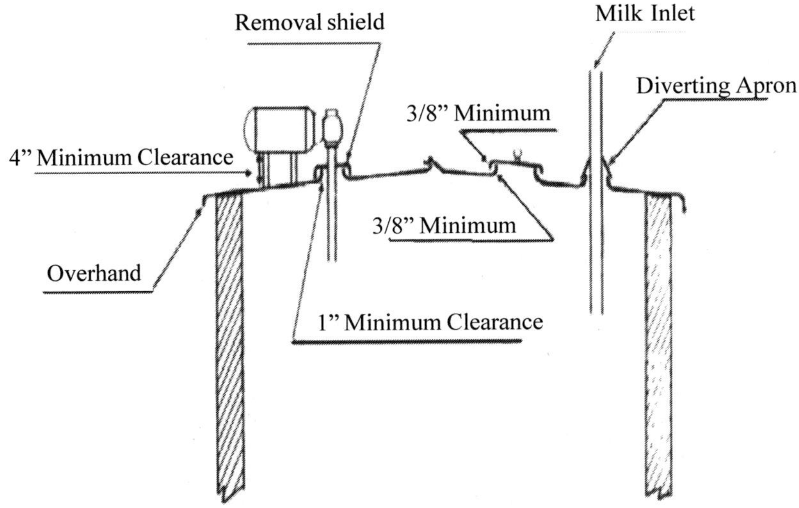

Fig. 8: Acceptable shoe box design openings and covers (FDA, 2000).

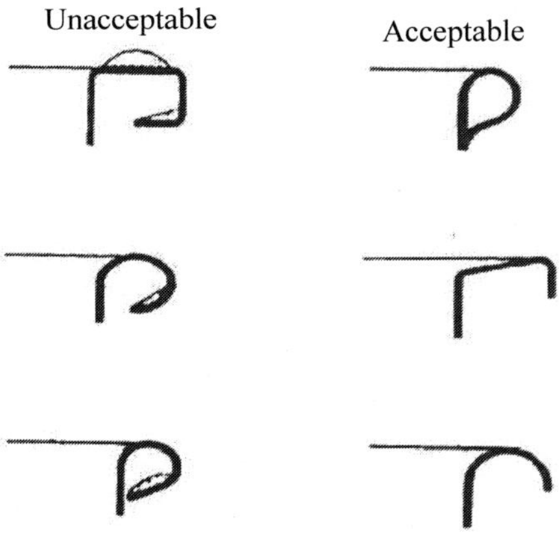

Fig. 9: Top rim of food equipment (FDA, 2000)

3.4 Non-Product Contact Surfaces

Non-product contact surfaces of food equipment are a well-documented source for environmental contamination of a food facility with pathogens (especially *Listeria monocytogenes*). These areas can also be harborage areas for insects and rodents. Therefore, care should be used in evaluating these surfaces of equipment with regard to hygienic construction and design. In general, non-product surfaces of equipment should be constructed with appropriate materials and fabricated in such a manner as to be reasonably cleanable, corrosion resistant, and maintenance free. As much as is practicable, tubular steel equipment framework should be entirely sealed and not penetrated (e.g., bolts, studs), to avoid creating niches for microorganisms (Fig. 10). Whenever practicable, attachments should be welded to the surface of the tubing and not attached via drilled and tapped holes. Ledges or areas where dust can collect should be avoided. Tops of equipment, shields, covers, or boxes, should be sloped at a 45 degree angle or more. To avoid niche areas for microbiological growth, the legs of equipment should be sealed at the base and not be of hollow design.

Fig. 10: Tubular Framework with Bolted Attachments Potential Microbial Niche (Marconnett, 2004)

3.5 Surface Finish

Product contact surfaces must be finished to a degree of surface roughness that is smooth enough to enable them to be easily cleaned and disinfected. The surface finish must be such that there are no cracks, pits or cavities were water or soil might remain. For food contact, stainless steel surfaces are usually finished through polishing, grinding or other means to obtain a smooth finish. Most hygiene standards require that food contact surfaces have a roughness average (Ra) of 0.8 μm or less, determined using a profilometer, which corresponds to a No. 4 finish on stainless steel (Tuthill & Avery, 1992). Stainless steel with a 2B or milled finish is acceptable, with limitations (Bilgili, 2006). The 2B finish is used for its superior fat release properties in equipment intended to process and handle higher fat products (e.g., butter, meats). Surface roughness, Ra, of enclosures in hygienic production areas should not exceed 2.5 μm. Surfaces will deteriorate making cleaning more difficult (Hauser, 2004a).

3.6 Food Equipment Installation

Food equipment should be installed in a logical sequence to avoid cross contamination. Space around and between equipment and between equipment, and walls should be adequate enough to allow for sufficient cleaning. There should be no potential harborages for insects and rodents. Unless sealed to walls, food equipment should be at least 4 inches from walls. Floor mounted equipment should be sealed to the floor, platform, or pedestal or should be no less than 6 inches from the floor. All legs, levelers and related supports should be designed and constructed to have no hollow areas, penetrated framework or exposed threads that are not of cleanable design.

3.7 Cleaning and Sanitation

Food equipment should be operated in a way that ensures effective cleaning and does not allow, cross connections between product and other solutions (e.g., cleaning solutions, allergens, raw food materials). The majority of the food equipments are cleaned and sanitized using mechanical or clean-in-place (CIP) systems. However, it should be noted that not all food equipments are designed for total automated CIP cleaning and should be partially disassembled for manual cleaning as required.

- Cleaning is an integral part of food processing operation.
- The process should ensure the microbiological safety of final products.
- After cleaning, the surface should be washed with hot water and left to dry.

3–A standards for cleaning in place are as follows:

- Using alkali or acid solutions appropriate for the product and equipment surface.
- Providing a time of exposure of 10 to 60 min to remove substances without damage to the metal.
- Utilizing a velocity of flow of 1.5m/s (1 to 3m/s).
- Maintaining a slope of surface and tubing to provide for drainage (5 to 10mm/m).
- Avoiding dead ends for flows.
- Using connections and joints that are cleanable (welded joints, clamp-type joints, appropriate gaskets).

4. Legislation

4.1 Indian Standards

FSSAI has provided guidelines for auditing of food factories for food safety assessments. However, elaborate guidelines are missing on food factory design, layout & on sanitary equipment design. Even BIS also does not have these aspects. In absence of "appropriate & elaborate" guidelines, it will be good to study and adopt the suitable guidelines available in Europe/ US as well as by ISO/Codex/WHO etc. under Indians conditions.

4.2 European Machinery Legislation and Sanitary Standards

Food equipment intended to be sold in European countries and designing operations in food factories must comply with (Moerman, 2011):

- European Machinery Legislation, consisting of the Machine Directives 2006/42/EC & 98/37/EC
- Guide to application of the Machine Directive 2006/42/EC, published by the Industry and Enterprise department of the European Commission
- Materials and Articles intended to come into contact with Food Directive 89/109/EEC
- Materials and Articles intended to come into contact with Food Regulation EC N° 1935/2004
- Council of Europe Guideline on Metals and Alloys used as Food Contact Materials.
- Plastics and Materials in Contact with Food Regulations Directives 2002/16/EC & 2002/72/EC
- prEN 1672-1 and EN 1672-2 standard
- Regulation (EC) No 852/2004 & Directive 93/43/EEC
- EU commission - Scientific Committee on Veterinary Measures relating to Public Health: Cleaning and Disinfection of Knives in the Meat and Poultry Industry
- Several EN Food Machinery-specific Standards, applicable to specific food production equipment (e.g. mixers, cutters, cooking equipment, etc.), developed by CEN /TC153
- 41 EHEDG (European Hygienic Engineering & Design Group) guidelines

Annex I of the Machine Directive 2006/42/EC & 98/37/EC (formerly 89/392/EEC and its amendments91/368/EEC & 93/44/EEC) requires that all equipment used to handle food should be hygienically designed: (a) be so constructed, be of such materials and be kept in such good order, repair and condition as to minimize any risk of contamination of the food; (b) with the exception of nonreturnable containers and packaging, be so constructed, be of such materials and be kept in such good order, repair and condition as to enable them to be kept thoroughly cleaned and, where necessary, disinfected, sufficient for the purposes intended; (c) be installed in such a manner as to allow adequate cleaning of the surrounding area.

prEN1672-1 and EN1672-2 are Harmonized European standards specifying machinery, safety, and hygienic requirements for various food industries, drawn up by the Technical Committee CEN/TC 153 of the ComitéeEuropéen de Normalisation (CEN). prEN 1672-1 deals especially with how to arrange interlocking of guards to allow safe cleaning according to the hygiene requirements (coded magnetic switches), how to apply electrical safeguards in wet environments and during hose-down operations, how to contain product to avoid slip risks, and how to proceed safe hopper feeding and product loading. prEN 1672-1 also provides the user instructions for safe and effective clearing blockage, cleaning, setting up and maintenance. EN 1672-2 sets design principles and requires the choice of a design which meets both safety and hygiene objectives. These two standards are supported by around forty EN food machinery-specific Standards.

EHEDG guidelines are developed by members of European research institutes and universities, food companies and food equipment manufacturers. EHEDG was founded in 1989 to provide European food equipment manufacturers and Food manufacturer's guidance in the implementation of the hygienic requirements defined in the Machine Directives 2006/42/EC & 98/37/EC, and the EN standard 1672-2. Several members of EHEDG participate in CEN/TC 153 to develop EN standards with respect to the construction of safe and hygienic food equipment.

Regulation (EC) No 852/2004 on the hygiene of foodstuffs that replaces Directive 93/43/EEC, set out the framework for standards of food hygiene and food control. Both directives describe general requirements for food premises, specific requirements for rooms where food is prepared, particular requirements for transport, equipment, food waste, water supply, personal hygiene, storage/handling and training. To fulfil all these requirements, Directive 93/43/EEC and Regulation (EC) No 852/2004 have adopted the principles of HACCP as tool to identify and control food safety hazards (EC, 1993 &2004). Therefore, the EC has published a Guidance document to facilitate the implementation of the HACCP principles in food and food related businesses (EC, 2005).

4.3 British Sanitary Standards

In Great Britain, the following hygienic standards are developed:

- Campden Food & Chorleywood Research Association Guidelines;
- Chilled Food Association - Hygienic Design Guidelines 2002
- Institute of Food Science & Technology's Food and Drink – Good Manufacturing Practice: A guide to its Responsible Management, 5th edition, 2007.

4.4 US Sanitary Standards

In the US, the following Government Agencies and Private Organizations have published sanitary standards for food processing equipment (Moerman, 2011):

- US Dept. of Agriculture (USDA): Food Safety and Inspection Service (FSIS) 11.000 series: Facilities, Equipment & Sanitation;
- USDA Guidelines for the Sanitary Design and Fabrication of Dairy Processing Equipment;
- US Public Health Service: Food and Drug Administration (FDA): Code of Federal Regulations, Title 21, § 110.40: Equipment, Utensils & cGMP;
- International Association of Milk, Food, and Environmental Sanitarians, Inc. (IAMFES): committee on Sanitary Procedures "3-A Sanitary Standards";
- American Society of Mechanical Engineers (ASME): ANSI-ASME F2-1: "Food, Drug and Beverage Equipment" & ASME Bioprocess Equipment International Standard (ASME BPE-2009);
- Baking Industry Sanitation Standards Committee: ANSI-BISSC Sanitation Standards;
- AFDOUS (Association of Food and Drug Officials of the United States): "AFDOUS Frozen Food Code";
- NSF international: a) Food Service Equipment Standards; b) Food preparation and Service Equipment;
- American Meat Institute (AMI) Equipment Design Task Force: 10 principles of Sanitary Equipment Design;
- American Meat Institute (AMI) checklists, to allow processors to conduct a sanitary design audit of the equipment based on assigned points. To develop US sanitary standards, both NSF and 3-A cooperate with EHEDG.

4.5 International Standards

Several international operating organisations have developed hygienic standards on their own (Moerman, 2011):

- ISO/TS 22002-1:2009 (replacement of the British Standard Institution standard, PAS220:2008;
- ISO/TS 22002-4 : 2013 Contains specific prerequisites for food packaging manufacturing.
- ISO/TS 22003 : 2013 provides guidelines for audit and certification bodies.
- ISO/TS 22004: 2014 provides generic advice on the application of ISO 22000
- ISO 14159:2002 Safety of Machinery - Hygienic Requirements for the Design of Machinery;
- ISPE Baseline® Guides, ISPE Guides, ISPE Good Practice Guides;
- Codex Alimentarius (developed by Food and Agricultural Organization (FAO) of the United Nations and the World Health Organization);
- Codex HACCP Code;
- GMP – WHO standards;

4.6 Three-A Sanitary Standards (3-A-SSI)

3-A Sanitary Standards are written by a group of volunteer state and federal dairy regulators, dairy equipment manufacturers and dairy industry personnel. 3-A SSI formulates standards and practices for the sanitary design, fabrication, installation and cleanability of dairy and food equipment or systems used to handle, process and package consumable products where a high degree of sanitation is required. Sanitary codes and guidelines issued by regulatory agencies for equipment are often based on 3-A Sanitary Standards. Oversight of 3-A Standards and guides is maintained by the 3-A Steering Committee which is responsible for establishing standard operating procedures and setting priorities for the development of new or revised 3-A standards.

5. Conclusion

Food equipment hygienic design is more important than ever before and is addressed in a general manner in most regulatory and industry food safety programs. However, the terms used are only broadly defined, and interpretation of acceptability is left to the individual auditor and her or his particular aptitude for equipment evaluation.

Microbes (bacteria, yeasts, molds, viruses etc.) are ubiquitous in nature and generally cannot be seen by necked eye, they have ability to grow at normal environmental conditions (mesophiles) as well as under different and sometimes in extreme environmental conditions e.g. at low temperature (psychrophilic, psychrotrophs), high temperature (thermophiles), low water activity/humidity (xerophiles), under acidic (acidophiles) and alkaline conditions (alkalophiles), in presence of air (aerobes) as well as in absence of air (anaerobes). Unwanted and higher number of microbes will be responsible for reducing/ limiting the shelf life of food products and presence of pathogenic organisms will be responsible for spreading disease to the consumer. These types of situations may results into product recalls.

Quality of raw materials or foods ingredients, proper processing, packaging and storage of finished products decides the quality of the food products. An engineer's work to contribute towards quality begins as early as first lines for planning of the plant are drawn. Planning for plant and equipment layout, its design, services (water, air, refrigeration, steam), waste disposal etc. are some of the critical factors, which contributes to quality. During routine production food engineer's role is to see that equipment, pipe etc., are properly cleaned, sanitized and preventive maintenance is done regularly. Food engineers from time to time; along with team of technologists, chemists and microbiologists have to diligently work together to ascertain the quality of food products. Sanitary design of food equipment is therefore of first and paramount importance for production of quality food product and should be given due weightage.

References

Anonymous, 2016. European Hygienic Equipment Design Group (EHEDG). www.ehedg.org (accessed December 9, 2016)

Anonymous, 2016. Food and Drug Admin. 2004b. Food Code. www.fda.gov(accessed December 9, 2016)

Bilgili, S. F. 2006. Sanitary/hygienic processing equipment design. *Worlds Poult Sci. J.,* 62: 115–122.

Food and Drug Admin. 2000. Milk and Milk Product Equipment— A Guideline for Evaluating Construction.www.fda.gov (accessed December 9, 2016)

Graham, D. J. 1992. A Mind Set. Dairy Food Env. San.(April): 234-235; (May.):296-297.

Hauser, G., Curiel, G.J., Bellin, H.-W., Cnossen, H.J., Hofmann, J., Kastelein, J., Partington, E., Peltier, Y., Timperley, A.W. (2004a). 'Hygienic Equipment Design Criteria', EHEDG Guideline N° 8, 2nd ed., EHEDG subgroup Design Principles, EHEDG, Frankfurt, Germany, pp. 1-16.

ISO. 1984. Surface roughness — terminology — Part 1~ Surface and its parameters. ISO 42871, International Organization for Standards, Geneva, Switzerland.

Lewan M., and Partington E. 2014. Food processing equipment construction materials (Ch. 5). In: Lelieveld H. L. M., Mostert M. A., Holah J., and Napper D. (Eds.), Hygiene in Food Processing: Principles and practice, 2nd ed., Woodhead Publishing, Cambridge, England, pp. 142-154.

Marconnett, G. 2004. Sanitary Design Challenges. Presented at 3A Sanitary Standards Annual Meeting, Milwaukee, WI.

Moerman, F. 2011. 'Hygienic design of piping for food processing support systems in food factories", Ch. 21, in Lelieveld, H.L.M. and Holah, J. (eds.), Hygienic Design of Food Factories, Woodhead Publishing, Cambridge, England, pp. 471- 493.

Tuthill, A. and R. Avery. 1992. Specifying stainless steel surface treatments. Adv Mater Process December:34–38.

11

Modification of Starch by Gamma Irradiation: A Novel Approach

Khalid Bashir, Kulsum Jan and Shumaila Jan

Abstract

Tremendous hike inworld population has increased thrust on the limited resources which has considerably affected the viability of the food. The emerging challenge for policy makers and food scientists is to put forward viable solutions. Utilization of underutilized crops/plants that act as good sources of starch could be explored in a better way for the sustenance of the limited sources like food crops/plants. The demand for starch and the foods containing starch has been increasing continually. Since, the starch in its native form has certain limitations in its functional properties to be used for different applications. Therefore, it becomes important to explore certain technologies which could be used for modification of starch. Among different technologies gamma irradiation ensures food safety while inducing physicochemical changes of the components. Although, the chemical modifications have been used widely so far but the concerns related to the chemical residues left are diminishing their demand. Hence, the physical processes particularly the gamma irradiation process has emerged as an efficient alternative with some benefits over other process like eco-friendly, economical, reliable and safe for altering the physico-chemical and biological characteristics of the product. Gamma Irradiation of starch has been successfully employed for the achievement of some desired physico-chemical, biological and functional properties of the foods and other related items. In this chapter, valuable impact of gamma irradiation on the physico-chemical, biological and functional properties of starch has been summarized.

Keywords: Gamma irradiation, modification, physico-chemical, starch, underutilized

1. Introduction

Starch is the primary source of stored energy in cereal grains. Starch is a semi-crystalline, present in granular form in the chloroplasts of green leaves and the amyloplast of tubers and seeds (Ellis *et al.*, 1998). Starch is being consumed on a large scale because of its widespread availability, comparatively low cost and capability to impart a wide range of functional properties to the food as well as non-food items. It is a polysaccharide, derived from roots, tubers and seeds of plant kingdom and acts as a chief dietary source of carbohydrates for humans (Han, 2007). The major chemical components of starch are amylose and amylopectin made of glucosyl units. Minor components include protein, phosphorus, lipids, and ash (Perez and Bertoft, 2010). The size, functional and physico-chemical properties of the starch granules vary from species to species because of the differences in the chemical composition (Tharanathan 1995).The starch can be divided into three main groups which include: *native starch* (includes thatstarch which after its extraction from its source is not subjected to any treatment, it is white odourless and colourless either powder or liquid), *modified starch* (includes that starch in which if any one or more of the original characteristics of the native starch has been altered or modified with any of the treatments like physical, chemical or enzymatic or combination of these as per the Good Manufacturing Practices), *hydrolysed starch* (includes that starch in which the polymeric chains are broken into simple sugars like maltose) (Tegge, 1987; BeMiller and Whistler, 2009).

2. Chemical Composition of Starch

The major chemical components of starch are amylose and amylopectin made of glucosyl units. Minor components include protein, phosphorus, lipids, and ash (Perez and Bertoft, 2010). Free radicals generated by γ-irradiation (commonly detected by electron paramagnetic resonance (EPR) (Aleksieva and Yordanov, 2012) in the granules react with starch components to produce diverse radiolytic productssuch as acids and aldehydes. The formation of free radicals and various chemical products from g-irradiation has been reviewed previously in detail (Sokhey and Hanna, 1993; Tomasik and Zaranyika, 1995) and is not a focus here. Recent studies have confirmed some of these observations, in particular, the oxidised component of starch most reported. γ-irradiation greatly increased the carboxyl content of corn, potato, and bean starches at 50 kGy (Chung and Liu, 2009). Similar results have been reported on lotus stem starch (Gani, *et al*., 2013) and kidney bean, broad bean, and Indian horse chestnut starches (5e20 kGy) (Gani *et al*., 2012; Sofi, *et al*., 2013; Wani *et al*., 2014). A lower dose rate of irradiation resulted in lower carboxyl contents of corn starch (Chung and Liu, 2009).

3. Modification of Starch

Starch in its native form has certain limitations *viz.*, propensity towards retrogradation, high viscosity even at low concentrations, handling problems, poor freeze-thaw stability, low process tolerance and gel opacity that prevent its use in food processing. In order to overcome these problems starch granules are modified prior to their final use as food or food ingredient. Starch modification has resulted an increase in one or more of the following properties: increased digestibility, emulsifying agent, emulsion stabilizer, encapsulating agent, cold-water swellability, charged starch molecules, increased cooking characteristics, film formation, wall materials for encapsulation, improved gel characteristics (freeze-thaw stability, viscoelasticity, viscosity, adhesiveness), pH, temperature and shear tolerance, water-holding capacity etc. due to which its applications in the food and other industries has increased (Shi and BeMiller 2000, Tester *et al.,* 2004). The modified starch has gained attention in food business because of its ability to be used as dietary fat replacer. Also the consumption of starch within adequate limits has been linked with the prevention of cancer, diverticulitis, coronary heart diseases (Asp and Bjorck 1992, Lopez *et al.*, 2001).

At present there are several techniques which are being used for the production of modified starch (Jacobs and Delcour 1998); they include:

1. Chemical methods (such as cross-linking, graft copolymerization, cationization, stabilization/substitution, conversion, trans-glycosidation involving the use of various chemicals like phosphoryl-chloride, sodiumtri-polyphosphate, vinylchloride, mono-sodiumphosphate, epichlorohydrin) (Zhang *et al.*, 2006; Gunaratne *et al.*, 2007; Marcoa *et al.*, 2008; Segura-Campos *et al.*, 2008).
2. Enzymatic methods (including enzymes such as amylomaltases, α and β-amylases, transglucosidase, cyclo-maltodextrinase) (Rajan and Abraham, 2006; Yadav *et al.*, 2007; Tester *et al.*, 2008).
3. Genetic methods (resulting into amylose free starch, high amylose starch, starch with altered amylopectin structure) (BeMiller and Whistler, 2009)
4. Physical methods (*e.g.* pre-gelatinization, ball milling (pulverizing), annealing, heat-moisture treatment, dry heating of starch, radiation treatments, shear modification) (Lawal, 2005; Huang *et al.*, 2007b; Pimpa *et al.*, 2007; Mustapha *et al.*, 2014).

The enzymatic methods being complicated and time consuming have limited applications in the food industry and related sectors. The chemical methods although being faster,pose risks because of leaving certain chemical residues into the final product. Now-a-days there has been an escalating interest in physical methods particularly radiation processing which is considered to be a cold process and has been reported as one of the suitable techniques for starch modification. Radiation processing has emerged as an environment-friendly and an economical technique which can be used for bringing about certain changes in some of the physico-chemical and functional properties of certain components of food products. Radiation processing besides having other applications for food processing, is widely employed for the enhancement of the shelf life of food products. Since it is highly effective against all bacteria, insects and other pests, today the use of radiation technology is widely accepted in the international markets for its various applications in the food industries (Kaur *et al.*, 2012).

4. Effect of Gamma Irradiation on Physico-chemical, Thermal and Functional Properties of Starch

Studies pertaining to the starch modification by related to the impact of gamma irradiation on starch (modification, functional properties, thermal properties and physicochemical properties) have been summarized. Kertez *et al.* (1959), studied the effect of gamma irradiation at a dose level of 1 and 5 kGy on the maize starch. They found that the relative viscosities decreased when compared to the reference sample treated with high temperature of 140 °C for 30 min. Saini (1968) also carried the research studies on the effects of gamma irradiation on corn starch granules. They found that the starch macromolecules were depolymerised and the severity increased as the dose was increased. Several other studies revealed the structural changes and an increase in maltose, maltotetrose, maltotriose and other related saccharide content in wheat and rice starch, when subjected to gamma irradiation. An increase in starch solubility, decreased viscosity, dough stability, swelling capacity and amylograph peak viscosity was also reported as the dosage level increased (Ananthaswamy *et al.*, 1970, ElSaadany *et al.*, 1974, MacArthur and D Appolonia 1983, Rao *et al.*, 1975, Ng *et al.*, 1989). The molecular disintegration in starch and proteins of gamma irradiated wheat was reported along with high amylose fraction, decreased amylopectin, formic acid production and elevated retrogradation, which influenced the dough properties, rheological properties, baking qualities of the flour but having almost nil impact on the nutritional value (Vakil *et al.*, 1973, Abd Allah *et al.*, 1974). Gamma irradiation increases the proportions of rapidly digestible and enzyme resistant starch. Moreover, induced modification increases the radical scavenging activity and ferric reducing power, hence, an increase in antioxidant activity (Hussain *et al.*, 2014).

The compositional changes in the gamma irradiated (1 Mrad) starch extracted from the pigeon pea (*Cajan uscajan)* was evaluated by Nene *et al.* (1975). The results revealed decrease in gelatinization temperature, a progressive increase in maltose content with time, increased sensitivity of irradiated starch towards α-amylase. A study on the effects of low-dose gamma irradiation (0, 50, 100, 200, and 300 Krad) on the starch extracted from the three red spring cultivars of wheat was carried out by MacArthur *et al.* (1984). The starch properties were analysed and it was found that there was a decreasing trend in the peak viscosity and intrinsic viscosity values as the dose was increased. In a study carried out by Kashani and Valadon (1984) on the gamma irradiated *Pistacia vera* kernals, the authors revealed that the dosage up to 10kGy did not produce any significant effect on the total available carbohydrates (total starch, dextrin or on any of the individual free sugars).

Bhatty *et al.* (1988) treated the scout hull-less barley with gamma irradiation (10 Mrad) and it was found that viscoamylogram properties were completely lost. Although, Scanning Electron Microscopy results showed no significant alterations in outer structure of the starch granules, the granules were found internally broken. The irradiated starch was also found more susceptible to hydrolysis by both alpha- and beta amylase as compared to the non-irradiated starch. Rayas *et al.* (1993) irradiated starch extracted from northern bean (*Phaseolus vulgaris*) and it was observed that reducing maltose value of the starch molecule was increased besides increased solubility in both water and ethanol. Ciesla *et al.* (1999) irradiated starch extracted from potato and wheat ûour with high doses of gamma rays (20kGy). They found that the gelatinization temperatures varied between the irradiated starch and non-irradiated one. The differences between the gelatinization temperature was ascribed to the irradiation induced deformation of the amylopectin structures which resulted in the destruction of the crystalline structures. The viscosities of porridges made from gamma irradiated maize, beans and their composite flours decreased with increase in dosage level (0 to 10kGy) (Rombo *et al.*, 2001). They also found that starch digestibility was higher at dosage of 2.5kGy in case of maize, with subsequent increase in the dosage level the starch digestibility was reduced. The digestibility of the maize was found higher as compared to the bean starch for the same treatments.

5. Inferences from the Studies

Gamma Irradiation can be successfully employed for the modification of the starch. However, the dose required depends upon the intended use of the starch. The effect of gamma irradiation depends on the dose, dose rate, moisture content, temperature and atmosphere during irradiation of the native starch. A radiation dose of higher than 5 kGy induced a significant change in the physico-chemical and thermal properties (like viscosity, gelatinization, freeze-thaw stability, digestibility, solubility) of the starch (Raffi *et al.*, 1981; Roushdi *et al.*, 1983). Studies have also reported that gamma irradiation increases the proportions of both rapidly digestible starch and enzyme resistant starch. Gamma irradiation induced modification increases the radical scavenging activity and ferric reducing power indicating an increase in antioxidant activity (Hussain *et al.,* 2014).

6. Conclusion

The pace of growth of human population is a serious concern for sustainable food supply. To achieve the sustainable supply, underutilized crops or plants that are good sources of the starch need to be explored. In 2000, the starch production was 48.5 million tonnes, while in 2008, the production was about 66 million tonnes which reached to about 75 million tonnes in 2012 and is expected to reach 95 million tonnes by 2020. The annual market growth rate for the starch in India and China is expected to be around 4.5%, while for US and EU it is around 2% and 3% for the rest of the world. It becomes quite evident that the demand for the modified starch is going to rise at a faster rate. To achieve it, a safe and inexpensive method needs to be developed and gamma irradiation has proved till now as an efficient alternative for the chemical and microbial modification of starch. In future research needs to be done for using the ionizing radiations in combinations in order to have efficient cross linking and desired functional properties of modified starch. Further standards need to be set for giving the dosage and also development of techniques to check whether the food has been irradiated or not. It is evident from the research available that starch modification by gamma irradiation is a booming sector in the area of food technology.

References

Abd Allah, M. A., Foda, Y. H., El Saadany, R. 1974. Effect of gamma rays on starch extracted from irradiated wheat flour. *Starch Stärke*, 26(3):89-93.

Aleksieva, K. and Yordanov, N.D., 2012. EPR investigation of some gamma-irradiated excipients. *Radiation Effects and Defects in Solids*, 167(9):685-689.

Ananthaswamy, H.N., Vakil, U.K. and Sreenivasan, A., 1970. Effect of gamma radiation on wheat starch and its components. *Journal of Food Science*, 35(6):795-798.

Asp NG, Bjorck I. 1992.Resistant starch. *Trends Food Sci Tech* 3:111–4.

BeMiller, J. N., Whistler, R. L. 2009. Starch: Chemistry and Technology. 3rd ed. A vol in Food Sc and Technology.

Bhatty, R. S., Macgregor, A. W. 1988. Gamma irradiation of hulless barley: effect on grain composition, â-glucans and starch. *Cereal Chem*, 65:463–70.

Chung, H.J. and Liu, Q., 2009. Effect of gamma irradiation on molecular structure and physicochemical properties of corn starch. *Journal of Food Science*, 74(5):C353-C361.

Chung, H.J. and Liu, Q., 2010. Molecular structure and physicochemical properties of potato and bean starches as affected by gamma-irradiation. *International Journal of Biological Macromolecules*, 47(2):214-222.

Cieœla, K., Svensson, E. and Eliasson, A.C., 1999. Preliminary studies using differential scanning calorimetry of radiation-induced transformations in starch and flour. *Journal of thermal analysis and calorimetry*, 56(3):1197-1202.

Data, A. and Gluten, W., 1983. Gamma Radiation of Wheat. I. Effects on Dough and Baking Properties1. *Cereal Chem*, 60(6):456-460.

El Saadany, R.M.A., El Saadany, F.M. and Foda, Y.H., 1974. Modification of rice starch by gamma irradiation to produce soluble starch of low viscosity for industrial purposes. *Starch Stärke*, 26(12):422-425.

Ellis, R.P., Cochrane, M.P., Dale, M.F.B., Duffus, C.M., Lynn, A., Morrison, I.M., Prentice, R.D.M., Swanston, J.S. and Tiller, S.A., 1998. Starch production and industrial use. *Journal of the Science of Food and Agriculture*, 77(3):289-311.

Gani, A., Bashir, M., Wani, S.M. and Masoodi, F.A., 2012. Modification of bean starch by ã-irradiation: Effect on functional and morphological properties. *LWT-Food Science and Technology*, 49(1):162-169.

Gani, A., Gazanfar, T., Jan, R., Wani, S.M. and Masoodi, F.A., 2013. Effect of gamma irradiation on the physicochemical and morphological properties of starch extracted from lotus stem harvested from Dal lake of Jammu and Kashmir, India. *Journal of the Saudi Society of Agricultural Sciences*, 12(2):109-115.

Gunaratne, A. and Corke, H., 2007. Influence of prior acid treatment on acetylation of wheat, potato and maize starches. *Food chemistry*, 105(3):917-925.

Han, J.A. and BeMiller, J.N., 2007. Preparation and physical characteristics of slowly digesting modified food starches. *Carbohydrate polymers*, 67(3):366-374.

Huang, Z-Q., Lu, J-P., Li, X-H., Tong, Z-F.2007b. Effect of mechanical activation on physicochemical properties and structure of cassava starch. *Carbohydr Polym* 68: 128–35.

Hussain, P.R., Wani, I.A., Suradkar, P.P. and Dar, M.A., 2014. Gamma irradiation induced modification of bean polysaccharides: Impact on physicochemical, morphological and antioxidant properties. *Carbohydrate polymers*, 110:183-194.

Jacobs, H. and Delcour, J.A., 1998. Hydrothermal modifications of granular starch, with retention of the granular structure: A review. *Journal of Agricultural and Food Chemistry*, 46(8):2895-2905.

Kashani, G.G. and Valadon, L.R.G., 1984. Effects of gamma irradiation on the lipids, carbohydrates and proteins of Iranian pistachio kernels. *International Journal of Food Science and Technology*, 19(5):631-638.

Kaur, B., Ariffin, F., Bhat, R. and Karim, A.A., 2012. Progress in starch modification in the last decade. *Food Hydrocolloids*, 26(2):398-404.

Kertesz, Z.I., Schulz, E.R., Fox, G. and Gibson, M., 1959. effects of ionizing radiations on plant tissues. iv. some effects of gamma radiation on starch and starch fractionsa, b. *Journal of Food Science*, 24(6):609-617.

Lawal, O.S., 2005. Studies on the hydrothermal modifications of new cocoyam (Xanthosoma sagittifolium) starch. *International journal of biological macromolecules*, 37(5):268-277.

Lopez, H.W., Levrat-Verny, M.A., Coudray, C., Besson, C., Krespine, V., Messager, A., Demigné, C. and Rémésy, C., 2001. Class 2 resistant starches lower plasma and liver lipids and improve mineral retention in rats. *The Journal of Nutrition*, 131(4):1283-1289.

MacArthur, L. A., D'Appolonia, B. L. 1984. Gamma radiation of wheat. II. Effects of low dosage radiations on starch properties. *Cereal Chem* 61:321–6.

Marcoa, C. and Rosell, C.M., 2008. Effect of different protein isolates and transglutaminase on rice flour properties. *Journal of Food Engineering*, 84(1):132-139.

Mustapha, M. B., Bousselmi, M., Jerbi, T., Bettaïebb, N. B., Fattoucha, S. 2014. Gamma radiation effects on microbiological, physicochemical and antioxidant properties of Tunisian millet (*Pennisetum glaucum*). *J of Food Chem,* 154: 230-237.

Nene, S. P., Vakil, U. K., Sreenivasan, A. 1975. Effect of gamma radiation on physico-chemical character of red gram (Cajanus cajan) Starch. *J Food Sci* 40:943–7.

Ng, P.K.W., Bushuk, W. and Borsa, J., 1989. Effect of gamma ray and high-energy electron irradiations on breadmaking quality of two Canadian wheat cultivars. *Canadian Institute of Food Science and Technology Journal*, 22(2):173-176.

Pérez, S. and Bertoft, E., 2010. The molecular structures of starch components and their contribution to the architecture of starch granules: A comprehensive review. *Starch Stärke*, 62(8):389-420.

Pimpa, B., Muhammad, S.K.S., Hassan, M.A., Ghazali, Z., Hashim, K. and Kanjanasopa, D., 2007. Effect of electron beam irradiation on physicochemical properties of sago starch. *Songklanakarin Journal of Science and Technology*, 29(3):759-768.

Rafû, J. J., Agnel, J. P. L., Thiery, C. J., Frejaville, C. M., Saint-Lebe, L. R. 1981. Study of ã -irradiated starches derived from different foodstuffs: a way for extrapolating wholesomeness data. *J Agric Food Chem,* 29:1227–32.

Rajan, A. and Abraham, T.E., 2006. Enzymatic modification of cassava starch by bacterial lipase. *Bioprocess and Biosystems Engineering*, 29(1):65-71.

Rao, S.R., Hoseney, R.C., Finney, K.F. and Shogren, M.D., 1975. Effect of gamma irradiation of wheat on breadmaking properties. *Cereal Chemistry*.

Rayas Duarte, P. and Rupnow, J.H., 1993. Gamma Irradiation Affects Some Physical Properties of Dry Bean (Phaseolus vulgaris) Starch. *Journal of Food Science*, 58(2):389-394.

Rombo, G.O., Taylor, J. and Minnaar, A., 2001. Effect of irradiation, with and without cooking of maize and kidney bean flours, on porridge viscosity and in vitro starch digestibility. *Journal of the Science of Food and Agriculture*, 81(5):497-502.

Roushdi, M., Harras, A., El Meligi, A. and Bassim, M., 1983. Effect of high doses of gamma rays on corn grains. Part II. Influence on some physical and chemical properties of starch and its fractions. *Starch Stärke*, 35(1):15-18.

Saini, V., 1968. Ionizing radiation effects on starch as shown by Staudinger index and differential thermal analysis. *Journal of Food Science*, 33(2):136-138.

Segura-Campos, M., Chel-Guerrero, L. and Betancur-Ancona, D., 2008. Synthesis and partial characterization of octenylsuccinic starch from Phaseolus lunatus. *Food Hydrocolloids*, 22(8):1467-1474.

Shi, X. and BeMiller, J.N., 2000. Effect of sulfate and citrate salts on derivatization of amylose and amylopectin during hydroxypropylation of corn starch. *Carbohydrate Polymers*, 43(4):333-336.

Sofi, B.A., Wani, I.A., Masoodi, F.A., Saba, I. and Muzaffar, S., 2013. Effect of gamma irradiation on physicochemical properties of broad bean (Vicia faba L.) starch. *LWT-Food Science and Technology*, 54(1):63-72.

Sokhey, A.S. and Hanna, M.A., 1993. Properties of irradiated starches. *Food Structure*, 12(4): p.2.

Tegge, G. 1987. Starch: properties and potential. Chichester, U.K.: John Wiley and Sons.

Tester, R.F., Yousuf, R., Karkalas, J., Kettlitz, B. and Röper, H., 2008. Properties of protease-treated maize starches. *Food chemistry*, 109 (2):257-263.

Tharanathan, R.N., 2005. Starch—value addition by modification. *Critical reviews in food science and nutrition*, 45(5):371-384.

Tomasik, P. and Zaranyika, M.F., 1995. Nonconventional methods of modification of starch. *Advances in Carbohydrate Chemistry and Biochemistry*, 51:243-318.

Vakil, U.K., Aravindakshan, M., Srinivas, H., Chauhan, P.S. and Sreenivasan, A., 1973. Nutritional and wholesomeness studies with irradiated foods: India's program. In *Radiation preservation of food*.

Wani, I.A., Jabeen, M., Geelani, H., Masoodi, F.A., Saba, I. and Muzaffar, S., 2014. Effect of gamma irradiation on physicochemical properties of Indian Horse Chestnut (*Aesculus indica* Colebr.) starch. *Food Hydrocolloids*, 35:253-263.

Yadav, A.R., Mahadevamma, S., Tharanathan, R.N. and Ramteke, R.S., 2007. Characteristics of acetylated and enzyme-modified potato and sweet potato flours. *Food chemistry*, 103(4):1119-1126.

Zhang, X., Hoobin, P., Burgar, I. and Do, M.D., 2006. Chemical modification of wheat protein-based natural polymers: cross-linking effect on mechanical properties and phase structures. *Journal of Agricultural and Food Chemistry*, 54(26):9858-9865.

12

Non Traditional and Analytical Instrument Based Approaches to Ascertain the Purity of Ghee

Tanmay Hazra, Priti Saha, Parmar Manish Kumar, Pratap Singh and Vivek Sharma

Abstract

Ghee means the pure clarified fat derived solely from milk or curd or from desi (cooking) butter or from cream to which no coloring matter or preservative has been added. It is the second largest dairy product prepared from milk and it is almost 35% of total milk production. Unfortunately, the producers or the middle-men involved in the ghee trade, tend to adulterate ghee with cheaper oils and fats like vegetable oils, animal body fats, hydrogenated fats and sometimes even the non-edible mineral oils, especially during lean season to earn more money. Recently, the problem of adulteration has assumed a very serious dimension. Such a situation has tarnished the image of dairy industry. Methods presently adopted by food law enforcing agencies to ensure the quality of ghee are mainly based on the physico-chemical constants, but all these methods have some limitations. So researchers are always in search of different innovative methods to check the quality of ghee.

Keywords: Ghee, Adulterants, physico-chemical constants, Fatty acids, Triglycerol.

1. Introduction

India is the largest producer of milk in the world, producing 140 million metric tons (MMT) in the year 2014-15, which estimated to be touched 146 million metric tons in the year 2016 (Anonymous, 2015). In India, ghee is the second largest dairy product prepared from milk and it is almost 35% of total milk production (GAIN report, 2014). Ghee (from Sanskrit ghrita meaning "sprinkled") is clarified milk fat and by far the most important product widely consumed in the Indian sub-continent since time immemorial. Its image as a natural product and its organoleptic attributes, nutritional value and functional properties make it suitable for numerous food applications. Ghee has been considered immensely superior to other fats, mainly because of the presence of characteristic short chain fatty acids, which are responsible for its better digestibility and anti-cancer property (Upadhay, 2014). Ghee performs a major and essential function as carrier of four fat soluble vitamins *viz.*, A, D, E, K and essential fatty-acids such as linolenic acid and arachidonic acid, apart from having rich and pleasant sensory attributes. Ghee is believed to be a coolant, capable of increasing mental power and physical appearance, curative of ulcers and eye-diseases (Rangappa and Achaya,1974).

According to FSSR (2011) "Ghee" means the pure clarified fat derived solely from milk or curd or from desi (cooking) butter or from cream to which no coloring matter or preservative has been added. It is estimated that in the year 2015-16 the production of ghee would be increased to 3 MMT to 5 MMT valued at Rs. 475 billion (GAIN report, 2014). Over 10% of this production comes from organized sector, half of which is contributed by the co-operative sector. About 60% ghee is packed in bulk and 40% in consumer packs (Aneja *et. al.*, 2002). Ghee production level varies from region to region, 57% in northern region, 9.5% in eastern, 23.5% in western and 10% in southern region, respectively

Unfortunately, the producers or the middle-men involved in the ghee trade, tend to adulterate ghee with cheaper oils and fats like vegetable oils, animal body fats, hydrogenated fats and sometimes even the non-edible mineral oils, especially during lean season to earn more money. Recently, the problem of adulteration has assumed a very serious dimension. Such a situation has tarnished the image of dairy industry, not only in India, but abroad also. Reports have been appearing in the print and electronic media, indicating the rampant malpractices of ghee adulteration on particularly in the central and northern parts of the country. It is not known as to what extent these types of malpractices of adulteration are prevailing in the ghee trade in our country and what quality of ghee is available to the consumers. Among all the adulterants, body fat is the most dangerous in Indian context, by adding animal body fats in ghee (the sacred holy food) the unscrupulous ghee traders are not only robbing the people of their money, but also playing with the religious sentiments, especially of the vegetarian section of the society. In order to ensure a genuine product to the consumer, the Government of India has prescribed the compositional standards for ghee (in table 1&2)', under FSSR (2011) and AGMARK rules (1981), but methods presently adopted by those food law enforcing agencies to ensure the quality of ghee are mainly based on the physico-chemical constants like [Butyro-refractometer reading (B.R – reading), Reichert-Meisslvalue (R.M – value) and Polenske Value (P- value), Phyto- sterol Acetate test (PA- test) and Baudouin - test]. These said methods are being used by enforcing agencies to ascertain the quality of milk fat but most of these standards are based on the physico-chemical parameters, that are subjected to be changeable from region wise (Table 1), also at the same time unscrupulous traders are developing such concoctions of adulterant fats so they pass the said tests. Therefore, in addition to these methods researchers are always in-search of new innovative techniques to tackle the menace of rampant adulteration in ghee. Hence, in this chapter some non-traditional as well modern instrumental approaches have been discussed to ensure the authenticity of ghee.

Table 1: FSSR (2011) Standards of Ghee

Sr.No.	States	BR AT 40ºC	RM value (min)	FFA (max % Oleic acid)	Moisture (% max)
1.	Bihar, Chandigarh, Delhi, Punjab, Haryana (areas other than cotton track), West Bengal (areas other than Bisnupur Subdivision), Sikkim, Jharkhand.	40-43	28	3.0	0.5
2.	Manipur, Meghalaya, Mizoram, Arupra, Orissa, Uttaranchal, Nagaland, Goa, Kerela, HP, U.P., J&K, Rajasthan, (areas other than jodhpur division), Haryana (cotton tract areas),\ Lakshadweep, Maharastra (areas other than cotton tract areas).	40-43	26	3.0	0.5
3.	Karnataka (Belgaum district), M.P. (areas other than cotton tract areas), Pondicherry, Chhatisgarh.	40-44	26	3.0	0.5
4.	A.P., Daman & Diu, Dadar& Nagar Haveli, Karnataka(areas other than Belgaum Dist	40-43	24	3.0	0.5
5.	Andaman & Nicobar island, T.N.	41-44	24	3.0	0.5
6.	Gujarat (cotton tract areas), M.P. (cotton tract areas), Maharashtra (cotton tract areas), Rajasthan (Jodhpur sub division), West Bengal (Bishnupur sub division)	41.5-45	21	3.0	0.5
7.	Gujarat (areas other than cotton tract)	40-43.5	24	3.0	0.5

Table 2: AGMARK (1981) Standards of Ghee

Parameters	Special grade	General grade
1. Baudouin test	Negative	Negative
2. Butyro-refractometer reading at 40ºC	41.5	45.0
3. Reichert Meissl value	Not less than 21	Not less than 21
4. Polenske value	0.5-1.2	0.5-1.2
5. Moisture content	0.3%	0.3%
6. %age of Free Fatty Acids (as oleicacid)	Not more than 1.4	Not more than 2.5

2. Non-Traditional Test-based on Physico-Chemical Properties of Milk Fat

Food law enforcing agencies adopted methods to ensure the quality of milk of ghee are mainly based on the physico-chemical constants. Patel (2011) reported that Reichert-Meissl value (RM–value) and Polenske Value (P-value) were not very much useful to ensure the quality of ghee for detection of body fat adulteration in ghee. At the same time variation of these physico-chemical constants on different region wise creates a great problem. So different non-traditional methods based on physico-chemical properties of milk fat is given here.

2.1 Titre Value

The Titre value of ghee represents the highest temperature reached when the liberated water insoluble fatty acids are crystallized under arbitrarily controlled conditions. For determination of Titre value of ghee, it is first saponified with glycerol-potassium hydroxide solution, thereafter the resulting soap is decomposed with sulphuric acid and the liberated water-insoluble fatty acids are separated, washed free from mineral acid and dried. Titre value of milkfat lies between 33 to 38°C (Hamilton and Rossell, 1986). Animal body fats such as beef tallow, lard and mutton tallow generally have a higher range (32-48°C). On the other hand, vegetable oils such as sunflower oil, safflower oil, soybean oil, groundnut oil, plam kernel oil, etc. generally have lower Titre values (15-32°C), except cottonseed oil (30-37°C) and palm oil (40-47°C). At one time, the Titre value was used for judging the quality of ghee produced in cotton tract areas, Moreover, its use is limited due to the introduction of more modern instrumental methods of analysis.

2.2. Bomer Value (BV)

Bomer value is defined as the sum of the melting point of saturated triglycerides (isolated by diethyl ether method) and twice the difference between this melting point and that of the fatty acids obtained after the saponification of these triglycerides. The Bomer value of both cow and buffalo ghee ranges from 63°C to 64°C, whereas those of animal body fats, e.g., goat, sheep and buffalo ranges from 68 to 69 and that of pig body fat from 75 to 76. Sharma and Singhal (1996) successfully applied this test for the detection of body fats (buffalo, goat and pig) and vanaspati added to buffalo ghee at 20 % (w/w) level.

2.3. Opacity Test

Singhal (1980) developed an opacity test to detect the adulteration of ghee with animal body fats. In this test 5.0 g of ghee use to take in a test tube (8 cm × 1.5 cm) to become opaque (OD>0.5) at 23°C using 590 nm (yellow) filter and observed that the normal ghee took more than 35 minutes, whereas animal body fats (buffalo, goat and sheep) took only 10 to 20 seconds to become opaque. In pure state, both cow and buffalo ghee took almost similar time to become opaque, but adulterated cow ghee took more time than the adulterated buffalo ghee to show a noticeable opacity.

Sharma and Singhal (1996) carried out the opacity test at 25°C for pure fats (ghee, body fats and vanaspati) and adulterated ghee samples (5, 10 and 20% level) and observed almost the similar results as reported earlier by Singhal (1980). Their study revealed that ghee took more than 35 min to become opaque, while vanaspati and lard (pig body fat) took 2 to 2.5 min and 6 to 7 min, respectively. On the other hand, tallow (buffalo and goat body fats) took very less time (<18 seconds) to become opaque. They did not find any significant difference in the opacity time of pure ghee and ghee samples adulterated with vanaspati and lard even up to 20 % level. However, in case of adulteration with buffalo and goat body fats, the opacity times were significantly reduced, thereby making the detection possible..

2.4. Apparent solidification test (AST)

The Apparent solidification test defined as time taken by completely melted fat sample to get apparently solidify at a particular temperature by below mentioned method that was given by Kumar *et al.* (2009)

The method is as follows 3.0 gm of the complete melted fat sample was taken in to the test tube (12×100mm) and kept it in oven maintained at 60 °C for 5min and thereafter put in water bath till apparent solidification of fat samples, time taken to become apparent solidify of a fat sample is called apparent solidification time. Kumar *et al.* (2009) reported that AST time taken for buffalo ghee ranges from 2 min 30 s to 2 min 48 s, whereas for cow ghee 2 min 56 s to 3 min 26 s and these authors reported any deviation from these range indicting the possibility of adulteration of ghee. Later some researchers (Hariyani 2010) reported that time of AST values for ghee varies from seasonal basis, so it is not possible to detect all adulterants in ghee by this method (Upadhay, 2014).

2.5. Critical Temperature of Dissolution (CTD)

Critical temperature of dissolution (temperature at which turbidity appears on gradual cooling of the fat dissolved in a warm solvent or solvent mixture) is a characteristic of a particular fat which depends upon the nature of the solvent, nature and amount of most insoluble glycerides (usually tri- saturated glycerides) present in a fat as well as the mutual solubilizing power exerted on these glycerides by the soluble glycerides (Boghra *et al.*, 1981). Bhide and Kane (1952) observed the CTD values for ghee and vanaspati in the range of 39 to

45°C and 62 to 72°C, respectively, employing a 2:1 (v/v) mixture of 95 % ethanol and iso-amyl alcohol, and reported that gross adulteration of ghee with vanaspati could easily be detected. Delforno (1964) reported the CTD values for butter as 50.5 to 57.5°C (Average 54°C), for coconut oil as 28 to 41°C (Average 33°C) and for other oils and fats as 67 to 82.5°C (Average 71-78°C). Similarly, the presence of body fats in ghee was detected by employing either a single solvent such as absolute alcohol (Delforno, 1964) or a solvent mixture of 95 % ethyl alcohol and iso-amyl alcohol in the ratio of 2:1 (Bhide and Kane, 1952). Likewise, CTD was used for the detection of adulteration of ghee with mineral oils by Kane and Ranadive (1951) using aniline as solvent. The CTD test seems to be simple, but its efficacy is greatly affected by the free fatty acid (FFA) and rancidity (peroxides) present in ghee.

2.6. Complete Liquification Time (CLT)

Complete liquification time test is based on melting behavior of pre-solidify fats/oils at a particular temperature. Normally, the fats which contain higher proportion of unsaturated fatty acids melt fast, while the fats which consist of more of saturated fatty acids melt slowly. The cow ghee showed slightly lower value of CLT as compared to buffalo ghee, which was probably due to the slightly higher content of unsaturated fatty acids in cow ghee than buffalo ghee, as reported by Kumar *et al.* (2011). Adulteration of cow as well as buffalo ghee with vegetable oil (soybean oil) decreased the CLT value and this decrease was dependent upon the amount of vegetable oil added to the pure cow and buffalo ghee. On the other hand, animal body fat (buffalo body fat) added to both cow and buffalo ghee increased the CLT value. It was also observed that addition of mixture of vegetable oil and animal body fat in equal proportion in both types of ghee caused increase in the CLT value. Higher the level of adulterant added, greater was the increase or decrease in the CLT value of ghee samples which was dependent on the type of adulterant used. Recently Upadhay *et al.* (2016) able to detect15%, w/w, groundnut oil and 10%, w/w, goat body fat in ghee.

2.7. Dilatation Behavior

This property is based on the thermal expansion behavior of milk fat. Using this property, Kalsi (1984) reported different solid and liquid fractions of milk fat from different species in the temperature range of 10 to 80°C and observed that solid and liquid fractions in equal proportions are obtained at 33, 30 and 24.5°C in case of buffalo, cow and goat milk fats, respectively. Kumar *et al.* (2007) applied this method for detection of adulteration in ghee. He studied the proportion of solid and liquid fractions of pure and adulterated ghee at 5, 10 and 15% level and observed that the ratio of solid to liquid fraction for pure cow and buffalo ghee was 2.37 and 3.10, respectively. On the basis of solid/liquid ratio, it was found that vegetable oils could be detected in cow ghee while body fats and Vanaspati could be detected in buffalo ghee.

3. Instrument Based Approaches for Detection of Adulteration in Ghee

Purity of ghee can be ascertained on the basis of physicochemical parameters, which require use of chemicals and solvents.This leads to potential health hazards and environmental pollution, moreover, these analytical methods are laborious and time consuming (Javidnia *et al.,* 2013), Researchers were also employing variousa nalytical techniques circumvent above said objections and now a days thesea nalytical techniques are gaining popularity due to their high specificity as well as precision.

3.1 Spectroscopic Methods

Spectroscopy deals with the production, measurements and interpretation of spectra arising from the interactions of electromagnetic radiation with matter. Spectroscopic methods based on the adsorption or emission of radiation in the ultraviolet, visible, infrared and radio (nuclear magnetic resonance) frequency ranges are most commonly encountered in traditional food analysis.

3.1.1 Tests Based on Visible Spectroscopy

Jha (1981) applied visible spectroscopy for the detection of Cheuri (*Madhuca butyracea*) fat in ghee, a common adulterant in Nepal. Pure ghee showed no absorption band in visible range (600-700 nm), whereas, Cheuri fat showed an absorption band with maxima between 640 and 680 nm. Jha (1981) reported even 5 % Cheuri fat content added to ghee could be detected in this range. In another study, Kumar *et al*. (2010) reported that visible spectroscopic methods were not so much useful for detection of adulteration in ghee as there were no significant difference absorption pattern between pure ghee as well as adulterants.

3.1.2 Tests Based on Ultraviolet (UV) Spectroscopy

Sharma (1989) scanned the UV spectra of cow ghee, buffalo ghee and animal body fats (buffalo, goat, pig and sheep) between 200 to 320 nm after dissolving the fats in n-hexane and observed a maximum absorption between 220 to 230 nm. However, cow ghee showed another small maximum at 270 nm. These workers also examined the UV spectrum of unsaponifiable matter extracted from ghee and animal body fats between 200 to 320 nm and observed an absorption maxima between 215 to 220 nm for both fats. However, the ghee samples showed a second maxima at 270 nm, which was shifted to 260 nm

(Singhal, 1973) or to 280 nm (Sharma, 1989) in case of animal body fats. But, on this basis, adulterated ghee could not be differentiated from pure ghee (Kumar, 2003).

3.1.3 Tests Based on Infra-Red (IR) Spectroscopy

The infra-red (IR) region which extends from 0.8 to 1,000 μm (14,000 to 20 cm^{-1} in wave number) is generally divided into three areas: near infra-red (0.8-2.5 μm), mid-infra-red (2.5 to 15.38 μm) and far infra-red (15-1,000 μm)

Sharma (1989) scanned the IR spectra of cow ghee, buffalo ghee, animal body fats (Buffalo, goat, sheep and pig) and ghee adulterated with body fats in the 4,000 to 600 cm^{-1} region and observed distinct differences between body fats and ghee in the region of 1300 to 1180 cm^{-1} and 1120 to 1100 cm^{-1}, respectively. Body fats showed the presence of 5 to 6 bands, while ghee showed only two bands. Ghee samples adulterated with body fats also showed 3 to 6 extra bands. Unsaponifiable matter extracted from the ghee, body fats and adulterated ghee samples also exhibited the similar pattern of bands as reported above for the whole fat. Hence the author concluded that the differences in IR spectrum of ghee and body fats could be used to detect ghee adulteration with body fats at 10 % level. Recently, Kumar (2003) reported that on the basis of increased level of trans isomers in ghee, as low as 5% of vanaspati added to ghee could be detected.Very recently Bency *et al.* (2016) differentiate cow and buffalo ghee using FT-IR.

3.1.4 Other spectroscopic methods

Nikhil and De (2015) used derivative spectroscopy to detect adulteration of tallow in ghee and they were reported to detect 20% level of buffalo tallow in pure ghee.

3.2 Differential Thermal Analysis (DTA) and Differential Scanning Calorimetry (DSC)

DTA and DSC are both closely related thermo-analytical techniques which measure the physical properties such as phase transition and specific heat of foods as a function of temperature. DTA measures the difference in temperature (Dt) between a sample and an inert reference material as a function of temperature. In DSC thermograms, the area delineated by the output curve is directly proportional to the total amount of energy transferred in or out of the sample.

Lambelet *et al.* (1980) detected goat body fat (more than 10%) in ghee by DTA technique on the basis of differences in melting diagram and crystallization patterns of goat body fat and ghee. Using DSC, detection of foreign fats like pig and buffalo body fats (Lambelet and Ganguly, 1983) and chicken fat (Coni *et al.*, 1994) in milk fat was reported. The method, however, failed to detect coconut oil, cotton tract ghee and other animal body fats.

Upadhay *et al.* (2016) reported that cow ghee added with goat body fat @5%,10% and 15% had different crystallization and melting curves from pure cow ghee, hence the author reported to detect 5% level of goat body fat in cow ghee.

3.3 Tests Based on Gas Liquid Chromatography (GLC) of Fatty Acids

Singhal (1987) reported that on GLC analysis of ratio of fatty acids, viz., $C_{15:0}$ / $C_{17:0}$ and $C_{16:0}$ / $C_{18:0}$ was lower in ghee samples adulterated with body fats even in the presence of vegetable oils. Sharma and Singhal (1996) analyzed the buffalo ghee samples adulterated with body fats (buffalo, goat, pig) and vanaspati at 20 % level and noted that short and medium chain fatty acids decreased while long chain fatty acids increased on adulteration. Panda and Bindal, (1997) employed this technique for the detection of adulteration in ghee with vegetable oils at level as low as 5 % using $C_{18:2}$ or $C_{22:1}$ as marker acid. Kumar (2003) found that the adulteration of ghee with body fats or vanaspati at 15 % level and above, could be detected using different fatty acid ratios like $C_{14:0}/C_{16:0}$ and $C_{18:0}/C_{18:1}$ whereas, presence of even 5 % vegetable oils (sunflower oil, soybean oil and groundnut oil) in ghee could be detected easily, using fatty acid ratios such as $C_{14:0}/C_{18:2}$, $C_{16:0}/C_{18:2}$, $C_{18:0}/C_{18:2}$, as well as linoleic acid ($C_{18:2}$) as a marker.

Upadhay (2014) reported that ratio of fatty acid C10:0/C18:2 could be a efficient marker for detection of goat body fat in ghee and even 15% of goat body fat could be detected by using this parameter. Kumar *et al.* (2015) claimed to detect 5 % level of animal fat in ghee (cow or buffalo) using GLC as oleic acid marker.

3.4 Tests Based on Gas Liquid Chromatography (GLC) of Triglycerol

For analysis of fatty acids using GLC based methods preparation of samples is very necessary and that is time consuming also fatty acids profile is dependent of milk is depends on environment factors as well as feed factors of animals, so instead of using fatty acid analysis recently triglycerol profiling getting popular to ascertain the purity of ghee.

Kala (2013) used capillary column based GLC for triglycerol analysis to asecertain the purity of ghee and the author concluded that triglycerol analysis is very much effective for ascerting the purity of ghee, also in another study Kala *et al.* (2016) concluded that triglycerol analysis using GLC also very much effective for ghee based products for ascertain its purity and quality.

4. Tests Based on the Nature and Content of Unsaponifiable Constituents

The unsaponifiable matter (USM) which can be obtained from oils and fats after saponification with alkali and subsequent extraction by a suitable organic solvent constitutes less than 2 % by weight of fat. It is a combination of so many valuable constituents, like sterols (cholesterol and phytosterols), fat-soluble vitamin (A, D, E and K), hydrocarbons such as squalene, pigments, etc. Milk fat contains USM in the range of 0.30 to 0.45 % by weight (Jenness and Patton, 1969) chiefly consisting of cholesterol (0.25 to 0.40% by weight of fat). Vegetable oils and animal body fats like lard and tallow have USM in the range of 0 to 2 and 0 to 1.0 %, respectively (Hamilton and Rossell, 1986).

Sterols and tocopherols are the two most important constituents of USM, which have been used to detect the vegetable fats in milk fat by using various techniques like GLC, TLC, paper chromatography, etc.

Kumar *et al.* (2013) & Anupama *et al.* (2013) reported to detect very low level of vegetable oil in ghee using RP-TLC, but Kumar *et al.* (2013) also reported that RP-TLC not able to detect animal body fat in ghee.

In a different study using HPLC (High Performance Liquid Chromatography) Anupama *et al.* (2015) reported that cholesterol and α-sitosterol as markers in the unsaponifiable could be used to detect even 1% vegetable oil in ghee.

5. Miscellaneous Methods

5.1 Tests for Mineral Oils

Adulteration of common edible oils and fats including milk fat with cheaper mineral oils, such as paraffin oil, heavy and light fuel oil, petroleum jelly, etc., has become a widespread phenomenon because of the price difference. Mineral oils also referred to as white oils are of different thickness and refractive indices. Unlike oils and fats, mineral oils are not saponifiable by alkali. This characteristic behaviour of mineral oils has been used as the basis for their detection in edible oils and fats. Venkatachalam and Sundaram (1957) could detect the presence of even 1 % of mineral oil in ghee by saponifying the test sample (1 ml) with aqueous potash followed by addition of alcohol (50%) and thorough shaking.

Besides the above reports of mineral oil detection in ghee, few reports have also appeared for their detection in vegetable oils and fats using turbidity test. Using Holde'stest , the presence of as little as 0.3 % of mineral oil in a fat can be detected by saponifying 10 drops of test sample (1 ml) with 5 ml of 0.5 N ethanolic potassium hydroxide solution and adding 5 ml of water to the hot soap solution and noting the appearance of turbidity (Winton and Winton, 1999). Kumar *et al.* (2003) have also reported the detection of liquid paraffin added to ghee at the rate of 0.5 % and above using Holde's test as described by Winton and Winton (1999).

5.2 Tests for Cottonseed Oils

Fatty acids containing cyclopropene ring, *viz*., malvalic ($C_{18:-0}$) and sterculic ($C_{19:0}$) acids which are altogether absent in milk fat, but are characteristic of cottonseed oil (Pandey and Suri, 1982) have been used as a tool by few workers (Christie, 1970) for the detection of cottonseed oil in milk fat and also to distinguish cotton tract ghee from normal ghee using Halphen test or methylene blue reduction test.

5.3 Halphen Test

This test is based on the development of a crimson colour due to the reaction between cyclopropenoic acids (constituents of cotton seed oil) and Halphen reagents (1% sulphur solution in CS_2 and equal volume of iso-amyl alcohol) after incubation for an hour in a boiling bath of saturated sodium chloride solution. This test finds its application for differentiating the cotton tract ghee from normal ghee (Singhal, 1980) as well as for the detection of cottonseed oil ghee.

5.4 Methylene Blue Reduction Test

Singhal (1980) developed a methylene blue reduction test for the identification of cotton tract ghee and reported that the colour of methylene blue dissolved in chloroform: methanol (1:1) was decolourised by cotton tract ghee or ghee added with cottonseed oil due to the presence of cyclopropenoic acids, while normal pure ghee did not reduce the colour of methylene blue dye.

5.5 Modified Bieber's Test

The Bieber's test, hitherto employed for the detection of almond oil adulteration with Kernel oil, was suitably modified by Sharma *et al.* (2007) to detect the adulteration of ghee with vegetable oils. Their results showed the presence of orange brown colour in case of refined vegetable oils & fats, whereas in case of pure ghee samples no colour was observed. By this method, adulteration of ghee with different vegetable oils to the tune of 5-7% could be detected.

6. DNA based Methodology for Quality Control in Food Products

Recently DNA based methodologies have proven their potential in ensuring the quality and origin of food and feed ingredients. Literature suggested that DNA is more thermo stable than many proteins and nucleic acid are less liable to be disrupted by processing of foodstuffs (Cunningham and Meghen, 2001). Furthermore, DNA is present in the majority of the cells of an organism, potentially enabling identical information to be obtained from any appropriate sample from the same source, regardless of the tissue of origin.

Nooratiny *et al.*(2013) developed a technique to isolate DNA from ghee using Epicentre Master DNA isolation kit followed by polymerase chain reaction (PCR) using cattle species-specific oligonucleotide primers which targeted the mitochondria DNA (mtDNA) of cytochrome b (cyt b) gene yielding 274 bp in size amplicon fragment for cattle. Hence, these authors reported that reported protocol was very efficient to prove the authenticity of ghee.

7. Conclusion

Ghee is a highly valuable and costlier product consumed allover India, as it imparts good sensory and nutritional properties. Therefore it is highly prone to adulteration with cheaper oils/fats. In recent years, the problem of adulteration has assumed a very serious dimension. Such a situation could tarnish the image of dairy Industry both in domestic and international market. So by adulterating ghee with cheaper oils and fat the unscrupulous traders are not only robbing the people of their money, but also playing with the cultural sentiments of people , besides adversely affecting their health.Detection of foreign fats in milk fat/ clarified milk fat (Ghee) is a very complex phenomenon, almost comparable with the detection of Pacific water in a sample of Atlantic water. Although several methods based on the physico-chemical characteristics of oils and fats have been developed to detect the various types of adulterant fats such as animal body fats and vegetable oils in milk fat, but most of the methods are quite tedious, time consuming and have one or the other limitation. The detection methods available till date are mainly based on the physico-chemical constants, fatty acid profile, sterol analysis, partial solidification behavior, etc. However, most of these methods fail when a mixture of body fats and vegetable oils & fats is added to milk fat. So researchers are always in search of new and innovative method to ascertain the purity of ghee.

References

AGMARK.1981. Ghee Grading and Marking Rules, 1938 (as amended).Government of India,Ministry of Food and Agriculture, Department of Agriculture, New Delhi.

Aneja, R.P., Mathur, B.N., Chandan, R.C., Banerjee, A.K.2002.*Technology of Indian Milk Product.*A airy India Publication, New Delhi, India.

Anonymous,2015.www.thehindu.com/business/Industry/milk-production-risesto140-million-tonnes-in-2013-14/article6085584.(Last accessed on 3/5/2016).

Anupama, R., Sharma, V., Arora, S. and Lal, D. 2015. Comparison of Rapid Reversed Phase High-Performance Liquid Chromatography (RP-HPLC) Method with Rapid Reversed Phase Thin Layer Chromatography Method for Detecting Vegetable Oils in Ghee (Clarified Milk Fat). *International Journal of Food Properties.*Doi10.1080/10942912.2015.1063065

Anupama, R. Sharma, V. Arora, S. Lal, D. and Kumar, A. 2013. A rapid reversed-phase thin layer chromatographic protocol for detection of adulteration in ghee (clarified milk fat) with vegetable oils. *Journal of Food Science & Technology*. 10: 2-6.

Bency, A., Sharma, S., Mehta, B.M., Ratnam, K. and Aparnathi, K.D. 2016. Comparison of transmittance and reflectance mode of FT -MIR and FT- NIRspectroscopy in application to clarified milk fat (*ghee*). *Indian Journal of Dairy Science,* 69:426-432.

Bhide, P.T. and Kane, J.G. 1952. Critical temperatures of dissolution of ghee and hydrogenated oils (vanaspati). *Indian Journal of Dairy Science*, 5: 183.

Boghra, V.R., Singh, S. and Sharma, R.S. 1981. Present status of the tests used for the detection of adulterants in ghee. *Dairy Guide*, 81: 21-31.

Christie, W.W. 1970. Cyclopropane and cyclopropene fatty acids. In: Topics in Lipid Chemistry. Vol. 1. Edited by F.D. Gunstone, Logos Press, London.

Coni, E., Pasquale, M.Di., Coppolelli, P., Bocca, A. and Di Pasquale, M.1994. Detection of animal fats in butter by differential scanning calorimetry: A pilot study. *Journal of American Oil Chemists Society*, 71:807 810.

Cunningham, E. P. and Meghen, C. M. 2001. Biological identification systems: Genetic markers. Revue scientifique et technique (International Office of Epizootics),20:491–499.

Delforno, G. 1964. Detection of foreign fats in butter using the crismer test. *Latte*, 38: 921 924.

FSSR. 2011. File No.1 94/FSSAI/SP/(Labelling). Food Safety and Standards Authority of India (Ministry of Health and Family Welfare). FDA Bhavan, KotlaRoad New Delhi-110002.

Gain Report 2014. (Global agriculture information Network). On "Dairy products Annual 2014". Report No.IN-4089. Published On-10/15/2014.

Hamilton, R.J. and Rossel, J.B.1986. Analysis of oils and fats. Elsevier Applied Science Publishers, London.

Hariyani, A. 2010. A study on physico-chemical qualities of market ghee. *Ph.D. Thesis* submitted to National Dairy Research Institute (Deemed University), Karnal, India

Javidnia, K., Parish, M., Karimi, S. and Hemmateenejad, B. 2013. Discrimination of edible oils and fats by combination of multivariate pattern recognition and FT-IR spectroscopy: A comparative study between different modeling methods. SpectrochimicaActa Part A: Molecule Biomolecule Spectroscopy, 104:175-181.

Jenness, R. and Patton, S. 1969. Principles of dairy chemistry. Wiley Eastern Pvt. Ltd., New Delhi.

Jha, J.S.1981.Spectrophotometeric studies of Cheuri (*Madhucabutyracea*) fat and ghee mixtures *.Journal of American Oil Chemistry Soc*iety, 58: 843-845.

Kala, A. 2013. Detection of possible adulteration in commercial ghee samples using low-resolution gas chromatography triglyceride profiles. *International Journal of Dairy Technology*. 3: 346–351.

Kala, A.L., Sabeena. and Havanur, P.P. 2016. Determination of triacyl glycerol and sterol components of fat to authenticate ghee based sweets. *Journal of Food Science Technology* DOI 10.1007/s13197-016-2182-3

Kalsi, P.S.1984. Dilatometeric study of solid/liquid fractions of milk fat from different species. MSc. Thesis submitted to National Dairy Research Institute(Deemed University) , Karnal.

Kane, J.G. and Ranadive, G.M.1951. Aniline point of some fats. *Journal of Science Industrial Research*, 10:62.

Kumar, A. 2003. Comparative studies on physico-chemical properties of various oils and fats with a view to detect adulteration in ghee. *Ph.D. Thesis* submitted to National Dairy Research Institute (Deemed University), Karnal, India.

Kumar, A. Lal, D. Seth, R. and Sharma, V. 2007. Dilatometric detection of body fats, vegetable oils and hydrogenated fat (vanaspati) added to milk fat. *International Journal of Dairy Science,* 60,pp.244-247.

Kumar, A., Upadhyay, N., Gandhi, K., Lal, D. and Sharma,V. 2013. Depot Fat in Ghee Using Normal-PhaseThin Layer Chromatography.*Indian Journal of Dairy Science*, 66:288-293.

Kumar, A., Upadhyay, N., Padghan, P. V., Gandhi, K., Lal, D and Sharma, V. 2015. Detection of Vegetable Oil and Animal Depot Fat Adulteration in Anhydrous Milk Fat (Ghee) using Fatty Acid Composition. *MOJ Food Processing & Technology*, 1:13-19.

Kumar, A., Lal, D., Kumar, A., Seth, R. and Sharma, V. 2011. Detection of added vegetable oils/ fats and animal body fats in milk fat on the basis of presence of marker fatty acids and different fatty acid ratios. *Indian Journal of Dairy Science*.64:388-395.

Kumar, A., Kumar, A., Lal, D., Seth, R. and Sharma,V. 2010.Validation of ultra-violet and visible spectroscopic methodsfor detection of milk fat adulteration. *Journal of Dairying, Foods & Home Science*, 29 ,pp.8 – 14.

Kumar, A., Lal, D., Seth, R. and Sharma,V. 2009. Apparent solidification time test for detection of foreign oils and fats adulterated in clarified milk fat, as affected by season and storage. *International Journal of Dairy Technology*, 62:33 - 38.

Lambelet, P. and Ganguli, N.C. 1983. Detection of pig and buffalo body fat in cow and buffalo ghee by differential scanning calorimetry. *Journal of American Oil Chemists Society*, 60: 1005.

Lambelet, P., Singhal, O.P. and Ganguli, N.C. 1980. Detection of goat body fat in ghee by differential thermal analysis. *Journal of American Oil Chemists Society*, 57:364.

Nikhil, M.J. and De, S.2015. Detection of tallow adulteration in cow ghee derivative spectrophotometry. *Journal of Natural Science Biology and Medicine*, 5:317-319.

Nooratiny, I. , Sahilah A M , Alif Alfie A R and Mohd Farouk M. Y. 2013 .DNA extraction from ghee and beef species identification using polymerase chain reaction (PCR) assay. *International Food Research Journal* , 20:2959-2961.

Pandey, S.N. and Suri, L.K. 1982. Cyclopropenoid fatty acid content and iodine value of crude oils from Indian cottonseed. *Journal of American Oil Chemists Society*, 59:99-101.

Panda, D. and Bindal, M.P. 1997. Detection of adulteration in ghee with animal body fats and vegetable oils using GLC based on a marker fatty acid. *Indian Journal of Dairy Science*, 50: 129-135.

Patel, A.M .2011.Validation of methods for detection of ghee adulteration with animal body fat. *M.Tech Thesis* submitted to National Dairy Research Institute (Deemed University), Karnal, India.

Rangappa, K.S. and Achaya, K.T. 1974. Indian dairy products. Asia Publishing House, Mysore.

Saderi, M. Saderi, A. and Hand, R.G. 2013. Identification of bovine, ovine and caprine pure and binary mixtures of raw and heat processed meats using species specific size markers targeting mitochondrial genome. *Iranian Journal of Veterinary Research*, 14:29-34.

Sharma, R. and Singhal, O.P. 1996. Fatty acid composition, bomer value and opacity profile of ghee prepared from milk adulterated with foreign fats. *Indian Journal of Dairy Science*, 49: 62 67.

Sharma, S.K. 1989. Studies on unsaponifiable matter of ghee (clarified butterfat) and animal body fats with a view to detect adulteration. Ph.D. Thesis submitted to National Dairy Research Institute (Deemed University), Karnal, India

Sharma, V., Lal, D. and Sharma, R. 2007. Color based platform test for the detection of vegetable oils/fats in ghee. *Indian Journal of Dairy Science*,60:16-18.

Singhal, O.P. 1973. Studies on ghee (clarified butterfat) and animal body fats with a view to detect adulteration. Ph.D. Thesis submitted to Punjab University, Chandigarh.

Singhal, O.P.1980. Adulterants and methods for detection. *Indian Dairyman*, 32:771 774.

Singhal, O.P. 1987. Detection of adulteration in butterfat. NDRI Annual Report: 64-65.

Upadhay, N. 2014. Detection of Vegetable Oil and Animal Body Fat In Ghee Using Solvent Fractionation Technique. Ph.D. Thesis submitted to National Dairy Research Institute (Deemed University), Karnal, India.

Upadhay, N., Kumar, A., Goyal, A. and Lal, D. 2016. Complete liquification time test coupled with solvent fractionation technique to detect adulteration of foreign fats in ghee. *International Journal of Dairy Technology*, Doi: 10.1111/1471-0307.12323.

Upadhay, N., Kumar, A., Goyal, A. and Lal, D. 2016. Detection of adulteration by caprine body fat and mixtures of caprine body fat and groundnut oil in bovine and buffalo ghee using differential scanning calorimetry. *International Journal of Dairy Technology* · DOI: 10.1111/ 1471-0307.12336

Venkatachalam, V. and Sundaram, S. 1957. Test for mineral oil in edible oils and ghee. *Current Science,* 26:157.

Winton, A.L. and Winton, K.B. 1999. Techniques of food analysis. Allied Scientific Publishers, Bikaner.

13

Pulsed Electric Field and its Applications in Food Processing

Manvesh Kumar Sihag, Nitika Sandhu, Ankit Goyal
Nihir Shah, Beenu Tanwar and Ami Patel

Abstract

Consumers increased response to new products with high sensory, organoleptic and nutritional potentials has impelled a search for new substitutes to processing methods. For several years, thermal processing was the main technology for producing safe products with long shelf lives, although in most cases losses of fresh flavors, vitamins, and some physicochemical characteristics were the price of safety and long-term stability. Pulsed electric field (PEF) processing as a non-thermal technique has been proven to inactivate microorganisms with minimal losses of flavor and food quality, possibly making it the answer to present-day consumer demands. In addition, the low processing temperatures used in this non-thermal technology allow the process to be nutrient preserving, energy efficient, which translates into lower costs and fewer environmental impacts. In this chapter, the the configuration of various PEF equipment, their electric configuration and recent application of this technique in processing of foods have been discussed in detail.

Keywords: PEF Chambers, Juice, Milk, Egg Processing

1. Introduction

The fresh food is best to eat as it contains all the vital nutrients necessary for better healthiness but as it is not always possible to get the fresh foods, therefore need of preservation methods arises. Previously thermal processing was used as the most common preservation method in food industries to inactivate the spoilage microorganisms and enzymes. However, along with preservation, heat treatment is also responsible for degradation of color, flavor, aroma and heat sensitive nutrients. Now a day, customers are much more aware about the taste, color, flavor and the nutritional value of the food they buy.

Non-thermal approaches provide such choice because they offer fresh-like nominally processed foods with slight loss of color, flavor, and nutrients. Pulsed electric field (PEF) is one of the promising non-thermal processing techniques. Compared with thermal processing, PEF offers the advantages of low processing temperatures, low energy utilization and the retention of flavors, nutrients and a fresh-like taste, while inactivating a wide range of vegetative cells of the spoilage microorganisms and enzymes. In this method, the food sample to be preserved is placed between two electrodes and pulses of high voltage usually 20-80 KV/cm are passed through them for fraction of seconds. PEF through its specific impact on biological tissue provides the advantage of continuous processing of electrically conductive foods achieving deactivation of microbes (food pasteurization) and at the same time retaining nutritive valuable compounds. (Jeldrik *et al.*, 2012). This technique is basically used for preservation of semi-solid and liquid foods like juices, whole liquid eggs, soups, and dairy products.

2. Important Aspects in PEF Technology

The key components of this method are treatment chamber, which carries electrodes and sends a high voltage to a food sample, design of chambers and different type of pulse waveforms. Important aspects of the PEF technology are discussed here.

2.1 Pulsed Waveforms

PEF may be applied in the form of exponentially decaying, square wave, bipolar, or oscillatory pulses. Exponentially decaying wave is actually a unidirectional voltage that rises to a maximum value and decays. The rise is much rapid than the decay. Fig. 1A shows the circuit used often to generate an exponential decay voltage wave. The circuit consists of a capacitor bank, charging resister and a power supply source. The capacitor bank and the charging register are connected in series and a DC power source is used to provide supply to the capacitor bank. As the switch turns on, the stored charge from the capacitor flows through the food in the chamber.

A square waveform can be attained by means of a pulse-forming complex involving an array of capacitors and inductors and solid state switching scheme. Square pulse waves are further lethal and are additionally energy competent than exponential decaying pulses (Fig. 1B).

The instant-charge-reversal pulses are characterized by a positive part and negative part (Fig. 1C) with various widths and peak field strengths. An instant-charge-reversal pulse width with charge-reversal at the end of the pulse is substantially dissimilar from a standard bipolar pulse.

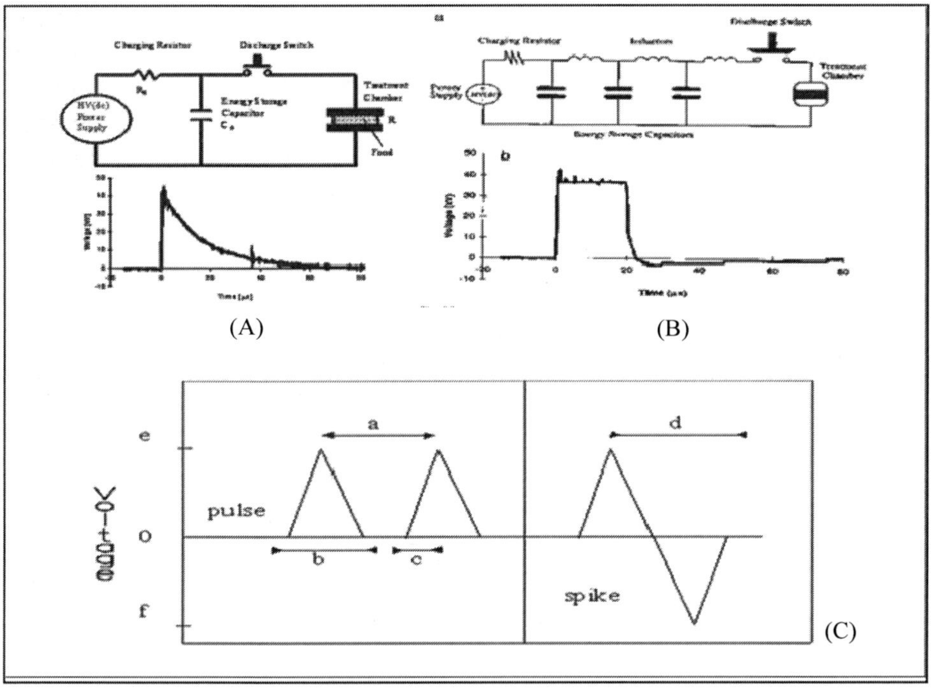

Fig. 1: (A) Electrical circuit for the creation of exponential decay waveforms; (B) Square pulse generator using a pulse-forming network of 3 capacitors inductor units and a voltage trace across the treatment chamber.; (C) A voltage (V) trace of an instant-charge-reversal pulse where (a) is pulse period (s), b is pulse width (μs), c is a pulse rise time(s) to reach e (kV), d is a spike width (s), e is a peak voltage (kV), and f is a spike voltage (kV) (Ho *et al.*, 1995).

In standard bipolar pulse, the polarity of the pulses is changed alternately with easing time amid pulses. Instant-charge-reversal pulses can extremely lessen energy necessities to as little as 1.3 J/ml. (EPRI, 1998). As the cell is avoided to be uninterruptedly open to a high intensity electric field for a prolonged time, therefore, Oscillatory decay pulses are the least efficient but they prevent the cell from irreversible breakdown also (Jeyamkondan *et al.*, 1999).

3. Treatment Chambers and Equipment

PEF technology is suitable for increasing the shelf life and maintaining organoleptic characteristics of liquid foods. Several pilot and commercial scale PEF treatment chambers, had been developed, constructed, manufactured by a number of universities, research groups and private industries and used for non-thermal treatment on microbial inactivation of molten foods. (Kang and Jianping, 2009).Currently, there are only two commercial scale systems available (by Pure Pulse Technologies, Inc. and by Thomson-CSF).

These chambers are categorized as static and continuous Static are further U-shaped polystyrene & glass coil static chambers and chamber with ion conductive membrane, chambers with baffles, enhanced electric field treatment chambers, and coaxial chambers comes under continuous chambers.

3.1 Static Chambers

3.1.1 U-shaped polystyrene

In this type of chamber, there is a U-shaped polystyrene spacer, Fig. 2. (A) in which two carbon electrodes are held by support of brass blocks. These brass blocks are also equipped with water jackets for recirculation and controlling temperature of the food during PEF treatment. Various spacers control the electrode region and volume of food to be preserved. This chamber could support electric field up to 30 kV/cm.

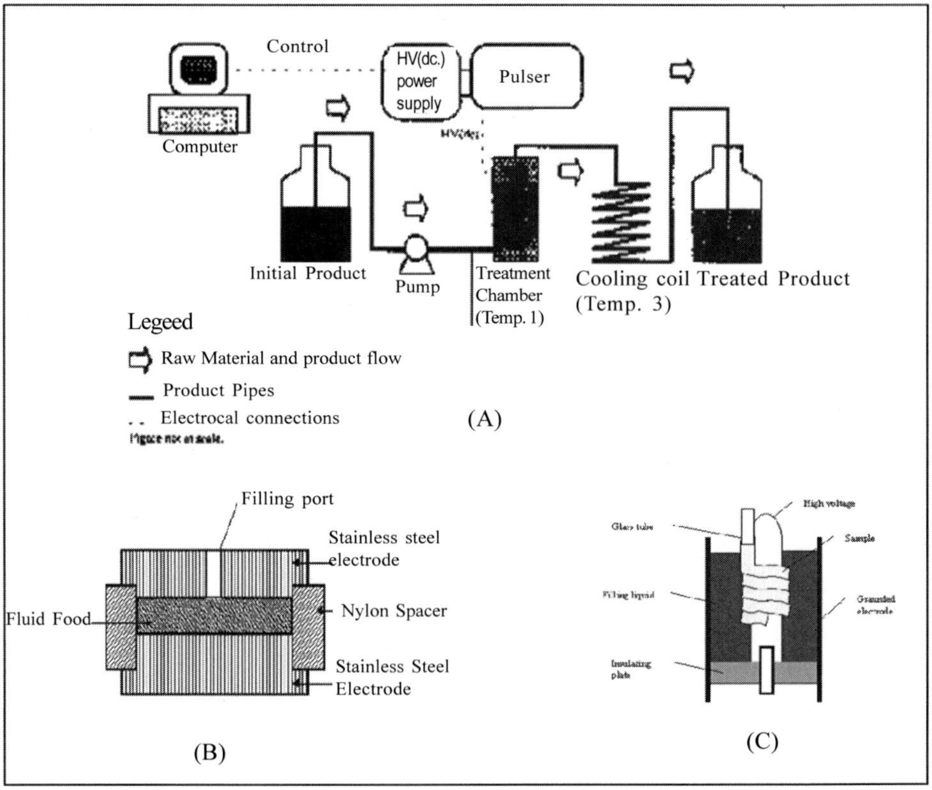

Fig. 2: (A) Static Chamber with carbon electrodes (Sale and Hamilton, 1967a b); (B): Cross-section of PEF static treatment chamber (Dunn and Pearlman, 1987); (C): Static chamber with glass coil surrounding the anode.

Dunn and Pearlman (1987) designed another model, Fig. 2 (B), which comprises of a chamber with 2cm height and 10cm inner diameter, one nylon spacer (cylindrical) and 2 electrodes (stainless steel, area 78cm^2). Another model proposed by (Barbosa-Cánovas and others 1999) comprised of two electrodes of stainless steel (round in shape, area 27cm^2). This chamber could support electric field up to 70 kV/cm. Polysulfone was used to provide insulation and provision of jackets for water circulation was also there.

3.1.2 Glass coil static chamber

Lubicki and Jayaram (1997) proposed Glass coil static chamber model. In this model the anode is surrounded by glass coil and the chamber is filled with a liquid usually silicon oil having similar conductivity and permittivity as the sample. The liquid is required for inactivation.

3.2 Continuous Pef Treatment Chambers

Continuous PEF treatment chambers are appropriate for large-scale operations and are more efficient than static chambers.

3.2.1 Continuous chamber with ion conductive membrane

Dunn and Pearlman (1987) proposed two designs, Fig. 3. (A) & Fig. 3. (B) for continuous chamber with ion conductive membrane. The first design comprised of two parallel plate electrodes, a dielectric spacer insulator, an electrolyte and a conductive membrane. The conductive membrane made of sulfonated polystyrene and acrylic acid copolymers is used to separate the electrodes from the foods. The electrical conduction between electrodes and ion permeable membrane is facilitated by the electrolyte. The second design comprised of electrode reservoir zones instead of electrode plates. Dielectric spacer insulators have slot-like openings (orifices) between which the electric field concentrates and liquid food are introduced under high pressure. The average residence time in each of these 2 reservoirs is as little as 1 min.

3.2.2 Enhanced electric continuous field treatment chambers

Yin *et al.*, (1997) applied the concept of improved electric fields in the dealing areas by development of a continuous co-field flow PEF chamber, Fig. 3. (C), with conical insulator, shaped to remove gas deposits inside the treatment volume. The conical sections were designed so that the voltage across the treatment zone could be almost equal to the supplied voltage. Other configurations with improved electric fields are showed in Fig. 3. (D) & Fig. 3. (E). In these designs the flow chamber can have several cross-section geometries that may be uniform or non-uniform. In this type of chamber configuration, the first electrode flow chamber, the insulator flow chamber, the second electrode flow chamber, the conducting insert members, and the insulating insert members are designed and aligned such that both the electrode flow and insulator flow chamber form a single tubular flow chamber though the device (Barbosa-Cánovas *et al.*, 1999).

3.2.3 Coaxial continuous PEF chambers

Coaxial chambers consist of two cylindrical electrodes, one inner cylindrical electrode of narrow diameter fitted in to another outer cylindrical electrode. The food passes through these two electrodes, Fig. 3. (F). The protruded surface of outer electrode heightens the electric field within the treatment zones and

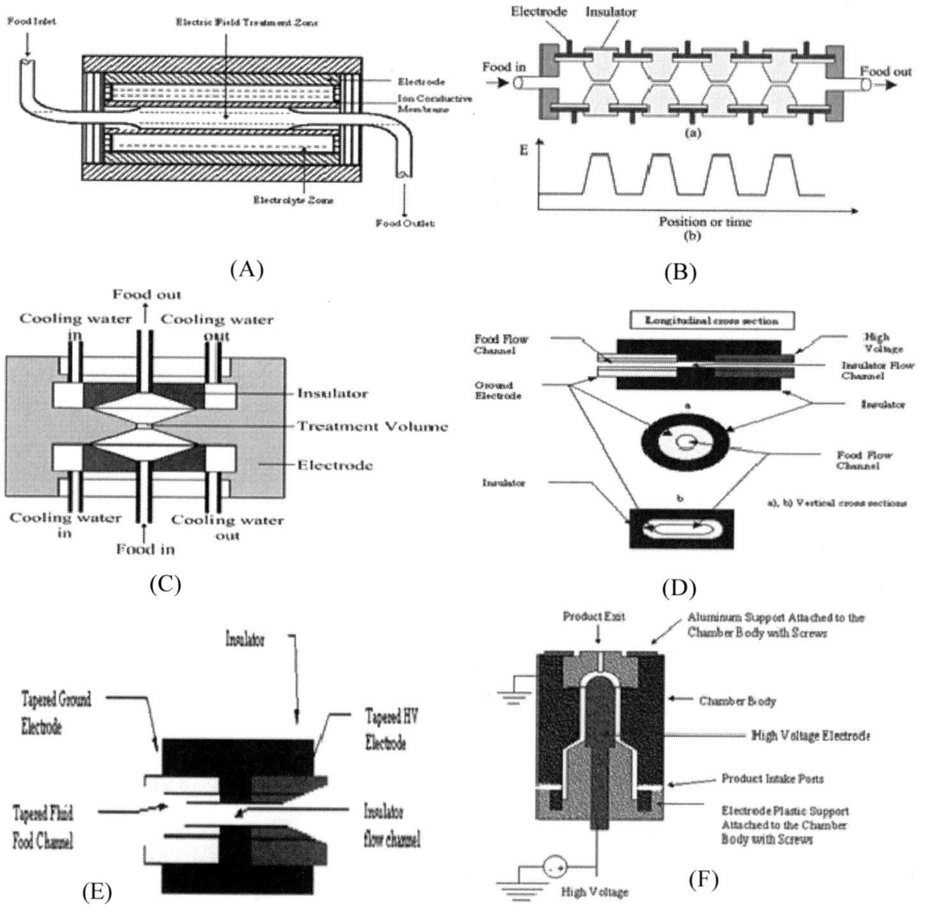

Fig. 3: (A) Continuous-treatment chamber with ion-conductive membranes separating the electrode and food; (B): Continuous treatment chamber with electrode reservoir zones. (Dunn and Pearlman, 1987); (C) A co-field continuous treatment chamber (Sensoy *et al.*, 1997); (D) Treatment chamber with different electrode geometries and enhanced electric fields in the insulator channel; (E) Treatment chamber with enhanced electric fields in the insulator channel and tapered electrodes; (F) Cross-sectional view of a coaxial treatment chamber (Pizzichemi and Occhialini, 2007).

decreases the field intensity in the remaining part of the chamber. The electrode configuration was acquired by boosting the electrode design with a numerical electric field computation. Using the optimized electrode shape, a recommended field distribution along the fluid path without an electric field enhancement point was determined. This treatment chamber has been used successfully in the deactivation of pathogenic and non-pathogenic bacteria, molds, yeasts, and enzymes present in liquid foods such as fruit juices, milk, and liquid whole eggs (Barbosa-Cánovas *et al.*, 1999).

4. Applications in Food Processing

Safe and nutritiously superior food productsuch as fruit juices, milk, eggs etc. with enhanced shelf life can be obtained by using the PEF processing technique. However, the intensity of pulse used (in terms of energy, number and electric field strength) and properties of the food matrix to be investigated are directly related with the degree of inactivation of microorganisms (Toepfl *et al.*, 2007). PEF in combination with mechanical pressing is a promising alternative to thermal processing and also provides good yield and quantity of the juice from fruits and vegetables such as grapes, apples and carrots (Grimi *et al.*, 2011; Jaeger *et al.*, 2012; Praporscic *et al.*, 2007). Recent reports suggests the increase in total phenol and anthocyanin content, higher cell disintegration index, decrease in freezing and thawing time and increase in DPPH (1,1-Diphenyl-2-picrylhydrazyl) activity of juices (Table-1). Similarly, PEF treatment of milk by different workers suggested less denaturation of xanthine oxidase & delta H of whey proteins, no effect on milk fat melting temperature, significant reduction of *Escherichia coli* and *Listeria innocua* count, increased casein protein content in serum and minor denaturation of whey proteins (Table 1). In case of eggs also PEF treatment is comparable to ultra-pasteurization to inactivate *Salmonella Senftenberg* 775W and *Listeria monocytogenes* (Table 1). Some of these recent applications of PEF with different pulse parameters in fruit juices, milk, eggs are discussed in the Table below.

5. Conclusion

PEF has an encouraging effect on the yield, antioxidant aspects and retrieval of bioactive compounds, enzymes, vitamins and micronutrients of liquid foods. This technology can be used alone or in combination with mild thermal processes for processing and preservation of foods. PEF offers an approach to select suitable process constraints and hence to guarantee product safety. Further work will be needed for optimization of suitable electrode geometry and material and, in specific the advance in impulse generating systems with adequate output voltage and repetition rate for high capacity treatment chambers, crucial conditions for a required industrial scale up of this mild preservation process.

Table 1: Application of PEF in food processing

S.N.	Experiment	Parameters	Significant findings	Reference
Processing of juices				
1	Raspberry (14g) were given PEF treatment in specifically designed chambers connected with electric field generators with different electric field strengths (1, 3 and 5 kV/cm) and specific energy values (1 to $12 KJKg^{-1}$).	Cell disintegration index, % juice recovery, total phenolic and anthocyanin content	Total phenolic and anthocyanin content increased to 22 & 27.5%, respectively as compared with control. Highest cell disintegration index and maximum juice recovery were achieved by applying 3 kV cm^{-1} electric field strength & from 3 up to 10 kJ kg^{-1} total specific energy and 3 kV cm-1 electric field strength and12 kJ kg^{-1} total specific energy	Lamanauskas *et al.*, 2016
2	Two fruit-milk beverages; fruit juice-whole milk (FJ-WM) & fruit juice-skim milk (FJ-SM) were prepared and subjected to HIPEF, thermal treatment and control (without any treatment)	Total phenol count (TPC) and total flavonoid count (TFC) were measured initially and after the storage period of 56 days.	Initially there was no significant difference between TPC & TFC of FJ-WM & FJ-SM prepared by any treatment, but at the end of the storage time, retention of TPC was 5-15% more in case of HIPEF processed juice	Morales de la Peña *et al.*, 2016
3	Apples were pre-treated with PEF before juice extraction by freezing assisted pressing method. Specifications for PEF treatment were: Rectangular shaped Bipolar pulses, electric field of 800 V/cm, distance between electrodes 5mm, pulse duration 100μs	Freezing time, Thawing time, nutritional profile of the juice obtained	Both freezing and thawing time of the PEF pretreated juice were reduced significantly, carbohydrates conc., TPC, TFC, Total antioxidant capacity were also significantly higher in PEF treated juice than the untreated	Carbonell-Capella *et al.*, 2016
4	PEF effect on fresh sugar canejuice at room temperature & refrigerated temperature (31°C & 4°C) with & without addition of lemon and ginger at	microbial content, chemical properties, nutrientcontent and shelf life	Significant ($p < 0.05$) decrease in pH (from 5.10 to 3.98), vitamin C (from 87.5 to 81.54mg%) and a significant ($p < 0.05$) increase in acidity(from 0.2 to 0.5%) of sugarcane juice	Kayalvizhi *et al.*, 2016

Contd.

S.N.	Experiment	Parameters	Significant findings	Reference
	different field strengths (30 kV cm^{-1} and 50 kV cm^{-1}) anddifferent pulse numbers (150, 300) wascompared with untreated sample for 30 days storage period		(without addition of lemon and ginger, stored at 31°CIn sugarcane juice, (without addition of lemon and ginger at 4°C), vitamin C content retained (87.5mg %) up to 7 days, when PEF at 30 kV cm^{-1}, 150 pulses was used. Higher field intensities caused significant ($p<0.05$) reduction in the ascorbic acid	
5	*Emblica officinalis* juice was inoculated with *Zygosaccharomyces bailii.* The juice was then given PEF treatment (1is monopolar pulses with electric field strength of 26kV/cm) and compared with heat treatment (90°C for 60 sec.) and control without any treatment for the storage period of 40 days at 4°C	Vitamin C,TPC, antioxidant capacity, non-enzymatic index, 5-hydroxymethyl-2-furfural (HMF)	Change in pH and Brix level was non-significant in both PEF and heat treatment, However, the concentration of vitamin C & TPC was found to be 797 & 228mg/100ml and 172 & 133 GAE/L in PEF and heat treated samples, respectively. HMF & browning index decreased relative to heat treated juice.	Bansal *et al.*, 2015
6	Grapefruit juice was treated with pulsed PEF (electric field strengths: 0, 5, 10, 15, 20 and 25 $kVcm^{-1}$; flow rate: 80 mL min ; pulse frequency: 1 kHz at 40 °C for 600 µs)	TPC, DPPH, total antioxidant capacity (TAC), total anthocyanins, total carotenoids	Increase in DPPH, TAC, TPC and total carotenoids and decrease in microbial load was observed with the increase in PEF strength relative to controltreatment	Aadil *et al.*, 2015
7	Apples were given PEF treatment with variation in following parameters: electric field strengths (0 to 5 kV/cm) and specific energy values (0 to 80 $KJKg^{-1}$), pulse number (0 to 100) and pulse width (0 to 24µs.	Freezing time, Thawing time, mass loss, textural properties and color change	Freezing and thawing time were reduced from 3.5 to 17.2% and thawing time up to 26.8%, respectively. More the intensity of the treatment, higher the mass loss. However, the mass loss was 1.6% less compared to control when treated by 10 pulses at 3 kV/cm, change in color of the PEF treated samples was also observed	Wiktor *et al.*, 2015

Contd.

S.N.	Experiment	Parameters	Significant findings	Reference
Processing of milk				
1	Milk was subjected to two treatments, treated thermally and with PEF with the following parameters: bipolar square wave pulses of 20 or 26 kV cm^{-1} for 34 is with or without pre-heating of milk (55 °C for 24 s)	Thermodynamics of milk fat, xanthine oxidase, caseins and whey proteins were studied	Milk fat melting temperature was not affected by PEF but increased 2-3°C by thermal treatment and there was 13% less xanthine oxidase denaturation in PEF treatment, delta H of whey protein denaturation was also less in PEF	Sharma *et. al.*, 2016
2	Milk was subjected to two treatments, treated thermally and with PEF with the following parameters: continuous mode PEF with electric field intensities of 15.9–26.2 kV cm^{-1} for 17–101 is	Bacterial count and enzyme inactivation	*Escherichia coli* and Listeria innocua count was reduced to 2 log cfu mL^{-1} from 6 log cfu mL^{-1} with at 20.7–26.2 kV cm^{-1}PEF. However, reduction in total plate count and indigenous alkaline phosphatase activity was similar to thermal treatment	Sharma *et. al.*, 2014
3	Reconstituted skim milk with different pH range (6.7 to 8.0) was subjected to PEF with following parameters: input voltage,9760 V; pulse width, 2 µs; pulsing frequency in bipolar pulsing mode, 1370 Hz; sample flow rate 240 mL/min	Particle size and Zeta potential of milk particles, total protein in serum and state of whey proteins	Samples with pHe"7.5 showed reduction in the size of milk particles and increased casein protein content in serum, Minor denaturation of whey proteins was also observed, no effect on Particle size and Zeta potential of milk particles	Liu *et al.*, 2015
Processing of Eggs				
1	Liquid whole eggs (LWE) were subjected to PEF plus heat treatment in presence of natural essential oils as an alternative of ultra-pasteurization	To checke ffectiveness against inactivation of *Salmonella Senftenberg* 775W and *Listeria monocytogenes*	PEF (25 kV/ and100 kJ/kg) accompanied by heat treatment at 60°C for 3.5 minutes in presence of lemon essential oil (200µl/L) was comparable to ultra-pasteurization to inactivate *Salmonella Senftenberg* 775W and *Listeria monocytogenes*	Espina *et al*., 2014

Contd.

S.N.	Experiment	Parameters	Significant findings	Reference
2	Effect of electric field strength on stability of egg white proteins was studied, samples were subjected to a constant electric field intensity of 25 kV/cmfor 200, 400, 600 and 800 μs, equivalent to treatment energies in 681.3, 1362.6, 2043.9 and 2726.3 kJ/L.	Soluble protein content, Poly disparity index (PDI) and Zeta potential	Soluble protein content and Zeta potential decreased significantly with the increase in time of treatment, no change in PDI	Wu *et al.*, 2014

References

Aadil, R. M., Zeng, X. A., Ali, A., Zeng, F., Farooq, M. A., Han, Z., Khalid, S. and Jabbar, S., 2015. Influence of different pulsed electric field strengths on the quality of the grapefruit juice. *International Journal of Food Science & Technology*, 50(10): 2290-2296.

Bansal, V., Sharma, A., Ghanshyam, C., Singla, M. L. and Kim, K. H., 2015. Influence of pulsed electric field and heat treatment on Emblica officinalis juice inoculated with Zygosaccharomyces bailii. *Food and Bioproducts Processing*, 95: 146-154.

Barbosa-Canovas, G. V., Go´ngora-Nieto, M. M., Pothakamury, U. R. and Swanson, B., 1999. Preservation of foods with pulsed electric fields. In: S. L. Taylor (Ed.), In Food science and technology international series. San Diego, CA, Academic Press.

Carbonell-Capella, J. M., Parniakov, O., Barba, F. J., Grimi, N., Bals, O., Lebovka, N. and Vorobiev, E., 2016. "Ice" juice from apples obtained by pressing at subzero temperatures of apples pretreated by pulsed electric fields. *Innovative Food Science & Emerging Technologies*, 33:187-194.

Dunn, J. E. and Pearlman, J. S., 1987. Methods and apparatus for extending the shelf-life offluid food products. US Patent No. 4,695,472.

EPRI, 1998. Pulsed electric field processing in the food industry. A status report on PEF. Report CR 109742. Industrial and agricultural technologies and services, Palo Alto, California

Espina, L., Monfort, S., Álvarez, I., García-Gonzalo, D. and Pagán, R., 2014. Combination of pulsed electric fields, mild heat and essential oils as an alternative to the ultra-pasteurization of liquid whole egg. *International Journal of Food Microbiology*, 189:119-125.

Grimi, N., Mamouni, F., Lebovka, N., Vorobiev, E., and Vaxelaire, J., 2011. Impact of apple processing modes on extracted juice quality, pressing assisted by pulsed electric fields. *Journal of Food Engineering*, 103:52-61.

Ho, S. Y., Mittal, G. S., Cross, J. D., and Griffiths, M. W., 1995. Inactivation of Pseudomonas fluorescens by high voltage electric pulses. *Journal of Food Science*, 60(6):1337-1343.

Jaeger, H., Schulz, M., Lu, P. and Knorr, D., 2012. Adjustment of milling, mash electroporation and pressing for the development of a PEF assisted juice production in industrial scale. *Innovative Food Science & Emerging Technologies*, 14: 46-60.

Jeldrik, M., Ana, B., Henry, J., Nicolas, M. and Dietrich, K., 2012. Investigating the potential of polyphenol oxidase as a temperature-time-indicator for pulsed electric field treatment. *Food Control*, 26:1-5.

Jeyamkondan, S., Jayas, D. S. and Holley, R. A., 1999. Pulsed electric field processing of foods, a review. *Journal of Food Protection*, 62(9): 1088-1096.

Kang, H. and Jianping, W., 2009. Designs of pulsed electric fields treatment chambers for liquid foods pasteurization process, A review. *Journal of Food Engineering*, 95:227-239.

Kayalvizhi, V., Pushpa, A. J. S., Sangeetha, G. and Antony, U., 2016. Effect of pulsed electric field (PEF) treatment on sugarcane juice. *Journal of Food Science and Technology*: 1-9.

Lamanauskas, N., Pataro, G., Bobinas, È., Šatkauskas, S., Viskelis, P., Bobinaite, R. and Ferrari, G., 2016. Impact of pulsed electric field treatment on juice yield and recovery of bioactive compounds from raspberries and their by-products. *Zemdirbyste (Agriculture)*, 103(1): 83-90.

Liu, Z., Hemar, Y., Tan, S., Sanguansri, P., Niere, J., Buckow, R. and Augustin, M. A., 2015. Pulsed electric field treatment of reconstituted skim milks at alkaline pH or with added EDTA. *Journal of Food Engineering*, 144:112-118.

Lubicki, P. and Jayaram, S., 1997. High voltage pulse application for the destruction of gram negative bacterium *Yersinia enterocolitica*. *Bio-electrochemistry Bioenergetics*, 43: 135-141.

Morales de la Peña, M., Salvia Trujillo, L., Rojas Graü, M.A. and Martín Belloso, O., 2016. Effects of high intensity pulsed electric Fields or thermal pasteurization and refrigerated storage on antioxidant compounds of fruit juice milk beverages. Part I, Phenolic Acids and Flavonoids. *Journal of Food Processing and Preservation.*doi,10.1111/jfpp.12912.

Pizzichemi, M., Occhialini, P.D.G., 2007. Application of pulsed electric fields to food treatment. Nuclear Physics B – Proceeding Supplements 172:314-316.

Praporscic, I., Lebovka, N., Vorobiev, E. and Mietton-Peuchot, M., 2007. Pulsed electric field enhanced expression and juice quality of white grapes. *Sep Purif Technology*, 52: 520-526.

Sensoy, I., Zhang, Q. H.and Sastry, S. K., 1997. Inactivation kinetics of Salmonella Dublin by pulsed electric field. *Journal of Food Process Engineering* 20 (5):367-381.

Sharma, P., Oey, I. and Everett, D. W., 2016. Thermal properties of milk fat, xanthine oxidase, caseins and whey proteins in pulsed electric field-treated bovine whole milk. *Food Chemistry*, 207:34-42.

Sharma, P., Oey, I., Bremer, P. and Everett, D.W., 2014. Reduction of bacterial counts and inactivation of enzymes in bovine whole milk using pulsed electric fields. *International Dairy Journal*, 39(1):146-156.

Grahl, Tand Markl, H.,1996. Killing of microorganisms by pulsed electric fields, *AppliedMicrobiology and Biotechnology*, 45: 148-157.

Toepfl, S., Heinz, V. and Knoor, D., 2007. High intensity pulsed electric fields applied for food preservation. *Chemical Engineering and Processing* 46: 537-546.

Wiktor, A., Schulz, M., Voigt, E., Witrowa-Rajchert, D. and Knorr, D., 2015. The effect of pulsed electric field treatment on immersion freezing, thawing and selected properties of apple tissue. *Journal of Food Engineering*, 146:8-16.

Wu, L., Zhao, W., Yang, R. and Chen, X., 2014. Effects of pulsed electric fields processing on stability of egg white proteins. *Journal of Food Engineering*, 139:13-18.

Yin, Y., Zhang, Q. H. and Sastri, S. H., 1997. High intensity pulsed electric field chambers for the preservation of liquid food products. U.S. Patent 5:690-978.

14

Food Adulteration: Types, their Effects and Control

Pardeep Kumar Sadh, Suresh Kumar Rohilla
Sandeep Kumar and Joginder Singh Duhan

Abstract

We are very fortunate to be born in a nation which is blessed with awesome decent variety of natural products, fruits, vegetables, cereals, pulses and so forth. The population of India expanded consistentlythat cause a genuine sustenance and shelter problem. The supply of food is not adequate to fulfill the demand of the consumers. This shortage of food is the root for adulteration of foodstuffs by the traders. Food adulteration is a procedure in which the nature of sustenance is brought down either by the addition of inferior quality material or by extraction of valuable ingredient. An adulterant is a chemical substance which should not be contained within other substances (food, beverages) for legal or other reasons. The addition of adulterants is called adulteration. Food is adulterated to increase the quantity and make more profit. The food is sucked of its nutrients and the place where the food is grown is often contaminated. For instance: milkis mixed with water. Vanaspati is utilized as an adulterant for ghee. Adulteration of food is unsafe as it may be toxic and causes serious health hazards to the consumer. To evade this issue government has passed an act which is known as preservation of Food Adulteration Act. It covers security from risks involved due to contamination of poisonous elements. Instead of government efforts the informed and aware consumers will have the capacity to dispense with this issue. So, here in the chapter adulterants their types, effect on human health, laws and control measurement were reviewed and discussed.

Keywords: Food adulteration; Food safety; Health effects

1. Introduction

In developing countries, as the population increase persistently the demand of food likewise increases. Food is any substance consumed to provide nutritional support for the body. It is usually of plant or animal origin, and contains essential nutrients, such as carbohydrates, fats, proteins, vitamins, or minerals. The substance is ingested by an organism and assimilated by the organism's cells to provide energy, maintain life, or stimulate growth. Rapid urbanization and sociological changes hadalso increases the impact on the life-style of a large segment of the population due toenhanced demand for pre-packaged and recooked ready-to-eat (RTE) foods (Vijayabaskar and Sundaram, 2012).

So in these nations food accounts for a large part of the family spending plan. Each customer needs to get the most extreme amount in a low cost as could be expected under the circumstances. This attitude of the consumers being coupled with the intension of the traders as well as the manufacturer to increase the margin of a profit as high as the variable market demand permits generates a vicious circle where the quality of the commodity gets reduced through addition of the baser substances and/or removal of vital elements, and the process is defined as adulteration. Food is said to be altered if the product sold by a vendor is not of the nature and if the product contains any prohibited colouring matter, preservatives, or contains any permitted colouring matter or preservative in excess of the prescribed limits.

Frederick Accum was the first to raise the alarm about food adulteration. Accumwas a German scientific expert who had come to London in 1793, and who quickly established himself as a chemical analyst, consultant and educator of science.The World Health Organization (WHO) has long been aware of the need to educate food handlers about their responsibilities for food safety. In the early 1990s, WHO developed the Ten Golden Rules for Safe Food Preparation, which were widely translated and reproduced. However, it became obvious that something simpler and more generally applicable was needed after consulting with food safety experts and risk communicators.

Even if a food article expires and its shelf life is overconsumption after that will also lead to unhealthy circumstances. Hence food perishability is a delicate issue and therefore has to be handled with utmost care. Adulteration of food effects on consumer and cause a serious hazard to health. Adulterated food is unsafe because it may be toxic or contaminated that result to various health problems. To maintain a strategic distance from this issue government has passed an act which is known as preservation of food Adulteration Act.

Recently to cover start to finish all aspects of food consumption, a central law of Food safety and Standards Act came into force. It has revoked all the earlier laws and taken a ground level to check on all the Food adulteration laws. With increasing awareness about Human Rights in the society, there have been many instances of PILs and writ petitions being filed in the Apex court in order that the judiciary interferes in the Administrative matter and questions them for injustice caused to the consumers and provide them justice.

2. Types of Adulterants (Paul *et al.*, 2015)

Adulterants can broadly be classified into three categories:

1. Intentional adulterants: Sand, marble, stones, mud etc.
2. Incidental adulterants: Pesticide residues, droppings of rodents
3. Metallic contaminants: Arsenic, Lead etc.

2.1 Examples of Adulteration

Milk: Cow/buffalo milk can be adulterated with starch, milk powder and urea

Laddu: Metanil yellow, a non-permitted color is a common adulterant in food items like laddu, tur dal and turmeric.

Ghee: Ghee essence is used in vanaspati or cheaper oils and passed off as pure ghee. This type of ghee will not solidify like normal ghee. It may also not have that grainy texture of pure ghee.

Sugar/Salt: With chalk powder and white sand.

Tea powder: With used tea leaves, dye or artificial colour, iron fillings.

Chilli powder: Sudan red,Red brick powder, grit, sand, dirt, non-permitted colors and saw dust.

Mustard seeds/ Vegetable oil: Argemone seeds and argemone oil.

Honey: Jaggery, Sugar, corn syrup

Coffee: Roasted powdered dates, Tamarind seed powder etc.

Green Vegetables: Malachite green

Vinegar: Sharpened' with sulphuric acid; often contained tin and lead dissolved when boiled in pewter vessels

Pickles: Copper salts for greening

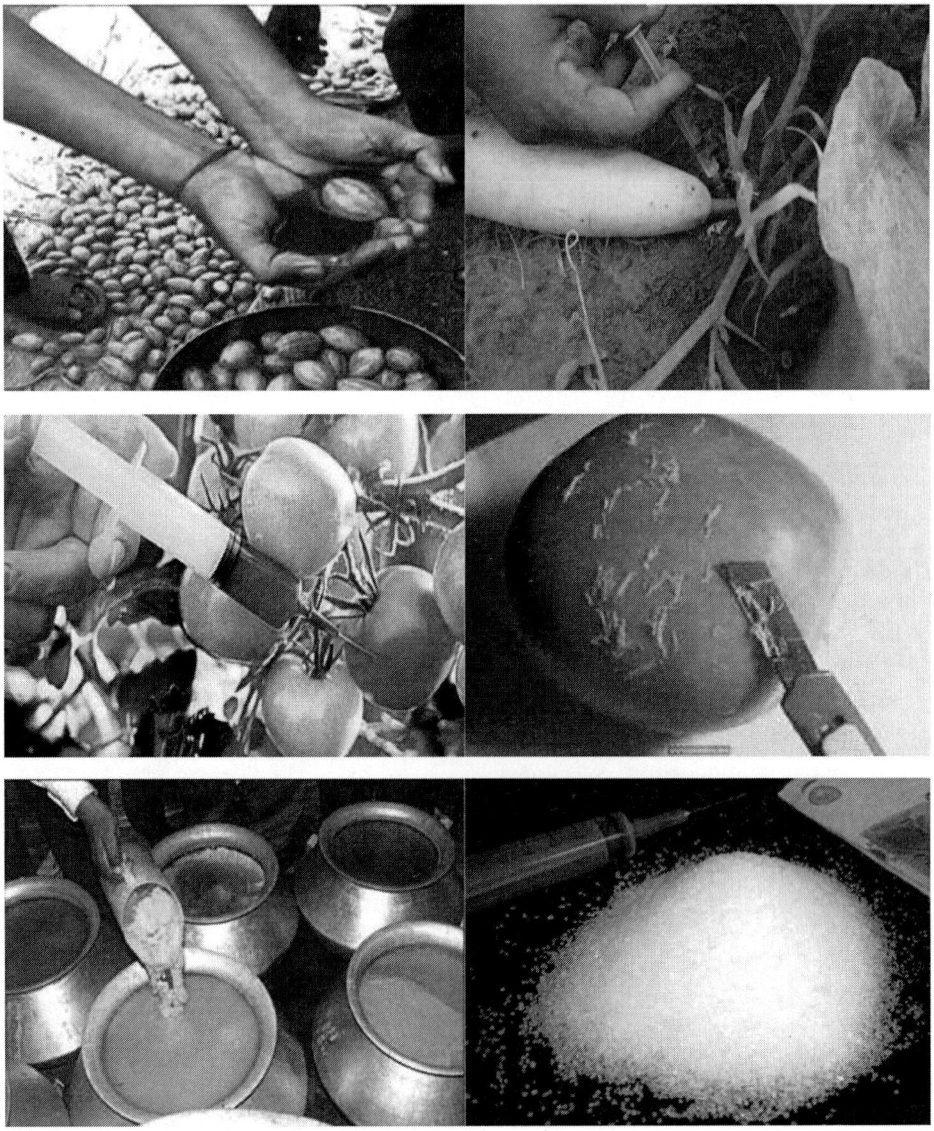

Fig. 1: Showing different adulteration in various food

3. How to Detect Food Adulteration

Several effective methods are employed to detect the adulterated foods such as:

- In case of black pepper seeds, the adulterate used i.e. papaya seeds. For detection of this adulteration, add some of the adulterated sample into glass water and found the floated seeds because papaya seeds can float while pepper seeds don't.

- Chalk, white sand and stone powders are utilized as adulterate in sugar and common salt. For check the adulterant in sugar and salt, dissolve sugar in a glass of water, chalk, white sand, stone powder will settle down as these are immiscible in water.
- In most of the honey, water and sugar/jaggery are mixed with honey and decreased the quality of the product. So, a simple method is used for detecting the adulterant *i.e.* a cotton wick dipped in pure honey burns when ignited with a matchstick. Presence of water will not allow the honey to burn, and if it does, it will produce a cracking sound.
- Malachite green, an adulterant is used in various green vegetables like chilli, peas etc. For detecting the impurities with malachite green, Take a small part of the sample and place it over a moistened white blotting paper. Colour impressions on paper indicate the presence of Malachite green.
- Kesari dal is an adulterant in arahar dal and chana dal. Kesari dal pointed and wedge shaped.chana dal/ arahar dal is smooth and round.
- Starch is used as an adulterant in milk, paneer, khoya etc. For detecting the starch adulterant Take a small portion of the product in a test tube adds water and boil. Cool to room temperature. Add 1-2 drops Iodine solution. Blue colour indicates the presence of starch. Likewise, adulteration in milk can be detected simply by rubbing the milk by bare hands. The appearance of oily hands indicates adulteration of milk.
- Old used spices are often blended with spices sold as fresh. Smell the spice no or less smell indicates the adulteration.
- In pulses viz., dals, like moong, channa etc. Metanil Yellow or Lead Chromate are used as an adulterant. To detecting this adulterant in pulses extract the colour with luke warm water from the sample of pulses. Add few drops of HCl. A pink colour indicates presence of Metanil Yellow / Lead Chromate.

4. Impact of Adulteration on Human Health

Food adulteration is common in almost all developing countries. The utilization of non-permitted and unsafe adulterants in the preparation of homemade processed foods for sale. The common use of toxic coloring agents as an adulterant for fruits, vegetables, sweets are very dangerous when it comes to health of a person. It can prompt serious health issues like cancer, cardiac problems, insomnia and paralysis and other neurological disorder or sometimes death as well. Table 1 shows different health effects from various adulterants in foods and their products.

Table 1: Health effects from different adulterants

Food Item/ Ingredients	Adulterant	Health Effects
Honey	Cane sugar High fructose corn syrup	Diabetics Foot ulcers Nerve damages
Turmeric	Lead chromate	Anemia Paralyses Mental retardation
Oils	Rancid oil	Destroys vitamin A andE
Mercury fungicide treated seed grains or mercury infected fish	Mercury	Brain damage Paralysis Death
Solvent extracted oil, oilcake etc.	Excessive solventresidue	Carcinogenic effect
Milk	Starch Urea	Cancer Renal failure
Ghee	Vanaspati	Acute renal failure
Sugar/Salt	Chalk, White sand	Stomach disorder
Tea powder	Used tea leaves Artificial colour	Cancer Tetanus
Chilli powder	Red brick powder Non permitted colour	Stomach disorder Carcinogenic
Sweets	Metanil yellow	Tumor and cancer
Mustard seeds	Argemone seeds	Epidemic dropsy
Black pepper	Dried papaya seeds	Stomach irritation Liver damage, Cancer
Jeera	Stone Alike seeds from wild plants	Stomach disorder Liver damage
Cereals	Stone pieces, mud, ergot seeds	Stomach disorder
Arahar dal	Yellow dye Kesari dal	Leprosy Paralysis
Potatoes	Solanine	Solanine poisoning (vomiting, abdominal pain, diarrhoea)
Drinking water	Flouride Mercury	Excess fluoride causes fluorosis (mottling of teeth, skeletal andneurological disorders) Minimata
Yellow rice	Toxins from*Penicillium*,*Fusarium*, *Rhizopus*, *Aspergillus*	Toxic mouldy rice disease
Food preservative	Sulphur dioxide and sulphate beyond safe limit	Acute irritation of the gastrointestinaltracts etc.
Alcoholic liquors	Methanol	Blurred vision, Blindness, Death
Fruit juices, soft drinks,	Cadmium	'Itai-itai (ouch-ouch) disease, Increased salivation, acutegastritis, liver and kidneydamage, prostrate cancer
Flavoured food	Food flavours beyond safe limit	Liver cancer

5. Notable Food Adulteration Incidents in India

- Adulteration in mustard oil in 1998 cause dropsy, therefore 31 people were passed on(www.hinduonnet.com/folio/fo9910/99100220.htm).
- In 1999, Bureau of Indian Standards (BIS) raided several products of different brands, as per regulation given by the Prevention of Food Adulteration (PFA) Act and against claims made by the producers (www.hinduonnet.com/folio/fo9910/99100220.htm).
- State Health department and its Food Adulteration wing in 2003 collected soft drinks samples from different parts of the state and found that the soft drinks are not fulfill the standards provided by the government. The Democratic Youth Federation of India launched a statewide "direct action" program against the multinational soft drink (www.hindu.com/the hindu/2003/08/08/stories).
- In 2008, food sample survey was conducted in the various cities across the country indicates an alarming increase in the adulteration levels with devastating consequences. ISO-9001-2000 certified laboratory which also has the approval from Agmark, Government of India (www.thehindu.com/2008/03/22/stories).
- A huge stock of adulterated spices was found in 2008 from the unit, Mayur Masala Products, Nagpur (Source:Times of India).
- In July 2009, Rajasthan Food Department seized over 10 quintals of adulterated pulses that were processed and polished to give fine appearance by using of toxic colouring agents and soapstone powder. Colour agents like tetrazene were used which is also not at all permissible as an additive. (Source: Times of India).
- The FDA collected samples from Pune, Satara, Kolhapur and Sangli and found 80% of the milk adulterated with detergent, fat, edible oil, urea and diluted with water.
- The FDA had collected 81 samples of milk from Mumbai and Thane and found out that six well-known brands including Amul, Gujarat Co-op Milk Federation used many adulterants.
- High coconut oil prices pave way for adulterated Coconut oil sale in Kerala amounting to 70% of the oil being impure and adulterated.
- In Bihar 25 primary students died and many fell ill after having adulterated mid day meal in the School after being contaminated with pesticide.

- On July 5th and 7th, 2014 cases of children becoming sick in Bihar districts due to the mid day meals containing worms and lizard led to a lot of protests.
- Recently the controversy over the Nestle's Maggi noodles began May 2015, are facing a ban inIndia after food inspectors found dangerous levels of lead or monosodium glutamate (MSG) in certain batches of the product. The FDA (FoodSafety and Drug Administration) reported that all the packets of instant noodles tested in the laboratory were contaminated. They found a lead concentration of 17.2 ppm, nearly seven times the permissible limit. The acceptable limit of lead ranges between 0.01 ppm and 2.5 ppm (Ravichandran, 2015).

6. Constitutional Provisions

6.1 Article 21 – Right to Life and Liberty

6.1.1 Includes - Right to pure food and health

- "Maintenance and improvement of public health have to rank high as these are indispensable to the very physical existence of the community and on the betterment of these depends the building of the society of which the Constitution makers are envisaged. Attending to public health, in our Opinion, therefore is of high priority – perhaps the one at the top" (M.P Jain, 2010).

1.6.2 Article 47 – Public Health and Nutrition

- This article obligates the state to regard as among its primary duties, the raising of level of nutrition and standard of living of its people and the improvement of public health. In particular, the state is to endeavour to bring about prohibition of the consumption except for medicinal purposes, of intoxicating drinks and drugs which are injurious to health (M.P Jain, 1991).
- This Article makes improvement of Public health a primary duty of the State. Hence the court should enforce this duty against a defaulting local authority on pain of penalty prescribed by law, regardless of the financial resources of such authority. " In case of need the local authorities should approach the state government to frant loan or aid , and the latter should supply the required money in view of the primary duty of the state under the Article 47"(V. Vardichand AIR, 1980).

The Prevention of Food Adulteration Act 1954 has been replaced by a broad based food safety law and a body called Food Safety and Standards Authority of India. But the change has made no difference at the ground level. Instead of tackling adulteration and the issue of food safety, the authority appears preoccupied with issues connected with packaged food Industry, labeling, processing, etc. It's high time that food regulator tightened its belt. The government of India introduced the food safety and Standards Act 2006 to overcome the deficiencies in the Prevention of food adulteration act, 1954. The Food Safety and Standards Authority of India has been established under this act. The Act aims to establish a single reference point for all matters relating to food safety and standards by moving from multi-level, multi-departmental control to a single line of command. The FSSAI and the state food authorities shall enforce various provisions under the act (Paul *et al.*, 2015).

7. Food Laws in India

The Indian Parliament has in 2006 passed the Food Safety and Standards Bill, 2006, which overrides all other food laws, when it comes into effect:

- The Prevention of Food Adulteration Act, 1954
- The Fruit Products Order, 1955
- The Meat Food Products Order, 1973
- The Vegetable Oil Products (Control) Order, 1947
- The Edible Oils Packaging (regulation) Order, 1988
- The Milk and Milk Products Order, 1992
- Any other order issued under the Essential Commodities Act, 1955, relating to food.

8. Control of Food Adulteration

Before going towards the control measurement of food adulteration, firstly we should know the categories of food adulteration. These categories are as follows:

- **Replacement:** Complete or partial replacement of a food ingredient or valuable authentic constituent with less expensive substitute with the intention of circumventing on "origin" and false declaration of the "process".
- **Addition:** Addition of small amounts of non-authenticated substances to mask inferior quality ingredient.
- **Removal:** Removal of authentic and valuable constituent without purchasers' knowledge.

9. Control Approaches

Food Quality Control Services: In India there is a three-tier system is function for ensuring food quality and food safety. They are as follows:

- Government of India
- State/UT Governments
- Local Bodies.

Government of India applies various act and laws to control the adulteration in foods because of its harmful effects on health.Prevention of Food Adulteration rules have been amended several times and quality standards for about 250 food articles, which are commonly consumed in India have been fixed. Implementation of food standards in corporation/municipal area rests with the local Bodies. These bodies employ their own food inspectors for examination and maintenance of standards. They are responsible for licensing of food industries/establishments as well.

In the District/Regional or State level there are 72 food laboratories and at the Central level there are four Central Food Laboratories. One or more laboratories are there in every state. However there are several constraints in this programme such as shortage of Food inspectors at the States/Local Bodies, deficiencies in the testing laboratories (lack of trained manpower, insufficient testing facilities, non-availability of sophisticated equipment).

10. Important Miscellaneous Provisions to Control Food Adulteration (agmarknet.nic.in)

- If any extraneous additions of colouring matter are added, the same should be indicated on the labels.
- Sale of kesari gram individually or as an admixture is prohibited.
- Prohibition of use of carbide (acetylene) gas in ripening is prohibited.
- Sale of admixture of ghee or butter is prohibited.
- Addition of artificial sweetener should be mentioned on the label.
- Sale of food colours without license prohibited.
- Food prepared in rusted containers, chipped enamel containers and untinned copper/brass utensils are treated as unfit for human consumption.
- Store of insecticides in the same premises where food articles are stored is prohibited.

- Milk powder or condensed milk can be sold only with ISI mark.
- Use of more than one type of preservative is prohibited.
- Crop contaminants beyond certain specified level is treated as adulterant.
- Naturally occurring toxic substances in the food material beyond certain level is considered as unfit for human consumption.
- No anti-oxidant, emulsifiers and stabilising agent is permitted beyond the prescribed level.

11. Precautions

By taking a few precautions, we can escape from consuming adulterated products (agmarknet.nic.in).

- Take only packed items of well known companies.
- Buy items from reliable retail shops and recognized outlets.
- Check the ISI mark or Agmark.
- Buy products of only air tight popular brands.
- Avoid craziness for artificially coloured sweets and buy only from reputed shops.
- Do not buy sweets or snacks kept in open.
- Avoid buying things from street side vendors.

12. Conclusion

The increasing number of food producers and the out standing amounts of imported food stuffs enables the producers to mislead and cheat consumers. Adulteration often considered as a one of the major problem of to days life and its ill effects on health from their daily meal item, either, in cereals, pulses, fruits and vegetables or in milk and milk products and spices. The adulteration in everyday item spoils our will to eat but turning a blind eye to these items is not the answer, you may feel it now but the opinion may change if you are unfortunate enough to land in a hospital. To avoid this problem government as well as local efforts are required to eliminate this problem. With a little planning of awareness among peoples and proper execution the adulteration scan be totally escaped from the society.

References

An Exhaustive Commentary on - The Prevention of Food Adulteration Act & Rules (Central and States with State Amendments) - A Book Review.

Bharat Paul, Puja Patel, Jasbir Singh Malik, Vivek Gera. Food safety: 2015. The Indian perspective. *National Journal of Community Medicine*. 6(2):153-155.

Indian Constitutional Law with constitutional documents by M.P Jain, 6th edition, 2010 Published by LexisNexis and Wadhwa, Pg. 1639.

M. Vijayabaskar and N. Sundaram. 2012. A study on purchasing attitude towards Ready-to-eat/ cook products by health conscious consumers in Southern India with respect to Tier-I cities. *International Journal of Physical and Social Sciences* 2 (4): 417-436.

R.V. Bhat. Food Safety Evaluation: National and International Perspectives. Nutrition Foundation of India, (1997) New Delhi, India.

S. P. Vasireddi. Food Adulteration & Control Mechanism. At the Workshop on Food Defense Awareness for Food Business Operators and Exporters. February 5, 2013 – Hyderabad.

S. Ravichandran. 2015. Food adulteration has taken away the joy of life. *International Journal of MediPharm Research*, 13(3):150-154.

Times of India article -07/04/2015, page 2.

V. Lakshmi. 2012. Food adulteration. *International Journal of Science Inventions Today*. 1(2): 106-113.

WHO Media Centre News release. Available from http://www.who.int/mediacentre/news/releases/ 2015/food-safety/en/.

WHO World Health Day Campaign toolkit. Available from:http://www.who.int/campaigns/world-healthday/2015/campaign-toolkit-en.pdf.

www.hindu.com/the hindu/2003/08/08/stories.

www.hinduonnet.com/folio/fo9910/99100220.htm.

www.sitaramdixit.4t.com

www.thehindu.com/2008/03/22/stories.

15

Advancement in Chromatographic Detection of Organophosphorus Pesticides in Food and Agricultural Samples

Prince Chawla, Ravinder Kaushik and Naveen Kumar

Abstract

Agriculture is the major sector for the livelihood of the billions of people worldwide. Increasing population and decreasing arable lands are the major concern for the fulfillment of the desired food production. After green revolution more production in the crop is obtained by worldwide. Several insects and pests are responsible for the inhibition of desired production in agriculture. Therefore, pesticides play a major role in the control of destructive insects and pests. After ban of organochlorine pesticides, organophosphorus pesticides has been used vigorously. Beside the effective pest management in agriculture, residual organophosphorus pesticides are more lethal for human and other living creature. Monitoring of these compounds is very much essential in the food and agricultural samples. Chromatographic techniques are well adopted techniques for the hundreds of residual pesticides. Introduction of various analyzers in chromatographic techniques improve the monitoring of the residual pesticides from different samples. Therefore, recent advancement in residual pesticides isolation and chromatographic techniques has been discussed in this book chapter.

Keywords: Organophosphates, LC-MS, QuEChERS, Chromatography, Pesticides

1. Introduction

World's population is growing immensely and it will be 10 billion by 2050. Arable lands for agriculture is also decreasing every year (FAO, 2016). Accomplish the demand of food is a foremost apprehension for both developed and developing countries (Liu *et al.*, 2017; Singh *et al.*, 2017). In addition, world's most of the population directly depend upon the agriculture for their daily nutrient requirement and livelihood (FAO, 2017). Therefore, to overcome the problem of production of more agriculture produces in limited arable land significant techniques, process are required (Fu *et al.*, 2017). Due to green revolution significant changes has been occurred in the production of agricultural crops with the help of more scientific and technical approaches (Abhilash and Singh, 2009). Although researchers and farmers are working significantly for the desirable production of agriculture crops but there are some major issues which are directly reducing the production (Bala *et al*, 2017). Among these insects and pests are major reason for the deterioration of almost 30 % production of the crop every year. Approximately 9000 species of insects and mites are known worldwide which are directly destroying the crop every year. Thus, to improve the production of agriculture produces control and monitoring on disparaging insects is an essential chore(Pimentel, 2009; Moreno-Gonzalez *et al.*, 2014; Fan *et al.*, 2015). In this perspective,pesticides are used as primary tool for effective insect control since ancient time (Davies *et al.*, 2007). A broader depletion of plant protection agents and chemicals was started in the middle of the 19th century with the invention of DDT as highest contact poison for various insects (Bate, 2007). Era of DDT in plant protection was over in the second half of the 20th century as it was effective in action and precarious not only against pest insects but also for many other groups of organisms, such as mammals, birds, and reptiles and it was completely replaced by a period of widespread use of organophosphate compounds (Zhang *et al.*, 2012; Fan *et al.*, 2014). Henceforth, wide range of organophosphorus pesticides with significant benefit in effective pest management has been come under the spotlight (Li *et al.*, 2012; Giannoulis *et al.*, 2014; Wu, 2017). Hundreds of organophosphate compounds are meritoriously used for the crop protection. Beside these significant effects organophosphorus compounds are very much lethal for the all living creatures including human being (Zhang *et al.*, 2016; Yue *et al.*, 2016; Bala *et al.*, 2017).

These organophosphorus compounds are found in tremendous amount in food and environmental samples. Due to consumption of these compounds with food several life threatening diseases occur and therefore, it is necessary to monitor and detection of these pesticides from food and environmental samples (Liang *et al.*, 2012; Zhao *et al.*, 2014; Liu *et al.*, 2015; Yu *et al.*, 2016; Qiu *et al.*, 2016; Wu, 2017; Rastogi *et al.*, 2017). Consequently, this book chapter consist of Indian scenario of pesticides and various chromatographic detection techniques for the assessment of the residual pesticides from the food matrix.

2. Indian Scenario of Pesticides

Majorly India is an agricultural society and according to Statistics time Gross Development Product growth for agriculture and allied sector shared 17.1% of total Indian economy during the year 2015-2016. India is destined to be global leader in production of agricultural produces due to large vegetarian population which is significantly depend upon the cereals and legumes to fulfil their nutritive requirements (Singh *et al.*, 2017). At present stage, Indian population is in log phase and development in agriculture sector is principal objective in policy of the Indian government (Abhilash and Singh, 2009). Therefore, to increase the agricultural productivity and to boost the development in agriculture pesticides have become important tools as a crop protection agent. Chemical pesticides played significant role to increase the agricultural yield by controlling pests and various plant related diseases (Gupta, 2004). To increase the required food production globally one of the major and effective strategies is pest management because more than 50 % of annual food production is lost due to pest infestation (Abhilash and Singh, 2009). In India use of synthetic pesticides started in 1948-49 with the use of organochlorines like DDT and BHC to control the malaria and locust, respectively in human health sector (Gupta, 2004). Kolkata was the first place (1952) where Indian pesticide production industry started for the production of BHC that followed by other units for the manufacturing of organochlorine pesticides (Gupta, 2004; Abhilash and Singh, 2009). Union Carbide started manufacturing of DDT in 1969 in Bhopal and this unit was the part of green revolution in India. Main aim of India's green revolution was to increase the productivity of crops in major regions of India. It is one the few remaining countries which is affianced in the production of toxic chlorinated pesticides such as DDT, HCH and PCP at large extent. Even in the 1990 more than 70% of the gross tonnage of pesticides used in agricultural applications in India consisted of formulations which are banned or severely restricted in the east and west regions of world (Abhilash and Singh, 2009). According to a Green Peace report, India is now producing more than 100000 metric tons of pesticides as the largest industry of Asia and twelfth largest in entire world. On the other hand the rampant use of pesticides has played havoc with human and other life forms. Pesticides account for a small but significant fraction of acute human poisonings. Due to high biological activity of pesticides and their persistency in the environment excessive use of pesticides may cause undesired effects on human health, environment and other living creatures. Moreover, pesticides play a vital role in rural health programs in countries which are mainly use to control biting, noxious, irritating, annoying or contaminating insects and other pests, which infest human and animal at large extent. Pesticide residue in food and feed crops, meat and poultry, fish and aquaculture as well as milk products generally arise from their indiscriminate use in agriculture and public health. Fortunately, there are encouraging trends towards phasing out the toxic and persistent group of pesticides. Although India has national standards for equipment used for spraying of pesticides and these standards are followed by the manufactures of pesticides and spraying equipment. But there are several manufacturers which are producing pesticides and equipments without following the national standards. Due to less awareness in safety aspects of pesticides, Indian farmers are using locally made products at large extent and they are more prone to the exposures of pesticides. In recent years, broad-spectrum organophosphorus pesticides are used for pest management and improvement of agricultural yields in India (Abhilash and Singh, Bala *et al.*, 2017, Singh *et al.*, 2017).

3. Detection and Monitoring of Pesticides with Chromatographic Techniques

3.1 Advancement in Quick, Easy, Cheap, Effective, Robust and Safe (QuEChERS) Technique

Several chromatographic techniques are well established and existing for the detection of the hundreds of the organophosphorus pesticides from food and environmental samples (Gao *et al.*, 2015; He *et al.*, 2015; Reichert *et al.*, 2015; Lan *et al.*, 2016; Bala *et al.*, 2017; Wu, 2017). Fractionation and isolation of the residual pesticides from food matrix and environmental sample is very much essential process. For this purpose several isolation methods such as supercritical fluid extraction (SFE), solid phase extraction (SPE), solid phase micro-extraction (SPME), microwave assisted extraction (MAE), accelerated solvent extraction (ASE), matrix solid phase extraction (MSPE), dispersive liquid-liquid micro-extraction (DLLME) and quick, easy, cheap, effective, robust and safe (QuEChERS), respectively are used. Various researchers have been reported detailed process and principle of these techniques for the isolation of residual pesticides from various food matrix (Malato *et al.*, 2011; Tran *et al.*, 2012; Barganska *et al.*, 2013; Botero-Coy *et al.*, 2013; Moreno *et al.*,2015; He *et al.*, 2015; Yu *et al.*, 2016; Gonzalez *et al.*, 2017). Currently, among all separation techniques QuEChERS technique is used immensely for the fractionation of the residual pesticides (Jiang *et al.*, 2017). Here in this chapter we are discussing about the recent advancements in QuEChERS technique for the fractionation of the pesticides. QuEChERS technique was primarily acquaint by the bunch of the scientists Michelangelo Anastassiades (visiting scientist from Chemisches und *Veterinaruntersuchungsamt*, Stuttgart, Germany), Steven J. Lehotay (US Department of Agriculture, Philadelphia, Pennsylvania, USA), Darinka Stajnbaher (Public Health Institute, Maribor, Slovenia), and Frank J. Schenck (U.S. Food and Drug Administration, Atlanta, Georgia, USA) as an unconventional method for the extraction of residual pesticides from vegetables and fruits. Primarily this method comprises of two different steps i.e. solid liquidextraction with a salting out effect and dispersive solid-phaseextraction (d-SPE) for sample cleanup purposes (Lehotay, 2011; Gonzalez -Curbelo *et al.*, 2015;Schmidt and Snow, 2016).Although these both steps had been immensely utilized in the detection and analysis of a vast diversity of the residual pesticides from different food matrix but in combination these techniques was a great rebellion in the analysis of residual pesticides (Martinez-Dominguez *et al.*, 2016; Schmidt and Snow, 2016). In addition, for the purpose of the high recovery, several modifications has been introduced in the QuEChERS technique (Bruzzoniti *et al.*, 2014; Gonzalez-Curbelo *et al.*, 2015). These modifications in this respective techniques are carried out by different components. In first type of modification pH adjustment is done by using acetate and citrate buffer to inhibit the base-sensitive pesticide degradation of the isolated pesticides. Other than acetate and citrate buffers formate and phosphate buffered saline are used for the adjustment of the pH for stability of the other pesticides (Xing *et al.*, 2016; Norambuena-Subiabre *et al.*, 2016; Martinez-Dominguez *et al.*, 2016). In second type of modification extraction solvents are used for the proper extractions of the residual pesticides. For this purpose mixture of solvent such as acetonitrile:methanol, acetonitrile:hexane, methanol:water, respectively are used (Liua *et al.*, 2016; Eslamizad *et al.*, 2016; Yu *et al.*, 2016; Chen *et al.*, 2017).During LLE reduction of ionization of analyte is a major issue, therefore to evade the ionization of components of pesticidesN-propylethylendiamine in combination with C_{18}(Herrmann and Poulsen, 2015; Xing *et al.*, 2016; Ramos *et al.*, 2016; Yu *et al.*, 2016)and N-propylethylendiamine in combination with graphitized carbon black are used (Boudra *et al.*, 2015; Yu *et al.*, 2016; Pang *et al.*, 2016; Rubies *et al.*, 2016; Chen *et al.*, 2017).

In addition, combination of C_{18} and graphitized carbon blackwith or without N-propylethylendiamine could be considered as a crucial fragment of the current QuEChERS method(Liu *et al.*, 2016; Rejczakand Tuzimski, 2017). Salts such as sodium chloride and magnesium sulphates are used in this technique for the eradication of the extra water from the extracted component. Low temperatures or freeze –out-step process is also used in QuEChERS method to prohibit the exothermic hydration reactions (Han *et al.*, 2014; Gonzalez-Curbelo *et al.*, 2015).In advanced form of the QuEChERS method alumina used as sorbent for the inhibition of lipophilic components, magnesium silicate i.e. florisil is used for the separation of polar and nonpolar components of the pesticides (Lozowicka *et al.*, 2016; Munaretto *et al.*, 2016). Furthermore, zirconium based components such as Z-Sep and Z-Sep+, multiwalled carbon nanotubes, trimethylaminopropyl-functionalized silica particles, styrene-divinylbenzene are most innovative and new sorbents used in the QuEChERS method (Han *et al.*, 2014; Cvetkovic *et al.*, 2016; Sawicki *et al.*, 2016).With these modifications QuEChERS method become more useful and essential process for the accurate fractionation of the residual pesticides from the complex food matrixes. Food and agriculture organization, European Union and Food Safety and Standard Authority of India established the maximum residue levels of pesticides which are permitted in different food products of plants or animal source envisioned for human and animal consumptions. Therefore, to assess the low concentrations of pesticides from real food samples chromatographic techniques are very much promising.

3.2 Advancement in Chromatographic Techniques

Chromatographic techniques are widely accepted by different laboratories due to their higher selectivity and sensitivity for the residual pesticides from food as well as environmental samples (Gonzalez-Curbelo *et al.*, 2017; Surma *et al.*, 2017). Gas and liquid chromatographic (GC and LC) techniques with three different detectors *i.e.* electron capture detector (ECD) (Banerjee *et al.*, 2013; Sivaperumal *et al.*, 2015), nitrogen and phosphorus detector (NPD), (Guerrero *et al.*, 2009; Dong *et al.*, 2011; Banerjee *et al.*, 2013; Sivaperunal *et al.*, 2015) and photometric detector (FPD) (Sivaperunal *et al.*, 2015) are immensely used for the detection and analysis of the residual pesticides. GC equipped with ECD, NPD and FPD detectors with high sensitivity and selectivity are used for specific pesticides such as organochlorine pesticides, organophosphorus and nitrogenated pesticides, Sulphur and phosphorous pesticides, respectively (Guerrero *et al.*, 2009; Dong *et al.*, 2011; Banerjee *et al.*, 2013; Sivaperunal *et al.*, 2015).On the other hand UV and diode array detector (DAD) are used in LC techniques for the assessment of numerous residual pesticides (Banerjee *et al.*, 2013; Sivaperunal *et al.*, 2015). In addition, in both GC and LC techniques use of mass spectroscopy (MS) is enormously used for the valuation of residual pesticides due to its higher sensitivity and selectivity (Fu *et al.*, 2017; Jiang *et al.*, 2017). Advanced techniques and analyzers such as single quadrupole (Q) triple quadrupole (QqQ) ion trap (IT) hybrid quadrupole ion trap (QTrap) time of flight (TOF) and Orbitrap are most commonly used in tandemMS (MS/MS) and high resolution MS (HRMS) techniques (Li *et al.*, 2012; Liua *et al.*, 2016; Eslamizad *et al.*, 2016; Yu *et al.*, 2016; Chen *et al.*, 2017).Various researchers used these advanced techniques for the assessment of residual pesticides from different real food samples such as spinach, cauliflower, tomato, cabbage, milk, grapes, honey, rice, wines etc. (Fan *et al.*, 2014; Reichert *et al.*, 2015; Liu *et al.*, 2016; Rejczak *et al.*, 2017). Moreover, for the pesticide detection from the food matrix the most conformistGC-MS detector is single quadrupole (Banerjee *et al.*, 2013). Some researchers used ion trap (IT) as alternative to the single quadrupole and presently combinations of MS analyzers *i.e.* tandem-

MS (QqQ) are used in tedious analysis of the residual pesticides from food matrix. Also, tandem-MS provides the probability of measuring in very selective acquisition mode i.e. selected reaction monitoring (SRM) (Reichert *et al.*, 2015; Lozowicka *et al.*, 2016; Han *et al.*, 2016; Cvetkovic *et al.*, 2016; Sawiciki *et al.*, 2016). Moreover, due to the polar nature of some residual pesticides reversed phase is used in liquid chromatographic techniques with the improvement in ionization capacity by using several additives such as ammonium formate, formic acid, ammonium acetate in the mobile phase (Zhang *et al.*, 2011; Banerjee *et al.*, 2013; Sivaperunal *et al.*, 2015). In LC-MS techniques ionization of analyte is achieved by atmospheric pressure ionization (API) sources such as electrospray (ESI). API exhibit soft ionization process and, therefore API-LC could be directly equipped with tandem-MS analyzers (QqQ or Qtrap) (Xing *et al.*, 2016; Chen *et al.*, 2017). In addition, the QTOF and Qorbitrap are vastly used in HRMS analyzers for the accurate measurements of the residual pesticides in very low concentrations by increasing the consistency of the analyte detection by achieving extra selectivity by elemental composition of parent and fragment ion spectra. On the other hand, some residual pesticides exhibit high polarity and strong ionic strength. For the assessment of these particular compounds some advance approaches directly based upon LC has been introduced. Several methods such as reduction in polarity by derivatization, addition of ion conjugation compounds, use of hydrophilic interaction liquid chromatography (HILIC) with carbon or ion exchange, respectively are used for the accurate detection of these components (Reichert *et al.*, 2015; Lozowicka *et al.*, 2016; Han *et al.*, 2016; Cvetkovic *et al.*, 2016; Sawiciki *et al.*, 2016; Xing *et al.*, 2016; Chen *et al.*, 2017). Although the efficiency of these technique is indubitable but these methods could not able to measure all the residual components with desired accuracy in a single run. Miscellany in the chemical characteristics and behavior of the different pesticides is a major reason for this. Therefore, more scientific approaches are still required to develop analytical methods for a single component of a pesticide of similar group.

4. Conclusion

Monitoring of organophosphorus compounds is very much essential in the food and agricultural samples. For this purpose chromatographic techniques are well adopted measures for the hundreds of residual pesticides. With various modifications QuEChERS technique become more useful and essential process for the accurate fractionation of the residual pesticides from the complex food matrixes. Introduction of various analyzers such as single quadrupole (Q) triple quadrupole (QqQ) ion trap (IT) hybrid quadrupole ion trap (Q Trap) time of flight (TOF) and Orbitrap are most commonly used in tandemMS (MS/MS) and high resolution MS (HRMS) techniquesin chromatographic techniques improve the monitoring of the residual pesticides from different samples. More scientific approaches are still required to develop analytical methods for a single component of a pesticide of similar group.

References

Abhilash, P. C., & Singh, N. 2009. Pesticide use and application: an Indian scenario. *Journal of hazardous materials*, 165(1): 1-12.

Anastassiades, M., Lehotay, S. J., Štajnbaher, D., &Schenck, F. J. 2003. Fast and easy multiresidue method employing acetonitrile extraction/partitioning and "dispersive solid-phase extraction" for the determination of pesticide residues in produce. *Journal of AOAC international*, 86(2: 412-431.

Bala, R., Dhingra, S., Kumar, M., Bansal, K., Mittal, S., Sharma, R. K., &Wangoo, N. 2017. Detection of organophosphorus pesticide–Malathion in environmental samples using peptide and aptamer based nanoprobes. *Chemical Engineering Journal*, 311, 111-116.

Banerjee, K., Mujawar, S., Utture, S. C., Dasgupta, S., &Adsule, P. G. 2013. Optimization of gas chromatography–single quadrupole mass spectrometry conditions for multiresidue analysis of pesticides in grapes in compliance to EU-MRLs. *Food chemistry*, 138(1): 600-607.

Bargañska, ¯., Œlebioda, M., &Namieœnik, J. 2013. Pesticide residues levels in honey from apiaries located of Northern Poland. *Food Control*, 31(1: 196-201.

Bate, R. (2007). The rise, fall, rise, and imminent fall of DDT.

Botero-Coy, A. M., Ibáñez, M., Sancho, J. V., and Hernández, F. 2013. Direct liquid chromatography–tandem mass spectrometry determination of underivatized glyphosate in rice, maize and soybean. *Journal of Chromatography A*, 1313: 157-165.

Boudra, H., Rouillé, B., Lyan, B., &Morgavi, D. P. 2015. Presence of mycotoxins in sugar beet pulp silage collected in France. *Animal Feed Science and Technology*, 205: 131-135.

Bruzzoniti, M. C., Checchini, L., De Carlo, R. M., Orlandini, S., Rivoira, L., & Del Bubba, M. 2014. QuEChERS sample preparation for the determination of pesticides and other organic residues in environmental matrices: a critical review. *Analytical and bioanalytical chemistry*, 406(17): 4089-4116.

Chen, H., Marín-Sáez, J., Romero-González, R., &Frenich, A.G. 2017. Simultaneous determination of atropine and scopolamine in buckwheat and related products using modified QuEChERS and liquid chromatography tandem mass spectrometry. *Food chemistry*, 218: 173-180.

Cvetkovic, J. S., Mitic, V. D., Jovanovic, V. P. S., Dimitrijevic, M. V., Petrovic, G. M., Nikolic-Mandic, S. D., &Stojanovic, G. S. 2016. Optimization of the QuEChERS extraction procedure for the determination of polycyclic aromatic hydrocarbons in soil by gas chromatography-mass spectrometry. *Analytical Methods*, 8(7): 1711-1720.

Davies, T. G. E., Field, L. M., Usherwood, P. N. R., & Williamson, M. S. 2007. DDT, pyrethrins, pyrethroids and insect sodium channels. *IUBMB life*, 59(3): 151-162.

Dong, J., Pan, Y. X., Lv, J. X., Sun, J., & Gong, X. M. 2011. Multiresidue method for the determination of pesticides in fruits and vegetables using gas chromatography-negative chemical ionization-triple quadrupole tandem mass spectrometry. *Chromatographia*, 74 (1-2): 109.

Eslamizad, S., Kobarfard, F., Javidnia, K., Sadeghi, R., Bayat, M., Shahanipour, *et al*. 2016. Determination of Benzo [a] pyrene in Traditional, Industrial and Semi-industrial Breads Using a Modified QuEChERS Extraction, Dispersive SPE and GC-MS and Estimation of its Dietary Intake. *Iranian journal of pharmaceutical research: IJPR*, 15(Suppl): 165.

Fan, S., Zhao, P., Yu, C., Pan, C., & Li, X. 2014. Simultaneous determination of 36 pesticide residues in spinach and cauliflower by LC-MS/MS using multi-walled carbon nanotubes-based dispersive solid-phase clean-up. *Food Additives & Contaminants: Part A*, 31(1): 73-82.

Fan, Y., Lai, K., Rasco, B. A., and Huang, Y. 2015. Determination of carbaryl pesticide in Fuji apples using surface-enhanced Raman spectroscopy coupled with multivariate analysis. *LWT-Food Science and Technology*, 60(1): 352-357.

FAO (2016). Summary report on world fertilizer trends and outlook to 2019.

FAO (2017). The future of food and agriculture: Trends and challenges.

Fu, Y., Yang, T., Zhao, J., Zhang, L., Chen, R., & Wu, Y. 2017. Determination of eight pesticides in Lyciumbarbarum by LC-MS/MS and dietary risk assessment. *Food chemistry*, 218: 192-198.

Gao, J., Wang, J., Zuo, M., Ma, L., Cui, Y., Yang, T., & Ding, M. 2015. A highly sensitive method for simultaneous determination of the quaternary ammonium pesticides chlormequat and mepiquat in pears and potatoes by modified QuEChERS-high performance liquid chromatography-tandem mass spectrometry. *RSC Advances*, 5(8): 5895-5903.

Giannoulis, K. M., Giokas, D. L., Tsogas, G. Z., &Vlessidis, A. G. 2014. Ligand-free gold nanoparticles as colorimetric probes for the non-destructive determination of total dithiocarbamate pesticides after solid phase extraction. *Talanta*, 119: 276-283.

González-Curbelo, M. Á., Socas-Rodríguez, B., Herrera-Herrera, A. V., González-Sálamo, J., Hernández-Borges, J., & Rodríguez-Delgado, M. Á. 2015. Evolution and applications of the QuEChERS method. *TrAC Trends in Analytical Chemistry*, 71: 169-185.

González-Curbelo, M. Á., Socas-Rodríguez, B., Herrero, M., Herrera-Herrera, A. V., & Hernández-Borges, J. 2017. Dissipation kinetics of organophosphorus pesticides in milled toasted maize and wheat flour (gofio) during storage. *Food Chemistry*, 229: 854-859.

Guerrero, E. D., Mariìn, R. N., Mejiìas, R. C., & Barroso, C. G. 2009. Traceability of phytosanitary products in the production of a Sherry wine vinegar. *Journal of agricultural and food chemistry*, 57(6): 2193-2199.

Gupta, P. K. 2004. Pesticide exposure—Indian scene. *Toxicology*, 198(1): 83-90.

Han, L., Sapozhnikova, Y., &Lehotay, S. J. 2014. Streamlined sample cleanup using combined dispersive solid-phase extraction and in-vial filtration for analysis of pesticides and environmental pollutants in shrimp. *Analyticachimicaacta*, 827: 40-46.

He, Z., Peng, Y., Wang, L., Luo, M., & Liu, X. 2015. Unequivocal Enantiomeric Identification and Analysis of 10 Chiral Pesticides in Fruit and Vegetables by QuEChERS Method Combined With Liquid Chromatography Quadruple/Linear Ion Trap Mass Spectrometry Determination. *Chirality*, 27(12): 958-964.

Herrmann, S. S., &Poulsen, M. E. 2015. Clean-up of cereal extracts for gas chromatography–tandem quadrupole mass spectrometry pesticide residues analysis using primary secondary amine and C18. *Journal of Chromatography a*, 1423: 47-53.

Jiang, Z., Li, H., Cao, X., Du, P., Shao, H., Jin, F *et al*. 2017. Determination of hymexazol in 26 foods of plant origin by modified QuEChERS method and liquid chromatography tandem-mass spectrometry. *Food Chemistry*, 228: 411-419.

Lan, M., Guo, Y., Zhao, Y., Liu, Y., Gui, W., & Zhu, G. 2016. Multi-residue detection of pesticides using a sensitive immunochip assay based on nanogold enhancement. *Analyticachimicaacta*, 938: 146-155.

Lehotay, S. J. 2011. QuEChERS sample preparation approach for mass spectrometric analysis of pesticide residues in foods. *Mass Spectrometry in Food Safety: Methods and Protocols*, 65-91.

Li, C., Jin, F., Yu, Z., Qi, Y., Shi, X., Wang, M., *et al*., 2012. Rapid Determination of Chlormequat in Meat by Dispersive Solid-Phase Extraction and Hydrophilic Interaction Liquid Chromatography (HILIC)–Electrospray Tandem Mass Spectrometry. *Journal of agricultural and food chemistry*, 60(27): 6816-6822.

Liang, Y., Wang, W., Shen, Y., Liu, Y., & Liu, X. J. 2012. Effects of home preparation on organophosphorus pesticide residues in raw cucumber. *Food Chemistry*, 133(3): 636-640.

Liu, L., Suryoprabowo, S., Zheng, Q., Song, S., &Kuang, H. 2017. Rapid detection of aldicarb in cucumber with an immunochromatographic test strip. *Food and Agricultural Immunology*, 28(3): 427-438.

Liu, X. Q., Li, Y. F., Meng, W. T., Li, D. X., Sun, H., Tong, L., & Sun, G. X. 2016. A multi-residue method for simultaneous determination of 74 pesticides in Chinese material medica using modified QuEChERS sample preparation procedure and gas chromatography tandem mass spectrometry. *Journal of Chromatography B*, 1015: 1-12.

Liu, Z. Y., Yang, K., Chen, F. H., Long, X. M., Deng, Y. B., Kuang, G. W., & Sun, Z. L. 2015. Development of a Rapid Method for the Confirmatory Analysis of Flunixin Residue in Animal Tissues Using Liquid Chromatography–Tandem Mass Spectrometry. *Food analytical methods*, 8(2): 352-362.

Lozowicka, B., Ilyasova, G., Kaczynski, P., Jankowska, M., Rutkowska, E., Hrynko, *et al.* 2016. Multi-residue methods for the determination of over four hundred pesticides in solid and liquid high sucrose content matrices by tandem mass spectrometry coupled with gas and liquid chromatograph. *Talanta*, 151: 51-61.

Malato, O., Lozano, A., Mezcua, M., Agüera, A., & Fernandez-Alba, A. R. 2011. Benefits and pitfalls of the application of screening methods for the analysis of pesticide residues in fruits and vegetables. *Journal of Chromatography A*, 1218(42): 7615-7626.

Martínez-Domínguez, G., Romero-González, R., &Frenich, A. G. 2016. Multi-class methodology to determine pesticides and mycotoxins in green tea and royal jelly supplements by liquid chromatography coupled to Orbitrap high resolution mass spectrometry. *Food chemistry*, 197: 907-915.

Moreno-González, D., Huertas-Pérez, J. F., García-Campaña, A. M., & Gámiz-Gracia, L. 2014. Determination of carbamates in edible vegetable oils by ultra-high performance liquid chromatography–tandem mass spectrometry using a new clean-up based on zirconia for QuEChERS methodology. *Talanta*, 128: 299-304.

Moreno-González, D., Pérez-Ortega, P., Gilbert-López, B., Molina-Díaz, A., Juan, F., &Fernández-Alba, A. R. 2017. Evaluation of nanoflow liquid chromatography high resolution mass spectrometry for pesticide residue analysis in food. *Journal of Chromatography A*.

Munaretto, J. S., Yonkos, L., & Aga, D. S. 2016. Transformation of ionophore antimicrobials in poultry litter during pilot-scale composting. *Environmental Pollution*, 212: 392-400.

Norambuena-Subiabre, L., González, M. P., & Contreras-Lynch, S. 2016. Uptake and depletion curve of Diflubenzuron in marine mussels (Mytiluschilensis) under controlled conditions. *Aquaculture*, 460: 69-74.

Pang, N., Wang, T., & Hu, J. 2016. Method validation and dissipation kinetics of four herbicides in maize and soil using QuEChERS sample preparation and liquid chromatography tandem mass spectrometry. *Food chemistry*, 190: 793-800.

Pimentel D. 2009a. Pesticides and pest control. In: Integrated Pest Management: Innovation-Development Process (Vol. 1) (P Rajinder and A Dhawaneds): Springer, 83-87

Qiu, J., Chen, G., Zhou, H., Xu, J., Wang, F., Zhu, F., & Ouyang, G. 2016. In vivo tracing of organophosphorus pesticides in cabbage (Brassica parachinensis) and aloe (Barbadensis). *Science of the Total Environment*, 550: 1134-1140.

Ramos, S., Silva, J. A., Homem, V., Cincinelli, A., Santos, L., Alves, A., &Ratola, N. 2016. Solvent-saving approaches for the extraction of siloxanes from pine needles, soils and passive air samplers. *Analytical Methods*, 8(27): 5378-5387.

Rastogi, L., Dash, K., &Ballal, A. 2017. Selective colorimetric/visual detection of Al 3+ in ground water using ascorbic acid capped gold nanoparticles. *Sensors and Actuators B: Chemical*, 248: 124-132.

Reichert, B., Pizzutti, I. R., Costabeber, I. H., Uclés, A., Herrera, S., &Fernández-Alba, A. R. 2015. Validation and application of micro flow liquid chromatography–tandem mass spectrometry for the determination of pesticide residues in fruit jams. *Talanta*, 134: 415-424.

Rejczak, T., &Tuzimski, T. 2017. QuEChERS-based extraction with dispersive solid phase extraction clean-up using PSA and ZrO 2-based sorbents for determination of pesticides in bovine milk samples by HPLC-DAD. *Food chemistry*, 217: 225-233.

Rúbies, A., Guo, L., Centrich, F., and Granados, M. 2016. Analysis of non-steroidal anti-inflammatory drugs in milk using QuEChERS and liquid chromatography coupled to mass spectrometry: triple quadrupole versus Q-Orbitrap mass analyzers. *Analytical and bioanalytical chemistry*, 408(21): 5769-5778.

Sawicki, T., Surma, M., Zieliñski, H., &Wiczkowski, W. 2016. Development of a new analytical method for the determination of red beetroot betalains using dispersive solid phase extraction. *Journal of separation science*, 39(15): 2986-2994.

Schmidt, M. L., & Snow, N. H. 2016. Making the case for QuEChERS-gas chromatography of drugs. *TrAC Trends in Analytical Chemistry*, 75: 49-56.

Singh, S., Tripathi, P., Kumar, N., & Nara, S. 2017. Colorimetric sensing of malathion using palladium-gold bimetallic nanozyme. *Biosensors and Bioelectronics*, 92: 280-286.

Sivaperumal, P., Anand, P., &Riddhi, L. 2015. Rapid determination of pesticide residues in fruits and vegetables, using ultra-high-performance liquid chromatography/time-of-flight mass spectrometry. *Food chemistry*, 168, 356-365.

Surma, M., Sadowska-Rociek, A., Cieœlik, E., &Sznajder-Katarzyñska, K. 2017. Optimization of QuEChERS sample preparation method for acrylamide level determination in coffee and coffee substitutes. *Microchemical Journal*, 131: 98-102.

Tran, K., Eide, D., Nickols, S. M., Cromer, M. R., Sabaa-Srur, A., & Smith, R. E. 2012. Finding of pesticides in fashionable fruit juices by LC–MS/MS and GC–MS/MS. *Food chemistry*, 134(4): 2398-2405.

Uclèis Moreno, A., Herrera Loìpez, S., Reichert, B., Lozano Fernaìndez, A., Hernando Guil, M. D., &Fernaìndez-Alba, A. R. 2014. Microflow Liquid Chromatography Coupled to Mass Spectrometry? An Approach to Significantly Increase Sensitivity, Decrease Matrix Effects, and Reduce Organic Solvent Usage in Pesticide Residue Analysis. *Analytical chemistry*, 87(2): 1018-1025.

Wu, C. C. 2017. Multiresidue method for the determination of pesticides in Oolong tea using QuEChERS by gas chromatography-triple quadrupole tandem mass spectrometry. *Food Chemistry*, 229: 580-587.

Xing, Y., Meng, W., Sun, W., Li, D., Yu, Z., Tong, L. and Zhao, Y. 2016. Simultaneous qualitative and quantitative analysis of 21 mycotoxins in Radix Paeoniae Alba by ultra-high performance liquid chromatography quadrupole linear ion trap mass spectrometry and QuEChERS for sample preparation. *Journal of Chromatography B*, 1031: 202-213.

Yu, R., Liu, Q., Liu, J., Wang, Q., & Wang, Y. 2016. Concentrations of organophosphorus pesticides in fresh vegetables and related human health risk assessment in Changchun, Northeast China. *Food Control*, 60: 353-360.

Yue, G., Su, S., Li, N., Shuai, M., Lai, X., Astruc, D., and Zhao, P. 2016. Gold nanoparticles as sensors in the colorimetric and fluorescence detection of chemical warfare agents. *Coordination Chemistry Reviews*, 311: 75-84.

Zhang, K., Wong, J. W., Yang, P., Hayward, D. G., Sakuma, T., Zou, Y., and Oulkar, D. 2012. Protocol for an electrospray ionization tandem mass spectral product ion library: development and application for identification of 240 pesticides in foods. *Analytical chemistry*, 84(13): 5677-5684.

Zhang, S. X., Xue, S. F., Deng, J., Zhang, M., Shi, G., & Zhou, T. 2016. Polyacrylic acid-coated cerium oxide nanoparticles: An oxidase mimic applied for colorimetric assay to organophosphorus pesticides. *Biosensors and Bioelectronics*, 85: 457-463.

Zhao, X., Kong, W., Wei, J., & Yang, M. (2014). Gas chromatography with flame photometric detection of 31 organophosphorus pesticide residues in Alpiniaoxyphylla dried fruits. *Food chemistry*, 162:270-276.